Get the eBooks FREE!

(PDF, ePub, Kindle, and liveBook all included)

We believe that once you buy a book from us, you should be able to read it in any format we have available. To get electronic versions of this book at no additional cost to you, purchase and then register this book a

Go to https://www.mann … follow the instructions to complete your pBook registration.

That's it!
Thanks from Manning!

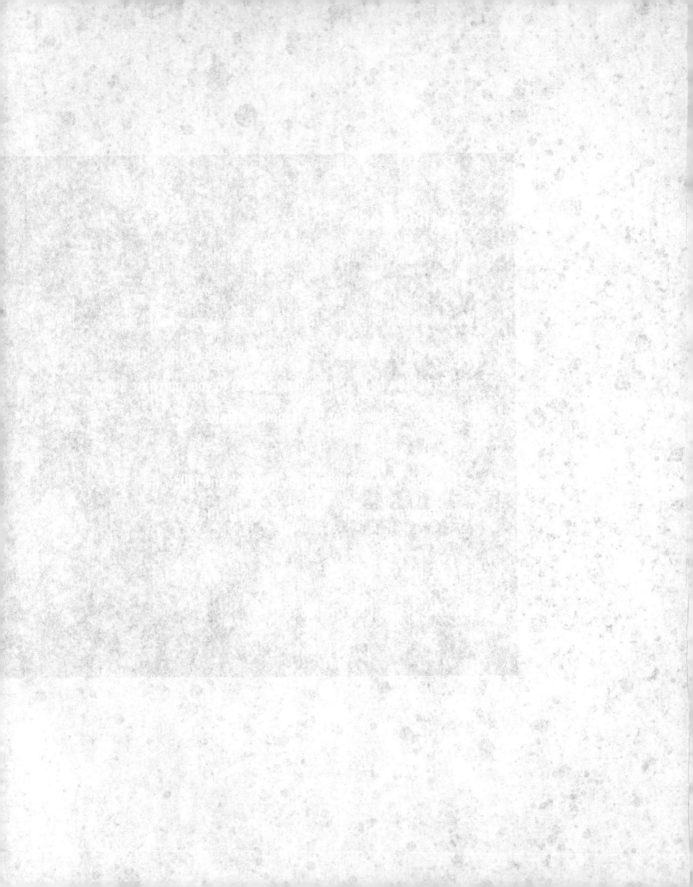

Electron in Action

Electron in Action

STEVEN KINNEY

MANNING
SHELTER ISLAND

For online information and ordering of this and other Manning books, please visit www.manning.com. The publisher offers discounts on this book when ordered in quantity. For more information, please contact

Special Sales Department
Manning Publications Co.
20 Baldwin Road
PO Box 761
Shelter Island, NY 11964
Email: orders@manning.com

Manning Publications Co.
20 Baldwin Road
PO Box 761
Shelter Island, NY 11964

Development editor: Helen Stergius
Technical development editor: Nickie Buckner
Review editor: Aleksandar Dragosavljević
Project editor: Lori Weidert
Copy editor: Pamela Hunt
Proofreader: Elizabeth Martin
Technical proofreader: Doug Warren
Typesetter: Dennis Dalinnik
Cover designer: Marija Tudor

ISBN: 9781617294143
Printed in the United States of America
1 2 3 4 5 6 7 8 9 10 – DP – 23 22 21 20 19 18

This book is dedicated to my wife, Logan, and my sons, Wes and Jack.
You are the loves of my life.

brief contents

contents

preface

Electron is one of the technologies that I'm most excited about right now. That excitement is something that I hope you catch on to as you read *Electron in Action.* As I'll explain ad nauseam throughout this book, Electron allows web developers the ability to create desktop applications with capabilities that are not available in the browser. It allows you to create graphical user interfaces for our command-line tools, opening our creations to a wider audience that may not be familiar with the terminal. Electron enables you to build applications with web technologies that you couldn't build otherwise.

Electron hits a sweet spot that's rare in open source. It's low-level enough that you will quickly wrap your head around the basics, and powerful enough to allow you to build incredibly sophisticated applications. It abstracts over some of the more tedious things you'd need to do to build a desktop application, while not falling into the trap of relying on too much black magic. The platform is supported by an enthusiastic community that has provided libraries that will help you accomplish a wide range of features with ease.

You might have heard of Electron through Atom, Slack, Visual Studio Code, or any of the other big-name applications that use it. But I wrote this book for the hobbyist or indie developer who wants to build something original and new. Electron is popular among larger teams, but it's also great for the single developer who wants to build an application that only they might use, or for the small team that needs to build tools for internal use.

It's a tool that, as you become familiar with it, opens up new avenues that wouldn't otherwise be possible. When you're becoming comfortable with Electron, it immediately seems cool, but it might be hard to come up with a use case at first. Let it sink in, and you'll soon catch yourself walking down the street coming up with ideas for applications you can build.

That's how it happened for me and I've taught Electron to enough people to develop a strong suspicion that that's how it will work for you as well. *Electron in Action* came to be as I was traveling around the United States and to Colombia, teaching workshops on building cross-platform desktop applications with Electron. Manning invited me to write a book on the topic and I jumped at the opportunity. The book informed the workshops, and delivering the workshops gave me new insights that helped improve the book.

If left to my own devices, I would have kept refining this book in perpetuity. It has helped me clarify my own thinking about building Electron applications and became a working diary as I tackled new challenges and implemented features in my projects. It's a virtuous cycle that I'll miss, although, I will be happy to have my nights and weekends back.

acknowledgments

One thing that surprised me most about writing a book is how much work it is. Second is how many people are involved in making it happen. First and foremost, I need to thank my wife, Logan, who tolerated my working on this book during nights and weekends that I should have been spending with my family. Her tolerance and support have been crucial in producing this book.

Thank you to Helen Stergius, who put up with deadlines whizzing by as I balanced my family, my day job, and this book—often poorly. Helen kept a positive attitude regardless of how stressed out I was at any given moment. Thank you to Nickie Buckner who ran through the code as I was writing the book, provided encouragement, and fixed my typos along the way. Thanks to Doug Warren who did a final technical pass as the book was nearing completion. Thanks to Brian Sawyer for reaching out and inviting me to write this book in the first place, as well as Marjan Bace who green-lit the project.

Thank you to Marc Grabanski of Frontend Masters for letting me workshop this content in front of a global audience and providing insightful feedback. Thanks to Jeff Casimir for giving me a platform to teach an endless stream of budding software engineers. Thank you to Meeka Gayhart, Louisa Barrett, Jhun de Andreas, Brenna Martenson, and Brittany Storoz for tolerating me as I dropped the ball on various things they were relying on me for, as well as putting up with me in general.

Thank you to the following reviewers, who read this book as it was being developed, and left feedback in the forums: Aiden Mark Humphreys, Alan Bogusiewicz, Alexey Galiulin, Anto Aravinth, Ashwin Raj, Buu Nguyen, Daniel Posey, Frederic

Flayol, Harald Kuhn, Hari Khalsa, Iain Shigeoka, Jay Kelkar, Jim McGinn, Jimmy Qiu, Jon Riddle, Matteo Gildone, Mladen Đurić, Philippe Charrière, Raq Khan, and William Wheeler. You helped me improve the content and catch mistakes along the way.

Thank you to Cheng Zhao and all of the people who maintain Electron. Without all of your incredible work, this book would not exist. In addition, your careful attention to detail and user-first mindset made it easy for me explain how to implement features that might otherwise be difficult on another platform. As you read *Electron in Action,* there will be many times where I just reach for some API that is built-in to Electron to tackle a tricky problem. Thank you to the wonderful community that provides an ecosystem of third-party libraries to help with Electron applications. In the rare case where Electron can't do something out of the box, there is invariably a library out there that will solve your problem for you. A platform is only as good as the community around it.

Lastly, thank you to Novo Coffee in Denver and their cold brew for giving me a place to write, and the caffeine required to get the words out.

about this book

The primary goal of *Electron in Action* is to get you started building Electron applications quickly. We explore many of the foundational concepts by learning them as we put them to practice in code. This book seeks to not only introduce you to the basics of Electron, but also provide you with inspiration and ideas for applications of your own.

Who should read this book

The book is for anyone who wants to build applications that defy the limits put in place in the browser. It's a book for anyone who wants to scratch their own itch and build desktop applications without having to learn a new programming language or framework. It's a book for small teams punching above their weight and delivering applications that run on multiple operating systems from one code base. Nearest to my heart, this book is for anyone who wants to take a command-line application and provide a GUI or remove the requirement that a user have Node.js installed on their computer in order to use their application or tool.

I'll assume that you're familiar with JavaScript, but will guide you through any parts of the web platform or Node.js that might be unfamiliar to you, since you might only have experience in one of those areas depending on your background.

Roadmap

This book is split into sixteen chapters. It's true that many chapters continue from where the last one left off, but my hope is that you'll be able to read the chapters out of order if you're simply looking to implement a specific feature in your application.

In chapter 1, we'll cover what Electron is, as well as what it isn't. We'll look at some of the things that you can do with Electron that you couldn't do with either the browser or Node.js alone.

In chapter 2, we start with a very simple Electron application. The goal here is to get our hands dirty and demonstrate that it's easy to get started with Electron.

Chapter 3 introduces you to one of the main applications in this book: Fire Sale, which is an application that allows users to open Markdown files on their filesystem and edit them.

In chapter 4, we use native system dialogues and alerts that will allow users to select a file from their filesystem for editing in Fire Sale. The application will blur the lines between the DOM and Node's standard library, coordinating between both to implement this feature.

In chapter 5, we will add multi-window support to your application, which introduces a set of challenges that you're not used to dealing with in a single browser tab or in Node.js, where there aren't any windows to speak of.

Chapter 6 brings further integration into the native operating system. We'll append the documents opened in Fire Sale to the operating system's list of recently opened files, set up listeners to see if other applications have changed the contents of files you have open, and update the title bar of the window based on whether or not the file has unsaved changes.

Chapter 7 explores techniques for building native applications that are shared across all of the windows in your desktop application and context menus that are available upon right-clicking in the application.

In chapter 8, we look into how to update the application menu based on the state of the application—enabling and disabling menu items as appropriate.

In chapter 9, we switch gears and create a new type of application, one that lives in the menu bar on macOS or the system tray in Windows. This is not a place we're used to building web applications. In this chapter, you build Clipmaster, which is a small clipboard manager that can read and write to the system clipboard, respond to global hotkeys, and display notifications.

Chapter 10 ups the ante and uses a third-party library to create a version of Clipmaster that has DOM-based UI—just like Fire Sale. Clipmaster 9000, as it's called, is able to access GitHub's Gist API and publish clippings with a single keystroke.

Up until chapter 11, we have been using vanilla JavaScript to implement features in our Electron application. In this chapter, I'll show you how easy it is to use compile-to-JavaScript tools like Babel, TypeScript, and CoffeeScript in your application as well as Sass and Less for styling. In this chapter, you'll build a packing list application called Jetsetter using React.

In chapter 12, we'll look at strategies for persisting data beyond just writing to the filesystem. I'll demonstrate how to set up an SQLite database that you can read from and write to from your client-side code. We'll then take a second swing at the problem using the browser-based IndexedDB.

Chapter 13 introduces Spectron, which allows you to write Selenium tests for your Electron application. We'll write a set of tests for the Clipmaster 9000 application we created earlier.

In chapter 14, we'll look at tools that help us package our Electron applications for distribution to users that aren't interested in starting the application up using the command line—pretty much everyone who is not a developer and, frankly, many developers as well.

Chapter 15 covers how to sign your application for macOS, create an installer for Windows, and set up a simple server for collecting error logs and crash reports.

In chapter 16, I step through the process of getting your application into the Mac App Store. This isn't a required step if you prefer to distribute your application on your own, but is certainly useful if you don't have experience with Apple's process.

About the code

This book contains many examples of source code both in numbered listings and in line with normal text. In both cases, source code is formatted in a `fixed-width font like this` to separate it from ordinary text. Sometimes code is also **`in bold`** to highlight code that has changed from previous steps in the chapter, such as when a new feature adds to an existing line of code.

In many cases, the original source code has been reformatted; we've added line breaks and reworked indentation to accommodate the available page space in the book. In rare cases, even this was not enough, and listings include line-continuation markers (➥). Additionally, comments in the source code have often been removed from the listings when the code is described in the text. Code annotations accompany many of the listings, highlighting important concepts.

All of the code for this book is available from the publisher's website at www.manning.com/books/electron-in-action and also on Github at https://github.com/electron-in-action. In most cases, there is a branch for each chapter. For some of the later chapters where we pick up an application from earlier in the book, I have provided a branch for the starting point at the beginning of the chapter as well as one for where we left the code at the end of the chapter. If the final code for a chapter is short, I have included it at the end of the chapter. Code for chapters with longer examples can be found in the appendix of this book. In May of 2018, GitHub announced a web service and npm package that make it easy to implement auto-updating for open-source Electron applications published using GitHub releases (https://electronjs.org/blog/autoupdating-electron-apps). If your application meets those criteria, you might consider using update-electron-app. Chapter 15 covers how to roll your own solution in the event that you cannot or do not want to use update-electron-app.

One of the scariest parts of writing a book is that a new version of Electron, Node.js, or Chromium—even a minor version—might break one of the examples. This happened more than once as I was writing the book.

I am committed to keeping this code up-to-date and will provide any errata in the README.md on that chapter's branch. If something does not work as expected in the book itself, be sure to check the repository on GitHub or check the book's forum.

Book forum

Purchase of *Electron in Action* includes free access to a private web forum run by Manning Publications where you can make comments about the book, ask technical questions, and receive help from the author and from other users. To access the forum, go to https://forums.manning.com/forums/electron-in-action. You can also learn more about Manning's forums and the rules of conduct at https://forums.manning.com/forums/about.

Manning's commitment to our readers is to provide a venue where a meaningful dialogue between individual readers and between readers and the author can take place. It is not a commitment to any specific amount of participation on the part of the author, whose contribution to the forum remains voluntary (and unpaid). We suggest you try asking the author some challenging questions lest his interest stray! The forum and the archives of previous discussions will be accessible from the publisher's website as long as the book is in print.

About the author

STEVE KINNEY a principal engineer at SendGrid, an international speaker, and an organizer of DinosaurJS—a JavaScript conference in Denver, Colorado, Previously, he was the founding Director of the Front-End Engineering program at the Turing School of Software and Design and a New York City teacher for seven years.

about the cover illustration

The figure on the cover of *Electron in Action* is captioned "A Gypsy Woman." The illustration is taken from a collection of costumes of people, both simple and grand, of the Ottoman Empire, published on January 1, 1802, by William Miller of Old Bond Street, London. The title page is missing from the collection, and we've so far been unable to track it down. The book's table of contents identifies the figures in both English and French, and each illustration also bears the names of two artists who worked on it, both of whom would no doubt be surprised to find their art gracing the front cover of a computer programming book 200 years later.

The collection was purchased by a Manning editor at an antiquarian flea market in the "Garage" on West 26th Street in Manhattan. The seller was an American based in Ankara, Turkey, and the transaction took place just as he was packing up his stand for the day. The Manning editor didn't have on his person the substantial amount of cash that was required for the purchase, and a credit card and check were both politely turned down. With the seller flying back to Ankara that evening, the situation seemed hopeless. What was the solution? It turned out to be nothing more than an old-fashioned verbal agreement sealed with a handshake. The seller proposed that the money be transferred to him by wire, and the editor walked out with the bank information on a piece of paper and the portfolio of images under his arm. Needless to say, we transferred the funds the next day, and we remain grateful and impressed by this unknown person's trust in one of us. It recalls something that might have happened a long time ago.

The pictures from the Ottoman collection, like the other illustrations that appear on Manning's covers, bring to life the richness and variety of dress customs of two centuries ago. They recall the sense of isolation and distance of that period—and of every other historic period except our own hyperkinetic present. Dress codes have changed since then, and the diversity by region, so rich at the time, has faded away. It's now often hard to tell the inhabitant of one continent from that of another. Perhaps, viewed optimistically, we've traded a cultural and visual diversity for a more varied personal life. Or a more varied and interesting intellectual and technical life.

We at Manning celebrate the inventiveness, the initiative, and, yes, the fun of the computer business with book covers based on the rich diversity of regional life as it was two centuries ago, brought back to life by the pictures from this collection.

Part 1

Getting started with Electron

Have you used Slack recently? Maybe you've written some code in Atom or Visual Studio Code or sent a message to a friend using the WhatsApp desktop application. If so, then you've used an Electron application. So, what is Electron? The short version is that it's a platform for building desktop applications that run on macOS, Windows, and Linux using web technologies. Electron combines Node.js with Chromium—the open source foundation of Google Chrome. The long answer is the focus of this book in general and chapter 1 in particular.

If you're part of a small team tasked with building desktop applications for multiple platforms, Electron is a great way to build your product without the hassle of managing two or three distinct code bases, squashing related bugs on two or three platforms, or implementing the same feature two or three times. If you're a Node.js developer who wants to get your command-line application in front of a wider audience, Electron makes it easy to build a graphical user interface (GUI) without having to learn an entirely new skill set. If you're a web developer who has grown accustomed to building your own solutions to problems, Electron makes it easy to access the parts of your computer that exist outside of the browser's sandbox.

In my experience, learning Electron has both short- and long-term implications. It's immediately gratifying to see an icon appear in your dock or task bar when you start it up or trigger a native file dialog box from the operating system using JavaScript. But, as you become more and more comfortable with Electron, you'll find ideas for applications that you couldn't build with either the browser or Node.js alone. You'll be able to build a new class of applications that you may not have been able to build otherwise. My hope is that the examples in this book provide inspiration rather than merely guidelines as you embark on your journey as a desktop application developer.

In part 1, we'll tease out exactly what Electron is and isn't. We'll look at some of the big players using it in the wild. I'll elaborate on what makes it different from browser-based applications in chapter 1. In chapter 2, we'll build a simple Electron application in a thinly veiled attempt to convince you that building applications with Electron is both easy and fun.

1 Introducing Electron

This chapter covers

- Understanding what Electron is
- Learning which technologies Electron is built on
- Understanding how using Electron differs from traditional web applications
- Structuring Electron applications
- Using Electron in production to build real-world applications

One of the big things that the web has going for it is ubiquity. It's an amazing platform for creating collaborative applications that can be accessed from a wide range of devices running different operating systems. That said, entire classes of applications can't be built in the browser environment. Web applications can't access the filesystem. They can't execute code that isn't written in JavaScript. They can't hook into many of the operating system APIs that desktop applications can. Most web applications aren't available when there isn't a reliable internet connection.

For a long time, building for the desktop has involved adopting a completely different skill set. Many of us don't have the bandwidth to take on the long learning curve necessary for learning new languages and frameworks. With Electron, you can use your existing skills as a web developer to build applications that have many of the capabilities of a native desktop application.

1.1 What is Electron?

Electron is a runtime that allows you to create desktop applications with HTML5, CSS, and JavaScript. It's an open source project started by Cheng Zhao (aka zcbenz), an engineer at GitHub. Previously called Atom Shell, Electron is the foundation for Atom, a cross-platform text editor by GitHub built with web technologies.

You may have heard of—or used—Apache Cordova or Adobe PhoneGap for building web applications—wrapped in native shells—for mobile operating systems such as iOS, Android, and Windows Phone. If so, then it might be helpful to think of Electron as a similar tool for building desktop applications.

Electron allows you to use the web technologies you already know to build applications that you wouldn't otherwise build. In this book, you'll learn how to build applications that hook into native operating system APIs on Windows, macOS, and Linux.

Electron combines the Chromium Content Module and Node.js runtimes. It allows developers to build GUIs with web pages as well as access native operating system capabilities on Windows, macOS, and Linux through an OS-agnostic API.

Chromium and Node are both wildly popular application platforms in their own right, and both have been used independently to create ambitious applications. Electron brings the two platforms together to allow you to use JavaScript to build an entirely new class of application. Anything you can do in the browser, you can do with Electron. Anything you can do with Node, you can do with Electron.

The exciting part is what you can do with the two technologies together. You can build applications that take advantage of both platforms and build applications that wouldn't otherwise be possible on only one. That's what this book is all about. Electron is not only a great choice for building web applications that behave like native desktop applications; it's also a great choice for building a GUI around Node applications that would otherwise be limited to a command-line interface. See figure 1.1.

Let's say that you want to build an application that allows you to view and edit a folder of images on your computer. Traditional browser applications can't access the filesystem. They couldn't access the directory of photographs, load any of the photographs in the directory, or save any of the changes that you made in the application. With Node, you could implement all those features, but you couldn't provide a GUI, which would make your application difficult to use for the average user. By combining the browser environment with Node, you can use Electron to create an application where you can open and edit photographs as well as provide a UI for doing so. See figure 1.2.

Electron isn't a complicated framework—it's a simple runtime. Similar to the way you might use `node` from the command line, you can run Electron applications using the `electron` command-line tool. You don't have to learn many conventions to get started, and you're free to structure your application however you'd like—although I'll provide tips and best practices throughout this book.

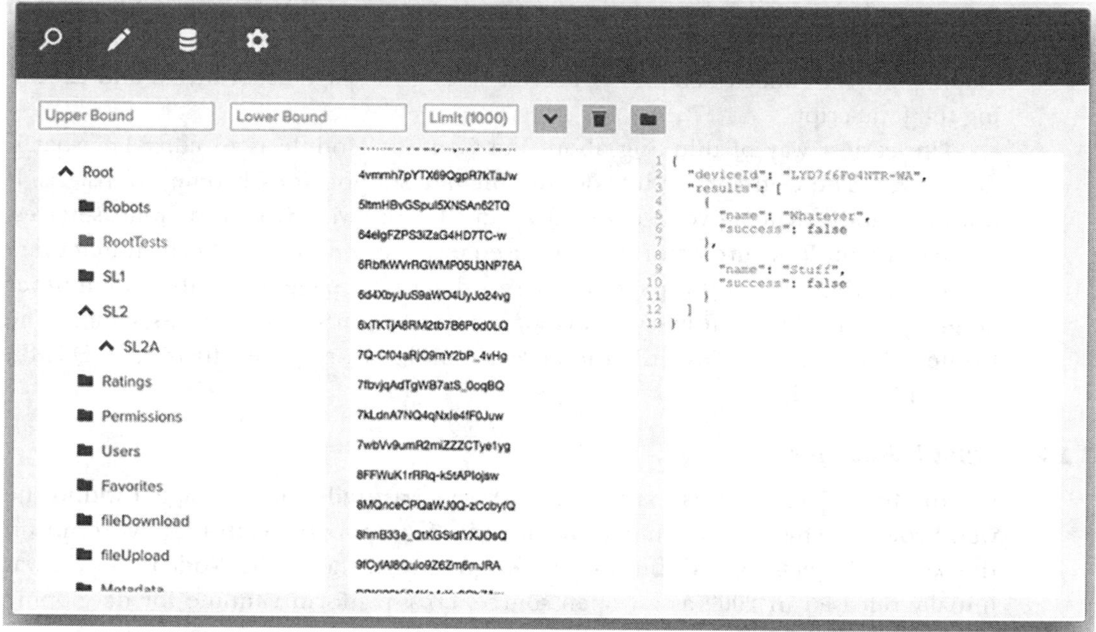

Figure 1.1 LevelUI is a GUI for Node's LevelUp database built with Electron. You couldn't build this application in a traditional browser because it wouldn't have the ability to access a local database on the user's computer. It also couldn't use the LevelUI library because it's a compiled C++ module, which only Node—and not the browser—can use.

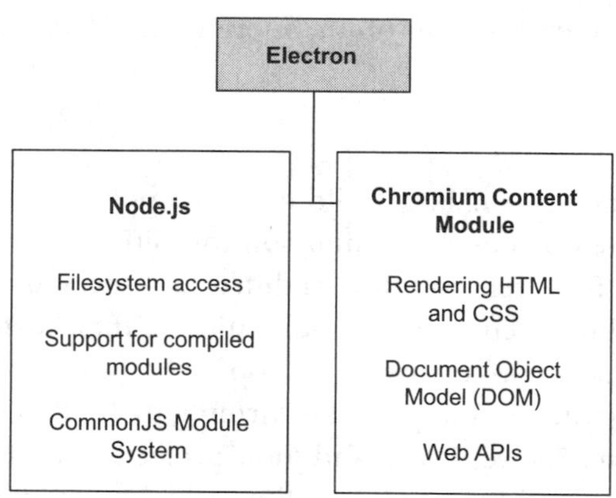

Figure 1.2 Electron combines the core web browsing component of Chromium with the low-level system access of Node.

1.1.1 *What is the Chromium Content Module?*

Chromium is the open source version of Google's Chrome web browser. It shares much of the same code and features with a few minor differences and different licensing. The Content Module is the core code that allows Chromium to render web pages in independent processes and use GPU acceleration. It includes the Blink rendering engine and the V8 JavaScript engine. The Content Module is what makes a web browser a web browser. It handles fetching and rendering HTML from a web server, loading any referenced CSS and JavaScript, styling the page accordingly, and executing the JavaScript.

The easiest way of thinking about the Content Module is to consider what it doesn't do. The Content Module doesn't include support for Chrome extensions. It doesn't handle syncing your bookmarks and history with Google's cloud services. It doesn't handle securely storing your saved passwords or automatically filling them in for you when you visit a page. It doesn't detect if a page was written in another language and subsequently call on Google's translation services for assistance. The Content Module includes only the core technologies required to render HTML, CSS, and JavaScript.

1.1.2 What is Node.js?

For the first 15 years of its existence, JavaScript was traditionally isolated within the web browser. There wasn't much in the way of support for running JavaScript on the server. Projects existed, but they never got any traction. The Node.js project was initially released in 2009 as an open source, cross-platform runtime for developing server-side applications using JavaScript. It used Google's open source V8 engine to interpret JavaScript and added APIs for accessing the filesystem, creating servers, and loading code from external modules.

Over the last few years, Node has enjoyed a surge of interest and popularity and is used for a wide range of purposes, from writing web servers to controlling robots to—you guessed it—building desktop applications. Node comes bundled with a package manager called npm, which makes it easy to lean on the more than 250,000 libraries available in its registry.

1.2 Who's using Electron?

Electron is used by companies, large and small, to build desktop applications. As discussed earlier, it was originally developed as the foundation for GitHub's Atom text editor. Atom needed access to the filesystem to fulfill its duties as a text editor. Similarly, other companies have turned to Electron as the foundation of their text-editing applications. Facebook released Nuclide as a package on top of Atom that turns the text editor into a full-fledged integrated development environment (IDE) with first-class support for working with React Native, Hack, and Flow projects. Microsoft also uses Electron for its cross-platform Visual Studio Code editor, which runs on macOS, Windows, and Linux.

You can build more than text editors with Electron. Slack, the popular messaging application, uses Electron for its Windows and Linux versions. Nylas used Electron for its N1 email client, which is designed to look beautiful across all the major platforms. It also supports a JavaScript plugin architecture that allows third-party developers to add features and extend the UI.

Particle, which produces development kits for creating custom hardware, uses Electron for its IDE, which lets users write code and deploy it to hardware devices through a cellular or Wi-Fi network. Using Mapbox Studio, users can import data stored locally and process it on their computers without having to send it over the internet to Mapbox's servers. The result is a faster and better experience that allows designers to create custom maps easily.

Dat is an open source tool for sharing, syncing, and versioning decentralized data. The grant-funded project consists of a team of three web developers. Despite being a relatively small team, Dat released a desktop application for the project using Electron. In 2015, Wiredcraft—a software consultancy—used Electron to build an offline-friendly Windows application for collecting and correcting voter registration information in Myanmar. The firm needed an application that could store the collected data offline and then publish it when the device was connected to the network. The company chose Electron as an alternative to building it using C++ because it allowed Wiredcraft to take advantage of its existing HTML, CSS, and JavaScript prowess instead of relearning those skills for a different ecosystem.

Brave—a new browser focused on speed and security by Brendan Eich, the creator of JavaScript—is itself built on top of Electron. See figure 1.3. That's right, you can even use web technologies to build a web browser.

New projects built on top of Electron are being released every day as companies and developers see the value in building products that use the power afforded to desktop applications while still maintaining the web's intrinsic platform agnosticism. By

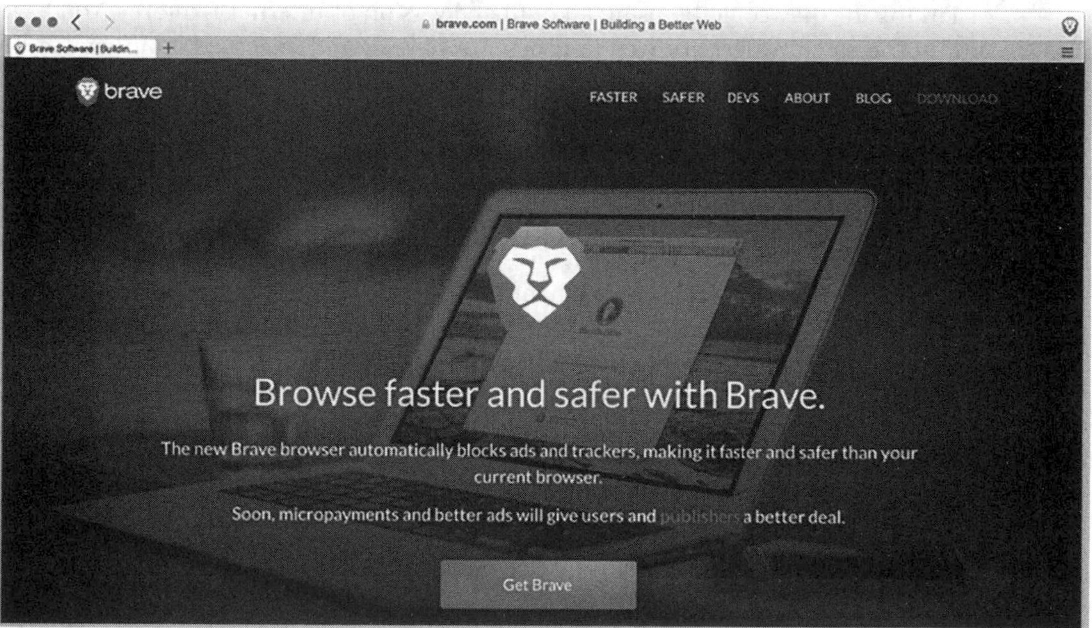

Figure 1.3 Brave is an entire web browser built on top of Electron.

the end of this book, you'll take your existing web development skills and apply them to create new applications that wouldn't have been possible in the traditional browser environment.

1.3 What do I need to know?

Let's start with what you don't need to know. This book is for web developers who want to use their existing skill set to create desktop applications that wouldn't be possible in the traditional browser environment. You don't need any experience building desktop applications to get value out of this book.

That said, you should be comfortable with writing JavaScript, HTML, and CSS, but by no means do you need to be an expert. I won't be covering variables or conditionals in this book, but if you're familiar with general language features of JavaScript, then you probably have the requisite skills to follow along. It's also helpful if you're familiar with some of the conventions and patterns from Node.js, such as how the module system works. We'll explore these concepts as we come across them.

1.4 Why should I use Electron?

When you're writing applications for a web browser, you have to be conservative in what technologies you choose to use and cautious in how you write your code. This is because—unlike many server-side situations—you're writing code that will be executed on someone else's computer.

Your users could be using the latest version of a modern browser such as Chrome or Firefox, or they could be using an outdated version of Internet Explorer. You have little to no say in where your code is being rendered and executed. You have to be ready for anything.

You typically must write code for the lowest common denominator of features that have the widest support across all versions of all browsers in use today. Even if a better, more efficient, or generally more appealing solution exists to a problem, you might not be able to use that approach. When you decide to reach for a modern browser feature, you usually need to implement a contingency plan of graceful fallbacks, feature detection, and progressive enhancement that adds a nontrivial amount of friction to your development workflow.

When you build your applications with Electron, you're packaging a particular version of Chromium and Node.js, so you can rely on whatever features are available in those versions. You don't have to concern yourself with what features other browsers and their versions support. If the build of Chromium included with your application supports the Service Worker API, for example, then you can confidently rely on that API in your application. See figure 1.4.

Electron allows you to use cutting-edge web platform features because it includes a relatively recent version of Chromium. Generally speaking, the version of Chromium in Electron is about one to two weeks behind the most recent stable release—and a

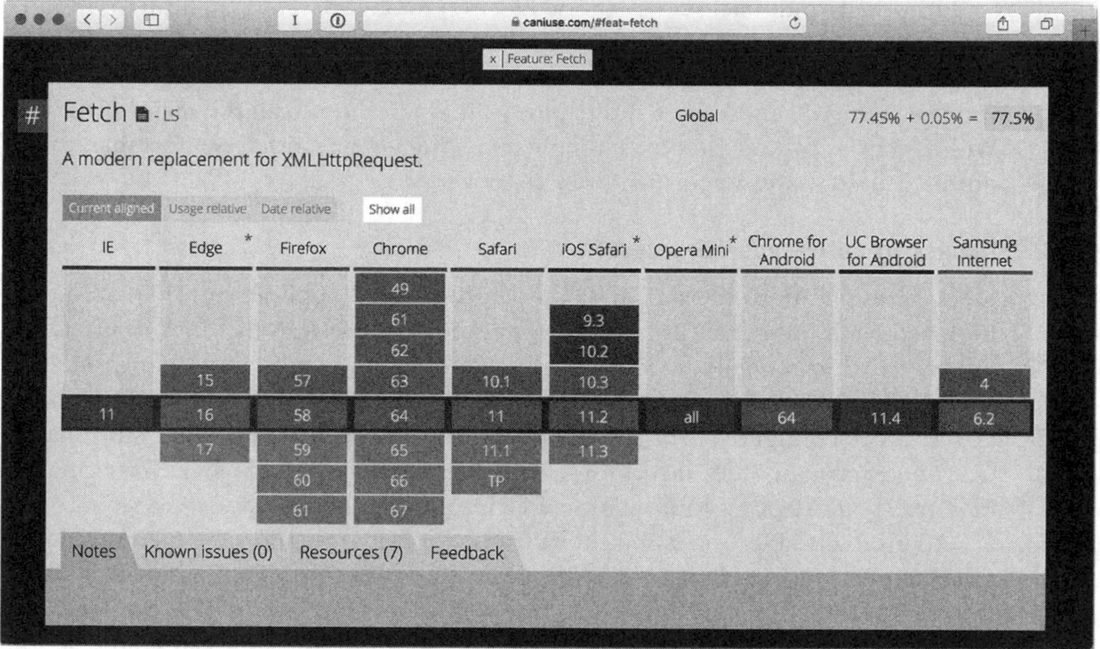

Figure 1.4 In a browser-based web application, it might not be practical to rely on the Fetch API, given its inconsistent support. But in your Electron applications, you're bundling the current stable build of Chromium with full support for the Fetch API.

new stable release comes out every six weeks. Electron typically includes new versions of Node.js about a month after they're released to ensure it contains the most recent version of V8. Electron already includes a modern build of V8 from Chromium and can afford to wait for minor bug fixes before upgrading to the latest version of Node.

1.4.1 Building on your existing skill set

If you're like me, you probably have much more experience building web applications than desktop applications. You'd love to add the ability to create desktop applications to your set of tools, but you don't have the bandwidth to learn not only a new programming language but likely a new framework as well.

Learning a new language or framework is an investment that's not to be taken lightly. As a web developer, you're used to writing applications that work equally well for all your users—even if that means fighting with idiosyncrasies of a particular browser or screen size. But when you're contemplating building traditional desktop applications, you're talking not only about learning one language and framework. You're also looking at learning at least three different languages and frameworks if you want to target Windows, macOS, and Linux.

Individuals and small teams can use Electron to offer desktop applications in situations where they couldn't otherwise. For a small team, hiring a developer skilled in building applications for each of those platforms may not be an option. Electron lets you use your existing skill set and deploy your application to all the major platforms. With Electron, you can support multiple operating systems with less effort than you're normally used to for supporting multiple browsers.

1.4.2 Access to native operating system APIs

Electron applications are similar to any other desktop application. They live in the filesystem with the rest of your native applications. They sit in the dock in macOS or taskbar in Windows and Linux where all the other native applications hang out. Electron applications can trigger native Open and Save File dialog boxes. These dialog boxes can be configured to allow the operating system to select only files with a particular file extension, whole directories, or multiple files at the same time. You can drag files onto your Electron applications and trigger different actions.

Additionally, Electron applications can set custom application menus like any other application. See figure 1.5. They can create custom context menus that spring into action when the user right-clicks from within the application. You can use Chromium's notification API to trigger system-level notifications. They can read from the system clipboard and write text, images, and other media to it as well.

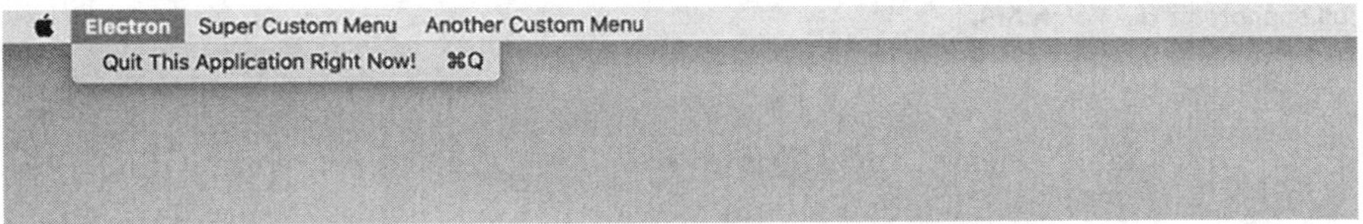

Figure 1.5 Electron allows you to create custom application menus.

Unlike traditional web applications, Electron applications aren't limited to the browser. You can create applications that live in the menu bar or the system tray. See figure 1.6. You can even register global shortcuts to trigger these applications or any of their abilities with a special keystroke from anywhere in the operating system.

Electron applications have access to system-level information—such as whether the computer is on battery power or plugged into the wall. They can also keep the operating system awake and prevent it from going into power-saving mode, if necessary.

1.4.3 Enhanced privileges and looser restrictions

The web is the largest distributed application platform in history. It's so ubiquitous that web developers take many of the associated headaches for granted. Building web applications involves carefully choreographing the communication between the server-side application and the potentially thousands of instances of the client-side application. Your client-side code runs in the user's web browser—far removed from the server.

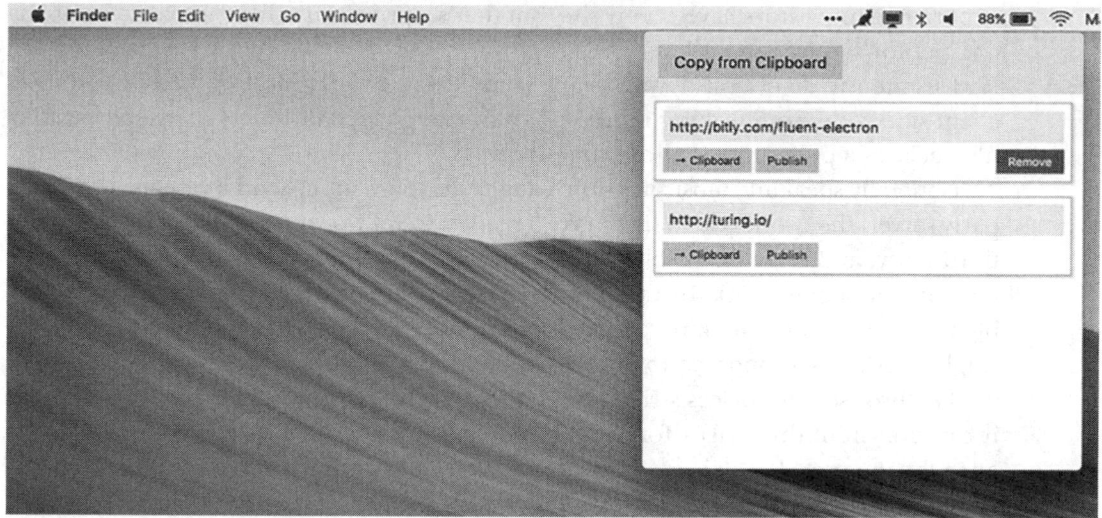

Figure 1.6 You can create an application that lives in the operating system's menu bar or system tray.

Anything that happens in the client is unique to that browser session unless the changes are sent back to your server. By the same token, if anything changes on your end, you have to wait until the client sends another HTTP request asking for updates; or you can potentially send the updates over WebSockets, if you've implemented that capability on both the client and the server.

Desktop applications enjoy a wider range of abilities and fewer restrictions on what they're allowed to do because the user explicitly went out of their way to download, install, and open the application. When you're browsing the web, however, you don't have the same amount of agency. You're executing code that you didn't choose to install on your computer. As a result, web applications have many limits on what they're allowed to do.

When the browser visits a page on the web, it happily downloads all the assets referenced in the HTML code of the document it's loading, as well as any additional dependencies added by those first assets, and then begins executing the code. Over the years, browser vendors have added restrictions to what the browser can do to prevent malicious code from harming the user or other sites on the internet.

I'm not a bad person, but let's say—for the sake of argument—that I am. Let's also say that I run a popular site that sells artisanal, hand-crafted widgets. One day, a competitor pops onto my radar selling equally pretentious widgets at a steep discount. My site is still getting more traffic for now, but this new challenger is affecting my beauty sleep.

Being a bad person, I decide to add JavaScript to my website that fires off an AJAX request every few milliseconds to my competitor's site with the hope that the thousands of visitors to my site will download this code and effectively flood my sworn enemy's server and make it unable to handle any legitimate request. It will also degrade the experience my visitors have on my site, but that's a price I'm willing to pay to bring my competitor's website to its knees.

Despite the diabolical nature of my plan, it won't work. Modern browsers restrict client-side code from making requests to a third-party server unless that server explicitly declares a policy that it allows such requests.

Generally speaking, most sites don't do this. If you want to send a request to a third-party server, then you have to first make a request to your own server, have it contact the third party, and relay the results back to the client. In the previous example, this adds my server as a bottleneck for those thousands of requests, which would make it infeasible for me to launch this kind of attack and trivially easy for my competitor to block my single IP address as opposed to the IPs of the thousands of visitors to my site.

The browser also places strict limits on what client-side code has access to and what it can do. All of this makes for a safer, more secure, and—ultimately—better experience for the user. It's all incredibly practical and is part of what makes the web such a fantastic and approachable platform for users.

That said, all these useful and important security restrictions severely limit the kinds of applications you can build using web technologies. The user explicitly downloads and installs Electron applications like any other native application. You're free to access the filesystem like any native desktop application or server-side Node process would. You're also free to make requests to third-party APIs without going through a Node server because you have access to the same privileges and capabilities as any other Node process. See figure 1.7.

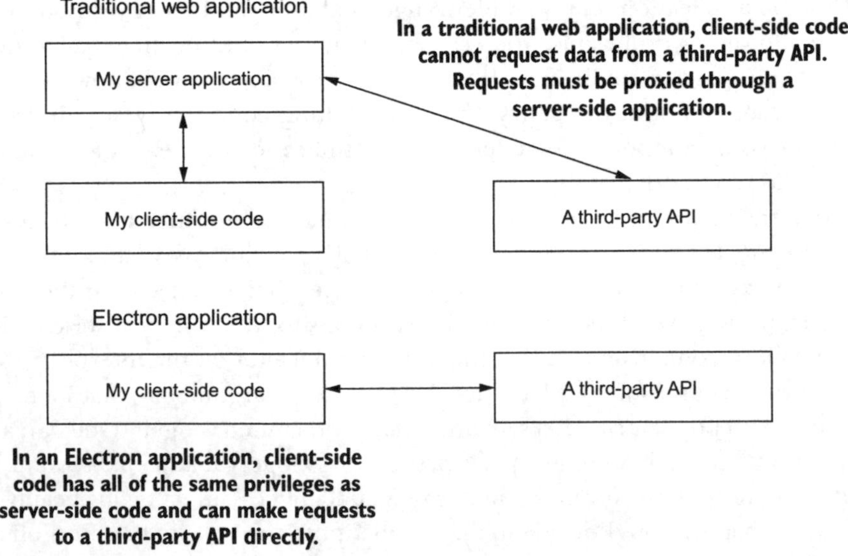

Figure 1.7 Electron applications can use their Node.js runtimes to make requests to third-party APIs.

1.4.4 Accessing Node from the browser context

Along with granting access to the filesystem and the ability to fire up a web server, Node.js uses a module system based on the CommonJS modules specification. From its earliest incarnations, Node has supported the ability to break out code into multiple modules and explicitly include ones you require from within a given file.

Packaging any nontrivial amount of JavaScript code for the browser hasn't always been so easy. For a small amount of code, you can include it in your markup between a matching pair of opening and closing `<script>` tags. For larger blocks of code, you can use the `src` attribute to reference an external JavaScript file. You're welcome to do that as many times as you wish, but you'll have to pay the performance penalties as the browser fires off an additional request to fetch each external asset.

You're welcome to use a build tool such as webpack or Browserify if you like, but it's often not necessary in Electron applications because all of Node's global properties (for example, `require`, `module`, and `exports`) are available in the browser content. You can use Node's module system on what you'd traditionally think of as the client side without needing to add a build process to your application.

You can access all of Node's APIs from the browser context of your Electron application. On top of taking advantage of Node's module system, you can also use compiled modules with native extensions, access the filesystem, as well as do a bevy of other things that aren't typically supported in the browser environment.

1.4.5 Offline first

As anyone who has ever taken a computer on a transcontinental flight can attest, most browser-based web applications aren't much good without a connection to the internet. Even advanced web applications using any of the popular client-side frameworks like Ember, React, or Angular typically need to connect to a remote server to download their assets.

Electron applications have already been downloaded to the user's computer. Typically, they load a locally stored HTML file. From there, they can request remote data and assets if a connection is available. Electron even provides APIs that allow you to detect if a connection is available. No special manifests or bleeding-edge technologies are necessary to build an offline application using Electron—it's the default state unless the application explicitly requests something from the internet. Barring a special circumstance—you're building a chat client, for example—Electron applications work as well offline as any other application.

1.5 How does Electron work?

Electron applications consist of two types of processes: the main process and zero or more renderer processes. Each process plays a different role in the application. The Electron runtime includes different modules to assist you in building your application. Certain modules, such as the ability to read and write from the system's clipboard, are available in both types of processes. Others, such as the ability to access an operating system's APIs, are limited to the main process. See figure 1.8.

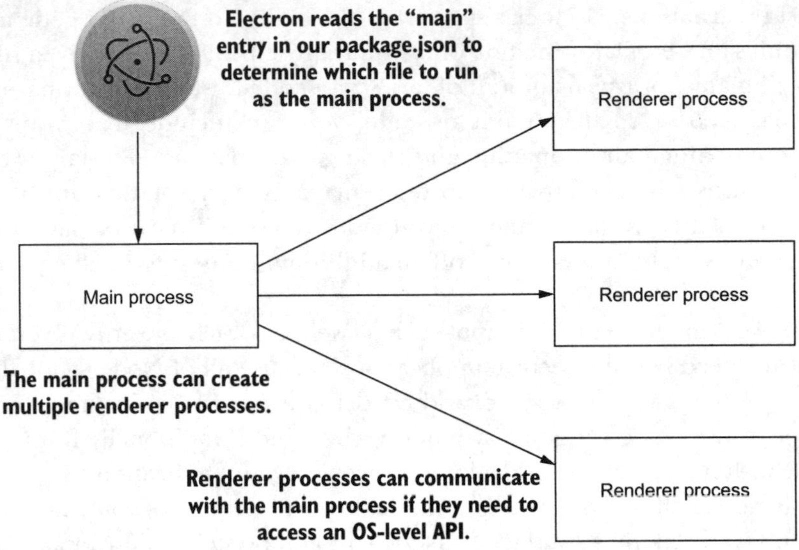
Electron reads the "main" entry in our package.json to determine which file to run as the main process.
Renderer process
Main process
Renderer process
The main process can create multiple renderer processes.
Renderer processes can communicate with the main process if they need to access an OS-level API.
Renderer process

Figure 1.8 Electron's multiprocess architecture

When Electron starts up, it turns to the start entry in your package.json manifest included in your project to determine the entry point of your application. This file can be named anything you'd like, as long as it's included properly in package.json. Electron runs this file as your main process.

1.5.1 The main process

The main process has a few important responsibilities. It can respond to application lifecycle events such as starting up, quitting, preparing to quit, going to the background, coming to the foreground, and more. The main process is also responsible for communicating to native operating system APIs. If you want to display a dialog box to open or save a file, you do it from the main process.

1.5.2 Renderer processes

The main process can create and destroy renderer processes using Electron's `BrowserWindow` module. Renderer processes can load web pages to display a GUI. Each process takes advantage of Chromium's multiprocess architecture and runs on its own thread. These pages can then load in additional JavaScript files and execute code in this process. Unlike normal web pages, you have access to all the Node APIs in your renderer processes, allowing you to use native modules and lower-level system interactions.

Renderer processes are isolated from each other and unable to access operating system integration APIs. Electron includes the ability to facilitate communication between processes to allow renderer processes to communicate with the main process in the event that they need to trigger an Open or Save File dialog box or access any other OS-level integration.

1.6 Electron vs. NW.js

Electron is similar to another project called NW.js (previously known as node-webkit). The two have much in common. In fact, zcbenz was a heavy contributor to NW.js before starting work on Electron. That said, they're different in several important ways, as shown in table 1.1.

Table 1.1 A comparison of some of the main differences between Electron and NW.js

	Electron	NW.js
Platform	Officially supported Chromium Content Module from recent build	Forked version of Chromium
Process model	Separate processes	Shared Node process
Crash reporting	Built in	Not included
Auto-updater	Built in	Not included
Windows support	Windows 7 and later	Windows XP and later

NW.js uses a forked version of Chromium. Electron uses Chromium and Node.js but doesn't modify them. This makes it easier for Electron to keep pace with the most recent versions of Chromium and Node. Electron also includes modules for automatically downloading updates and reporting crashes. NW.js doesn't.

NW.js applications start from an HTML page. Each browser window shares a common Node process. If more than one window is opened, they all share the same Node process. Electron keeps the Node and browser processes separate. In Electron, you start a main process from Node. This main process can open browser windows, each of which is its own process. Electron provides APIs for facilitating communication between the main process and the browser windows, which we call *renderer processes* throughout this book.

If backward compatibility is a concern, then NW.js might be a better choice because it supports Windows XP and Vista. Electron supports only Windows 7 and later. For multimedia-focused applications, Electron is typically a better choice because Chromium's FFmpeg library is a statically linked dependency, so Electron supports more codecs out of the box. With NW.js, you need to manually link the FFmpeg library.

Summary

- Electron is a runtime for building desktop applications using web technologies.
- The project began at GitHub as the foundation for the Atom text editor.
- Electron combines the Chromium Content Module, which is a stripped-down version of the Chrome web browser with Node.
- This combination allows you to build applications that can access the filesystem and compiled modules, as well as render a UI and use web APIs.
- Electron is used by applications large and small such as Atom, Microsoft's Visual Studio Code, and Slack.
- Electron is great for individuals or small teams who may want to target more than one platform without having to learn three or more languages, as well as each platform's frameworks.
- Electron allows web developers to use their existing skill set to build applications that wouldn't otherwise be possible within the browser environment.
- Electron ships with a modern version of Chromium and Node, which means you can use the latest and greatest features of the web platform.
- Electron applications can access operating system APIs such as application and context menus, File Open and Save dialog boxes, battery status and power settings, and more.
- Electron applications are permitted enhanced privileges and have fewer restrictions imposed on their capability as compared to browser-based web applications.
- Electron applications consist of one main process and one or more renderer processes.
- The main process handles OS integration, manages the lifecycle of the application, and creates renderer processes.
- Renderer processes display the UI and respond to user events.
- Electron differs from NW.js in that it uses the officially supported content module from Chromium as opposed to NW.js, which uses a custom fork of Chromium.

2 Your first Electron application

This chapter covers

- Structuring and setting up an Electron application
- Generating a package.json, and configuring it to work with Electron in development
- Including a prebuilt version of Electron for your platform in your project
- Configuring your package.json to start up your main process
- Creating renderer processes from your main process
- Taking advantage of Electron's relaxed sandboxing restrictions to build functionality that normally would not be possible inside of the browser
- Using Electron's built-in modules to side-step some common issues

In chapter 1, we discussed what Electron is at a high level. That said, this book is called *Electron in Action*, right? In this chapter, we learn the ropes of Electron by setting up and building a simple application from the ground up to manage a list of bookmarks. The application will take advantage of features available only in the most modern browsers.

In that high-level discussion from the previous chapter, I mentioned that Electron is a runtime like Node. That's still true, but I want to revisit that point for a moment. Electron is *not* a framework—it does not provide any scaffolding or have strong rules about how you structure your application or name your files. Those choices are left up to us, the developers. On the bright side, it also doesn't enforce any conventions, and we have less conceptual boilerplate information to discuss before getting our hands dirty.

2.1 Building a bookmark list application

Let's start by building a simple and somewhat naive Electron application to reinforce everything we've covered. Our application accepts URLs. When the user provides a URL, we fetch the title of the page that the URL refers to and save it in our application's `localStorage`. Finally, we display all the links in the application. You can find the completed source code for this chapter on GitHub (https://github.com/electron-in-action/bookmarker).

Along the way, we uncover some of the advantages of building an application in Electron, such as the ability to bypass the need for a server and use cutting-edge web APIs that do not have wide support across all the browsers but are implemented in modern versions of Chromium. Figure 2.1 is a wireframe of the application we build in this chapter.

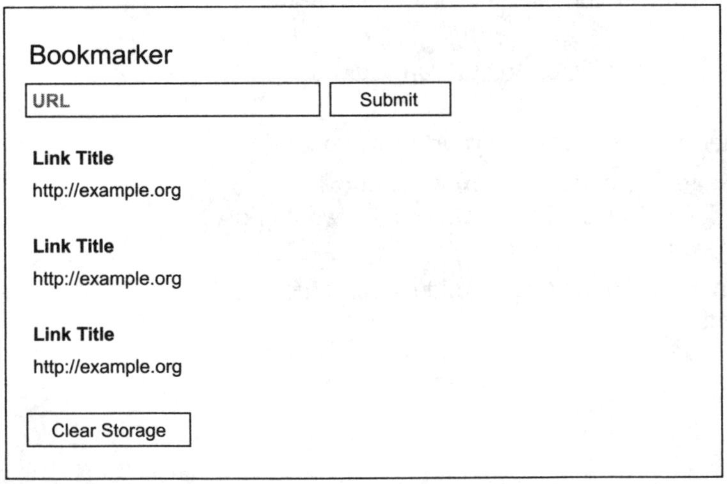

Figure 2.1 A wireframe of the application we build in this chapter

When users add the URL of a website that they would like to save to the list below the input fields, the application sends a request to the website to fetch the markup. After it successfully receives the markup, the application pulls the title of the website and appends both the title and URL to the list of websites, which is stored in the browser's `localStorage`. When the application starts, it reads from `localStorage` and restores the list. We add a button with a command to clear `localStorage` in case anything goes wrong. Because this simple application is designed to help you get comfortable with Electron, we won't implement advanced moves, such as removing individual websites from the list.

2.1.1 Structuring the Electron application

How you choose to structure your application is up to your team or the individual working on the application. Many developers take slightly different approaches. Looking at some of the more established Electron applications, we can discern common patterns and make decisions on how we'd like to approach our applications in this book.

For our purposes, let's agree upon a file structure for the remainder of this book. We have an app directory where we store all of our application code. We also have a package.json that will store a list of dependencies, metadata about our application, and scripts and declare where Electron should look for our main process. After we install our dependencies, we end up with a node_modules directory that Electron creates on our behalf, but we won't include that in the initial setup.

As far as files are concerned, let's start with two files in our app: main.js and renderer.js. These are purposely simple filenames so we can track the two types of processes. The start of all the applications that we build in this book roughly follows the directory structure shown in figure 2.2. (If you're running macOS, you can install the `tree` command using `brew install tree`.)

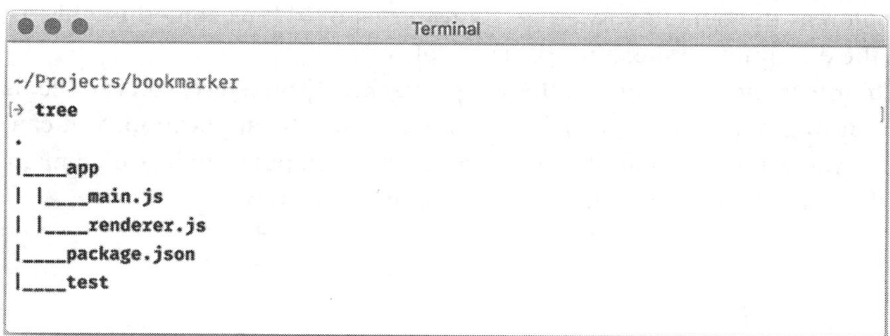

Figure 2.2 The file tree structure for our first Electron application

Make a directory called "bookmarker," and navigate to it. You can create this structure quickly by running the following two commands from the command line. You will generate a package.json file later using `npm init`.

```
mkdir app
touch app/main.js app/renderer.js app/style.css app/index.html
```

Electron doesn't require this structure, but it is inspired by some of the best practices established by other Electron applications. Atom keeps all of the application code in an app directory and all of its stylesheets and other assets such as images in a static directory. LevelUI has an index.js and a client.js on the top level and keeps all the dependent files in an src directory and stylesheets in a styles directory. Yoda keeps all of its files—including the file that loads the rest of the application—in an src directory. app, src, and lib are common names for the folder that holds the majority of the application's code, and styles, static, and assets are common names for the directory that holds the static assets used in the application.

2.1.2 package.json

The package.json manifest is used in many—if not most—Node projects. This manifest contains important information about the project. It lists metadata such as the name of the author as well as their email address, which license the project is released under, the location of the project's git repository, and where to file issues. It also defines scripts for common tasks such as running the test suite or—pertinent to our needs—building the application. The package.json file also lists all of the dependencies used to run and develop the application.

In theory, you could potentially have a Node project that does not have a package.json. But Electron relies on this file and its main property to figure out where to start when it loads or builds your application.

npm, the package manager that ships with Node, comes with a helpful tool for generating package.json. From the "bookmarker" directory you created earlier, run `npm init`. If you leave a prompt blank, npm uses whatever is in the parentheses after the colon as the default answer. Your answers should look something like figure 2.3, with the exception of the author's name, of course.

Of note is the main entry in the sample package.json. Here, you can see that I set it to point to ./app/main.js, based on how we set up the application. You can point to any file you want. The main file we're going to use happens to be called main.js, but it could be named anything (e.g., sandwich.js, index.js ,app.js).

```
Terminal
~/Projects/bookmarker
→ npm init
This utility will walk you through creating a package.json file.
It only covers the most common items, and tries to guess sensible defaults.

See `npm help json` for definitive documentation on these fields
and exactly what they do.

Use `npm install <pkg> --save` afterwards to install a package and
save it as a dependency in the package.json file.

Press ^C at any time to quit.
name: (bookmarker)
version: (1.0.0)
description: Our very first Electron application
entry point: (index.js) ./app/main.js
test command:
git repository:
keywords:
author: Steve Kinney
license: (ISC)
About to write to /Users/stevekinney/Projects/bookmarker/package.json:

{
  "name": "bookmarker",
  "version": "1.0.0",
  "description": "Our very first Electron application",
  "main": "./app/main.js",
  "scripts": {
    "test": "echo \"Error: no test specified\" && exit 1"
  },
  "author": "Steve Kinney",
  "license": "ISC"
}


Is this ok? (yes)
```

Figure 2.3 `npm init` **provides a series of prompts and sets up a package.json file**

2.1.3 Downloading and installing Electron in our project

We have the basic structure of our application set up, but Electron is nowhere to be found. Building Electron from source takes a while and can be tedious. We rely on prebuilt versions of Electron for each platform (macOS, Windows, and Linux) and both architectures (32- and 64-bit). We install Electron using npm.

npm allows us to install binaries globally or locally to each project. Installing Electron globally seems convenient, but it can cause trouble down the road if we have multiple applications using different versions of Electron. We're better off specifying and installing a unique version of Electron for each project we work on.

Downloading and installing Electron is easy. Run the following command from inside the project directory where you ran `npm init` previously:

```
npm install electron--save
```

This command will download and install Electron in your project's node_modules directory. (It will also create the directory if you don't already have one.) The `--save` flag adds it to the list of dependencies in our package.json. This means that if someone downloads the project and runs `npm install`, they will get `electron` by default.

> **A word on electron-prebuilt**
>
> As you acclimate yourself to the world of Electron, you may see blog posts, documentation, and even earlier versions of this book that refer to the `electron-prebuilt` package instead of `electron`. In the past, the former was the preferred way to install a precompiled version of Electron for your operating system. The latter is the new preferred way. As of early 2017, `electron-prebuilt` is no longer supported.

npm also lets you define shortcuts for running common scripts in your package.json. When you run a script defined in your package.json, npm automatically adds `node_modules` to the path. This means that it will use the locally installed version of Electron by default. Let's add a start script to our package.json.

Listing 2.1 Adding a start script to package.json

```
{
  "name": "bookmarker",
  "version": "1.0.0",
  "description": "Our very first Electron application",
  "main": "./app/main.js",
  "scripts": {
    "start": "electron .",
    "test": "echo \"Error: no test specified\" && exit 1"
  },
  "author": "Steve Kinney",
  "license": "ISC",
  "dependencies": {
    "electron": "^2.0.4"
  }
}
```

What npm will run when we use npm start. (annotation on the `"start"` line)

Now when we run `npm start`, npm uses our locally installed version of `electron` to start the Electron application. You'll notice that not much seems to happen. You should see the following code in your terminal application:

```
> bookmarker@1.0.0 start /Users/stevekinney/Projects/bookmarker
> electron .
```

You'll also see a new application in your dock or task bar—the Electron application we just set up—as shown in figure 2.4. Right now, it's called simply "Electron," and it uses Electron's default application icon. In later chapters, we'll see how we can customize these properties, but the default is good enough for now. All of our implementation files are completely blank. As a result, there isn't a lot going on with this application, but it exists and starts up correctly. We count that as a win for the time being. Closing all windows of the application on Windows or selecting Quit from the application menu terminates the process. Alternatively, you can press Control-C in the Windows Command prompt or Terminal to quit the application. Pressing Command-Period terminates a process on macOS.

Figure 2.4 The application in the dock isn't just any Electron application; it's the Electron application we just set up.

2.2 Working with the main process

Now that we have an Electron application, it would be cool if we could actually get it to do something. If you recall from chapter 1, Electron starts with a main process that can create one or more renderer processes. We start by writing code in main.js to get our application off the ground.

To work with Electron, we need to import the `electron` library. Electron comes with a number of useful modules that we use throughout this book. The first—and arguably, most important—is the `app` module.

Listing 2.2 Adding a basic main process: ./app/main.js

```
const {app} = require('electron');

app.on('ready', () => {                          // Called as soon as the application has fully launched.
  console.log('Hello from Electron');
});
```

`app` is a module that handles the lifecycle and configuration of our application. We can use it to quit, hide, and show the application as well as get and set the application's properties. The `app` module also runs events—including `before-quit`, `window-all-closed`, `browser-window-blur`, and `browser-window-focus`—when the application enters different states.

We cannot work with our application until it has completely started up and is ready to go. Luckily, app fires a ready event. This means we need to wait patiently and listen for the application to start the ready event before we do anything. In the previous code, we logged into the console, which is something we could easily do without Electron, but this code highlights how to listen for the ready event.

2.3 Creating a renderer process

Our main process is a lot like any other Node process. It has access to all of Node's built-in libraries as well as a special set of modules provided by Electron, which we explore over the course of this book. But, like any other Node process, our main process does not have a DOM (Document Object Model) and cannot render a UI. The main process is responsible for interacting with the operating system, managing state, and coordinating with all the other processes in our application. It is not in charge of rendering HTML and CSS. That's the job of the renderer processes. One of the primary reasons we signed up for this whole Electron adventure is that we wanted to create a GUI for Node processes.

The main process can create multiple renderer processes using the BrowserWindow module. Each BrowserWindow is a separate and unique renderer process that includes a DOM, access to the Chromium web APIs, and the Node built-in module. We can access the BrowserWindow module the same way we got our hands on the app module.

Listing 2.3 Requiring the BrowserWindow module: ./app/main.js

```
const {app, BrowserWindow} = require('electron');
```

You may have noticed that the BrowserWindow module starts with a capital letter. According to standard JavaScript convention, this usually means that we call it as a constructor with the new keyword. We can use this constructor to create as many renderer processes as we like or our computer can handle. When the application is ready, we create a BrowserWindow instance. Let's update our code as follows.

Listing 2.4 Creating a BrowserWindow: ./app/main.js

```
const {app, BrowserWindow} = require('electron');

let mainWindow = null;                      <- Creates a variable in the
                                               top-level scope for the main
                                               window of our application
app.on('ready', () => {
  console.log('Hello from Electron.');
  mainWindow = new BrowserWindow();         <- When the application is ready, creates
});                                            a browser window, and assigns it to the
                                               variable created in the top-level scope
```

We declared mainWindow outside the ready event listener. JavaScript uses function scope. If we declared mainWindow inside the event listener, mainWindow would be eligible for garbage collection because the function assigned to the ready event has run to completion. If garbage is collected, our window would mysteriously disappear. If we run this code, we see a humble little window displayed in the center of our screen, as shown in figure 2.5.

Figure 2.5 An empty `BrowserWindow` without an HTML document loaded

It's a window, but it's not much to look at. The next step is to load an HTML page into that `BrowserWindow` instance we created. All `BrowserWindow` instances have a `webContents` property, which has several useful features, such as loading an HTML file into the renderer process's window, sending messages from the main process to the renderer process, printing the page to either PDF or a printer, and much more. Right now, our biggest concern is loading content into that boring window we just created.

We need an HTML page to load, so create an `index.html` in the app directory of your project. Let's add the following content to the HTML page to make it a valid document.

Listing 2.5 Creating index.html: ./app/index.html

```
<!DOCTYPE html>
<html>
<head>
<meta charset="UTF-8">
<meta http-equiv="Content-Security-Policy"
```

```
          content="
            default-src 'self';
            script-src 'self' 'unsafe-inline';
            connect-src *
          "
>
<meta name="viewport" content="width=device-width,initial-scale=1">
<title>Bookmarker</title>
</head>
<body>

<h1>Hello from Electron</h1>

</body>

</html>
```

It's simple, but it gets the job done and gives a good foundation on which to build. We add the following to `app/main.js` to tell the renderer process to load this HTML document inside of the window we created earlier.

Listing 2.6 Loading an HTML document into the main window: ./app/main.js

```
app.on('ready', () => {
  console.log('Hello from Electron.');
  mainWindow = new BrowserWindow();
  mainWindow.webContents.loadFile('index.html');
});
```

Tells the browser window to load an HTML file located in the same directory as the main process

We use the `file://` protocol and the `__dirname` variable, which is globally available in Node. `__dirname` is the full path to the directory where our Node process is being executed. In my case, `__dirname` expands to `/Users/stevekinney/Projects/bookmarker/app`. It's like typing `pwd` in macOS and Linux or `chdir` in Windows.

Now, we can use `npm start` to start our application and watch it load our new HTML file. If all goes well, you should see something resembling figure 2.6.

2.3.1 Loading code from the renderer process

From the HTML file loaded by the renderer process, we can load any other files we might need just like we would in a traditional browser-based web application—namely, `<script>` and `<link>` tags.

What makes Electron different from what we're used to in the browser is that we have access to all of Node—even from what we would normally consider "the client." This means that we can use `require` or even Node-only objects and variables like `__dirname` or the `process` module. At the same time, we have all the browser APIs available as well. The division between what we can do only on the client and what we can do only on the server begins to fade away.

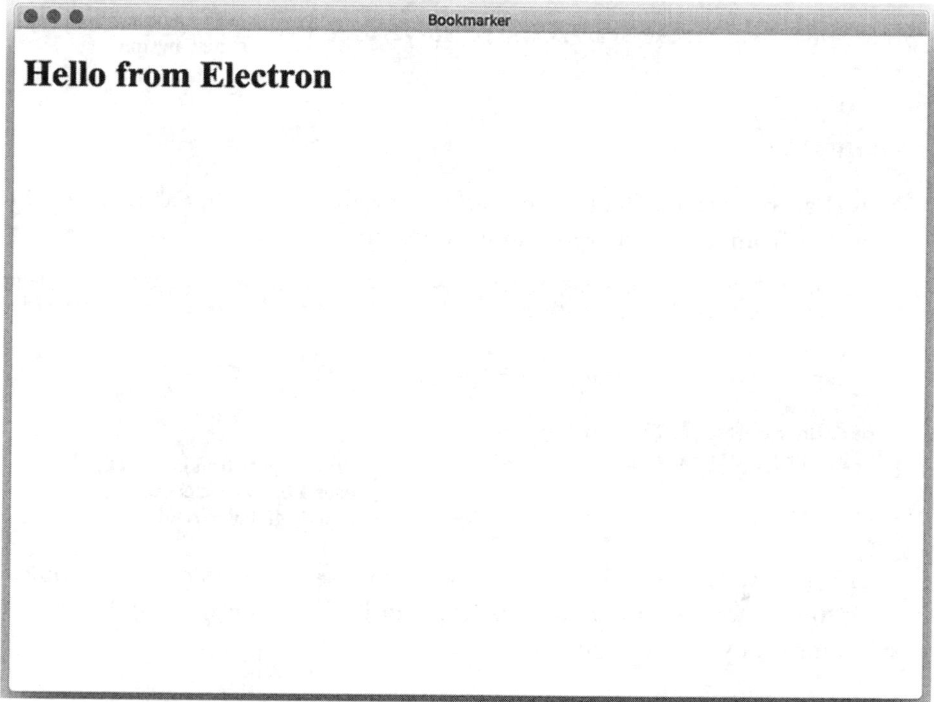

Figure 2.6 A `BrowserWindow` with a simple HTML document loaded

Let's look at this in action. `__dirname` is not available in the traditional browser environment, and `document` or `alert` are not available in Node. But in Electron we can seamlessly use them together. Let's add a button to the page.

Listing 2.7 Adding a button to an HTML document: ./app/index.html

```
<!DOCTYPE html>
<html>
<head>
<meta charset="UTF-8">
<meta http-equiv="Content-Security-Policy"
      content="
            default-src 'self';
            script-src 'self' 'unsafe-inline';
            connect-src *
          "
>
<meta name="viewport" content="width=device-width,initial-scale=1">
<title>Bookmarker</title>
</head>
<body>

<h1>Hello from Electron</h1>
```

```
<p>
<button class="alert">Current Directory</button>    This is our new button.
</p>

</body>

</html>
```

Now that we have our button, let's add an event listener that alerts us to the current directory from which our application is running.

Listing 2.8 Adding script with Node.js global in the browser context: ./app/index.html

```
<script>
  const button = document.querySelector('.alert');

  button.addEventListener('click', () => {
    alert(__dirname);         When the button is clicked, uses a browser alert to display a Node global variable
  });
</script>
```

`alert()` is available only in the browser. `__dirname` is available only in Node. When we click the button, we are treated to Node and Chromium working together in sweet, sweet harmony, as shown in figure 2.7.

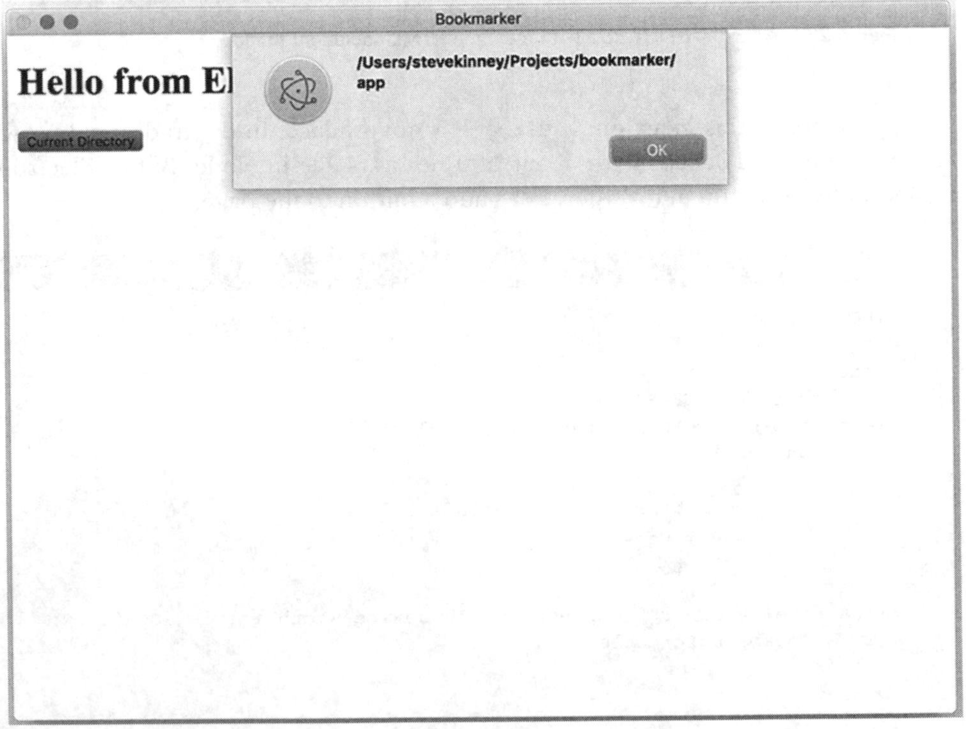

Figure 2.7 The `BrowserWindow` executing JavaScript from the context of the renderer process.

2.3.2 Requiring files in the renderer process

Writing code in our HTML file clearly works, but it's probably not hard to imagine a situation where our code might grow to the point where this method is no longer feasible. We can add script tags with `src` attributes to reference other files, but this also becomes cumbersome quickly.

This is where web development gets tricky. Although modules were added to the ECMAScript specification, no browsers currently have a working implementation of a module system. On the client, this is the point where we might consider some kind of build tool like Browserify (http://browserify.org) or the module bundler, webpack, and possibly a task runner like Gulp or Grunt.

We can use Node's module system with no additional configuration. Let's move all of the code from inside those `<script>` tags to our—currently empty—app/renderer.js file. Now we can replace the contents inside of the `<script>` tags with just a reference to renderer.js.

Listing 2.9 Loading JavaScript from renderer.js: ./app/index.html

```
<script>
  require('./renderer');
</script>
```

Uses Node's require function to load additional JavaScript modules into the renderer process

If we start up our application, you'll see that its functionality hasn't changed. Everything still works as it should. That rarely happens in software development. Let's briefly savor that feeling before moving on.

2.3.3 Adding styles in the renderer process

Few surprises occur when we reference stylesheets in our Electron applications. Later, we talk about using Sass and Less with Electron. Adding a stylesheet in an Electron application isn't much different than it would be with a traditional web application. That said, a few nuances are worth talking about.

Let's start by adding a style.css file to our app directory. We add the following content to that style.css.

Listing 2.10 Adding basic styles: ./app/style.css

```
html {
  box-sizing: border-box;
}

*, *:before, *:after {
  box-sizing: inherit;
}

body, input {
  font: menu;
}
```

Uses the default system font for the operating system the page is running on

That last declaration might look a little unfamiliar. It is unique to Chromium and allows us to use the system font in CSS. This ability is important to make our application fit in with its native siblings. On macOS, it's the only way to use San Francisco, the system font that ships with El Capitan 10.11 and later.

We should consider one other important distinction when working with CSS inside of our Electron applications. Our applications will run only in the version of Chromium that we ship with the application. We don't have to worry about cross-browser support or legacy compatibility. As mentioned in chapter 1, Electron ships with a relatively recent version of Chromium. This means we can freely use technologies like flexbox and CSS variables.

We reference our new stylesheet just like we would in the traditional browser environment, then add the following to the `<head>` section of index.html. I'll include the HTML tag for linking to a stylesheet—because, in my 20 years as a web developer, I still can never remember how to do it on the first try.

Listing 2.11 Referencing a stylesheet in the HTML document: ./app/index.html

```
<link rel="stylesheet" href="style.css" type="text/css">
```

2.4 Implementing the UI

We start by updating our index.html with the markup that we need for the UI.

Listing 2.12 Adding the markup for the UI of the application: ./app/index.html

```
<h1>Bookmarker</h1>

<div class="error-message"></div>

<section class="add-new-link">
  <form class="new-link-form">
    <input type="url" class="new-link-url" placeholder="URL"size="100"
     required>
    <input type="submit" class="new-link-submit" value="Submit" disabled>
  </form>
</section>

<section class="links"></section>

<section class="controls">
  <button class="clear-storage">Clear Storage</button>
</section>
```

We have a section for adding a new link, a section for displaying all of our wonderful links, and a button for clearing all links and starting over. The `<script>` tag in your application should be just as we left it earlier in this chapter, but just in case it isn't, here is what it should look like at this point:

```
<script>
  require('./renderer');
</script>
```

With our markup in place, we can now turn our attention to the functionality. Let's clear away anything we might have in app/renderer.js and start fresh. Throughout our time together, we're going to need to work with a few of the elements we added to the markup, so let's start by querying for those selectors and caching them into variables. Add the following to app/renderer.js.

Listing 2.13 Caching DOM element selectors: ./app/renderer.js

```
const linksSection = document.querySelector('.links');
const errorMessage = document.querySelector('.error-message');
const newLinkForm = document.querySelector('.new-link-form');
const newLinkUrl = document.querySelector('.new-link-url');
const newLinkSubmit = document.querySelector('.new-link-submit');
const clearStorageButton = document.querySelector('.clear-storage');
```

If you look back at listing 2.12, you'll notice that we set the input element's type attribute to `"url"` in the markup. Chromium will mark the field as invalid if the contents do not match a valid URL pattern. We can style valid and invalid states of the element and even check its state using JavaScript. Unfortunately, we don't have access to the built-in error message popups in Chrome or Firefox. Those popups are not part of the Chromium content module and—as a result—not part of Electron. For now, we disable the start button by default and then check to see if we have a valid URL pattern every time the user types a letter into the URL field.

If the user has provided a valid URL, then we flip the switch on that submit button and allow them to submit the URL. Let's add this code to app/renderer.js.

Listing 2.14 Adding an event listener to enable the submit button: ./app/renderer.js

```
newLinkUrl.addEventListener('keyup', () => {
  newLinkSubmit.disabled = !newLinkUrl.validity.valid;
});
```

When a user types in the input field, this uses Chromium's ValidityState API to determine if the input is valid. If so, removes the disabled attribute from the submit button.

Now is also a good time to add a small helper function to clear out the contents of the URL field. In a perfect world, we call this whenever we've successfully stored the link.

Listing 2.15 Adding a helper function to clear out form input: ./app/renderer.js

```
const clearForm= () => {
  newLinkUrl.value = null;
};
```

Clears the value of the new link input field by setting its value to null.

When the user submits a link, we want the browser to make a request for that URL and then take the response body, parse it, find the title element, get the text from that title element, store the title and URL of the bookmark in `localStorage`, and then—finally—update the page with the bookmark.

2.4.1 Making cross-origin requests in Electron

You may or may not feel some of the hairs on the back of your neck begin to stand at attention. You might even be thinking to yourself, "There is no way that this plan will work. You can't make requests to third-party servers. The browser doesn't allow this."

Normally, you'd be right. In a traditional browser-based application, you're not allowed to have your client-side code make requests to other servers. Typically, your client-side code makes a request to your server which in turn proxies the request to the third-party server. When it hears back, it proxies the response back to the client. We discussed some of the reasoning behind this in chapter 1.

Electron has all the abilities of a Node server along with all the bells and whistles of a browser. This means that we're free to make cross-origin requests without the need for a server to get in the way.

Another perk of writing this application in Electron is that we're able to use the up-and-coming Fetch API to make requests to remote servers. The Fetch API spares us the hassle of setting up `XMLHttpRequests` by hand and gives a nice, promise-based interface for working with our requests. As of this writing, Fetch has limited support among the major browsers. That said, it has full support in the current version of Chromium, which means we can use it.

We add an event listener to the form to spring into action whenever the form has been submitted. We don't have a server, so we need to be sure to prevent the default action of making a request. We do this by preventing the default action. We also cache the value of the URL input field for future use.

Listing 2.16 Adding an event listener to the submit button: ./app/renderer.js

```
newLinkForm.addEventListener('submit', (event) => {
  event.preventDefault();

  const url = newLinkUrl.value;

  // More code to come…
});
```

Tells Chromium not to trigger an HTTP request, the default action for form submissions

Grabs the URL in the new link input field. We'll need this value shortly.

The Fetch API is available as a globally available `fetch` variable. Fetching a URL returns a promise object, which will be fulfilled when the browser has completed fetching the remote resource. With this promise object, we could handle the response differently depending on if we decided to fetch a webpage, an image, or some other kind of content. In this case, we're fetching a webpage, so we convert the response to text. We start with the following code inside our event listener.

Listing 2.17 Using the Fetch API to request a remote resource: ./app/renderer.js

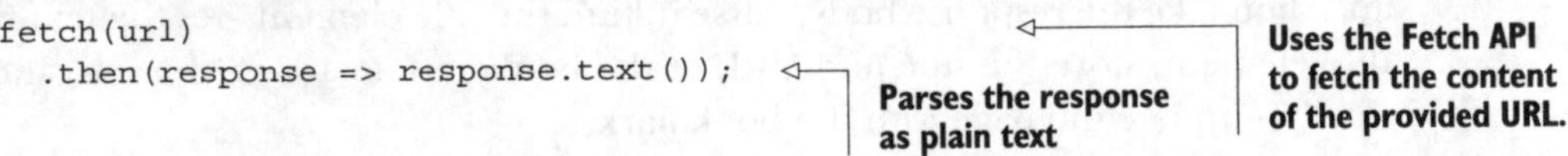

```
fetch(url)
  .then(response => response.text());
```

Uses the Fetch API to fetch the content of the provided URL.

Parses the response as plain text

Promises are chainable. We can take the return value of the previous promise and tack on another call to then. Additionally, response.text() itself returns a promise. Our next step will be to take the big block of markup that we received and parse it to traverse it and find the <title> element.

2.4.2 Parsing responses

Chromium provides a parser that will do this for us, but we need to instantiate it. At the top of app/renderer.js, we create an instance of DOMParser and store it for later use.

Listing 2.18 Instantiating a DOMParser: ./app/renderer.js

```
const parser = new DOMParser();
```

Creates a DOMParser instance. We'll use this after fetching the text contents of the provided URL.

Let's set up a pair of helper functions that parse the response and find the title for us.

Listing 2.19 Adding functions for parsing response and finding the title: ./app/renderer.js

```
const parseResponse = (text) => {
  return parser.parseFromString(text, 'text/html');
}

const findTitle = (nodes) =>{
  return nodes.querySelector('title').innerText;
}
```

Takes the string of HTML from the URL and parses it into a DOM tree.

Traverses the DOM tree to find the <title> node.

We can now add those two steps to our promise chain.

Listing 2.20 Parsing response and finding the title when fetching a page: ./app/renderer.js

```
fetch(url)
  .then(response => response.text())
  .then(parseResponse)
  .then(findTitle);
```

At this point, the code in app/renderer.js looks like this.

Listing 2.21 Current contents of app/renderer.js

```
const parser = new DOMParser();

const linksSection = document.querySelector('.links');
const errorMessage = document.querySelector('.error-message');
const newLinkForm = document.querySelector('.new-link-form');
const newLinkUrl = document.querySelector('.new-link-url');
const newLinkSubmit = document.querySelector('.new-link-submit');
const clearStorageButton = document.querySelector('.clear-storage');

newLinkUrl.addEventListener('keyup', () => {
  newLinkSubmit.disabled = !newLinkUrl.validity.valid;
});
```

```
newLinkForm.addEventListener('submit', (event) => {
  event.preventDefault();

  const url = newLinkUrl.value;

  fetch(url)
    .then(response => response.text())
    .then(parseResponse)
    .then(findTitle)
});

const clearForm = () => {
  newLinkUrl.value = null;
}

const parseResponse = (text) => {
  return parser.parseFromString(text, 'text/html');
}

const findTitle = (nodes) => {
  return nodes.querySelector('title').innerText;
}
```

2.4.3 Storing responses with web storage APIs

`localStorage` is a simple key/value store that is built into the browser and persists between sessions. You can store simple data types like strings and numbers under an arbitrary key. Let's set up another helper function that will make a simple object out of the title and URL, convert it into a string using the built-in JSON library, and then store it using the URL as the key.

Listing 2.22 Creating a function to persist links in local storage: ./app/renderer.js

```
const storeLink = (title, url) => {
  localStorage.setItem(url, JSON.stringify({ title: title, url: url }));
};
```

Our new `storeLink` function needs the title as well as the URL to get its job done, but the previous promise returns only the title. We use an arrow function to wrap our call to `storeLink` in an anonymous function that has access to the `url` variable in scope. If that is successful, we clear the form as well.

Listing 2.23 Storing a link and clearing the form upon fetching remote resource: ./app/renderer.js

```
fetch(url)
    .then(response => response.text())
    .then(parseResponse)
    .then(findTitle)
    .then(title => storeLink(title, url))    <-- Stores the title and URL into localStorage.
    .then(clearForm);
```

2.4.4 Displaying request results

Storing the links is not enough. We also want to display them to the user. This means that we need to create the functionality to go through all the links that we stored, turn them into DOM nodes, and then add them to the page.

Let's start with the ability to get all the links out of `localStorage`. If you recall, `localStorage` is a key/value storage. We can use `Object.keys` to get all the keys out of an object. We have to give ourselves another helper function to get all the links out of `localStorage`. This isn't a huge deal because we needed to convert them from strings back into real objects anyway. Let's define a `getLinks` function.

Listing 2.24 Creating a function for getting links from local storage: ./app/renderer.js

```
const getLinks = () => {
  return Object.keys(localStorage)
               .map(key => JSON.parse(localStorage.getItem(key)));
}
```

Gets an array of all the keys currently stored in localStorage

For each key, gets its value and parses it from JSON into a JavaScript object

Next, we take these simple objects and convert them into markup so that we can add them to the DOM later. We create a simple `convertToElement` helper that can take care of this as well. It's important to mention that our `convertToElement` function is a bit naive and does not try to sanitize user input. In theory, your application is vulnerable to script-injection attacks. It's a bit outside of the scope of this chapter, so we do just the bare minimum to render these links onto the page. I'll leave it as an exercise to the reader to secure this feature.

Listing 2.25 Creating a function for creating DOM nodes from link data: ./app/renderer.js

```
const convertToElement = (link) => {
  return `
<div class="link">
<h3>${link.title}</h3>
<p>
<a href="${link.url}">${link.url}</a>
</p>
</div>
`;
};
```

Finally, we create a `renderLinks()` function that calls getLinks, concatenates them, converts the collection using `convertToElement()`, and then replaces the `linksSection` element on the page.

Listing 2.26 Creating a function to render all links and add them to the DOM: ./app/renderer.js

```
const renderLinks = () => {
  const linkElements = getLinks().map(convertToElement).join('');
  linksSection.innerHTML = linkElements;
};
```

Converts all the links to HTML elements and combines them

Replaces the contents of the links section with the combined link elements

We can now add now add this final step to our promise chain.

Listing 2.27 Rendering links after fetching a remote resource: ./app/renderer.js

```
fetch(url)
  .then(response => response.text())
  .then(parseResponse)
  .then(findTitle)
  .then(title => storeLink(title, url))
  .then(clearForm)
  .then(renderLinks);
```

We also render all of the links when the page initially loads simply by calling `renderLinks()` at the top-level scope.

Listing 2.28 Loading and rendering links: ./app/render.js

```
renderLinks();
```

Calls the renderLinks() function we created earlier as soon as the page loads

One of the advantages of using promises in coordination with breaking out functionality into named helper functions is that it's very clear what our code is doing as it works through fetching the external webpage, parsing it, storing the result, and re-rendering the list of links.

The final thing we need to complete all of the functionality for our simple application is to wire up the Clear Storage button. We call the clear method on `localStorage` and then empty the list in `linksSection`.

Listing 2.29 Wiring the Clear Storage button: ./app/renderer.js

```
clearStorageButton.addEventListener('click', () => {
  localStorage.clear();
  linksSection.innerHTML = '';
});
```

Empties all the links from localStorage

Removes the links from the UI

With the Clear Storage button in place, it seems we have most of the functionality in place. Our application now looks something like figure 2.8. At this point, our code for our renderer process should look like listing 2.30.

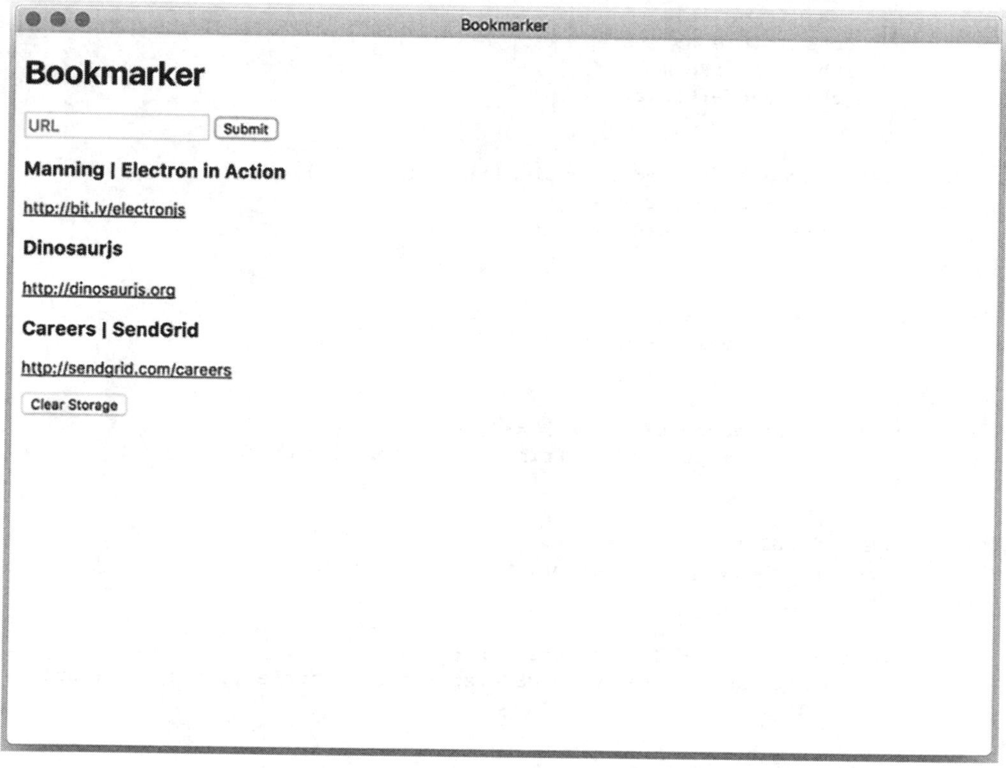

Figure 2.8 The complete Bookmarker application

Listing 2.30 Renderering process to fetch, store, and render links: ./app/renderer.js

```
const parser = new DOMParser();

const linksSection = document.querySelector('.links');
const errorMessage = document.querySelector('.error-message');
const newLinkForm = document.querySelector('.new-link-form');
const newLinkUrl = document.querySelector('.new-link-url');
const newLinkSubmit = document.querySelector('.new-link-submit');
const clearStorageButton = document.querySelector('.clear-storage');

newLinkUrl.addEventListener('keyup', () => {
  newLinkSubmit.disabled = !newLinkUrl.validity.valid;
});

newLinkForm.addEventListener('submit', (event) => {
  event.preventDefault();

  const url = newLinkUrl.value;

  fetch(url)
    .then(response => response.text())
    .then(parseResponse)
```

```
    .then(findTitle)
    .then(title => storeLink(title, url))
    .then(clearForm)
    .then(renderLinks);
});

clearStorageButton.addEventListener('click', () => {
  localStorage.clear();
  linksSection.innerHTML = '';
});

const clearForm = () => {
  newLinkUrl.value = null;
}

const parseResponse = (text) => {
  return parser.parseFromString(text, 'text/html');
}

const findTitle = (nodes) => {
  return nodes.querySelector('title').innerText;
}

const storeLink = (title, url) => {
  localStorage.setItem(url, JSON.stringify({ title: title, url: url }));
}

const getLinks = () => {
  return Object.keys(localStorage)
               .map(key => JSON.parse(localStorage.getItem(key)));
}

const convertToElement = (link) => {
  return `<div class="link"><h3>${link.title}</h3>
<p><a href="${link.url}">${link.url}</a></p></div>`;
}

const renderLinks = () => {
  const linkElements = getLinks().map(convertToElement).join('');
  linksSection.innerHTML = linkElements;
}

renderLinks();
```

2.4.5 The unhappy path

So far, everything appears to work. Our application fetches the title from the external webpage, stores the link locally, renders the links on the page, and clears them from the page when we ask it to.

But what happens if something goes wrong? What happens if we give it an invalid link? What happens if the request times out? We'll handle the two most likely cases: when the user provides a URL that passed the validation check on the input field but is not in fact valid, and when the URL is valid but the server returns a 400- or 500-level error.

The first thing we add is the ability to handle any error. Promise chains support a catch method, which is called into action in the event of an uncaught error. We define another helper method in this event.

Listing 2.31 Displaying an error message: ./app/renderer.js

```
const handleError = (error, url) => {
  errorMessage.innerHTML = `
There was an issue adding "${url}": ${error.message}
  `.trim();
  setTimeout(() => errorMessage.innerText = null, 5000);
}
```

Sets the contents of the error message element if fetching a link fails

Clears the error message after 5 seconds

We can add that to the chain. We use another anonymous function to pass along the URL with our error message. This is primarily for providing better error messages. It's not necessary if you don't want to include the URL in the error message.

Listing 2.32 Catching errors when fetching, parsing, and rendering links: ./app/renderer.js

```
fetch(url)
  .then(response => response.text())
  .then(parseResponse)
  .then(findTitle)
  .then(title => storeLink(title, url))
  .then(clearForm)
  .then(renderLinks)
  .catch(error => handleError(error, url));
```

If any promise in this chain rejects or throws an error, catches the error and displays it in the UI

We also add a step early on to the chain that checks to see if the request was successful. If so, it passes the request along to the next promise in the chain. If it was not successful, then we throw an error, which circumvents the rest of the promises in the chain and skips directly to the `handleError()` step. There is an edge case here that I didn't handle: the promise returned from the Fetch API rejects outright if it cannot establish a network connection. I leave that as an exercise to the reader to handle because we have a lot to cover in this book and a limited number of pages to do it in. `response.ok` will be false if its status code is in the 400- or 500-range.

Listing 2.33 Validating responses from remote servers: ./app/renderer.js

```
const validateResponse = (response) => {
  if (response.ok) { return response; }
  throw new Error(`Status code of ${response.status}
     ${response.statusText}`);
}
```

If the response was successful, passes it along to the next promise.

Throws an error if the request received a 400- or 500-series response.

This code passes the response object along if there is nothing wrong. But if there is something wrong, it throws an error, which is caught by `handleError()` and dealt with accordingly.

Listing 2.34 Adding `validateResponse()` to the chain: ./app/renderer.js

```
fetch(url)
  .then(validateResponse)
  .then(response => response.text())
  .then(parseResponse)
  .then(findTitle)
  .then(title => storeLink(title, url))
  .then(clearForm)
  .then(renderLinks)
  .catch(error => handleError(error, url));
```

2.4.6 An unexpected bug

We're not out of the woods yet—we also have an issue in the event that everything goes well. What happens if we click one of the links in our application? Perhaps unsurprisingly, it goes to that link. The Chromium part of our Electron application thinks that it is a web browser, and so it does what web browsers do best—it goes to the page.

Except our application is not really a web browser. It lacks important things like a Back button or a location bar. If we click any of the links in our application, we're pretty much stuck there. Our only option is to kill the application and start all over.

The solution is to open the links in a real browser. But this raises the question, which browser? How can we tell what the user has set as their default browser? We certainly don't want to take any lucky guesses because we don't know what browsers the user has installed and no one likes seeing the wrong application start opening just because they clicked a link.

Electron ships with the `shell` module, which provides some functions related to high-level desktop integration. The `shell` module can ask the user's operating system what browser they prefer and pass the URL to that browser to open. Let's start by pulling in Electron and storing a reference to its `shell` module at the top of app/renderer.js.

Listing 2.35 Requiring Electron's `shell` module: ./app/renderer.js

```
const {shell} = require('electron');
```

We can use JavaScript to determine which URLs we want to handle in our application and which ones we want to pass along to the default browser. In our simple application, the distinction is easy. We want all of the links to open in the default browser. Links are being added and removed in this application, so we set an event listener on the `linksSection` element and allow click events to bubble up. If the target element has an `href` attribute, we prevent the default action and pass the URL to the default browser instead.

Listing 2.36 Opening links in the user's default browser: /app/renderer.js

```
linksSection.addEventListener('click', (event) => {
  if (event.target.href) {
    event.preventDefault();
    shell.openExternal(event.target.href);
  }
});
```

Checks to see if the element that was clicked was a link by looking for an href attribute

If it was a link, don't open it normally.

Uses Electron's shell module to open a link in the user's default browser

With that relatively simple change, our code behaves as expected. Clicking a link will open that page in the user's default browser. We have a simple—yet fully functional—desktop application.

Our finished code should look something like the following code example. You may have your functions in a different order.

Listing 2.37 Completed application: ./app/renderer.js

```
const {shell} = require('electron');

const parser = new DOMParser();

const linksSection = document.querySelector('.links');
const errorMessage = document.querySelector('.error-message');
const newLinkForm = document.querySelector('.new-link-form');
const newLinkUrl = document.querySelector('.new-link-url');
const newLinkSubmit = document.querySelector('.new-link-submit');
const clearStorageButton = document.querySelector('.clear-storage');

newLinkUrl.addEventListener('keyup', () => {
  newLinkSubmit.disabled = !newLinkUrl.validity.valid;
});

newLinkForm.addEventListener('submit', (event) => {
  event.preventDefault();

  const url = newLinkUrl.value;

  fetch(url)
    .then(response => response.text())
    .then(parseResponse)
    .then(findTitle)
    .then(title => storeLink(title, url))
    .then(clearForm)
    .then(renderLinks)
    .catch(error => handleError(error, url));
});
```

```
clearStorageButton.addEventListener('click', () => {
  localStorage.clear();
  linksSection.innerHTML = '';
});

linksSection.addEventListener('click', (event) => {
  if (event.target.href) {
    event.preventDefault();
    shell.openExternal(event.target.href);
  }
});

const clearForm = () => {
  newLinkUrl.value = null;
};

const parseResponse = (text) => {
  return parser.parseFromString(text, 'text/html');
};

const findTitle = (nodes) => {
  return nodes.querySelector('title').innerText;
};

const storeLink = (title, url) => {
  localStorage.setItem(url, JSON.stringify({ title: title, url: url }));
};

const getLinks = () => {
  return Object.keys(localStorage)
               .map(key => JSON.parse(localStorage.getItem(key)));
};

const convertToElement = (link) => {
  return `<div class="link"><h3>${link.title}</h3>
<p><a href="${link.url}">${link.url}</a></p></div>`;
};

const renderLinks = () => {
  const linkElements = getLinks().map(convertToElement).join('');
  linksSection.innerHTML = linkElements;
};

const handleError = (error, url) => {
  errorMessage.innerHTML = `
    There was an issue adding "${url}": ${error.message}
  `.trim();
  setTimeout(() => errorMessage.innerText = null, 5000);
};

const validateResponse = (response) => {
  if (response.ok) { return response; }
```

```
  throw new Error(`Status code of ${response.status}
    ${response.statusText}`);
}

renderLinks();
```

Summary

- Electron does not recommend or enforce a particular project structure.
- Electron uses npm's package.json manifest to determine what file it should load as the main process.
- We can generate a package.json from a boilerplate by using `npm init`.
- We typically install Electron locally in each project we work on. This allows us to have project-specific versions of Electron.
- We can use `require('electron')` in Electron applications to access Electron-specific modules and functionality.
- The `app` module manages the lifecycle of our Electron application.
- The main process cannot render a UI.
- We can create renderer processes from the main process using the `BrowserWindow` module.
- Electron allows us to make requests from a third-party server directly from the browser without an intermediary server. Traditional web applications are not permitted to do this.
- Storing data in `localStorage` will allow it to persist when we quit and reopen the application.

Part 2

Building cross-platform applications with Electron

In part 1, I talked a bit about what makes Electron interesting and special, but our first run at building an Electron application was deliberately simple and—I'll admit—a bit uninspired. In part 2—which takes up the lion's share of this book—we'll start digging into Electron's more compelling abilities. In this section, we'll build three applications: a Markdown text editor with a live preview and direct access to the filesystem, a clippings manager that lives in your operating system's menu bar or system tray and can read and write to the system clipboard, and a travel packing list built with React that can read and write directly to a native database.

In part 2, I try to walk a fine line by having you build applications that are simple enough that you can understand them in short order while also having just enough complexity that we'll run into some of the problems waiting for us in larger, more complex applications.

In chapter 3, we'll lay the foundation for Fire Sale, our Markdown editor, by implementing the UI. We'll also look into the finer points of debugging an Electron application. In chapter 4, we'll explore the relationship between the main Node.js process and the one or more browser windows—which are called renderer processes—you can spawn. We'll read from and write to the filesystem and send data back and forth between processes. In chapter 5, I'll cover how to manage multiple windows and dig a bit deeper into Electron's interprocess communication model.

Chapter 6 covers some of the finer points of integrating with the native operating system. We'll determine whether a file has unsaved changes and update the title bar provided by the operating system accordingly. We'll append our documents to the operating system's list of recent documents and listen to see if another application has changed a file currently open in Fire Sale. Chapter 7 explores how to build native application and context menus, which is not normally something web and Node.js developers encounter often. In chapter 8, we'll put the finishing touches on Fire Sale by implementing additional integrations with the host operating system as well as dynamically updating menus by enabling and disabling menu items as the state of the application changes.

In chapter 9, we'll set out to build an application in a place where no web developer has gone before: the menu bar in macOS and the system tray in Windows. Clipmaster is a simple application that allows you to read text from the system clipboard and store it in memory. When an item is selected, it's written back to the clipboard for easy pasting. It's an application I used thoroughly in writing this book. In chapter 10, we'll burn the entire application down and start over from scratch, giving it a more robust UI in the process.

Until chapter 11, we use a very limited set of tools for manipulating the DOM. As you read through the chapters leading up to chapter 11, you may be getting grand ideas about how you would integrate your favorite frontend framework. Your patience will be rewarded as we see that implementing tools like Babel, TypeScript, or Sass are easier than you could have imagined. We'll build a simple list manager called Jetsetter that keeps track of the items you need to pack before your next great adventure. I'll be using React solely because it has the gentlest learning curve, but I assure you that there are great libraries for Ember, Angular, and Vue as well.

You may have used a tool like webpack or Browserify to pull dependencies from npm into your application. If so, you might have come across a set of modules, which typically use compiled C++ code, that are off limits. Browsers, generally speaking, can work only with JavaScript. But Electron applications are not mere browser applications. In chapter 12, we'll take Jetsetter and hook it directly to a portable SQLite database. We'll figure out how to correctly compile your modules for the version of Node.js that ships with Electron. I'll implement persistent storage in a browser-based IndexedDB database, in an effort to help you determine which approach you might prefer for your own applications.

Chapter 13 covers end-to-end testing using Spectron, which is based on Selenium. In this chapter, I'll show you how to write tests that spin up your Electron application and take it for a ride. By the end of part 2, you'll be comfortable with a large subset of everything Electron has to offer, and the creative juices will certainly be flowing.

3 Building a notes application

This chapter covers

- Introducing the application we'll build over the next few chapters
- Configuring our CSS stylesheet to look more like a native application
- Reviewing the relationship between the main and renderer processes in Electron
- Implementing the basic functionality for our main and renderer processes
- Accessing the Chrome Developer Tools in the renderer process in Electron

Our bookmark manager was a fine place to start, but it only scratches the surface of what we can do with Electron. In this chapter, we dig a little bit deeper and lay the foundation for an application with stronger ties to the user's operating system. Over the course of the next few chapters, we'll implement features that trigger the operating system's GUIs, read from and write to the filesystem, and access the clipboard.

We are building a simple note editor that allows us to create new or open existing Markdown files, convert them to HTML, and save the HTML to the filesystem and clipboard. Let's call the application Fire Sale as an only slightly clever play on price markdowns—because it's a Markdown editor after all. At the end of the chapter, we'll discuss the techniques and tools available for debugging our Electron applications when things go awry.

3.1 Defining our application

Let's start by setting goals for our humble, little application. Many of our features might seem a bit banal for a desktop application, and that's the point. They're standard fare for a desktop application but completely outside of the realm of abilities for traditional web applications, which cannot access anything outside of their isolated browser tab. Our application will consist of two panes: a left pane where the user can write or edit Markdown and a right pane that displays the user's Markdown rendered as HTML. Along the top we have a series of buttons, which will allow the user to load a text file from the filesystem as well as write the result to the clipboard or filesystem.

In the first phase of our application, we build a UI based on the wireframe in figure 3.1. We can also add additional UI elements to the wireframe—and subsequently our application—as we go along, but this is a good place to start.

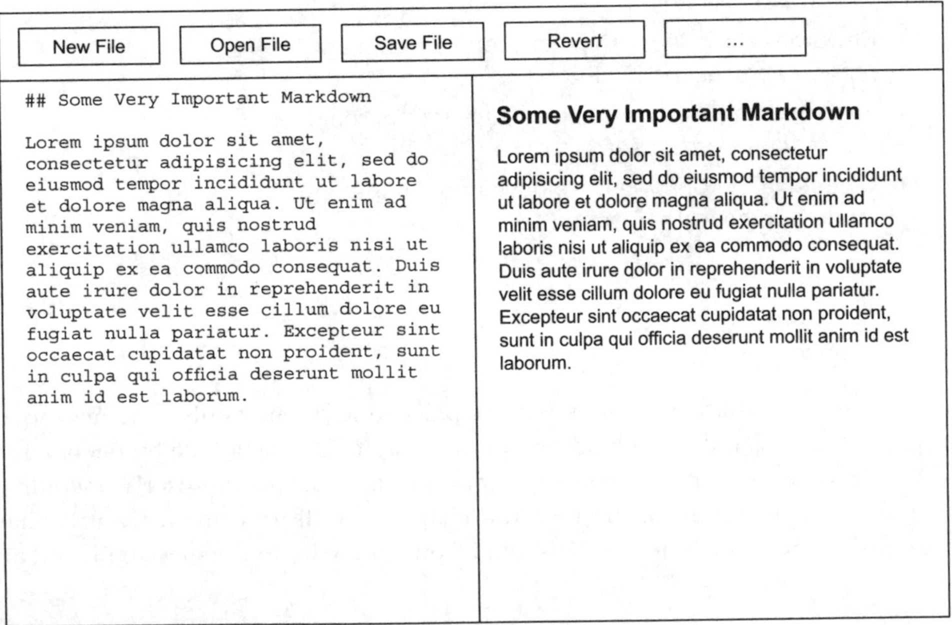

Figure 3.1 A wireframe of our application shows that the user can enter text in the left pane or load it from a file from the user's filesystem.

In this chapter, we lay the foundation for our application. We create the project's structure, install our dependencies, set up our main and renderer processes, build our UI, and implement the Markdown-to-HTML rendering when the user enters text into the left pane.

We build the remainder of the application in phases over the next several chapters. In each chapter, you'll download the current state of our application. This way you can flip to a chapter that covers the functionality you're interested in without having to build the entire application from scratch.

In the first phase, our application will be able to

- Open and save files to the filesystem
- Take Markdown content from those files
- Render the Markdown content as HTML
- Save the resulting HTML to the filesystem
- Write the resulting HTML to the clipboard

In later chapters, our application tracks recently opened documents using the native operating system APIs. We can drag Markdown files from the Finder or Windows Explorer onto our application and have the application immediately open that Markdown file. Our application will have its own custom application menu as well as custom context menus when we right-click on different areas of our application.

We also take advantage of OS-specific features such as updating the application's title bar to show the file that is currently open and whether it has been changed since the last time it was saved. We also implement additional features such as updating the content in the application if some other application on the computer changes the file while we have it open.

3.2 Laying the foundation

The file structure, shown in figure 3.2, is unsurprisingly similar to the structure we agreed upon and used for our bookmark manager in the previous chapter. For the sake of simplicity and clarity as we continue to get comfortable with Electron, we keep all of the code for the main process in app/main.js and all of the code for our single

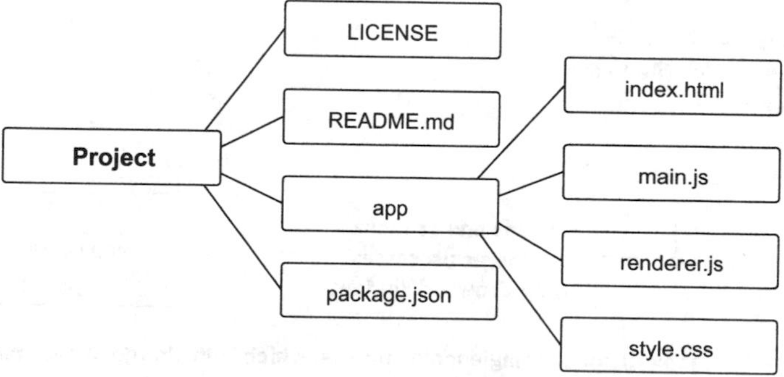

Figure 3.2 The structure of our project

renderer process in app/renderer.js. We store the app folder on a UNIX-based operating system so we can generate it quickly, as shown in the following listing. Alternatively, you can check out the master branch for this project on GitHub at https://github.com/electron-in-action/firesale.

Listing 3.1 Generating the application's file structure

```
mkdir app && touch app/index.html app/main.js app/renderer.js app/style.css
```

The parts of the project are

- index.html—Contains all of the HTML markup that provides structure for our UI
- main.js—Contains the code for our main process
- renderer.js—Contains all of the code for interactivity of our UI
- style.css—Contains the CSS that styles our UI
- package.json—Contains all of our dependencies and points Electron to main.js when it loads the main process on start-up

To keep things simple, we start with two dependencies in addition to Elcctron as our run time. We use a library called marked to handle the heavy lifting of converting Markdown to HTML.

To generate a package.json for this project, run `npm init --yes`. The `--yes` flag allows you to skip the prompts from the previous chapter. After you generate the package.json file, run the following command to install the necessary dependencies:

```
npm install electron marked --save
```

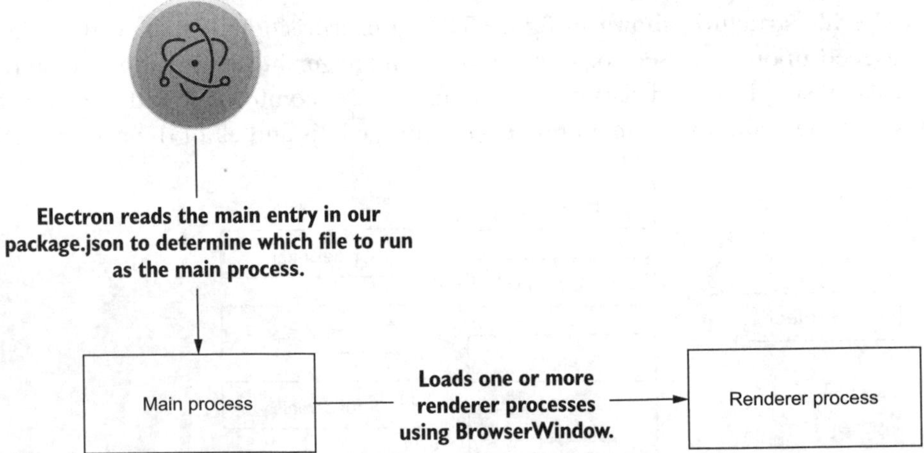
Electron reads the main entry in our package.json to determine which file to run as the main process.
Main process
Loads one or more renderer processes using BrowserWindow.
Renderer process

Figure 3.3 Electron starts by looking for our single main process, which is in charge of spawning one or more renderer processes in charge of displaying our UI.

3.3 Bootstrapping the application

The main entry in our package.json is configured to load index.js as the main process for our application shown in figure 3.3. We need to adjust this to app/main.js. We also need to fire up a renderer process to present the user with an interface for our application. In app/main.js, let's add the following code.

Listing 3.2 Bootstrapping the main process: ./app/main.js

```
const { app, BrowserWindow } = require('electron');

let mainWindow = null;

app.on('ready', () => {
  mainWindow = new BrowserWindow();

  mainWindow.loadFile('index.html');

  mainWindow.on('closed', () => {
    mainWindow = null;
  });
});
```

- `let mainWindow = null;` — Declares mainWindow at the top level so that it won't be collected as garbage after the "ready" event completes
- `mainWindow = new BrowserWindow();` — Creates a new BrowserWindow using the default properties
- `mainWindow.loadFile('index.html');` — Loads app/index.html in the BrowserWindow instance we just created
- `mainWindow = null;` — Sets the process back to null when the window is closed

This is enough to start up our application. That said, there is not a lot going on because our main process currently loads an empty file in the renderer process.

3.3.1 Implementing the UI

Implementing the requisite amount of HTML and CSS to get a workable version of the wireframe in figure 3.1 is fairly easy in Electron because we need to support only one browser, and that browser supports the latest and greatest features that the web platform offers, as shown in figure 3.4.

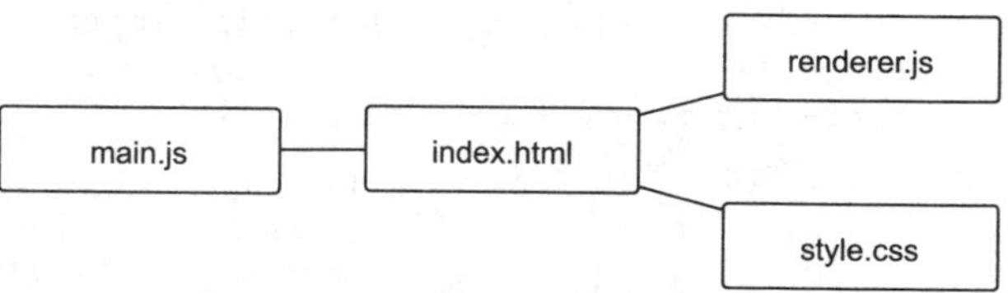

Figure 3.4 The main process will create a renderer process and tell it load index.html, which will then load CSS and JavaScript just as it would in the browser.

In index.html, we add the markup in listing 3.3 to create the browser window in figure 3.5.

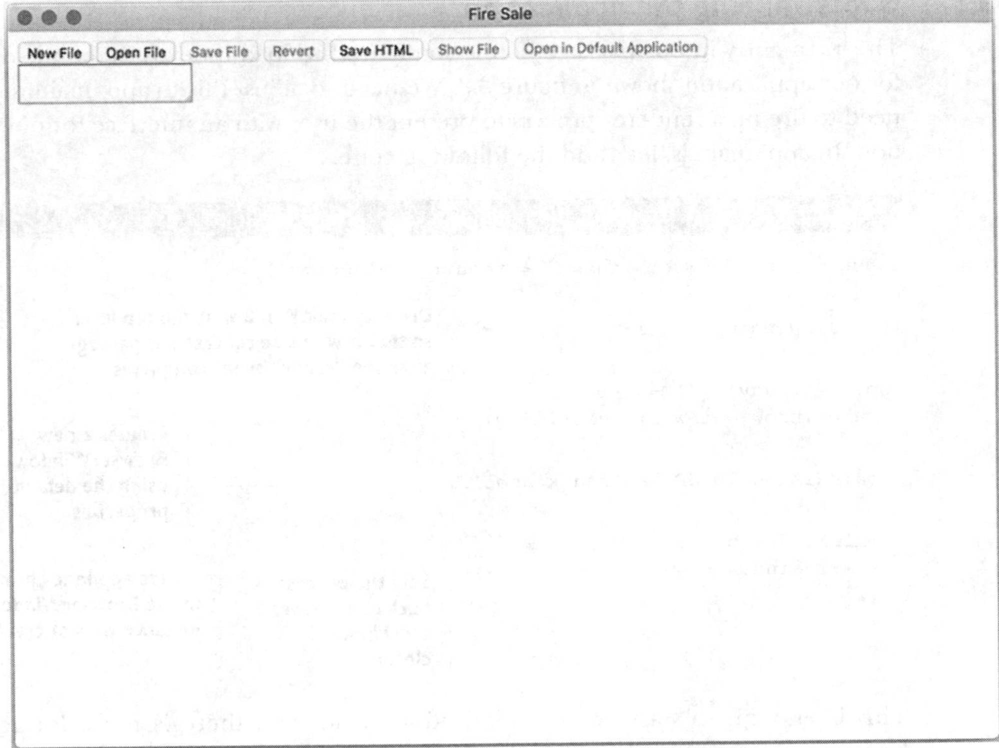

Figure 3.5 The unstyled beginnings our first Electron application

Listing 3.3 Our application's markup: ./app/index.html

```
<!DOCTYPE html>
<html>
  <head>
    <meta charset="UTF-8">
    <meta name="viewport" content="width=device-width,initial-scale=1">
    <title>Fire Sale</title>
    <link rel="stylesheet" href="style.css" type="text/css">
  </head>
  <body>

    <section class="controls">
      <button id="new-file">New File</button>
      <button id="open-file">Open File</button>
      <button id="save-markdown" disabled>Save File</button>
      <button id="revert" disabled>Revert</button>
      <button id="save-html">Save HTML</button>
      <button id="show-file" disabled>Show File</button>
      <button id="open-in-default" disabled>Open in Default
     ➥ Application</button>
    </section>
```

The .controls section added the buttons for opening and saving files along the top. We'll add functionality to these buttons later.

```
    <section class="content">
      <label for="markdown" hidden>Markdown Content</label>
      <textarea class="raw-markdown" id="markdown"></textarea>
      <div class="rendered-html" id="html"></div>
    </section>

  </body>
  <script>
    require('./renderer');
  </script>
</html>
```

The <label> tags are optional and included to make the application more accessible for visually impaired users.

In the <script> tags at the end of the file, we require the code for our renderer process, which lives in renderer.js in the same directory.

Our application allows us to write and edit content in the text area with the class of .raw-markdown and render that content in the div element with the class of .rendered-html.

Our application isn't much to look at just yet. If you're anything like me, you've been a bit skeptical about that two-column interface I introduced in the wireframe. The word *easy* is rarely used when discussing how to implement columns using HTML and CSS. Luckily, we can confidently use a new layout mode added to CSS3 called Flexbox to quickly define the two-column layout of our application. Flexbox makes it easy to create page layouts that behave predictably across a wide range of screen sizes, as shown in listing 3.4. It's relatively new to CSS and—until recently—was not supported by Internet Explorer. As we discussed in chapters 1 and 2, our applications are always coupled with a recent version of Chrome, so we can confidently use the Flexbox layout mode without having to worry about cross-browser compatibility.

Listing 3.4 Using Flexbox to create page layouts: ./app/style.css

```
html {
  box-sizing: border-box;
}

*, *:before, *:after {
  box-sizing: inherit;
}

html, body {
  height: 100%;
  width: 100%;
  overflow: hidden;
}

body {
  margin: 0;
  padding: 0;
  position: absolute;
}

body, input {
  font: menu;
}
```

Opts in to an updated CSS box model that will correctly set the width and height of elements

Passes this setting to every other element and pseudoelement on the page

Uses the operating system's default font throughout the application

```
textarea, input, div, button {
  outline: none;
  margin: 0;
}

.controls {
  background-color: rgb(217, 241, 238);
  padding: 10px 10px 10px 10px;
}

button {
  font-size: 14px;
  background-color: rgb(181, 220, 216);
  border: none;
  padding: 0.5em 1em;
}

button:hover {
  background-color: rgb(156, 198, 192);
}

button:active {
  background-color: rgb(144, 182, 177);
}

button:disabled {
  background-color: rgb(196, 204, 202);
}

.container {
  display: flex;
  flex-direction: column;
  min-height: 100vh;
  min-width: 100vw;
  position: relative;
}

.content {
  height: 100vh;
  display: flex;
}

.raw-markdown, .rendered-html {
  min-height: 100%;
  max-width: 50%;
  flex-grow: 1;
  padding: 1em;
  overflow: scroll;
  font-size: 16px;
}

.raw-markdown {
  border: 5px solid rgb(238, 252, 250);;
  background-color: rgb(238, 252, 250);
  font-family: monospace;
}
```

Removes the browser's default highlighting around active input fields (annotates `outline: none;`)

Uses Flexbox to align the two panes of our application (annotates `display: flex;` in `.content`)

Sets both panes to an equal width using Flexbox (annotates `flex-grow: 1;`)

We have two major goals for the stylesheet. First, we want to take advantage of modern CSS features like Flexbox to lay out our UI. Second, we want to take small steps toward making our application look and feel a bit more like a real web application (see figure 3.6).

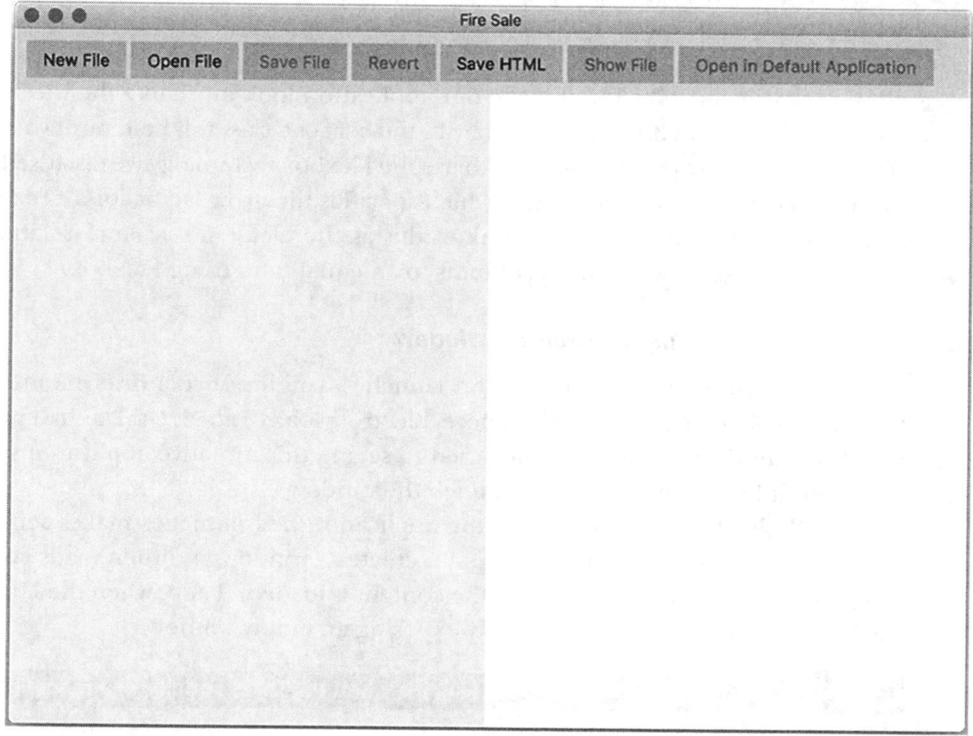

Figure 3.6 Our application has been given some basic styling using modern features of CSS.

The `box-sizing` property handles an historical oddity in CSS where adding 50 pixels of padding to an element with a width of 200 pixels would cause it to be 300 pixels wide (adding 50 pixels of padding on each side), with the same being true for borders as well. When `box-sizing` is set to `border-box`, our elements respect the height and width that we set them to. Generally speaking, this is a good thing. In this CSS rule, we also have every other element and pseudoelement respect the hard work we did by setting `box-sizing` to `border-box`.

We want our applications to fit in with their native colleagues. One important step in that direction is to use the system font that all of the other applications use. That's easier said than done. For example, despite the fact that macOS uses San Francisco as the default font throughout the operating system, it's not available as a regular font. We set the `font` property to `menu`, which defers to the operating system to use its default font—even if we wouldn't otherwise have access to it.

The browser puts a border around whatever UI element is currently active. In macOS, this border is a blue glow. You've probably never thought much about it, because we're used to it on the web, but it looks out of place when we're developing a desktop application. It looks especially bad in our application where one-half of the UI is effectively a large text input. By setting `outline` to none, we remove the unnatural glow around the active element.

In the `.content`, `.raw-markdown`, and `.rendered-html` rules, we implement a simple Flexbox layout, which will make our application look more like the wireframe we introduced in figure 3.1. The element with the `content` class will hold our two columns. We set the `display` property to `flex` to use the Flexbox technology we discussed earlier. In the next step, we set `flex-grow`, which specifies the grow factor for a `flex` item, of course. It's probably helpful to think of this as the element's scale in relation to its sibling. In this case, we set both columns to an equal ratio using Flexbox.

3.3.2 Gracefully displaying the browser window

If you look closely as your application launches, you'll notice a brief moment when the window is completely blank before Electron loads `index.html` and renders the DOM in the window. Users are not used to seeing this in native applications, and we can avoid it by rethinking how we launch the window.

The flash of nothingness when the application first launches makes sense if you consider the code in the main process: it creates a window and then loads content in it. What if we hide the window until the content is loaded? Then, when the UI is ready, we show the window and avoid briefly exposing an empty window.

Listing 3.5 Gracefully showing the window when the DOM's ready: ./app/main.js

```
app.on('ready', () => {
  mainWindow = new BrowserWindow({ show: false });

  mainWindow.loadFile('index.html');

  mainWindow.once('ready-to-show', () => {
    mainWindow.show();
  });

  mainWindow.on('closed', () => {
    mainWindow = null;
  });
});
```

Begin by hiding the window when it's first created.

Add a single event listener to the window's "ready-to-show" event.

Show the window when the DOM is ready.

We passed an object to the `BrowserWindow` constructor, setting it as hidden by default. When the `BrowserWindow` instance fires its `'ready-to-show'` event, we'll call its `show()` method, which will bring it out of hiding after the UI is fully ready to go. This approach is even more useful when the application is loading a remote resource over the network, which is likely to take much longer to initialize the page.

3.4 Implementing the base functionality

Let's put a stake in the ground by getting some of the basic functionality in place. For starters, we want to update the rendered HTML view in the right pane whenever the Markdown in the left pane changes (see figure 3.7). This is where our one dependency—`marked`—comes in to play.

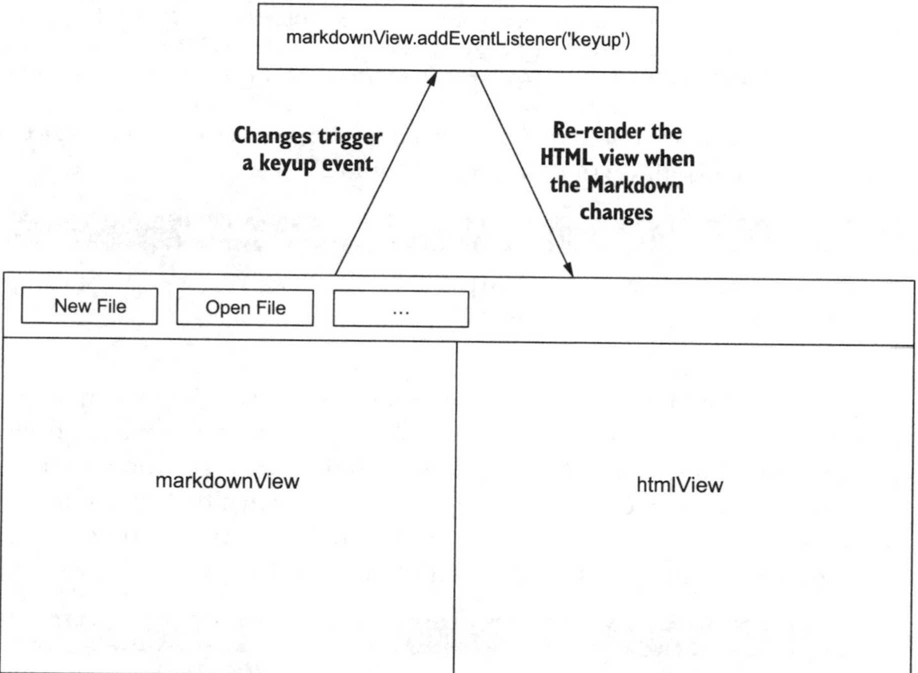

Figure 3.7 We'll add an event listener to the left pane that will render the Markdown as HTML and display it in the right pane.

Bringing in our dependencies is easy because we can use Node's `require` to pull in `marked`. Let's add the following in app/renderer.js.

Listing 3.6 Requiring our dependencies: ./app/renderer.js

```
const marked = require('marked');
```

Now, we have access to Marked using `marked`. Given our discussion of the application's functionality along with the diagram in figure 3.7, you've probably begun to suspect that we'll be working with the `#markdown` text area and the `#html` element a fair amount as we develop our application. Let's use a pair of variables to store a reference to each element so that they're easier to work with, as shown in listing 3.7. While we're at it, let's also create variables for each of the buttons along the top of the UI.

Listing 3.7 Caching DOM selectors: ./app/renderer.js

```
const markdownView = document.querySelector('#markdown');
const htmlView = document.querySelector('#html');
const newFileButton = document.querySelector('#new-file');
const openFileButton = document.querySelector('#open-file');
const saveMarkdownButton = document.querySelector('#save-markdown');
const revertButton = document.querySelector('#revert');
const saveHtmlButton = document.querySelector('#save-html');
const showFileButton = document.querySelector('#show-file');
const openInDefaultButton = document.querySelector('#open-in-default');
```

We also render Markdown into `htmlView` fairly frequently, so we want to give ourselves a function to make this easier for us in the future.

Listing 3.8 Converting Markdown to HTML: ./app/renderer.js

```
const renderMarkdownToHtml = (markdown) => {
  htmlView.innerHTML = marked(markdown, { sanitize: true });
};
```

`marked` takes the Markdown content we want to render as the first argument and an object of options as the second argument. We'd like to protect ourselves from accidental script injections, so we pass in an object with the `sanitize` property set to `true`.

Finally, we add an event listener to `markdownView` that on `keyup` will read its contents (which, in `textarea` elements, is stored in its `value` property), run them through `marked`, and then load them into `htmlView`. The result is shown in figure 3.8.

Listing 3.9 Re-rendering the HTML when Markdown changes: ./app/renderer.js

```
markdownView.addEventListener('keyup', (event) => {
  const currentContent = event.target.value;
  renderMarkdownToHtml(currentContent);
});
```

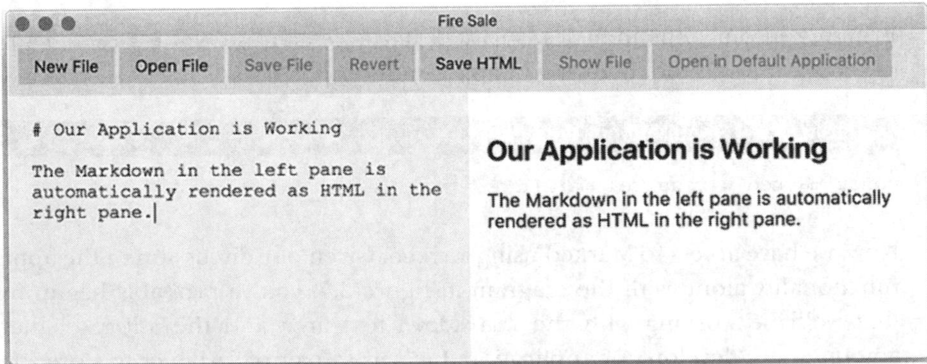

Figure 3.8 Our application takes the content typed by the user in the left pane and automatically renders it as HTML in the right pane. This content was provided by the user and is not part of our application.

The basic functionality is in place and we're ready to begin working on the features that would only be possible in an Electron application—starting with reading and writing files from and to the filesystem. When all is said and done, the renderer process of our application should look like this.

Listing 3.10 The renderer process: ./app/renderer.js

```
const marked = require('marked');

const markdownView = document.querySelector('#markdown');
const htmlView = document.querySelector('#html');
const newFileButton = document.querySelector('#new-file');
const openFileButton = document.querySelector('#open-file');
const saveMarkdownButton = document.querySelector('#save-markdown');
const revertButton = document.querySelector('#revert');
const saveHtmlButton = document.querySelector('#save-html');
const showFileButton = document.querySelector('#show-file');
const openInDefaultButton = document.querySelector('#open-in-default');

const renderMarkdownToHtml = (markdown) => {
  htmlView.innerHTML = marked(markdown, { sanitize: true });
};

markdownView.addEventListener('keyup', (event) => {
  const currentContent = event.target.value;
  renderMarkdownToHtml(currentContent);
});
```

3.5 Debugging an Electron application

In an ideal world, we'd never make mistakes when writing code. APIs and methods would never change between versions and your author wouldn't have to hold his breath every time a new version of a dependency used by the applications in this book was released. We don't live in that world. Thus, we have developer tools at our disposal to aide us in tracking down and—hopefully—eliminating bugs.

3.5.1 Debugging renderer processes

Everything has been going pretty smoothly so far, but it probably won't be long before we're going to have to debug some tricky situation. Because Electron applications are based on Chrome, it's no surprise that we have access to the Chrome Developer Tools when building Electron applications (figure 3.9).

Debugging the renderer process is relatively straightforward. Electron's default application menu provides a command for opening up the Chrome Developer Tools in our application. In chapter 6, we'll learn how to create our own custom menu and eliminate this feature in the event that you'd prefer not to expose it your users.

There are also two other ways to access the Developer Tools. At any point, you can press Command-Option-I on macOS or Control-Shift-I on Windows or Linux to open up the tools (figure 3.10). In addition, you can trigger the Developer Tools

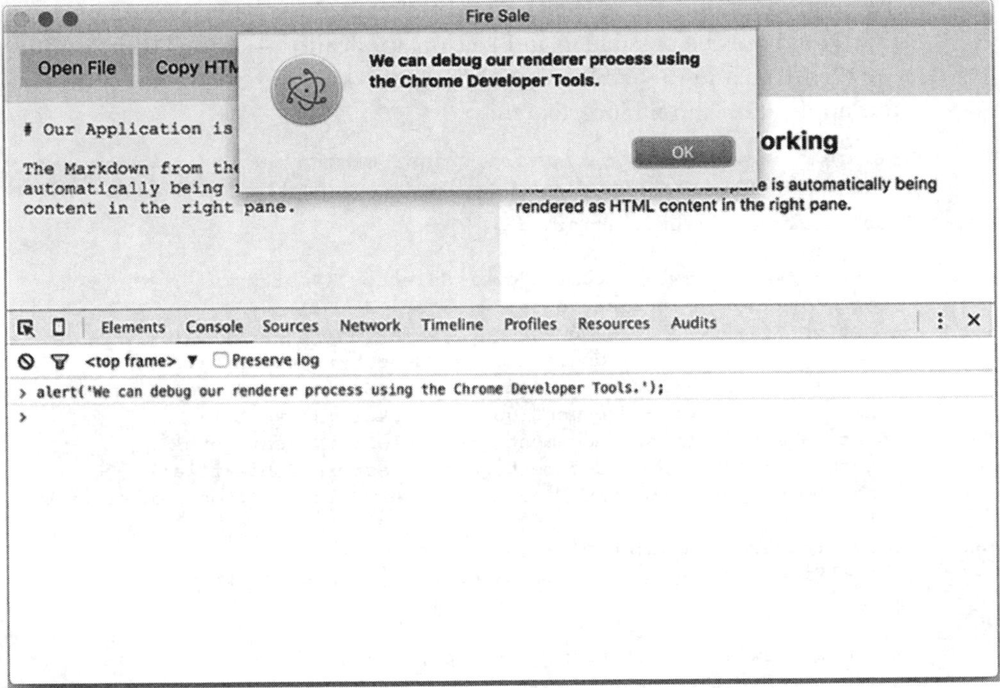

Figure 3.9 The Chrome Developer Tools are available in the renderer process just as they would be in a browser-based application.

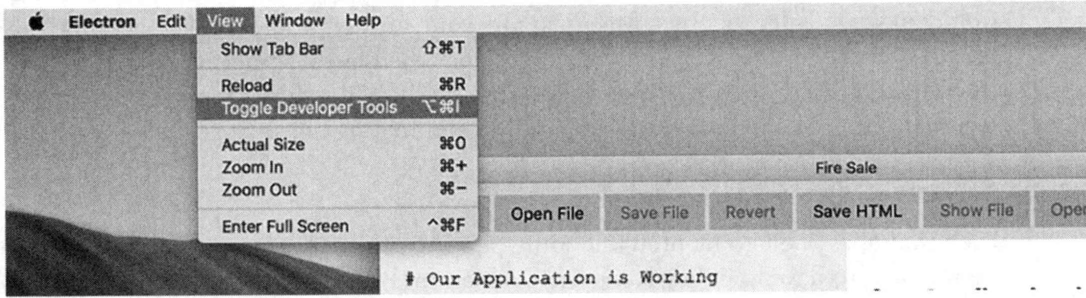

Figure 3.10 The tools can be toggled on and off in the default menu provided by Electron. You can also toggle them using Control-Shift-I on Windows or Command-Option-I on macOS.

programmatically. The `webContents` property on `BrowserWindow` instances has a method called `openDevTools()`. This method, as explained in listing 3.11, will open the Developer Tools in the `BrowserWindow` it's called on.

Listing 3.11 Opening the Developer Tools from the main process: ./app/main.js

```
app.on('ready', () => {
  mainWindow = new BrowserWindow();

  mainWindow.loadFile('index.html');

  mainWindow.once('ready-to-show', () => {
    mainWindow.show();
    mainWindow.webContents.openDevTools();
  });

  mainWindow.on('closed', () => {
    mainWindow = null;
  });
});
```

We can programmatically trigger the opening of the Developer Tools on the main window as soon as it's loaded.

3.5.2 Debugging the main process

Debugging the main process is not so easy. Node Inspector, a common tool for debugging Node.js applications, is not fully supported by Electron at this time. You can start your Electron application in debug mode using the `--debug` flag, which will—by default—enable remote debugging on port 5858.

Limited support for using Node Inspector with Electron is available in the official documentation. As this is still in a bit of flux for the time being, you should review the most recent version of the documentation if you are not using Visual Studio Code (http://electron.atom.io/docs/tutorial/debugging-main-process/). That said, I haven't found this technique particularly stable and wouldn't recommend it. Your mileage may vary.

3.5.3 Debugging the main process with Visual Studio Code

Visual Studio Code is a free, open source IDE available for Windows, Linux, and macOS and is—coincidentally—built on top of Electron by Microsoft. Visual Studio Code comes with a rich set of tools for debugging Node applications that make it much easier to debug Electron applications than noted previously. A quick way to set up a build task is to ask Visual Studio Code to build the application without a build task. Press Control-Shift-B on Windows or Command-Shift-B on macOS and you'll be prompted to create a build task, as shown in figure 3.11.

Clicking on the Configure Build Task menu item will prompt you to select whether you want to create a "start" or "test" task. Choosing "start" will generate a task that calls `npm start`. Choosing "test" will generate `npm test`. Listing 3.12 is an example of what a "start" task looks like.

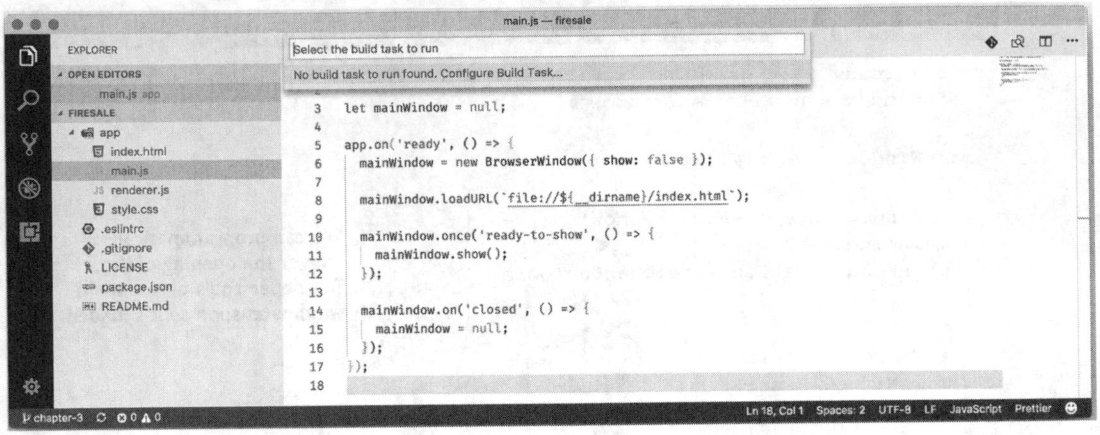

Figure 3.11 Triggering the build task without one in place will prompt Visual Studio Code to create one on your behalf.

Listing 3.12 Setting up a build task in Visual Studio Code for Windows: tasks.json

```
{
  // See https://go.microsoft.com/fwlink/?LinkId=733558
  // for the documentation about the tasks.json format
  "version": "2.0.0",
  "tasks": [
    {
      "type": "npm",
      "script": "start",
      "group": {
        "kind": "build",
        "isDefault": true
      }
    }
  ]
}
```

Now, when you press Control-Shift-B on Windows or Command-Shift-B on macOS, your Electron application will start up. Not only is this important in order to set up debugging within Visual Studio Code, it's also a convenient way to start up your application in general. The next step is to set up Visual Studio Code to launch the application and connect it to its built-in debugger (figure 3.12).

To create a launch task, go the Debug tab in the left pane and click on the small gear in the upper-left corner. Visual Studio Code will ask you what kind of configuration file you'd like to create. Select Node and replace the contents of the file with listing 3.13.

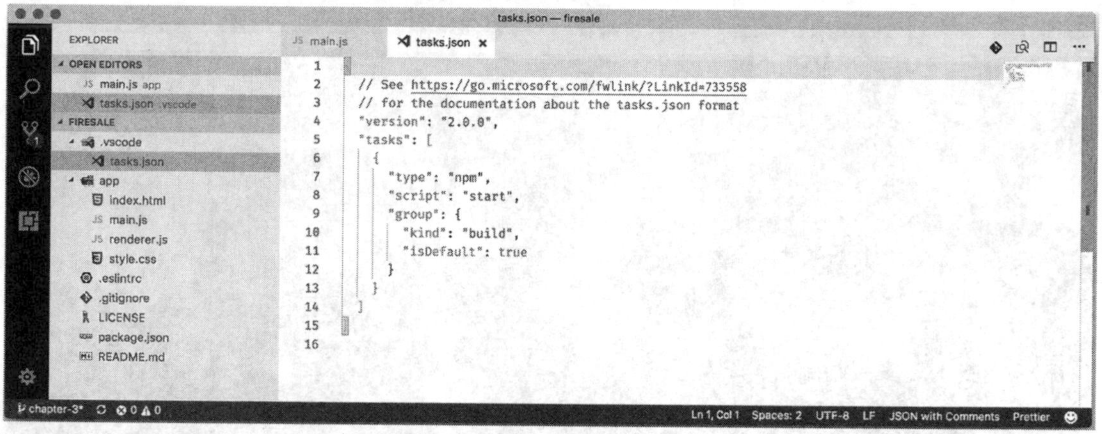

Figure 3.12 Inside the Debug tab, click on the gear and Visual Studio Code will create a configuration file for launching the debugger on your behalf.

Listing 3.13 Setting up a launch task for Visual Studio Code for Windows: launch.json

```
{
  "version": "0.2.0",
  "configurations": [
    {
      "name": "Debug Main Process",
      "type": "node",
      "request": "launch",
      "cwd": "${workspaceRoot}",
      "runtimeExecutable":
        "${workspaceRoot}/node_modules/.bin/electron",
      "windows": {
        "runtimeExecutable":
          "${workspaceRoot}/node_modules/.bin/electron.cmd"
      },
      "args":
        "."
      ]
    }
  ]
}
```

With this configuration file in place, you can click on the left margin of any line in your main process to set a breakpoint and then press F5 to run the application. Execution will pause at the breakpoint, allowing you to inspect the call stack, determine what variables are in scope, and interact with a live console. Breakpoints aren't the only way to debug your code. You can also watch for particular expressions or drop into the debugger whenever an uncaught exception is thrown (figure 3.13).

There is a high chance that you're not using Visual Studio Code. That's fine. It's not a prerequisite for this book and you will almost definitely be fine using the text

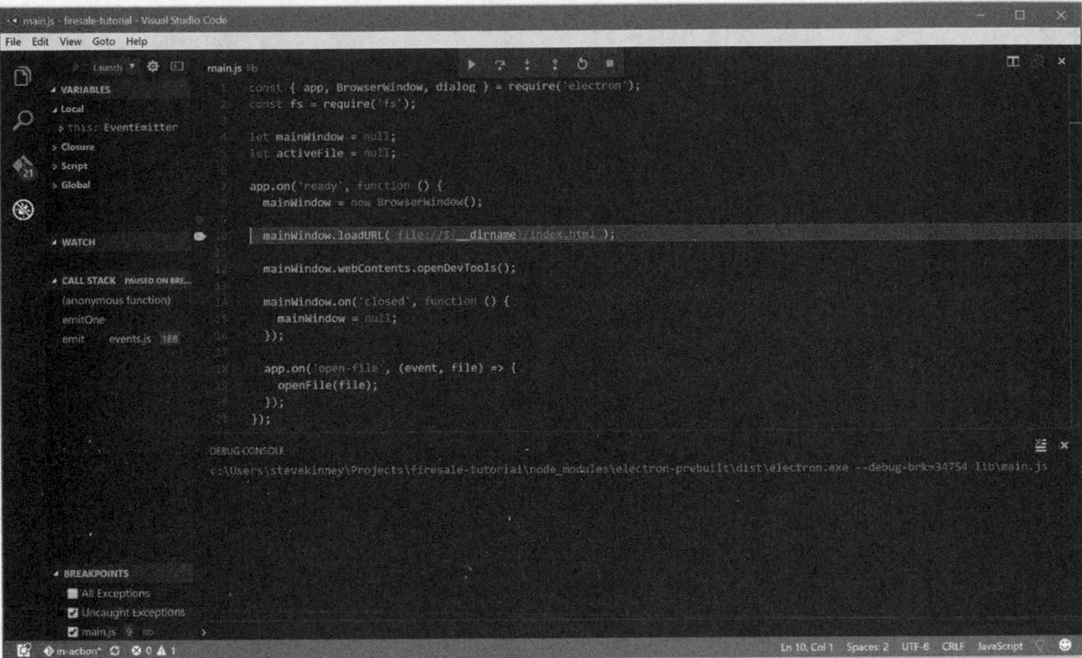

Figure 3.13 The debugger built in to Visual Studio Code allows you to pause the execution of your application and drop in to investigate bugs.

editor or IDE you're most comfortable with. In addition, Visual Studio Code isn't the only one with support for debugging the main process. For example, you can find details for configuring WebStorm here: http://mng.bz/Y5T6.

Summary

- Over the next few chapters, we'll be working on a Markdown-to-HTML renderer.
- Flexbox is supported by modern browsers and allows us to easily implement a two-pane interface that will adapt as the user changes the size of the window.
- Chrome Developer Tools are available in all renderer processes and can be triggered from the default application in Electron, a keyboard shortcut, or from the main process.
- The Node Inspector is not fully supported in Electron at this time.
- Visual Studio Code provides a rich set of tools for debugging problems in the main process of your application.

4 Using native file dialog boxes and facilitating interprocess communication

This chapter covers

- Implementing a native open file dialog box using Electron's `dialog` module
- Facilitating communication between the main process and a renderer process
- Exposing functionality from the main process to renderer processes
- Importing functionality from the main process into the renderer process using Electron's `remote` module
- Sending information from the main process to a renderer process using the `webContents` module and setting up a listener for messages from the main process using the `ipcRenderer` module

In the previous chapter, we laid the foundation for our first Electron project, a notes application that takes Markdown from the left pane and renders it as HTML in the right pane. We set up our main process and configured it to spawn a renderer. We set up package.json, installed the necessary dependencies, created the main and renderer processes, and laid out the UI. We also explored ways we can make our application feel like a desktop application, but we haven't added a feature that is far outside the scope of what a traditional web application could do yet.

Right now, the application allows the user to write in the Markdown view. When the user presses a key in the Markdown view, the application automatically renders the Markdown to HTML and displays it in the HTML view.

In this chapter, we'll add the ability to trigger a native file dialog box and select a text file from anywhere on the filesystem and load it into our application. By the end of the chapter, the Open File button in the renderer process's browser window will trigger the Open File dialog box from the main process. Before we can do that, it's important to discuss how to communicate between processes in a bit more depth. We start on the chapter-3 branch, which can be found at http://mng.bz/11Kd. The code at the end of the chapter can be found at http://mng.bz/0C34. Alternatively, you can pull down the master branch and check out either of these two branches.

```
git clone  https://github.com/electron-in-action/firesale.git chapter-3
git checkout -f chapter3
```

4.1 Triggering native file dialog boxes

An easy way to get started is to prompt the user for a file to open when the application first starts and emits its ready event, as shown in figure 4.1. Our application is already listening for the ready event before we create our `BrowserWindow` instance. Later in this chapter, we learn how to trigger this functionality from the UI. In the next chapter, we learn how to trigger it from the application menu as well.

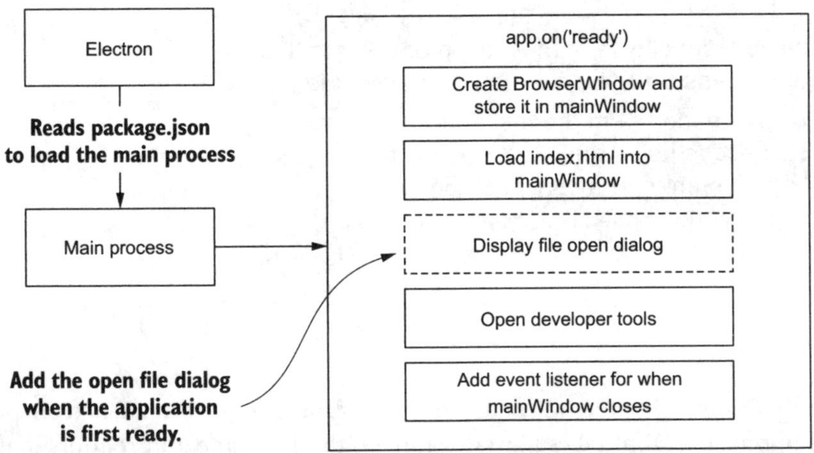

Figure 4.1 Our application will trigger the Open File dialog box when it starts. By the end of the chapter, this functionality will be replaced by the ability to trigger the dialog box from the UI.

You create native dialogs using Electron's `dialog` module. Add the code in listing 4.1 to app/main.js just beneath where the other Electron modules are required.

Listing 4.1 Importing the dialog module: ./app/main.js

```
const { app, BrowserWindow, dialog } = require('electron');
```

Eventually the application should trigger our file-opening functionality from multiple places. The first step is to create a function to reference later. Start by logging the name of the file selected to the console after it has been selected.

Listing 4.2 Creating a `getFileFromUser()` function: ./app/main.js

```
const getFileFromUser = () => {
  const files = dialog.showOpenDialog({
    properties: ['openFile']
  });

  if (!files) { return; }

  console.log(files);
};
```

- Triggers the operating system's Open File dialog box. We also pass it a JavaScript object of different configuration arguments to the function. (`dialog.showOpenDialog({`)
- The configuration object sets different properties on the Open File dialog. (`properties: ['openFile']`)
- If we don't have any files, return early from the function. (`if (!files) { return; }`)
- Logs the files to the console (`console.log(files);`)

Our `getFileFromUser()` function is a wrapper over `dialog.showOpenDialog()` that we can use in multiple places in our application without having to repeat ourselves. It will trigger the `showOpenDialog()` method on `dialog` and pass it a JavaScript object with different settings that we can adjust as needed. In JavaScript, an object's keys are called its properties. The properties of the object passed to `dialog.showOpenDialog()` configure certain characteristics of the dialog box we're creating. One such setting is the properties of the dialog box itself. The `properties` property on the configuration object takes an array of different flags we can set on the dialog box. In this case, we're activating only the `openFile` flag, which signifies that this dialog box is for selecting a file to open—as opposed to selecting a directory or multiple files. The other flags available are `openDirectory` and `multiselections`.

`dialog.showOpenDialog()` returns the names of the files selected. An array of the paths selected by the user are stored in a variable called `files`. If the user presses cancel, `dialog.showOpenDialog()` returns `undefined` and breaks if we try to call any methods on `files` while it's `undefined`. The `return` statement guards against that by leaving the function early if `files` is a false value—and `undefined` is, in fact, a false value.

`getFileFromUser()` must be called somewhere in our application to trigger the dialog box. Eventually, it will be called from the UI and the application menu. A convenient place to do this—for now—is when the application starts. Call `getFileFromUser()` when the app module fires its ready event, as shown in the following listing. This step will be removed when our UI is configured to trigger `getFileFromUser()` from the renderer process.

Listing 4.3 Invoking `getFileFromUser()` when the application is first ready

```
app.on('ready', () => {
  mainWindow = new BrowserWindow({ show: false });

  mainWindow.loadFile('index.html');

  mainWindow.once('ready-to-show', () => {
    mainWindow.show();
    getFileFromUser();
  });

  mainWindow.on('closed', () => {
    mainWindow = null;
  });
});
```

We'll call getFileFromUser() when the window is ready to show. getFileFromUser() is defined in listing 4.2.

When our application starts and the window is fully loaded, users immediately will see a File dialog box, which will allow them to select a file (see figure 4.2). We eventually remove this function call from the launch process and assign it to the Open File button in the UI.

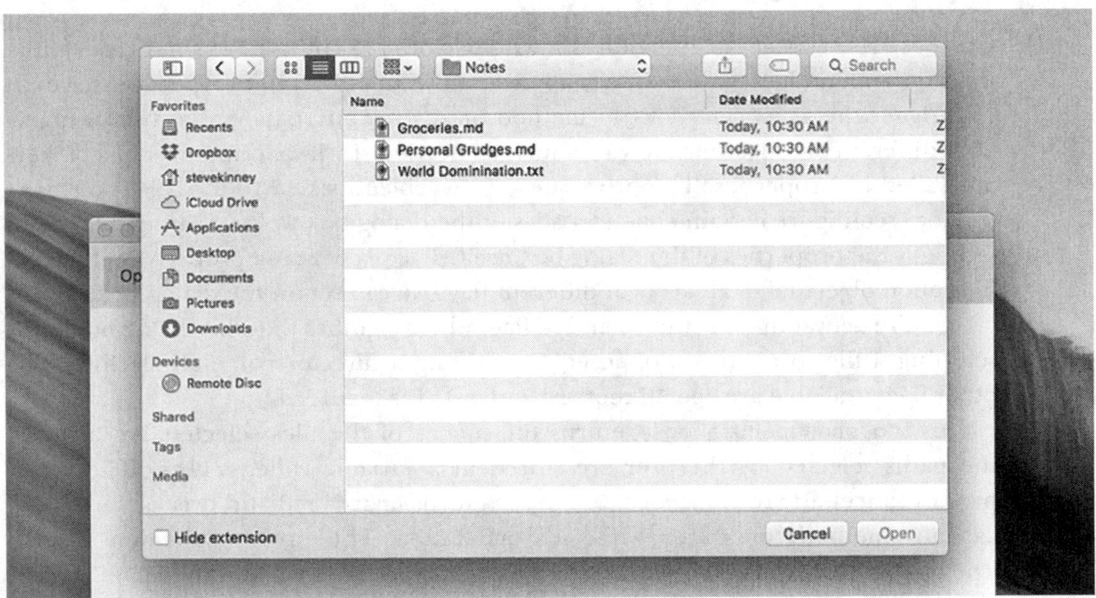

Figure 4.2 Electron is able to trigger native file dialog boxes in each of its supported operating systems.

In figure 4.3, we can see the results of our selection in the Open File dialog box displayed in our terminal. Notice that `dialog.showOpenDialog()` returns an array. If `multiselections` is activated in the dialog's `properties` array, the user can select multiple files. Electron always returns an array for consistency.

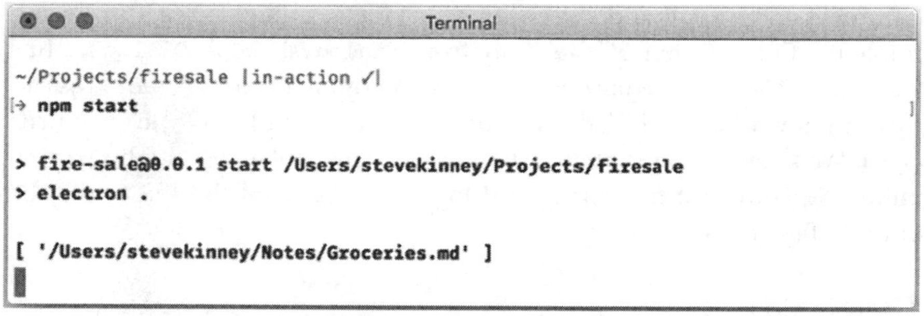

```
~/Projects/firesale |in-action ✓|
→ npm start

> fire-sale@0.0.1 start /Users/stevekinney/Projects/firesale
> electron .

[ '/Users/stevekinney/Notes/Groceries.md' ]
```

Figure 4.3 Upon selecting a file, the full path of the file is logged to the console in our terminal window.

4.2 Reading files using Node

`dialog.showOpenDialog()` returns an array consisting of the paths of the file or files that the user selected, but it does not read them on our behalf. Depending on what kind of file we're building, we might want to handle opening the file differently. In this application, the contents of the file are read and immediately displayed in the UI. A different application that handles copying images or uploads them to an external service might take a contrasting approach when the user selects a file. Still another application might add a large movie to a playlist to watch later. In this case, it would be wasteful to immediately start opening the large file.

Node comes with a set of tools for working with files in its standard library. The built-in `fs` library handles common filesystem operations such as reading and writing files, so you should require it near the top of app/main.js.

Listing 4.4 Importing Node's fs module: ./app/main.js

```
const { app, BrowserWindow, dialog } = require('electron');
const fs = require('fs');                    ← Requires Node's fs library.

app.on('ready', () => { … });                ← Code omitted for clarity.

const getFileFromUser = () => {
  const files = dialog.showOpenDialog(mainWindow, {
    properties: ['openFile']
  });

  if (!files) { return; }

  const file = files[0];                     ← Pulls the first file out of the array
  const content = fs.readFileSync(file).toString();   ← Reads from the file, and converts the resulting buffer to a string.

  console.log(content);
};
```

In listing 4.4, the application opens only one file at a time. `files[0]` selects the first—and only—file path out of the array from `dialog.showOpenDialog()`. In `fs.readFileSync(file)` the file path is passed as an argument to `fs.readFileSync()`. Node doesn't know what kind of file was opened, so `fs.readFileSync()` returns a buffer object. We know, however, that we typically work with plain text in this particular application. We convert it to a string and log the contents of the file to the terminal, as shown in figure 4.4.

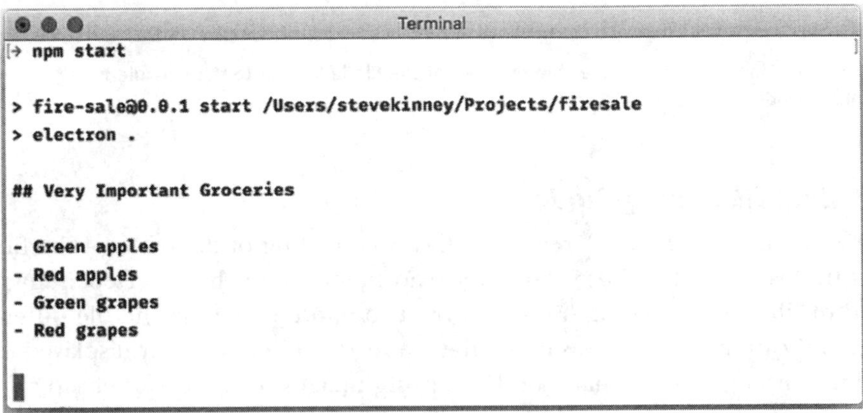

Figure 4.4 The contents of the file are logged to the user's terminal.

4.2.1 Scoping the Open File dialog

As you can see in figure 4.4, `getFileFromUser()` successfully logs the contents of a text file to the terminal. But there is a problem. By default, `dialog.showOpenDialog()` lets us open any file on our computer, with no consideration for what types of files we're prepared to handle. Figure 4.5 shows the problematic result when we open an image file instead of a text file through the dialog box.

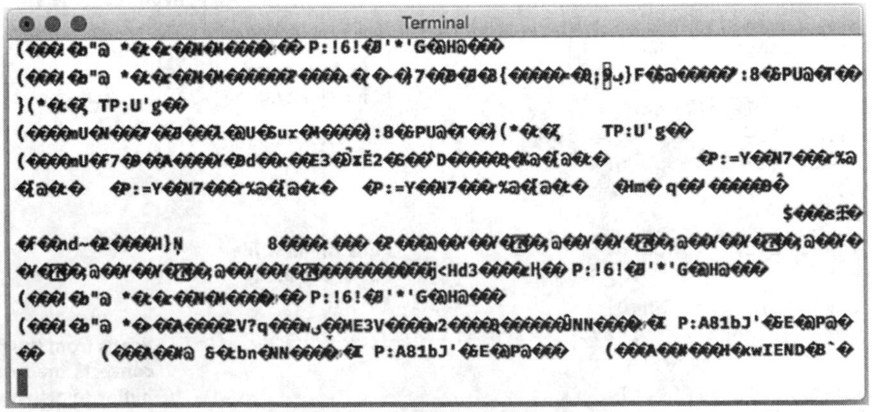

Figure 4.5 If the user selects a nontext file, the function logs the binary data.

Many desktop applications can limit the file types that the users can open. This is also true for applications built with Electron. Our application isn't suited for opening music files, so we should probably not let the user select MP3s. Additional options can be added to the configuration object passed to `dialog.showOpenDialog()` to restrict the dialog box to file extensions that we've whitelisted.

Listing 4.5 Whitelisting specific file types: ./app/main.js

```
const getFileFromUser = () => {
  const files = dialog.showOpenDialog({
    properties: ['openFile'],
    filters: [
      { name: 'Text Files', extensions: ['txt'] },
      { name: 'Markdown Files', extensions: ['md', 'markdown'] }
    ]
  });

  if (!files) { return; }

  const file = files[0];
  const content = fs.readFileSync(file).toString();

  console.log(content);
};
```

The filters property allows us to specify what types of files our application should be able to open and disables any file that doesn't match our criteria.

In the listing we added a second property to the object passed to `dialog.showOpenDialog()`. In Windows, the dialog displays the name Markdown Files in the drop-down menu, as seen in figure 4.6. In macOS, there is no drop-down menu, but we cannot select images that do not have one of the extensions, as shown in figure 4.7.

4.2.2 *Implementing dialog sheets in macOS*

Electron applications are designed to be cross-platform, meaning they work on macOS, Windows, and Linux. Electron provides interfaces to native features and APIs that exist in each of the supporting operating systems but do not exist in the others. We saw this earlier when we provided a name for our file extension filters. This name appears in Windows, but macOS does not have this capability. Electron takes advantage of this feature if it is available, but it still works in the cases where it isn't.

In macOS, we're able to display dialog boxes that drop down as sheets from the top of the window instead of being displayed in front of it (listing 4.6). We can create this UI easily in Electron by passing a reference to the `BrowserWindow` instance—which we've stored in `mainWindow`—as the first argument to `dialog.showOpenDialog()`, before the configuration object.

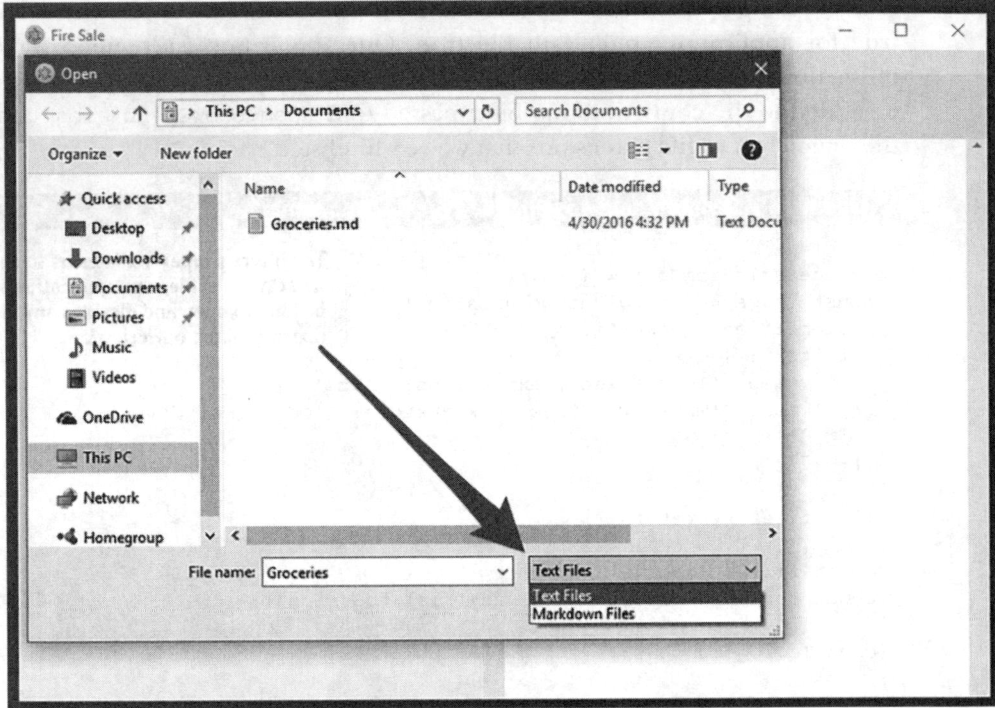

Figure 4.6 In Windows, we can switch between different types of files.

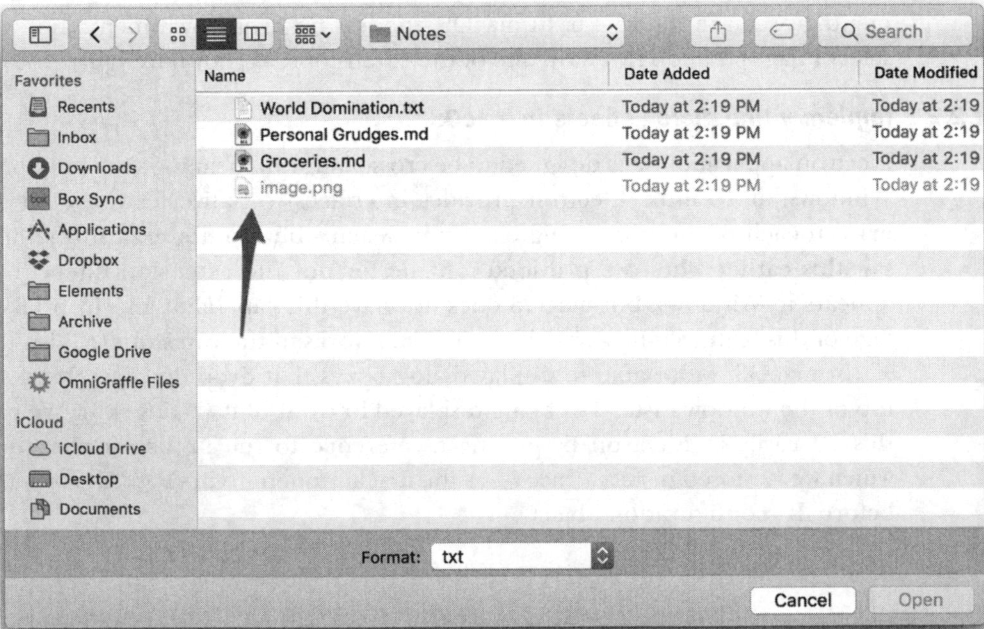

Figure 4.7 macOS does not support switching between types of files but does allow us to select any file that is eligible as defined by the filters option.

Listing 4.6 Creating sheet dialogs in macOS: ./app/main.js

```
const getFileFromUser = () => {
  const files = dialog.showOpenDialog(mainWindow, {
    properties: ['openFile'],
    filters: [
      { name: 'Text Files', extensions: ['txt'] },
      { name: 'Markdown Files', extensions: ['md', 'markdown'] }
    ]
  });

  if (!files) { return; }

  const file = files[0];
  const content = fs.readFileSync(file).toString();

  console.log(content);
};
```

Passing a reference to a BrowserWindow instance to dialog.showOpenDialog will cause macOS to display the dialog box as a sheet coming down from the title bar of the window. It has no effect on Windows and Linux.

With this simple change, Electron now displays the Open File dialog as a sheet that drops down from the window passed to the method, as shown in figure 4.8.

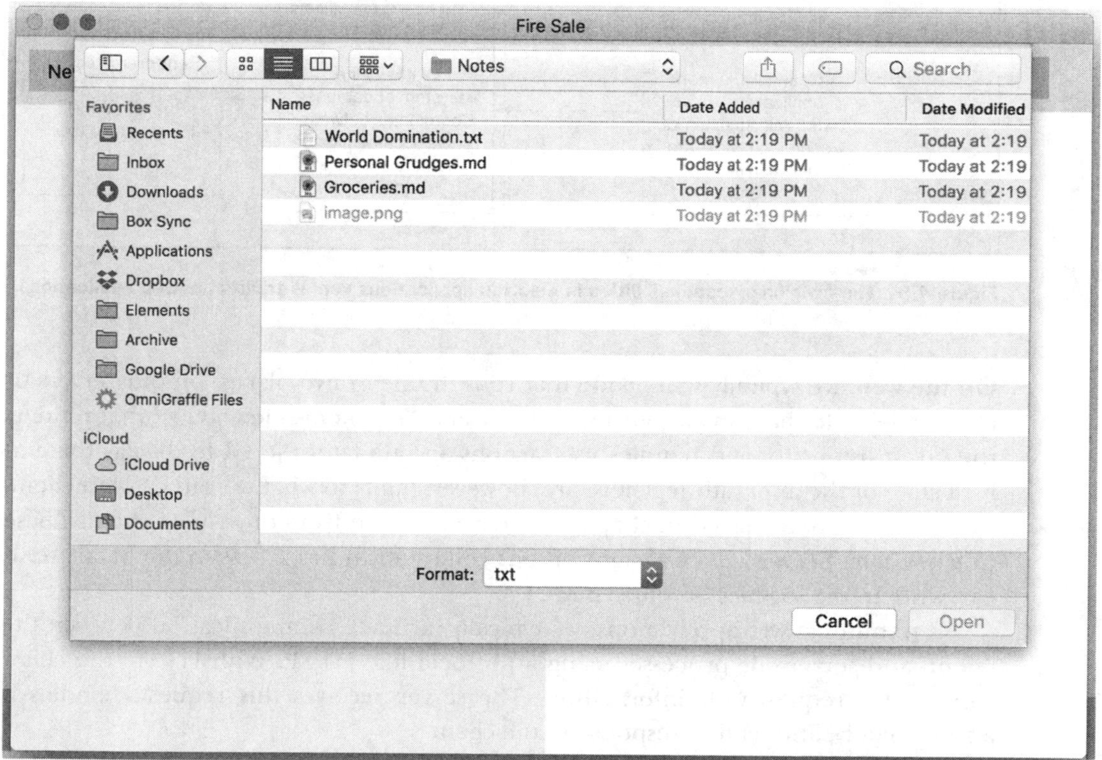

Figure 4.8 Instead of appearing as an additional window in front of our application's window, the Open File dialog box now drops down from the menu's title bar in macOS.

4.3 Facilitating interprocess communication

We've written all of the code for selecting files and reading files in our main process. But how do we send the contents of the file to the renderer process? How do we trigger the `getFileFromUser()` function in our main process from our UI?

We have to deal with similar issues when building traditional web applications. It's not exactly the same because all of the code runs on the client's computer, but thinking about how we usually build web applications can serve as a helpful metaphor for understanding how to structure our Electron applications. See figure 4.9.

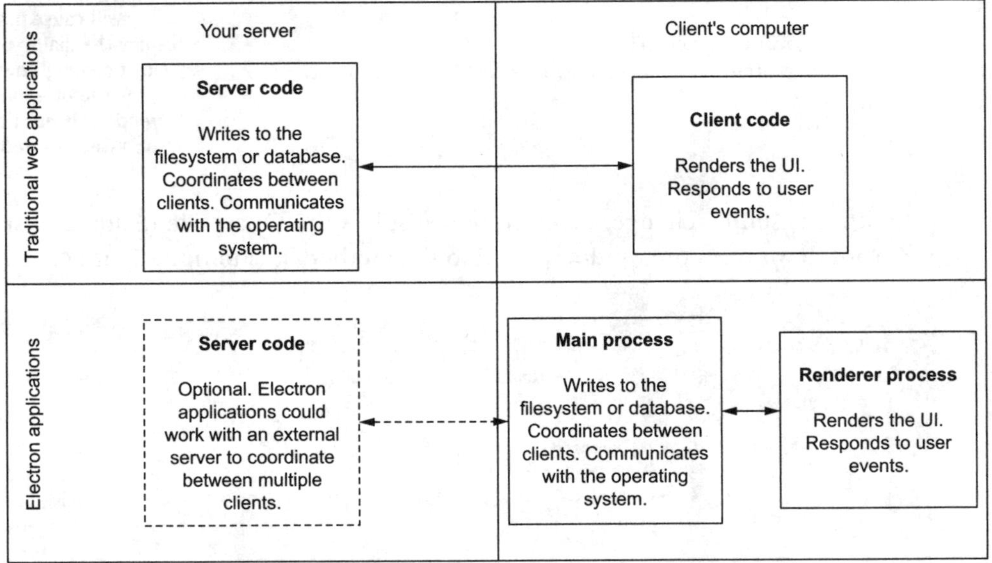

Figure 4.9 The division of responsibilities in Electron applications versus traditional web applications.

On the web, we typically write code that runs in one of two places: on our servers or client-side code that runs in our users' browsers. The client-side code is what renders the UI. It listens for and handles user actions and updates the UI to display the current state of the application. There are, however, limits to what we can do with client-side code. As we discussed in chapter 1, we cannot read from or write to the database or filesystem. Server-side code runs on our computer. It has access to the database. It can write to the log files on our system.

In traditional web applications, we typically facilitate communication between the client- and server-side processes using a protocol like HTTP. With HTTP, the client can send a request with information. The server receives this request, handles it appropriately, and sends a response to the client.

In Electron applications, things are a little different. As we've discussed in the previous chapters, Electron applications consist of multiple processes: one main process and one or more renderer processes. Everything runs on our computer, but there is a similar separation of roles to the client-server model. We don't use HTTP to communicate between processes. Instead Electron provides several modules for coordinating communication between the main and renderer processes.

Our main process is in charge of interfacing with the native operating system APIs. It's in charge of spawning renderer processes, defining application menus, displaying Open and Save dialog boxes, registering global shortcuts, requesting power information from the OS, and more. Electron enforces this by making many of the modules needed to perform these tasks available only in the main process, as shown in figure 4.10.

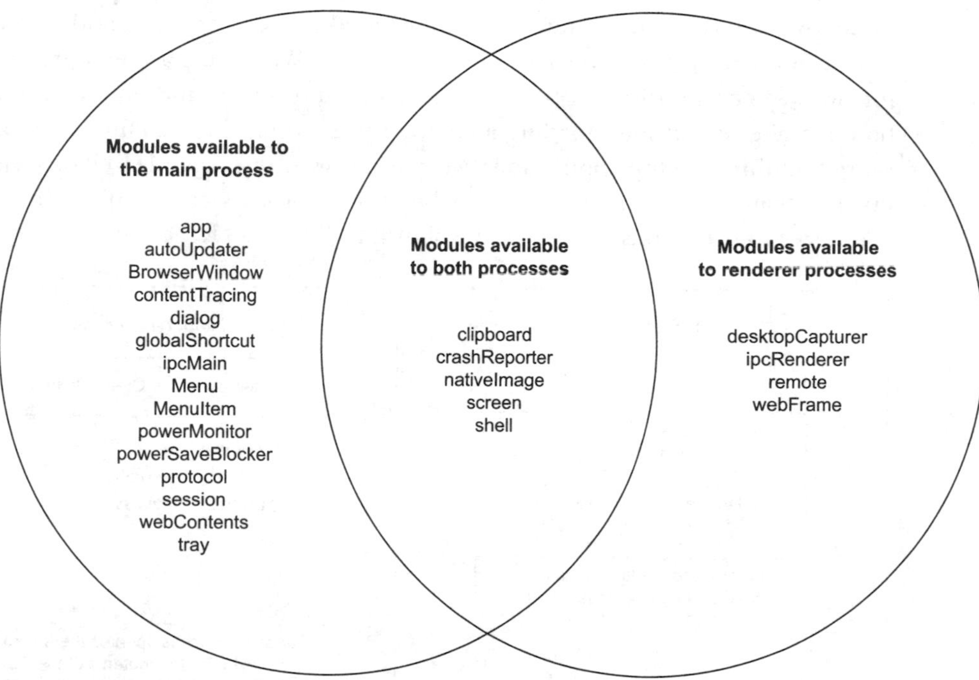

Figure 4.10 Electron provides different modules to the main and renderer processes. These modules represent the code capabilities of Electron. This list is likely to grow and may be incomplete by the time you read this. I encourage you to visit the documentation to see the latest and greatest features.

Electron provides only a subset of its modules to each process and doesn't keep us from accessing Node APIs that are separate from Electron's modules. We can access a database or the filesystem from the renderer process if we want, but there are compelling reasons to keep this kind of functionality in the main process. We could potentially have many renderer processes, but we will always have only one main process. Reading from and writing to the filesystem from one of our renderer processes could become problematic; we could end up in a situation where one or more processes try to write to the same file at the same time or read from a file while another renderer process is overwriting it.

A given process in JavaScript executes our code on a single thread and can do only one thing at a time. By delegating these tasks to the main process, we can be confident that only one process is performing reading or writing to a given file or database at a time. Other tasks follow the normal JavaScript protocol of patiently waiting in the event queue until the main process is done with its current task.

It makes sense that the main process handles tasks that call native operating system APIs or provides filesystem access, but the UI that likely triggers these operations is called in the renderer process. Even though all of the code is running on the same computer, we still have to coordinate the communication between our processes, just as we would have to coordinate communication between the client and server.

More recently, protocols like WebSockets and WebRTC have emerged that allow for two-way communication between the client and server, and even communication between clients, without needing a central server to facilitate communication. When we're building desktop applications, we typically won't be using HTTP or WebSockets, but Electron has several ways to coordinate interprocess communication, which we begin to explore in this chapter and is shown in figure 4.11.

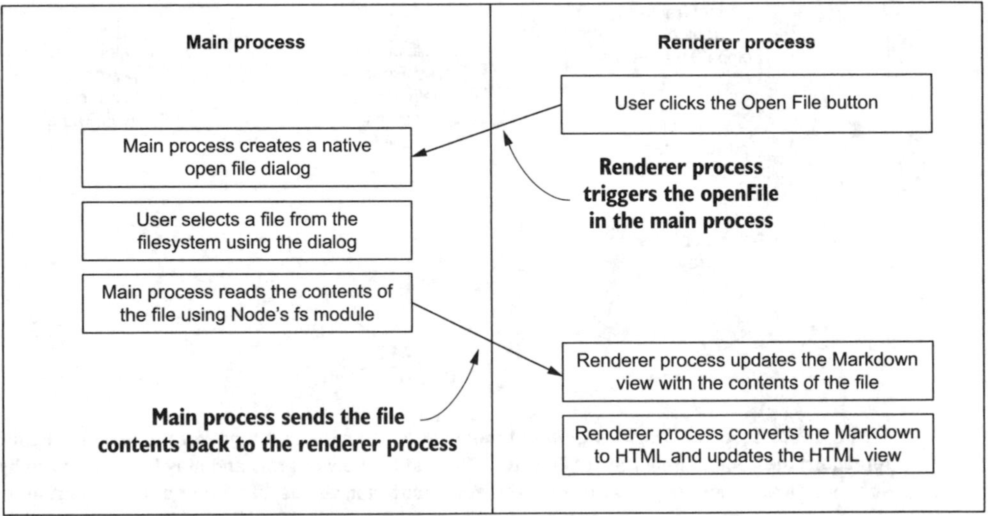

Figure 4.11 Implementing the Open File button involves coordinating communication between the renderer process and the main process.

Our UI contains a button with the label Open File. When the user clicks this button, our application should provide a dialog box allowing the user to select a file to open. After the user selects a file, our application should read the contents of the file, display them in the left pane of our application, and render the corresponding HTML in the right pane.

As you might have guessed, this requires us to coordinate between the renderer process, where the button was clicked, and the main process, which is responsible for displaying the dialog and reading the chosen file from the filesystem. After reading the file, the main process needs to send the contents of the file back over to the renderer process (next listing) to be displayed and rendered in the left and right panes, respectively.

Listing 4.7 Adding an event listener in the renderer process: ./app/renderer.js

```
const marked = require('marked');

const markdownView = document.querySelector('#markdown');
const htmlView = document.querySelector('#html');
const newFileButton = document.querySelector('#new-file');
const openFileButton = document.querySelector('#open-file');
const saveMarkdownButton = document.querySelector('#save-markdown');
const revertButton = document.querySelector('#revert');
const saveHtmlButton = document.querySelector('#save-html');
const showFileButton = document.querySelector('#show-file');
const openInDefaultButton = document.querySelector('#open-in-default');

const renderMarkdownToHtml = (markdown) => {
  htmlView.innerHTML = marked(markdown, { sanitize: true });
};

markdownView.addEventListener('keyup', (event) => {
  const currentContent = event.target.value;
  renderMarkdownToHtml(currentContent);
});

openFileButton.addEventListener('click', () => {
  alert('You clicked the "Open File" button.');
});
```

Opts in to an updated CSS box model that will correctly set the width and height of elements

Start by adding an event listener to the Open File button in our renderer process. With our event listener in place, it's time to coordinate with the main process to trigger the Open File dialog box we created earlier.

4.3.1 Introducing the remote module

Electron provides numerous ways to facilitate interprocess communication. The first one is the `remote` module—a simple way to perform interprocess communication from the renderer process to the main process. The `remote` module, available only in the renderer process, works as a proxy to the main process by mirroring the modules that are accessible in the main process. The `remote` module also takes care of communication to and from the main process when we access any of those properties.

Depicted in figure 4.12, the `remote` module has several properties that overlap with the modules available only to the main process. In our renderer process, we can require the `remote` module, and it provides access to objects and properties in the main process, as shown in figure 4.13.

When we call a method or property on the `remote` object, it sends a synchronous message to the main process, executes in the main process, and sends a message back

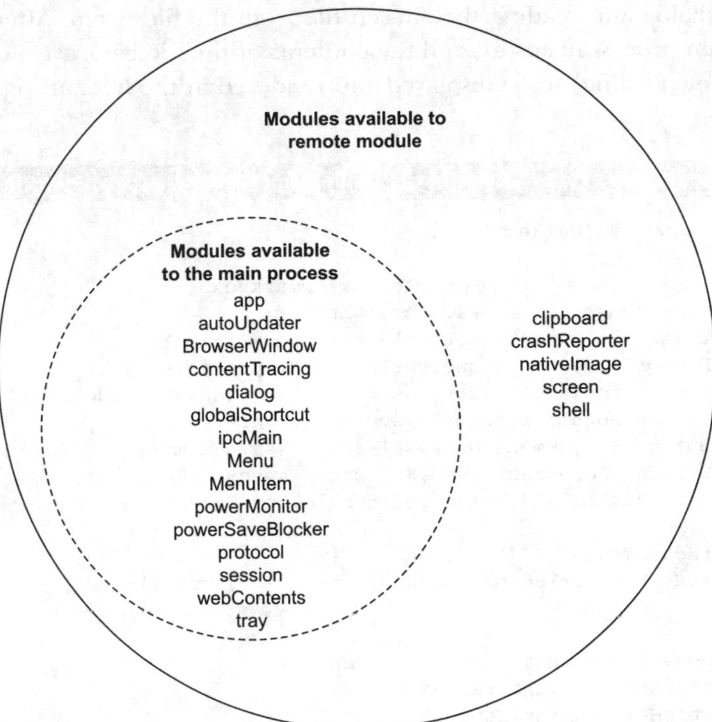

Figure 4.12 The `remote` module shares many of the same properties as the Electron module in the main process.

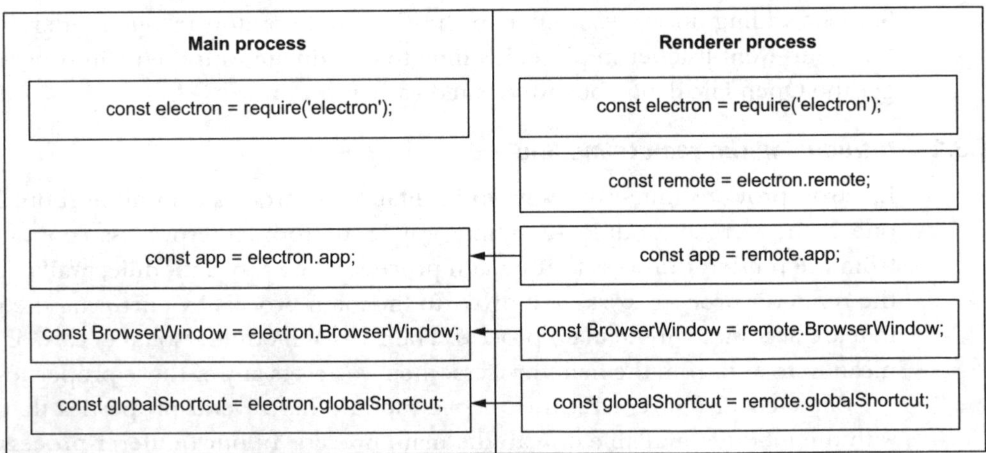

Figure 4.13 The `remote` module provides access to modules normally available only to the main process.

to the renderer process with the results. The `remote` module allows us to define functionality in the main process and easily makes it available to our renderer processes.

4.4 Triggering the Open File function using interprocess communication

The application can now trigger an Open File dialog box and read the contents of the file that the user selected in the main process. We've also added an event listener to the Open File button in the renderer process. Now it's just a matter of connecting them using the interprocess communication techniques we explored earlier.

4.4.1 Understanding the CommonJS require system

To use functionality from the main process using the `remote` module, we need to take advantage of Node's `CommonJS` module system to expose that functionality to other files in our application. We've used `require` in this book to pull in functionality from Electron, the Node standard library, and third-party libraries, but this is the first time we use it with our own code. Let's spend a few minutes reviewing how it works.

Node's module system consists of two primary mechanisms: the ability to require functionality from other sources, and the ability to export functionality to be consumed by other sources. When we require code from other sources, the other source could be a file we've written, a third-party module, a module from the Node, or a module provided by Electron. We've used Node's built-in `require` function at the top of both our main and renderer processes.

When we require a module, what exactly are we importing? In Node, we explicitly declare what functionality should be exported from the module, as shown in listing 4.8. This function is imported in listing 4.9. Every module in Node has a built-in object called `exports` that starts out as an empty object. Anything we add to the `exports` object is available when we require it from another file.

Listing 4.8 Exporting a function in Node: basic-math.js

```
exports.addTwo = n => n + 2;
```

Listing 4.9 Importing a function in Node

```
const basicMath = require('./basic-math');

basicMath.addTwo(4); // returns 6
```

4.4.2 Requiring functionality from another process

The built-in `require` function does not work across processes. When we're working in the renderer process, any functionality we use from the built-in `require` function to import will be part of the renderer process. When we're working in the main process, any functionality we require will be part of the main process. But what happens when we are in the renderer process and we want to require functionality from the main process?

Electron's `remote` module has its own `require` method that allows it to require functionality from the main process in our renderer process. Using `remote.require` returns a proxy object—like the other properties on the `remote` object. Electron takes care of all of the interprocess communication on our behalf.

To implement the functionality we set out at the beginning of this chapter, the main process must export its `getFileFromUser()` function so that we can import it into our renderer code. This listing updates a single line in app/main.js.

Listing 4.10 Exporting ability to open the file dialog from the renderer process: ./app/main.js

```
const getFileFromUser = exports.getFileFromUser  = () => {
  const files = dialog.showOpenDialog(mainWindow, {
    properties: ['openFile'],
    filters: [
      { name: 'Text Files', extensions: ['txt'] },
      { name: 'Markdown Files', extensions: ['md', 'markdown'] }
    ]
  });

  if (!files) { return; }

  const file = files[0];
  const content = fs.readFileSync(file).toString();

  console.log(content);
};
```

In addition to creating a constant in this file, we assign it as a property of the exports object, which will be accessible from other files—specifically, the renderer process.

The code takes the `getFileFromUser()` function we created and exports it as a property with the same name on the exports object. The render process needs to bring in Electron's `remote` module and then use the `remote.require` function to get a reference to the `getFileFromUser()` function from the main process in our renderer process. This is different from the built-in require function shown in listing 4.11 because the imported code is evaluated in terms of the main process, not the renderer process in which it was required. This is accomplished in four steps:

1. Require Electron in our renderer process.
2. Store a reference to the `remote` module.
3. Use `remote.require` to require the main process.
4. Store a reference to the `getFileFromUser()` function exported from the main process.

Listing 4.11 Requiring functions from the main process in the renderer process: ./app/renderer.js

```
const { remote } = require('electron');
const mainProcess = remote.require('./main.js');
```

We can now call the `getFileFromUser()` function we exported from the main process in our renderer process. Let's replace the functionality in our event listener to trigger the Open File dialog box instead of firing an `alert`.

Listing 4.12 Triggering `getFileFromUser()` in the main process from the UI: ./app/renderer.js

```
openFileButton.addEventListener('click', () => {
  mainProcess.getFileFromUser();
});
```

If we start our Electron application and click the Open File button, it correctly triggers the Open File dialog box. With that in place, we're still logging the files only to the console in the main process. To complete our feature, the main process must send the file's contents back to the renderer process to be displayed in our application.

4.5 Sending content from the main process to the renderer process

The remote module facilitates access to functionality from the main process in our renderer processes, but it doesn't allow for the inverse. To send the contents of the file that the user selected back to the renderer process to be rendered in the UI, we need to learn another technique for communicating between processes.

Each `BrowserWindow` instance has a property called `webContents`, which stores an object responsible for the web browser window that we create when we call `new BrowserWindow()`. `webContents` is similar to `app` because it emits events based on the lifecycle of the web page in the renderer process.

The following is an incomplete list of some of the events that you can listen for on the `webContents`object:

- `did-start-loading`
- `did-stop-loading`
- `dom-ready`
- `blur`
- `focus`
- `resize`
- `enter-full-screen`
- `leave-full-screen`

`webContents` also has a number of methods that can trigger different functions in the renderer process from the main process. In the previous chapter, we opened the

Chrome Developer Tools in the renderer process from the main process using `mainWindow.webContents.openDevTools()`. `mainWindow.loadURL('file://${__dirname}/index.html')`, an alias for `mainWindow.webContents.loadURL()`, loaded our HTML file into the renderer process when the application first launched. Figure 4.14 shows more aliases.

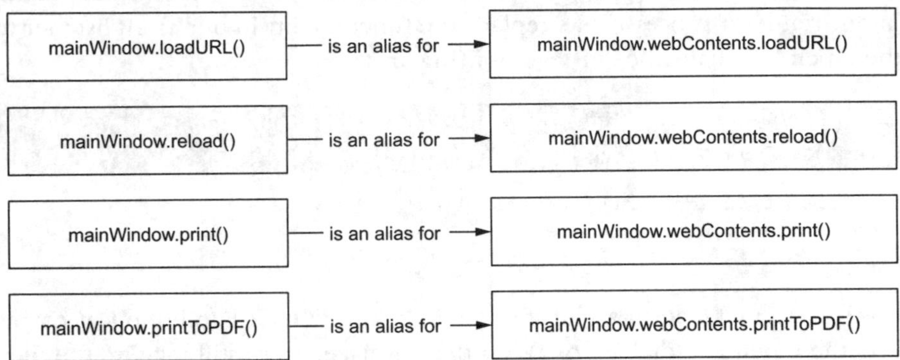

Figure 4.14 `BrowserWindow` instances have methods that are aliases to Electron's `webContents` API.

`webContents` has a method called `send()` which sends information from the main process to a renderer process. `webContents.send()` takes a variable number of arguments. The first argument, which is an arbitrary string, is the name of the channel on which to send the message. An event listener in the renderer process listens on the same channel. This flow will become clearer when we see it in action. All of the subsequent arguments after the first are passed along to the renderer process.

4.5.1 Sending the file contents to the renderer contents

Our current implementation reads the file that the user selected and logs it to the terminal. `mainWindow.webContents.send()` sends the contents of the file to the renderer process instead. The next chapter covers additional ways to open files that do not require a dialog box prompting the user to select a particular file because we do encounter situations where we will want to open a file without triggering the dialog box.

Listing 4.13 Sending content from the main to a renderer process: ./app/main.js

```
const getFileFromUser = exports.getFileFromUser =  () => {
  const files = dialog.showOpenDialog(mainWindow, {
    properties: ['openFile'],
    filters: [
      { name: 'Text Files', extensions: ['txt'] },
      { name: 'Markdown Files', extensions: ['md', 'markdown'] }
    ]
  });
```

```
    if (files) { openFile(files[0]); }
  };

  const openFile = (file) => {
    const content = fs.readFileSync(file).toString();
    mainWindow.webContents.send('file-opened', file, content);
  };
```

We'll send the name of the file and its content to the renderer process over the "file-opened" channel.

Previously, we interrupted the function with a return statement in the event that files were undefined. In this example, we'll flip that logic and pass the first file to Open File when dialog.showOpenFile() successfully returns an array of file paths.

The main process is now broadcasting the name of the file and its contents over the `file-opened` channel. The next step is to set up a listener on the `file-opened` channel in the renderer process using the `ipcRenderer` module. Electron comes with two basic modules for sending messages back and forth between processes: `ipcRenderer` and `ipcMain`. Each module is available only in the process type with which it shares a name.

`ipcRenderer` can send messages to the main process. More important to our immediate needs, it can also listen for messages that were sent from the main process using `webContents.send()`. It requires the `ipcRenderer` module in the renderer process.

Listing 4.14 Importing the `ipcRenderer` module: ./app/renderer.js

```
const { remote, ipcRenderer } = require('electron');
const mainProcess = remote.require('./main.js');
```

We'll import the ipcRenderer module in our renderer process.

With that in place, we can now set up a listener. `ipcRenderer` listens on the `file-opened` channel, adds the content to the page, and renders the Markdown as HTML.

Listing 4.15 Listening for messages on the `file-opened` channel: ./app/renderer.js

```
ipcRenderer.on('file-opened', (event, file, content) => {
  markdownView.value = content;
  renderMarkdownToHtml(content);
});
```

`ipcRenderer.on()` takes two arguments: the channel to listen on and a callback function that defines an action to take when the renderer process receives a message on the channel on which you're setting up the listener. The callback function is provided with a few arguments when it is called. The first is an `event` object, which is just like a normal event listener in the browser. It contains information about the event for which we set up the listener. The additional arguments are what were provided when using `webContents.send()` in the main process. In listing 4.13, we sent the name of the file and its contents. Those will be additional arguments passed to our listener.

With these new additions, the user can now click the Open File button, select a file using a native file dialog box, and render the contents in the UI. We've successfully implemented the feature that we set out to implement at the beginning of the chapter. The code for our main and renderer processes should look something like the following two listings.

Listing 4.16 Open File functionality implemented in the main process: ./app/main.js

```
const { app, BrowserWindow, dialog } = require('electron');
const fs = require('fs');

let mainWindow = null;

app.on('ready', () => {
  mainWindow = new BrowserWindow({ show: false });

  mainWindow.loadFile('index.html');

  mainWindow.once('ready-to-show', () => {
    mainWindow.show();
  });

  mainWindow.on('closed', () => {
    mainWindow = null;
  });
});

const getFileFromUser = exports.getFileFromUser = () => {
  const files = dialog.showOpenDialog(mainWindow, {
    properties: ['openFile'],
    filters: [
      { name: 'Text Files', extensions: ['txt'] },
      { name: 'Markdown Files', extensions: ['md', 'markdown'] }
    ]
  });

  if (files) { openFile(files[0]) }
};

const openFile = (file) => {
  const content = fs.readFileSync(file).toString();
  mainWindow.webContents.send('file-opened', file, content);
};
```

Listing 4.17 Open File functionality implemented: ./app/renderer.js

```
const { remote, ipcRenderer } = require('electron');
const mainProcess = remote.require('./main.js');

const marked = require('marked');

const markdownView = document.querySelector('#markdown');
const htmlView = document.querySelector('#html');
const newFileButton = document.querySelector('#new-file');
const openFileButton = document.querySelector('#open-file');
```

```
const saveMarkdownButton = document.querySelector('#save-markdown');
const revertButton = document.querySelector('#revert');
const saveHtmlButton = document.querySelector('#save-html');
const showFileButton = document.querySelector('#show-file');
const openInDefaultButton = document.querySelector('#open-in-default');

const renderMarkdownToHtml = (markdown) => {
  htmlView.innerHTML = marked(markdown, { sanitize: true });
};

markdownView.addEventListener('keyup', (event) => {
  const currentContent = event.target.value;
  renderMarkdownToHtml(currentContent);
});

openFileButton.addEventListener('click', () => {
  mainProcess.getFileFromUser();
});

ipcRenderer.on('file-opened', (event, file, content) => {
  markdownView.value = content;
  renderMarkdownToHtml(content);
});
```

Summary

- Electron provides the `dialog` module for creating a variety of native operating system dialogs.
- Open dialog boxes can be configured to allow for a single file or directory as well as multiple files or directories.
- Open dialog boxes can be configured to allow the user to select only certain file types.
- Open dialog boxes return an array consisting of the one or more files or directories selected by the user.
- Electron does not include an ability to read files. Instead, we use Node's `fs` module to read from and write to the filesystem.
- Each operating system offers a different set of features. Electron uses the features available while providing a graceful fallback if that feature does not exist in a given operating system.
- In macOS, we can have a dialog box drop down as a sheet from one of the windows by providing a reference to that window as the first argument in `dialog.showOpenDialog()`.
- Native operating system APIs and filesystem access should be handled by the main process, while rendering the UI and responding to user input should be handled by the renderer process.
- Electron provides a different set of modules to the main process and renderer processes.

- Electron provides a number of mechanisms for communicating between processes.
- The `remote` module provides a proxy to the main process modules and functions and makes that functionality available in our renderer processes.
- We can send messages from the main process to a renderer process using `webContents.send()`.
- We can listen for messages sent from the main processes in our renderer processes using the `ipcRenderer` module.
- We can namespace messages using channels, which are arbitrary strings. In this chapter, we used the `file-opened` channel to send and listen for messages.

5 Working with multiple windows

This chapter covers

- Tracking multiple windows using the JavaScript `Set` data structure
- Facilitating communication between the main process and multiple renderer processes
- Using Node APIs to detect what platform the application is running on

Right now, when Fire Sale starts up, it creates a single window for the UI. When that window is closed, the application quits. Although this behavior is perfectly acceptable, we typically expect to be able to open multiple, independent windows. In this chapter, we convert Fire Sale from a single-window application to one that supports multiple windows. Along the way, we'll explore new Electron APIs as well as some of JavaScript's more recent additions. We also explore solutions to problems that occur when taking a main process that is configured to communicate with one renderer process (see figure 5.1) and refactoring it to manage a variable number of processes (see figure 5.2). The completed code at the end of this chapter can be found at http://mng.bz/V145. We start from the `chapter-4` branch, however.

We start by instantiating a `Set` data structure, which was added to JavaScript in 2015 and tracks all of the user's windows. Next, we create a function that manages

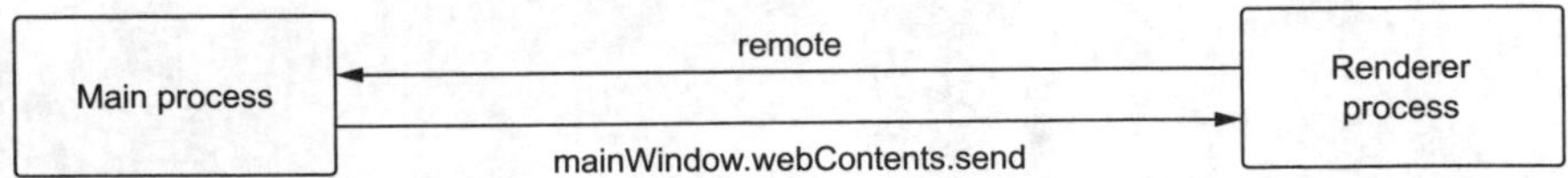

Figure 5.1 In chapter 4, we set up communication between the main process and one renderer process.

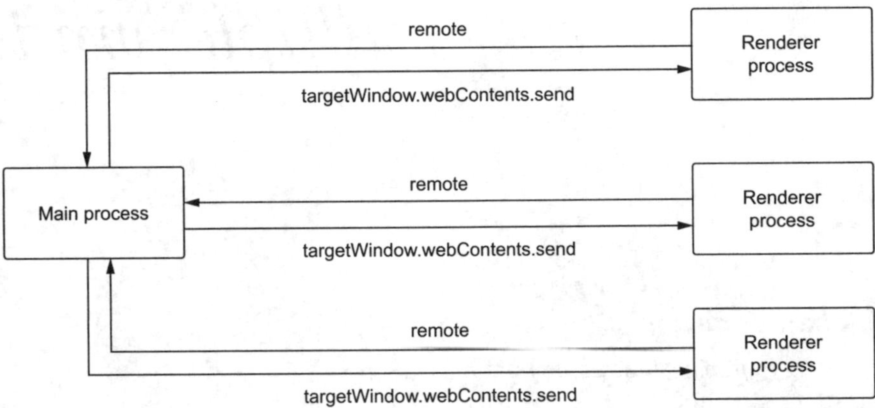

Figure 5.2 In this chapter, we update Fire Sale to support multiple windows and facilitate communication between them.

the lifecycle of an individual window. After that's in place, we modify the functions that we created in chapter 4 for prompting the user to select a file and opening it to target the correct window. In addition, we also take care of some common edge cases and other quirks that arise along the way, such as windows that eclipse each other.

5.1 Creating and managing multiple windows

`Set`s are a new data structure to JavaScript and were added in the ES2015 specification. A set is a collection of unique elements; an array can have duplicate values in it. I chose to use a set rather than an array because it's easier to remove an element. This listing shows how to create a `Set` in JavaScript.

Listing 5.1 Creating a `Set` to keep track of new windows: ./app/main.js

```
const windows = new Set();
```

With an array, we'd have to either find the index of the window and remove it, or create an array without that window. Neither approach is as simple as calling the `delete` method on the set and passing it a reference to the window that we want to remove.

With a data structure in place to track all of the application's windows, the next step is to move the process of creating a BrowserWindow (listing 5.2) out of the application's "ready" event listener and into its own function.

Listing 5.2 Implementing a function to create new windows: ./app/main.js

```
const createWindow = exports.createWindow = () => {
  let newWindow = new BrowserWindow({ show: false });

  newWindow.loadFile('index.html');

  newWindow.once('ready-to-show', () => {
    newWindow.show();
  });

  newWindow.on('closed', () => {
    windows.delete(newWindow);        // Removes the reference from the windows set when it has been closed
    newWindow = null;
  });

  windows.add(newWindow);        // Adds the window to the windows set when it has been opened
  return newWindow;
};
```

The createWindow() function creates a BrowserWindow instance and adds it to the set of windows that we created in listing 5.1. Next we repeat the steps for creating a new window from the previous chapters. Closing the window removes it from the set. Finally, we return a reference to the window that was just created. We need this reference in the next chapter.

When the application is ready, call the new createWindow() function, shown in the following listing. The application should start in the same manner as it did before we implemented this change, but it also sets the stage to create additional windows in other contexts.

Listing 5.3 Creating a window when the application is ready: ./app/main.js

```
app.on('ready', () => {
  createWindow();
});
```

The application starts as before, but if you try to click the Open File button, you'll notice that it's broken. This is because we're still referencing mainWindow in a few places. It's referenced in dialog.showOpenDialog() to display the dialog box as a sheet in macOS. More importantly, it is referenced in openFile() after the file's contents have been read from the filesystem and we send it to the window.

5.1.1 Communicating between the main process and multiple windows

Having multiple windows raises the question: to which window do we send the file path and contents? To support multiple windows, these two functions must reference the window where the dialog box should be displayed and the contents sent, as shown in figure 5.3.

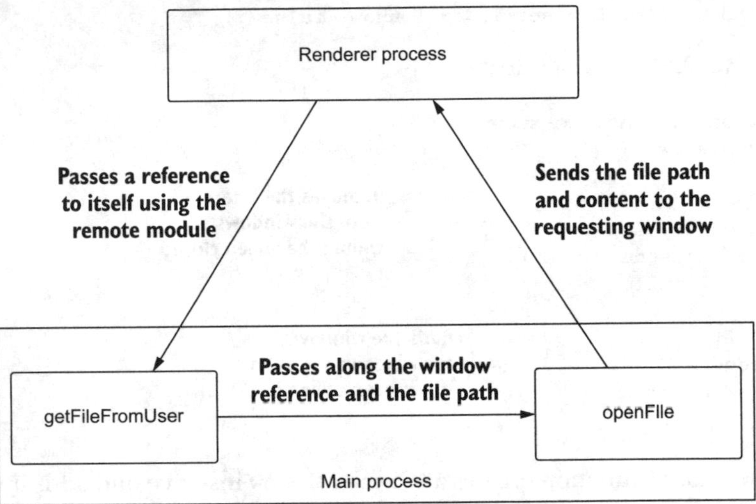

Figure 5.3 To figure out to which window to send the file's content, the renderer process must send a reference to itself when communicating to the main process to call `getFileFromUser()`.

In listing 5.4, let's refactor the `getFileFromUser()` function to accept a given window as an argument instead of always assuming that there is a `mainWindow` instance in scope.

Listing 5.4 Refactoring `getFileFromUser()` to work with a specific window: ./app/main.js

```
const getFileFromUser  = exports.getFileFromUser = (targetWindow) => {
  const files = dialog.showOpenDialog(targetWindow, {
    properties: ['openFile'],
    filters: [
      { name: 'Text Files', extensions: ['txt'] },
      { name: 'Markdown Files', extensions: ['md', 'markdown'] }
    ]
  });

  if (files) { openFile(targetWindow, files[0]); }
};
```

- dialog.showOpenDialog() takes a reference to a browser window object
- Takes a reference to a browser window to determine which window should display the file dialog and subsequently load the file selected by the user.
- The openFile() function takes a reference to a browser window object to determine which window should receive the contents of the file opened by the user.

In the code excerpt, we've modified `getFileFromUser()` to take a reference to a window as an argument. I avoided naming the argument `window` because it might be confused with the global object in the browser. After the user has selected a file, we pass the `targetWindow` to `openFile()` in addition to the file path, shown here.

Listing 5.5 Refactoring `openFile()` to work with a specific window: ./app/main.js

Sends the contents of the file to the browser window provided

Accepts a reference to a browser window object

```
const openFile = exports.openFile = (targetWindow, file) => {
  const content = fs.readFileSync(file).toString();
  targetWindow.webContents.send('file-opened', file, content);
};
```

5.1.2 Passing a reference to the current window to the main process

After the contents of the file have been read from the filesystem, we send the file's path and content to the window passed in as the first argument. This raises the question, though: How do we get a reference to thc window?

`getFileFromUser()` is called from the renderer process using the `remote` module to facilitate communication to the main process. As we saw in the previous chapter, the `remote` module contains references to all the modules that would otherwise be exclusively available to the main process. It turns out that `remote` also has a few other methods—notably, `remote.getCurrentWindow()`, which returns a reference to the `BrowserWindow` instance from which it was called, shown here.

Listing 5.6 Getting a reference to the current window in the renderer process: ./app/renderer.js

```
const currentWindow = remote.getCurrentWindow();
```

Now that we have a reference to the window, the last step necessary to complete the feature is to pass it along to `getFileFromUser()`. This lets the functions in the main process know which—of our soon to be many—browser windows they're working with.

Listing 5.7 Passing a reference to the current window to the main process: ./app/renderer.js

```
openFileButton.addEventListener('click', () => {
  mainProcess.getFileFromUser(currentWindow);
});
```

When we implemented the Markup for the UI in chapter 3, we included a New File button. We now have the `createWindow()` function implemented in and exported from the main process. We can quickly wire up that button as well.

Listing 5.8 Adding listener to `newFileButton`: ./app/renderer.js

```
newFileButton.addEventListener('click', () => {
  mainProcess.createWindow();
});
```

We can make a few more enhancements to our implementation of multiple windows in the main process, but we're finished in the renderer process for this chapter. The current state of the code in app/renderer.js follows.

Listing 5.9 `newFileButton` implemented in the renderer process: ./app/renderer.js

```
const { remote, ipcRenderer } = require('electron');
const mainProcess = remote.require('./main.js');
const currentWindow = remote.getCurrentWindow();

const marked = require('marked');

const markdownView = document.querySelector('#markdown');
const htmlView = document.querySelector('#html');
const newFileButton = document.querySelector('#new-file');
const openFileButton = document.querySelector('#open-file');
const saveMarkdownButton = document.querySelector('#save-markdown');
const revertButton = document.querySelector('#revert');
const saveHtmlButton = document.querySelector('#save-html');
const showFileButton = document.querySelector('#show-file');
const openInDefaultButton = document.querySelector('#open-in-default');

const renderMarkdownToHtml = (markdown) => {
  htmlView.innerHTML = marked(markdown, { sanitize: true });
};

markdownView.addEventListener('keyup', (event) => {
  const currentContent = event.target.value;
  renderMarkdownToHtml(currentContent);
});

newFileButton.addEventListener('click', () => {
  mainProcess.createWindow();
});

openFileButton.addEventListener('click', () => {
  mainProcess.getFileFromUser(currentWindow);
});

ipcRenderer.on('file-opened', (event, file, content) => {
  markdownView.value = content;
  renderMarkdownToHtml(content);
});
```

5.2 Improving the user experience of creating new windows

When clicking the New File button after implementing the event listener in the previous chapter, you might have been confused whether it was working. You may have noticed that the drop shadow around the window got darker, or you may have clicked and dragged the new window and revealed the previous window underneath.

The minor problem that we have right now is that each new window appears in the same default position as the first window and completely eclipses it. It might be more obvious that the new window is created if it is slightly offset from the previous window, as shown in figure 5.4. This listing shows how to offset the window.

Listing 5.10 Offsetting new windows based on the currently focused window: ./app/main.js

```
const createWindow = exports.createWindow = () => {
  let x, y;

  const currentWindow = BrowserWindow.getFocusedWindow();

  if (currentWindow) {
    const [ currentWindowX, currentWindowY ] = currentWindow.getPosition();
    x = currentWindowX + 10;
    y = currentWindowY + 10;
  }

  let newWindow = new BrowserWindow({ x, y, show: false });

  newWindow.loadFile('index.html');

  newWindow.once('ready-to-show', () => {
    newWindow.show();
  });

  newWindow.on('closed', () => {
    windows.delete(newWindow);
    newWindow = null;
  });

  windows.add(newWindow);
  return newWindow;
};
```

Gets the browser window that is currently active.

If there is a currently active window from the previous step, sets the coordinates of the next window down and to the right of the currently active window.

Creates the new window, hiding it at first with the x- and y-coordinates. These are set if the code in the previous step ran and are undefined if it did not, in which case the window is created in the default position.

In addition to instantiating instances with the `new` keyword, the `BrowserWindow` module also has methods of its own. We can use `BrowserWindow.getFocusedWindow()` to get a reference to the window with which the user is currently working. When the application is first ready and we call `createWindow()`, there isn't a focused window and `BrowserWindow.getFocusedWindow()` returns `undefined`. If there is a window, we call its `getWindow()` method, which returns an array with the *x*- and *y*-coordinates of the window. We'll store these values in two variables outside of the conditional block and pass them to the `BrowserWindow` constructor. If they're still undefined (for example, there was no focused window), then Electron uses the defaults, just as it did before we implemented this feature. Figure 5.4 shows a second window offset from the first.

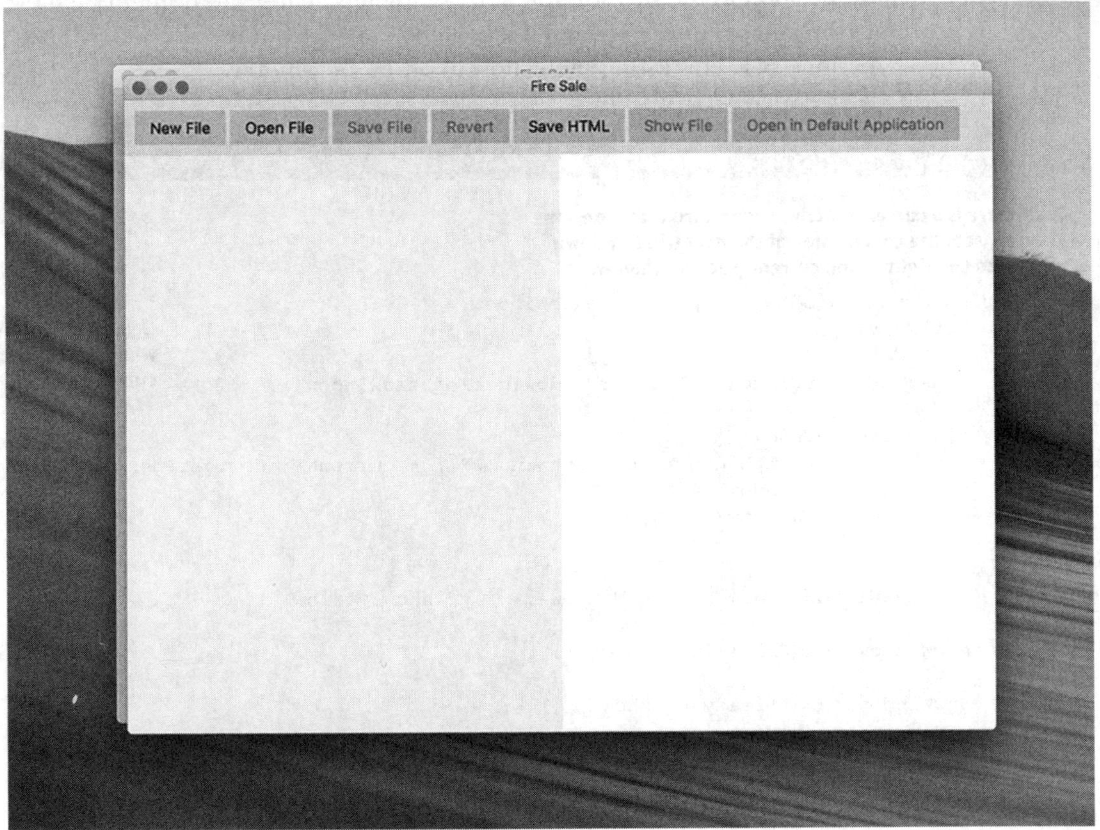

Figure 5.4 New windows are offset from the current window.

This isn't the only way to implement this feature. Alternatively, you could track an initial *x*- and *y*-position and increment those values on each new window. Or, you could add a slight bit of randomness to the default *x*- and *y*-values so that each window is slightly offset. I leave those methods as exercises to the reader.

5.3 Integrating with macOS

In macOS, many—but not all—applications remain open, even when all their windows are closed. For example, if you closed all your windows in Chrome, the application remains active in the dock and still appears in the application switcher. Fire Sale doesn't do that.

In earlier chapters, this might have been acceptable. We had one window and no way of creating additional windows. In this section, we enable the application to remain open only in macOS. By default, Electron quits the application when it fires its `window-all-closed` event. If we want to prevent this behavior, we must listen for this event and conditionally stop it from closing if we're running on macOS.

Listing 5.11 Keeping the application alive when all windows are closed: ./app/main.js

```
app.on('window-all-closed', () => {
  if (process.platform === 'darwin') {
    return false;
  }
  app.quit();
});
```

- Checks to see if the application is running on macOS
- If it is, returns false to prevent the default action
- If it isn't, quits the application

The `process` object is provided by Node and globally available without needing to be required. `process.platform` returns the name of the platform in which the application is currently executing. As of this writing, `process.platform` returns one of five strings: `darwin`, `freebsd`, `linux`, `sunos`, or `win32`. Darwin is the UNIX operating system that macOS is built on. In listing 5.11, we checked if `process.platform` is equal to `darwin`. If it is, then the application is running on macOS and we want to return `false` to stop the default action from occurring.

Keeping the application alive is half the battle. What happens if the user clicks the application in the dock and no windows are open? In this situation Fire Sale should open a new window and display it to the user as shown here.

Listing 5.12 Creating a window when application is opened and there are no windows: ./app/main.js

```
app.on('activate', (event, hasVisibleWindows) => {
  if (!hasVisibleWindows) { createWindow(); }
});
```

- Electron provides the hasVisibleWindows argument, which will be a Boolean.
- If there are no visible windows when the user activates the application, creates one.

The `activate` event passes two arguments to the callback function provided. The first is the `event` object. The second is a Boolean, which returns `true` if any windows are visible and `false` if all the windows are closed. In the case of the latter, we call the `createWindow()` function that we wrote earlier in the chapter.

The `activate` event fires only on macOS, but there are plenty of reasons why you might choose to have your application remain open on Windows or Linux, particularly if the application is running background processes that you want to continue even if the window is dismissed. Another possibility is that you have an application that can be hidden, or shown with a global shortcut, or from the tray or menu bar. We implement each of these in later chapters.

With these two additional events, we've converted Fire Sale from a single-window application to one that supports multiple windows. This listing shows the code for the main process in its current form.

Listing 5.13 Multiple windows implemented in the main process: ./app/main.js

```
const { app, BrowserWindow, dialog } = require('electron');
const fs = require('fs');

const windows = new Set();

app.on('ready', () => {
  createWindow();
});

app.on('window-all-closed', () => {
  if (process.platform === 'darwin') {
    return false;
  }
});

app.on('activate', (event, hasVisibleWindows) => {
  if (!hasVisibleWindows) { createWindow(); }
});

const createWindow = exports.createWindow = () => {
  let x, y;

  const currentWindow = BrowserWindow.getFocusedWindow();

  if (currentWindow) {
    const [ currentWindowX, currentWindowY ] = currentWindow.getPosition();
    x = currentWindowX + 10;
    y = currentWindowY + 10;
  }

  let newWindow = new BrowserWindow({ x, y, show: false });

  newWindow.loadFile('index.html');

  newWindow.once('ready-to-show', () => {
    newWindow.show();
  });

  newWindow.on('closed', () => {
    windows.delete(newWindow);
```

```
    newWindow = null;
  });

  windows.add(newWindow);
  return newWindow;
};

const getFileFromUser  = exports.getFileFromUser = (targetWindow) => {
  const files = dialog.showOpenDialog(targetWindow, {
    properties: ['openFile'],
    filters: [
      { name: 'Text Files', extensions: ['txt'] },
      { name: 'Markdown Files', extensions: ['md', 'markdown'] }
    ]
  });

  if (files) { openFile(targetWindow, files[0]); }
};

const openFile = exports.openFile = (targetWindow, file) => {
  const content = fs.readFileSync(file).toString();
  targetWindow.webContents.send('file-opened', file, content);
};
```

Summary

- When creating an Electron application with multiple windows, we can no longer hard-code a window for the main process to send data to.
- We can use Electron's `remote` module to ask the window in the renderer process for a reference to itself and send that reference along when communicating with the main process.
- Applications on macOS do not always quit when all the windows are closed. We can use Node's `process` object to determine on what platform the application is running.
- If `process.platform` is `darwin`, then the application is running on macOS.
- Returning `false` in a function that listens for `app`'s `windows-all-closed` event prevents the application from quitting.
- On macOS, `app` fires an `activate` event when the user clicks the dock icon.
- The `activate` event includes a Boolean called `hasVisibleWindows` as the second argument passed to the callback function. This is `true` if any windows are currently open, and `false` if there are none. We can use this to determine if a new window should be opened.

6 Working with files

This chapter covers

- Determining if the content has been edited and is unsaved
- Modifying the window's title based on the state of the currently active document
- Using custom interactions available to windows in applications running on macOS
- Implementing append documents to the operating system's list of recent documents
- Watching for changes to the current file from the operating system

Over the previous two chapters, we implemented the ability to read a file from the filesystem and display it in a browser window of our application. This exercise demonstrated how interprocess communication works in Electron, as well as Electron's ability to bridge the gap between a traditional browser-based application and a Node.js application. In the previous chapter, we also added support for multiple browser windows.

In the name of clarity, I kept our initial implementation naively simple. It turns out that users interact with files in a surprising number of different ways—even in a simple note-taking application like Fire Sale. A user might start writing a new note from the empty window spawned when the application initially launches, or they may choose to open an existing file from the filesystem. A user might click the Open File button we implemented earlier, or they might select the file from a list of recently opened documents. The path a user chooses impacts how our application behaves when they wish to save it. If it's a new file, then we must prompt the user to provide a location to write the new file. If it's an existing file, then the application should just overwrite the file the user originally selected from the Open File dialog box.

Users have come to expect several features from modern applications. Our application should provide visual indications that a file has been changed since it was originally opened or the last time it was saved. It should integrate with the operating system's list of recent documents and follow OS-level conventions for how the window's title bar should look, depending on the state of the file.

In this chapter, we rethink our approach to managing files as we implement the ability to save the Markdown text of our application, export the rendered HTML, and revert changes to unsaved files. We also explore additional ways to open files, such as using the HTML5 File API to implement a drag-and-drop feature to the left pane of the application. Finally, we don't want our users to end up in a situation where they edit a Markdown file in some other application and accidentally overwrite the changes when they save the file in Fire Sale. Therefore, we listen for external changes to the current file by other applications. Throughout this chapter, we implement all the functionality outlined in figure 6.1.

I'll be starting from the `chapter-5` branch of the repository as a starting point. You can also find the completed example in the `chapter-6` branch.

6.1 Keeping track of the current file

As we begin working with different files in our application, it's helpful to track the file with which we're currently working. This way, we know which file a user is working on if they ask to save it. Suppose that Mildred has an important stroke of inspiration and wants to record her genius idea into Fire Sale. She opens her list of important thoughts and jots down notes. Right now, Fire Sale doesn't know if Mildred is editing a new or existing file. The application also doesn't have a way to track what file Mildred is working on when she selects a file to open.

To solve this problem, we need to implement the ability to keep track of what file Fire Sale is currently working with. In chapter 4, whenever a new file was opened, we sent the contents of the file as well as the path of the file that was just opened from the main process to the renderer process that requested the file. We populated the right and left panes of the application with the content. Our next step is to enable the renderer process to track the path of the file that is currently being displayed to the user. Doing so allows us to save changes without prompting the user for a file location.

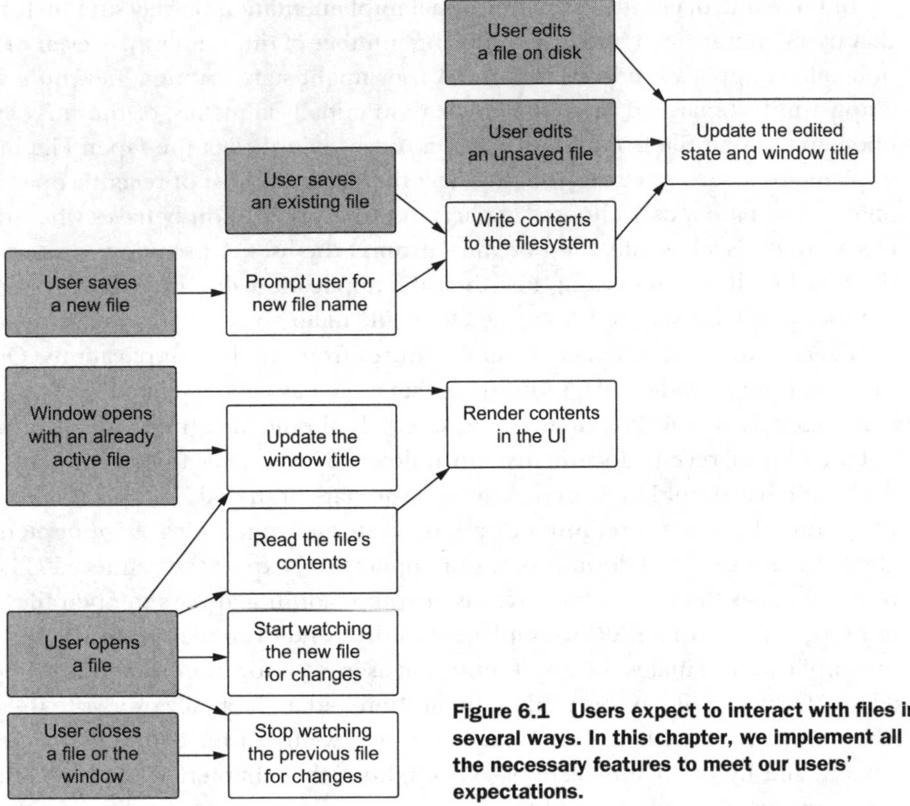

Figure 6.1 Users expect to interact with files in several ways. In this chapter, we implement all the necessary features to meet our users' expectations.

We also have a Revert button in the UI. If the user clicks this button, it should roll back any unsaved changes and return the content to its last saved state. A simple way to handle this action is to store a copy of the content whenever a file is opened. If the user clicks Revert, Fire Sale replaces the content in the UI with the cached content from the last time the file was opened.

Let's start with some sensible defaults for the case where the user opens a new window that isn't yet tied to a given file. We declare two variables in the top level of the renderer process to track the original content of the current file and its file path.

Listing 6.1 Declaring global variables for keeping track of the current file: ./app/renderer.js

```
let filePath = null;
let originalContent = '';
```

I chose to use an empty string instead of `null` for `originalContent` because that's the value of an empty `input` or `textarea` in the browser. Later in the chapter, this setting makes it easier for us to see if a new document has been edited.

Whenever a file has been opened and sent to the renderer process, we need to update these values. We take care of this in the IPC event listener on the `file-opened` channel we set up in chapter 4.

Listing 6.2 Updating global variables when a new file is opened: ./app/renderer.js

```
ipcRenderer.on('file-opened', (event, file, content) => {
  filePath = file;
  originalContent = content;

  markdownView.value = content;
  renderMarkdownToHtml(content);
});
```

- `filePath = file;` — Updates the path of the currently opened file stored in the top-level scope
- `originalContent = content;` — Updates the original content to determine if the file has unsaved changes
- `markdownView.value = content;` — Updates the Markdown content in the UI
- `renderMarkdownToHtml(content);` — Updates the HTML content in the UI

6.1.1 Updating the window title based on the current file

Mildred can open a file on her computer, edit it, and save the changes, but she currently has no way of knowing what file she is working with. Are these the meeting minutes from this week, or the meeting she missed while on vacation in Greenland? She has multiple windows open and can't tell which is which. In the previous section, we implemented a feature that allowed each window in Fire Sale to keep a reference to the current file, but we did not add anything to the UI to share that information with the user. The common pattern for desktop applications is to show the name of the file that is currently active in the title bar of the window, as shown in figure 6.2. In this section, we'll follow best practices and implement this pattern in Fire Sale.

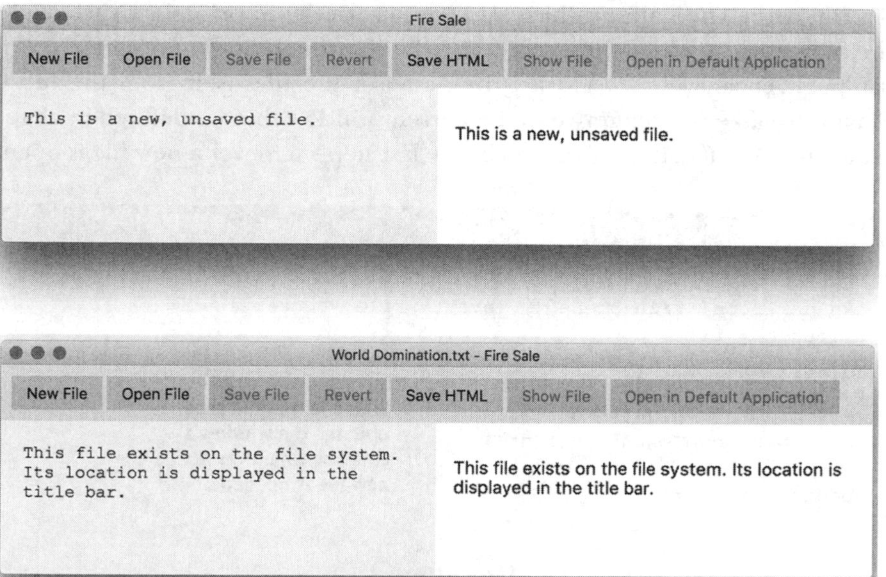

Figure 6.2 The name of file in the filesystem is displayed in the window's title.

By default, the application's window displays the title of the HTML page, which is defined in app/index.html. This is a reasonable default, but many native desktop applications display the name or path of the current file. One approach is to update the title of the window whenever the user opens a new file. In addition to displaying the name of the currently open file (as in listing 6.3), we may want to display other information in the window's title such as whether the current file has been edited since it was saved. We also need to update the window's title for a few different contexts, such as editing and saving the file.

All `BrowserWindow` instances have a method called `setTitle()` that allows us to programmatically manipulate the window's title. Later in this chapter, we display information about whether the file has been edited since the last time it was saved or since it was opened. We create a method called `updateUserInterface()` that eventually encapsulates all of this logic as well as some other features down the road like enabling the Save File and Revert buttons if the file contains unsaved changes.

Listing 6.3 Updating the window title based on the current file: ./app/renderer.js

```
const path = require('path');

const updateUserInterface = () => {
  let title = 'Fire Sale';
  if (filePath) { title = `${path.basename(filePath)} - ${title}`; }
  currentWindow.setTitle(title);
};
```

If a file is open, prepends the name of that file to the title

Updates the title of the window

We start with the default title. If a file is currently open, we modify the title to include the file path. The path can be long and most of the information, such as the root of the filesystem or where the users' folders are stored, is not important to our users. We use `path.basename()` to extract the name of the file itself from the full file path. Finally, we take the reference to the current window that we defined in chapter 5 and set its title. We'll call this function as the last step whenever a new file is opened.

Listing 6.4 Calling `updateUserInterface()` when a new file is opened: ./app/renderer.js

```
ipcRenderer.on('file-opened', (event, file, content) => {
  filePath = file;
  originalContent = content;

  markdownView.value = content;
  renderMarkdownToHtml(content);

  updateUserInterface();
});
```

Calls the method that updates the window's title bar whenever a new file is opened.

6.1.2 Determining whether the current file has changed

In the midst of taking important notes in Fire Sale, Mildred realizes that she's 20 minutes late for a meeting. She wants to close Fire Sale before rushing down to the fifth floor, but she is unsure if she has saved her recent changes to the file she was working on. We have lots of good reasons to track whether the user has edited the file since they opened it. We might want to prompt the user if they attempt to close the window and they have unsaved changes. Or, we might want to show only certain UI elements if the file has been modified (see figure 6.3).

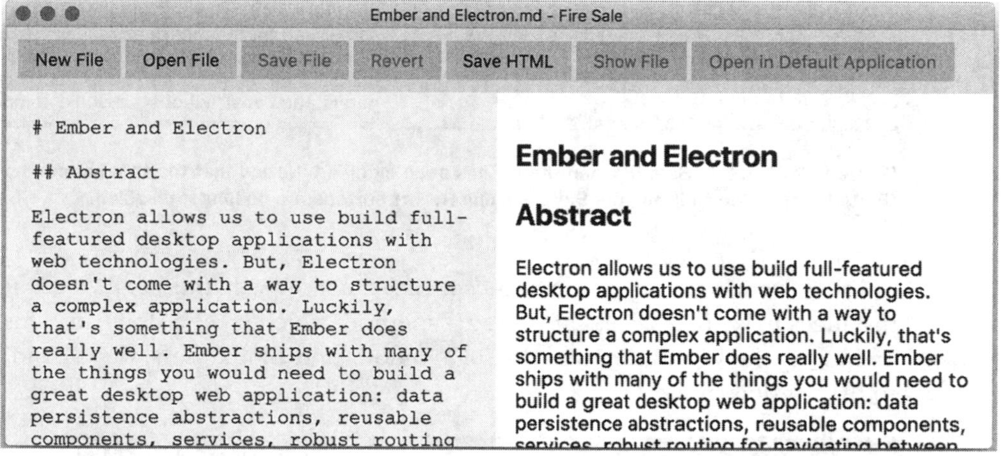

Figure 6.3 The Fire Sale UI when the file has not been modified. Notice that the Save File and Revert buttons have been disabled.

In this section, we add a visual cue in the UI. The Save File button is enabled only if the file has been modified. In addition, we append (Edited) to the title bar (see figure 6.4). To add this feature, we'll take advantage of the abstraction we began building earlier in this chapter and add functionality to detect if the file has been modified. We have a few approaches we could take.

A naive—and flawed—way to check if a file has changed is to listen for either a `keyup` or `change` event in our UI. If the user adds a character and then removes it, this approach still considers the file modified, which is not consistent with how other native desktop applications behave.

To determine whether the file has been modified, we need two pieces of information: the original and current contents of the file. We were crafty enough to store the original contents in listing 6.2. If those two pieces of information are identical, then the file has not changed. But if they differ, even slightly, then we know we have a modified file on our hands.

To implement this feature, modify `updateUserInterface()` to take an argument called `isEdited`. On `keyup`, we compare the current value of the `textarea` with the

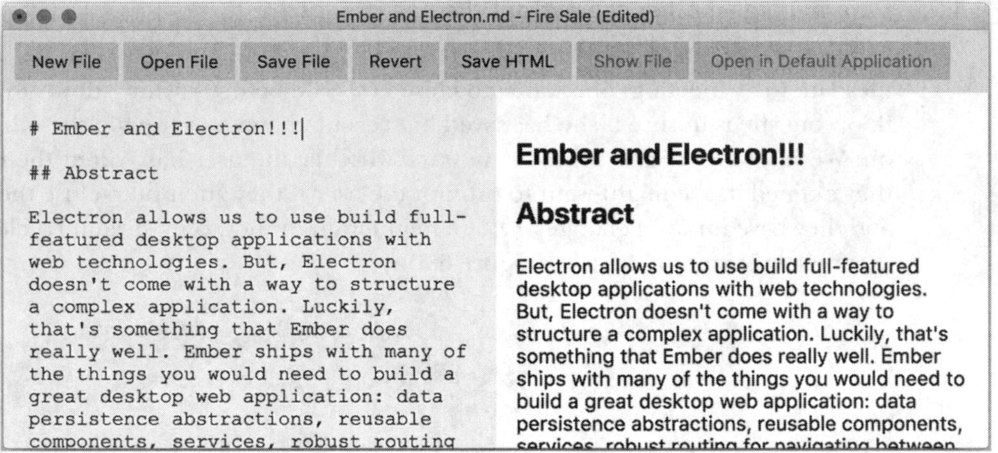

Figure 6.4 The Fire Sale UI when the file has been modified. Notice that the title bar content has (Edited) appended to it and the Save File and Revert buttons are no longer disabled.

`originalContent` and call `updateUserInterface()` with the result. `BrowserWindow` instances have a `setDocumentEdited()` method, which takes a Boolean. This will subtly modify the window on macOS; for Windows and Linux users, we append (Edited) to the window title.

Listing 6.5 Updating the UI if the document has unsaved changes: ./app/renderer.js

```
const updateUserInterface = (isEdited) => {
  let title = 'Fire Sale';

  if (filePath) { title = `${path.basename(filePath)} - ${title}`; }
  if (isEdited) { title = `${title} (Edited)`; }

  currentWindow.setTitle(title);
  currentWindow.setDocumentEdited(isEdited);
};
```

Passes in a Boolean that represents whether the document has unsaved changes

If isEdited is true, then updates the window accordingly

The last step is to have the renderer process call the `updateUserInterface()` method every time the user lifts their finger from a key while typing.

Listing 6.6 Checking for changes whenever the user types: ./app/renderer.js

```
markdownView.addEventListener('keyup', (event) => {
  const currentContent = event.target.value;
  renderMarkdownToHtml(currentContent);
  updateUserInterface(currentContent !== originalContent);
});
```

Whenever the user inputs a keystroke into the Markdown view, checks to see if the current content matches the content that we stored in a variable and updates the UI accordingly.

6.1.3 Enabling the Save and Revert buttons in the UI

With these steps in place, your application can tell if it is in an edited and unsaved state. But we have a problem. The Save File and Revert buttons are still disabled. These buttons should be enabled only if there are unsaved changes. It's easy to take care of this as we update the window itself.

Listing 6.7 Enabling the Save and Revert buttons when there are unsaved changes: ./app/renderer.js

```
const updateUserInterface = (isEdited) => {
  let title = 'Fire Sale';

  if (filePath) { title = `${path.basename(filePath)} - ${title}`; }
  if (isEdited) { title = `${title} (Edited)`; }

  currentWindow.setTitle(title);
  currentWindow.setDocumentEdited(isEdited);

  saveMarkdownButton.disabled = !isEdited;
  revertButton.disabled = !isEdited;
};
```

If the document is unedited, disables the Save button

If the document has no unsaved changes, disables the button that reverts unsaved changes

We implement the functionality for these buttons later in the chapter.

6.1.4 Updating the represented file on macOS

macOS windows support small representations of the current file in the window's menu bar. Hold and press Command while clicking the file icon to trigger a drop-down menu showing where the file exists in the filesystem's hierarchy, as shown in figure 6.5. You can also click and drag the icon—it acts as if you dragged the file from Finder. All `BrowserWindow` instances have a method called `setRepresentedFilename()`, which accepts a

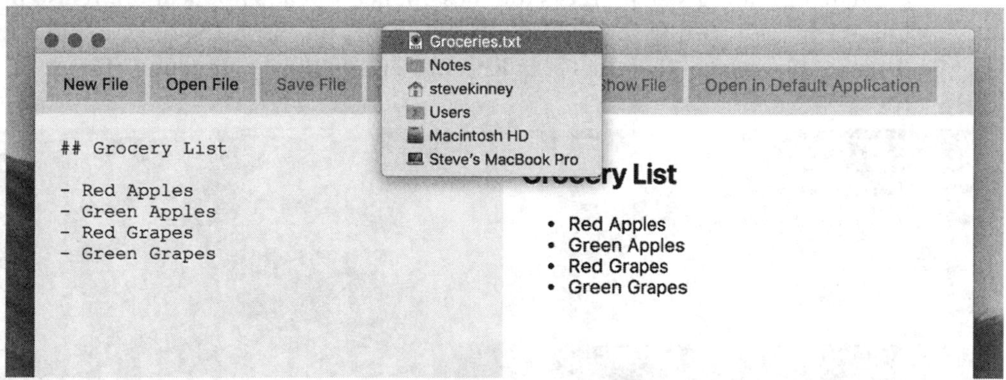

Figure 6.5 Pressing and holding Command while clicking the file icon in the title bar allows us to see its location on the filesystem. We can also drag and drop the icon as if it were the file itself.

valid file path as an argument. This method has no effect in Windows. Let's add this feature to our `updateWindowTitle()` method. Then we check to see if we have a valid path property and—if so—set it as the represented file for macOS windows.

This is unlike updating the title of the window with additional information, like whether the file has been edited. The represented file remains the same until the user opens another file in the same window. We don't need to update this value on `keyup`. We have two options: We could set the represented file in the main process before sending the path and content to the renderer process, or we could use the `currentWindow` reference in the renderer process after it has received the file. I'm going to go with the former, but both approaches are acceptable.

Listing 6.8 Setting the represented file in macOS: ./app/main.js

```
const openFile = exports.openFile = (targetWindow, file) => {
  const content = fs.readFileSync(file).toString();
  targetWindow.setRepresentedFilename(file);
  targetWindow.webContents.send('file-opened', file, content);
};
```

BrowserWindow instances have a method that allows you to set the represented file.

6.2 Tracking recently opened files

Now that Mildred is back from her meeting, she wants to get back to work. It was a long meeting, and she doesn't quite remember what notes she's been working on recently. Our current implementation doesn't have a way to help her out either. The operating system, however, does this stuff all the time. Whenever the user opens a file, let's have Electron notify the operating system that it should add the file to the list of recently opened files.

When opening a file in either macOS or Windows, Electron can add the file path to the operating system's list of recently opened documents. This list is available by right-clicking the Dock icon in macOS (figure 6.6) or the Taskbar icon in Windows (figure 6.7).

The operating system tracks the files opened by each application. It also provides a master list of recently opened files. In Windows, this list is found in the File Explorer. In macOS, you can find the list of Recent Items in the Apple menu (figure 6.8). When

Figure 6.6 Recent files in macOS

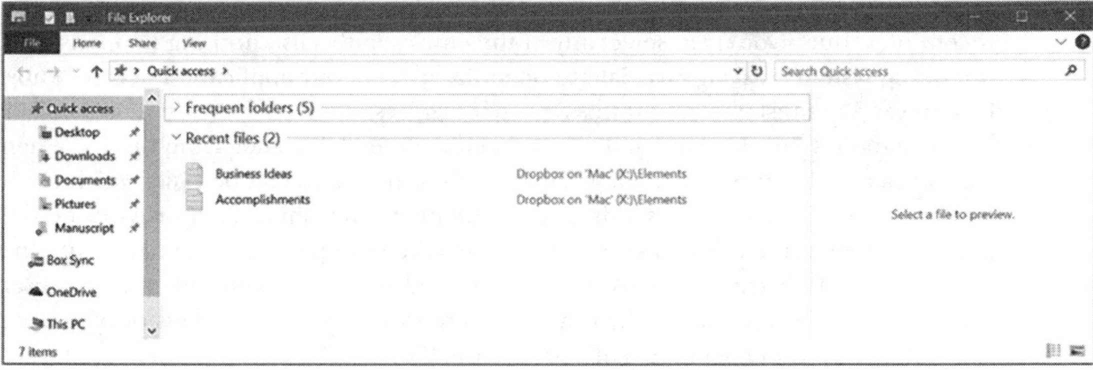

Figure 6.7 Recent files in Windows 10

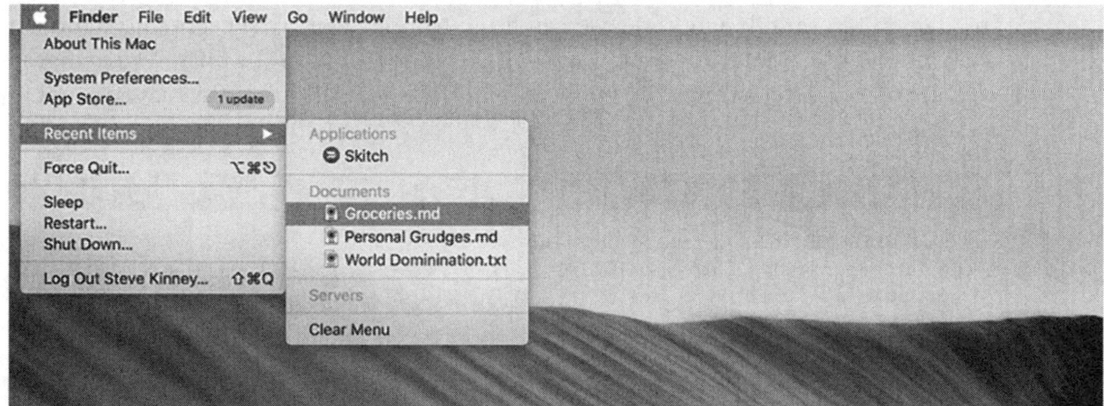

Figure 6.8 System-wide recent documents in macOS

a document is selected from the global list of recent documents, it is opened in the default application for that type of document. In this chapter, we primarily concern ourselves with the list of recent documents specific to our application.

You can add a file path to the recent documents list in Electron using `app.addRecentDocument()` and providing the file path as an argument. In the next listing, we add the path of the file we're opening with `openFile()` to the list of recent documents.

Listing 6.9 Appending to the list of recent documents: ./app/main.js

```
const openFile = exports.openFile = (targetWindow, file) => {
  const content = fs.readFileSync(file).toString();
  app.addRecentDocument(file);
  targetWindow.setRepresentedFilename(file);
  targetWindow.webContents.send('file-opened', file, content);
};
```

Electron's app module provides a method for appending to the operating system's list of recently opened documents. (annotates `app.addRecentDocument(file);`)

If you open a few files in Fire Sale, you see that they're being appended to the list of recent files. But if you try to select any of the entries in this list, nothing happens. The operating system is asking Fire Sale to open the file, but our application doesn't know how to yet. We must implement this feature ourselves.

In chapter 4 we added the ability to trigger an Open File dialog from the UI. When a user selects a file using the dialog, the file path is passed to an open file, which reads the contents of the file and sends those contents to the renderer process to be displayed in the left pane, which—finally—triggers the right pane to be updated with the resulting HTML. At the time, we briefly discussed that there were other ways a user might open a file, and that's why it makes sense to separate the process of triggering the dialog box from the process of opening the file.

Selecting an item from the Recent Documents menu is one instance where the user wants to open a file without being prompted with an Open File dialog box. Whenever a file is opened from outside of the application, Electron's `app` module fires an `open-file` event. In our code, we can listen for the `open-file` event and handle it accordingly. We should, however, wait until the application is fully up and running, so we'll set up our listener once the application fires its `will-finish-launching` event in app/main.js.

Listing 6.10 Responding to external requests to open a file: ./app/main.js

```
app.on('will-finish-launching', () => {
  app.on('open-file', (event, file) => {
    const win = createWindow();
    win.once('ready-to-show', () => {
      openFile(win, file);
    });
  });
});
```

Listens for the open-file event, which provides the path of the externally opened file, and then passes that file path to our openFile() function.

Now when the user selects a file in Fire Sale's list of recent documents, the application creates a new window and opens the file path in the new window—just as if you'd selected it using the Open File button in the UI that we implemented in chapter 4.

6.3 Saving files

Saving files with Electron is similar to opening files, but with one difference: users might want to save changes to the Markdown file, or they might want to export the HTML that was generated by their application.

If the user is saving a new file for the first time, then the application should ask where the user wants to save the file and what name they want to give it. After that, it should keep track of that name and update the window title as it if had originally opened the file from the filesystem. If the user is saving changes to an existing Markdown file, then the application does not need to prompt to specify a location and filename for the file. Implementing the ability to save files is more than just writing content to the filesystem. We must also update the UI to show where the current file is being saved and if it has been modified since the last time it was saved to the filesystem.

In the Fire Sale case, saving the HTML output is a bit more straightforward since the application doesn't allow the user to edit the HTML output after it has been saved. Exporting the generated HTML is a lot like saving a file for the first time, but we don't need to track where it was saved or reflect its new location in the UI. It's the easiest of the three to implement, so let's take care of that feature first.

6.3.1 *Exporting the rendered HTML output*

To allow for exporting the generated HTML, we add a `saveHtml()` function to the main process that asks the user where they'd like to save the HTML file, grabs the content from the HTML view, and then writes the file to the filesystem.

As you might expect, triggering the native dialog box for saving files is similar to triggering one for opening files. The biggest difference is that instead of prompting the user to select a specific file to open, we will ask the user for a filename and location to write to the filesystem. The contents of the file is passed as an argument to the `showSaveFileDialog()` function.

In the app/main.js, add the function shown in listing 6.11. When this function is run, Electron presents a dialog box asking the user to select a file path where the contents should be written. Once the user selects a file path, we use Node's built-in `fs` module to write the contents of the file to the filesystem.

Listing 6.11 Saving the generated output: ./app/main.js

```
const saveHtml = exports.saveHtml = (targetWindow, content) => {
  const file = dialog.showSaveDialog(targetWindow, {
    title: 'Save HTML',
    defaultPath: app.getPath('documents'),
    filters: [
      { name: 'HTML Files', extensions: ['html', 'htm'] }
    ]
  });

  if (!file) return;

  fs.writeFileSync(file, content);
};
```

Defaults to the user's "documents" directory as defined by the operating system

If the user selects cancel in the File dialog box, aborts the function.

In the example, `dialog.showSaveDialog()` takes two arguments. The first is a reference to a `BrowserWindow`, which is used to display the dialog box as a sheet in macOS only. The second argument is an options object that allows you to pass keys and values to configure the dialog box itself. The object provided to `dialog.showSaveDialog()` works with the following options:

- `title`: Sets the title of the dialog box. This will not appear in macOS.
- `defaultPath`: Sets the default directory for the Save dialog box.

- `buttonLabel`: Allows you to set custom text for the Save button.
- `filters`: Sets what files are enabled to select to overwrite. Electron also uses this option to set a default file extension, if the user does not provide one.

6.3.2 Common paths

We're implementing the ability to save files, but where should we prompt the user to save those files and how does it differ depending on which operating system they're using? Windows, macOS, and Linux organize their files differently. Ideally, a cross-platform Electron application should default to show the correct directory on each platform. Electron provides `app.getPath()`, which automatically returns the correct file path based on the user's platform, saving the developer from having to write error-prone conditional logic. In listing 6.11, we set the default path to `app.getPath('documents')`, which will be My Documents on Windows and the Documents folder in the user's home directory on macOS. Electron provides the following additional paths:

- `home` resolves to the user's home directory.
- `desktop`, `documents`, `downloads`, `pictures`, `music`, and `videos` each resolve to the corresponding path within the user's home directory.
- `temp` resolves to the operating system's temporary file directory.
- `exe` resolves to the location of the current executable.
- `appData` resolves to the user's application data directory. This would be %APPDATA% on Windows, ~/Library/Application/Support on macOS, and either $XDG_CONFIG_HOME or ~/.config on Linux.
- `userData` resolves to appData with the name of the application appended. For example, on macOS, `userData` would resolve to ~/Library/Application/Support/fire sale for the application in this chapter. This name comes from the name entry in your package.json.

You might want your application to override one of the defaults provided by `app.getPath()`. You can do this using `app.setPath()`, which takes two arguments: the name from the previous list and the new path to which you'd like it to resolve. It's important to note that you can override only paths from the previous list. If you're going to override one of these paths, you must do it before the application fires its "ready" event.

We didn't implement a default path in the `showOpenFile()` function in the previous chapter, but that's a good candidate for using this approach as well. It would make sense for a music player to default to the directory where users typically store their music, or a photograph management application to default to `app.getPath('pictures')`.

6.3.3 Saving files from the renderer process

Now we enable the Fire Sale application to save the rendered HTML content, shown in figure 6.9. To focus on learning the fundamentals of Electron, we'll simply take the HTML content of the right pane and pass it to `showSaveFileDialog()`. A more robust approach would be to add a `doctype` as well as `<html>`, `<head>`, and `<body>` tags to

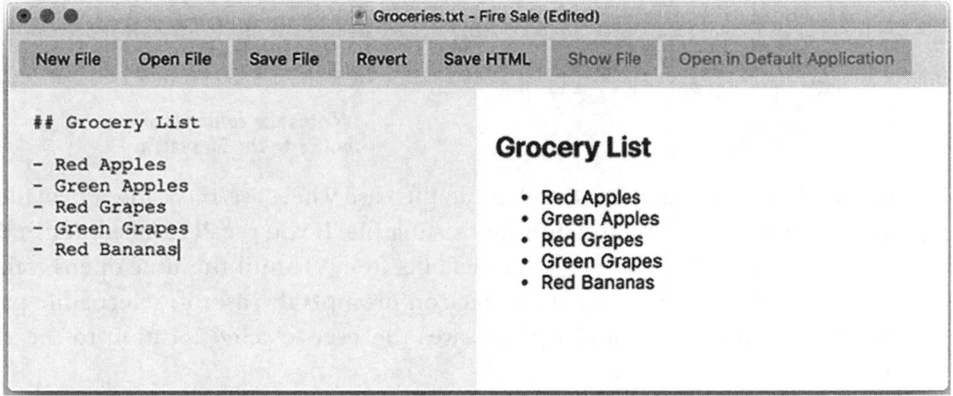

Figure 6.9 Fire Sale allows users to save their Markdown content in the left pane as well as the rendered HTML output shown in the right pane.

make it a valid HTML document. Additionally, we could add metadata about the document and a default style sheet, but that is beyond the scope of this book. In the next chapter, we add in the ability to trigger this functionality from the application's menu as well.

Listing 6.12 Triggering the Save File dialog box from the renderer process: ./app/renderer.js

```
saveHtmlButton.addEventListener('click', () => {
  mainProcess.saveHtml(currentWindow, htmlView.innerHTML);
});
```

6.3.4 *Saving the current file*

Saving the current file is like saving the HTML output with one small difference: if the file was opened from the filesystem, then the application does not need to prompt the user for a file path. Instead, the application just uses `filePath` as the location where the file should be written.

Listing 6.13 Saving the current file: ./app/main.js

```
const saveMarkdown = exports.saveMarkdown = (targetWindow, file, content) => {
  if (!file) {
    file = dialog.showSaveDialog(targetWindow, {
      title: 'Save Markdown',
      defaultPath: app.getPath('documents'),
      filters: [
        { name: 'Markdown Files', extensions: ['md', 'markdown'] }
      ]
    });
  }
```

If this is a new file without a file path, prompts the user to select a file path with a dialog box

```
  if (!file) return;

  fs.writeFileSync(file, content);
  openFile(targetWindow, file);
};
```

If the user selects Cancel in the File dialog box, aborts the function

Writes the contents of the buffer to the filesystem

This code is flexible enough to handle the case where we're saving a new file, as well as the case where we're updating an existing file. If you recall from earlier in the chapter, the `filePath` property's value defaults to `null` until the user opens a file. If the `filePath` property is `false`, then Electron prompts the user to select a file path using the native Save File dialog. It then saves the user-selected location to the `filePath` property.

Conversely, if it already knows where the file is located, then it moves forward and skips directly to writing the content to the filesystem. For the sake of brevity, I called `openFile()` on the file we just saved. If it's a new file that we're saving for the first time, then we would want to add it to the operating system's list of recent documents and set it as the represented file. Abstracting that out into its own function that we can call without having to read the file from disk again is an exercise that I leave to the reader.

No functionality is complete if there is no way to trigger it. The application needs an event listener on the Save File button that triggers our new functionality.

Listing 6.14 Adding an event listener to the Save File button: ./app/renderer.js

```
saveMarkdownButton.addEventListener('click', () => {
  mainProcess.saveMarkdown(currentWindow, filePath, markdownView.value);
});
```

6.3.5 *Reverting files*

Given the way we've structured our application so far, adding a feature is easy. When the user clicks the Revert button, we replace the value of the Markdown view with the original content of the file that we cached when we last opened or saved it, and then trigger the HTML view to be re-rendered with the cached content as well.

Listing 6.15 Reverting content in UI to last saved content: ./app/renderer.js

```
revertButton.addEventListener('click', () => {
  markdownView.value = originalContent;
  renderMarkdownToHtml(originalContent);
});
```

Later in the chapter, we'll prompt the user to make sure that they want to blow away all their changes before moving forward.

6.4 *Opening files using drag and drop*

Electron applications support the HTML5 File API, which allows us to create a feature for our application where users can drag a file onto certain elements in the DOM and drop them. You have seen this API used for uploading photographs in Twitter's web application or attaching a file to an email in Gmail. In Fire Sale, we take advantage of this API to allow the user to open files by dragging them onto the Markdown view of the UI.

6.4.1 Ignoring dropped files everywhere else

The default action of a web browser when a file is dropped into the browser window is to open the file in the browser itself. We can drag files onto our application and watch in terror as the contents of the file completely replace the UI. This is even more problematic when you consider that we don't have a Back button to rely on.

The first step to creating a drag-and-drop feature for our application is to disable the default behavior by adding an event listener to the document itself that prevents the default action. Later, we'll opt back in and customize the behavior for the Markdown pane in our UI.

Listing 6.16 Setting up foundation for drag-and-drop events: ./app/renderer.js

```
document.addEventListener('dragstart', event => event.preventDefault());
document.addEventListener('dragover', event => event.preventDefault());
document.addEventListener('dragleave', event => event.preventDefault());
document.addEventListener('drop', event => event.preventDefault());
```

6.4.2 Providing visual feedback

Though it's not necessary to implement the feature itself, it's often helpful to give the user a visual indication that they can drag a file onto an area within your application. We define two additional CSS classes that can be added and removed with JavaScript, depending upon whether the item being dragged is valid.

Listing 6.17 Adding styles for drag-and-drop functionality: ./app/style.css

```
.raw-markdown.drag-over {
  background-color: rgb(181, 220, 216);
  border-color: rgb(75, 160, 151);
}

.raw-markdown.drag-error {
  background-color: rgba(170, 57, 57,1);
  border-color: rgba(255,170,170,1);
}
```

This deep teal color signifies to the user that this a valid drop target.

This red color indicates that there is a problem with the file the user is dropping.

Before we begin implementing this feature, shown in listing 6.18, it would be nice to have some helper functions. I'm going to create two suspiciously similar functions: `getDraggedFile()` and `getDroppedFile()`. One important distinction between the two: When a user is dragging a file, we have access only to its metadata. Only after the user officially drops the file do we have access to the `File` object. `getDraggedFile()` will pick the file's metadata—in the form of a `DataTransferItem` object—out of the event object, which has a large number of other properties, such as where the mouse was when the event was fired and much more. `getDroppedFile()` pulls the first element from the files array, which was empty when the user was simply dragging the file.

This process might seem arduous, but it is all in the name of security. You might pass over windows that should not know about the file you're attempting to drop on your way to your intended application because that file could very well contain sensitive information. But once you've let go and dropped the file, then the browser assumes that this action is intentional and allows the application to read the file. `fileTypeIsSupported()` checks to see if the type of file being dragged is either of the two types supported by Fire Sale and returns a Boolean based on the result.

Listing 6.18 Helper methods: ./app/renderer.js

```
const getDraggedFile = (event) => event.dataTransfer.items[0];
const getDroppedFile = (event) => event.dataTransfer.files[0];

const fileTypeIsSupported = (file) => {
  return ['text/plain', 'text/markdown'].includes(file.type);
};
```

This is similar to the getDraggedFile(), but after the user has officially dropped the file, we have access to the file itself, not just its metadata.

This will always be an array in case the user selects multiple items. The application supports only one file at a time. We grab the first item in the array.

This helper function returns true or false if the file's type is in the array of supported file types.

When the user drags a file over the browser window, it rapid-fires `dragover` events until the user either leaves the target area—in which case, a `dragleave` event—or the user lifts their finger from the mouse or trackpad and drops the file onto the target area, which triggers a `drop` event.

During the `dragover` phase, we can give the user a visual clue as to whether the drop is going to be successful, as shown in figure 6.10. If the user is dragging a file type that we're not prepared to support, we can add the `.drag-error` class to the element (see figure 6.11). Otherwise, we'll add the `.drag-over` class to indicate that the user can drop a file here. When the user removes the file from the target area, we'll clean up any classes that were added and restore the UI to its default state.

Listing 6.19 Adding and removing classes on `dragover` and `dragleave`: ./app/renderer.js

```
markdownView.addEventListener('dragover', (event) => {
  const file = getDraggedFile(event);

  if (fileTypeIsSupported(file)) {
    markdownView.classList.add('drag-over');
  } else {
```

If the file type is supported, adds a CSS class to indicate this is a valid place to drop the file.

```
    markdownView.classList.add('drag-error');
  }
});

markdownView.addEventListener('dragleave', () => {
  markdownView.classList.remove('drag-over');
  markdownView.classList.remove('drag-error');
});
```

If the file type is not supported, adds a CSS class to indicate that although this is a valid place to drop a file, this file is not accepted.

If the user takes the file from the Markdown view, takes off the classes we added earlier.

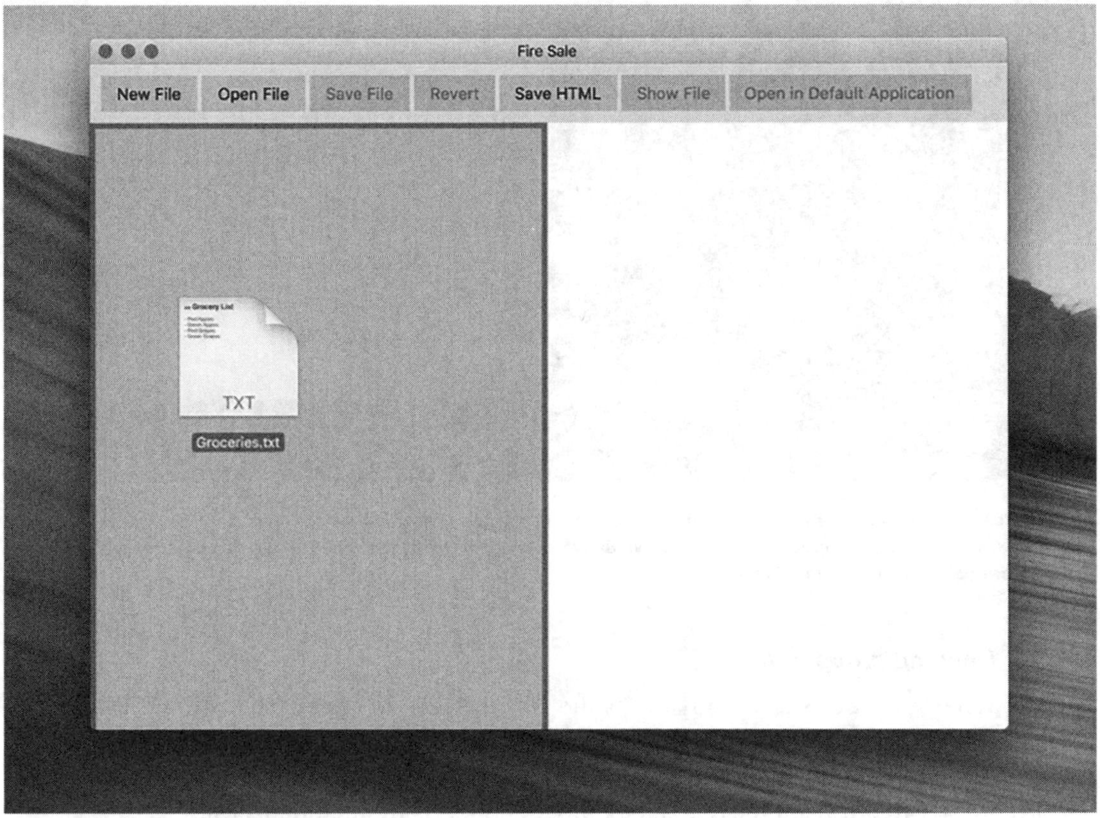

Figure 6.10 Adding a CSS class to the Markdown view provides a visual cue to the user that this is a valid place to drop this file.

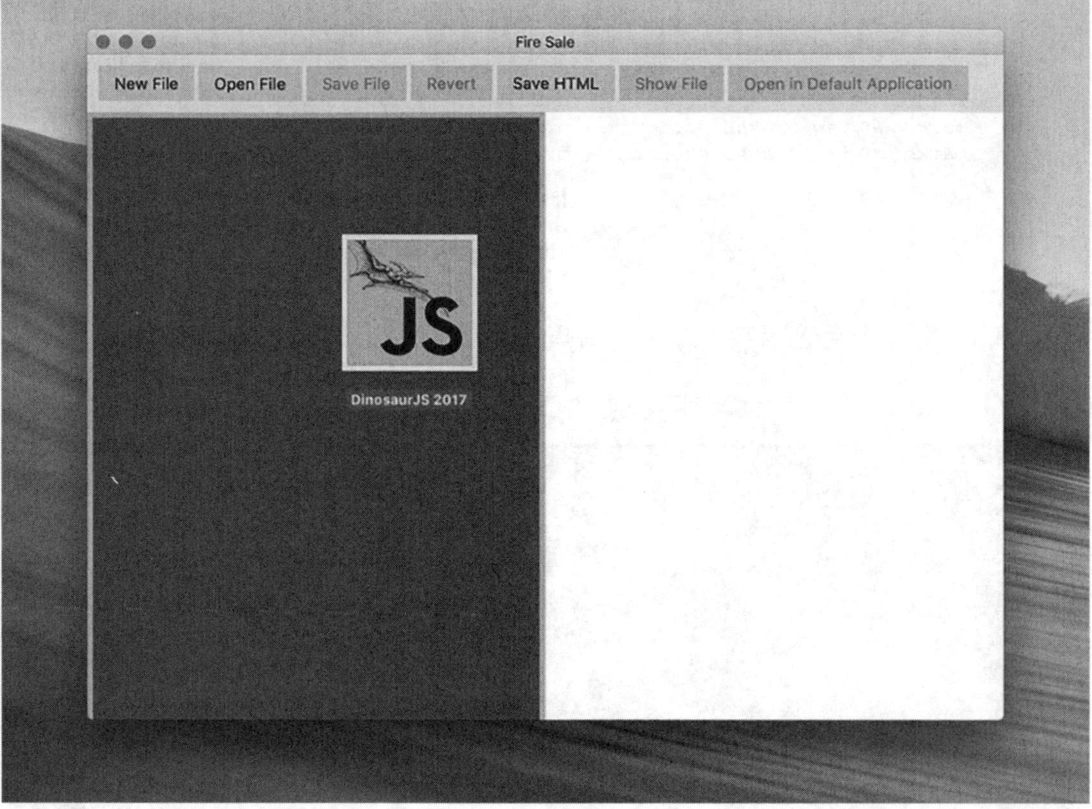

Figure 6.11 In the same vein, Fire Sale does not support images. The code we're about to write will reject any file that is not one of our supported types, but visually showing the user that the file won't be accepted allows them to cancel their action in advance.

6.4.3 Opening dropped files

When the user successfully drops the file onto the left pane, the code in listing 6.20 once again confirms that Fire Sale supports this type of file. If it does, we pass it over to the `activeFile` object in the main process that we created earlier, to be opened as if we selected it from the dialog box or from the recent documents list.

Listing 6.20 Drag-and-drop functionality: ./app/renderer.js

```
markdownView.addEventListener('drop', (event) => {
  const file = getDroppedFile(event);

  if (fileTypeIsSupported(file)) {
    mainProcess.openFile(currentWindow, file.path);
  } else {
    alert('That file type is not supported');
  }
```

- If the file type is supported, the renderer process communicates with the main process.
- If the file type is not supported, the application alerts the user.

```
  markdownView.classList.remove('drag-over');
  markdownView.classList.remove('drag-error');
});
```

With very little new code, we've successfully implemented a drag-and-drop feature reminiscent of a native desktop application.

6.5 Watching files for changes

A potentially dangerous edge case exists in our application right now. If we open a Markdown file in some other editor and make changes to it, Fire Sale is blissfully unaware. This means that if we save the file in Fire Sale after making changes in our other editor, it will destructively overwrite those changes.

We have a few ways around this. We could, for example, reread the file when Fire Sale comes back into focus. We could regularly check the file and see if its contents have changed. The way we approach it for now is to take advantage of Node's `fs.watchFile` feature, which uses operating system-specific libraries to monitor a file or directory and emit an event if the file changes.

The one caveat of this approach is that we must be careful to stop watching files when we open new ones. Otherwise, we keep adding watchers without letting any go, which is a memory leak. This is further complicated by the fact that we have multiple windows. If a file changes, we must make sure that we send it to the correct window. Our feature will work as follows:

1. Sets up a data structure for tracking our file watchers and the window that they're associated with.
2. Begins watching for file changes upon opening a file.
3. When opening subsequent files, closes the existing watcher before creating a new one.
4. Closes the watcher when the window is closed.

Our first task will be to figure out a way to manage the relationship between a window, the file currently displayed in the window, and/or the watcher for the file. In chapter 5, we used a `Set` to keep track of all the windows currently open in the application. In this section, we'll use another recent addition to the JavaScript language—a Map.

Maps are key-value stores, much like regular objects in JavaScript, with an important distinction. Objects can have only strings and numbers as keys. Maps can use any type of object or value as a key. To implement this feature, we instantiate a Map that uses `BrowserWindow` instances as keys and file watchers as values. When the user closes a window, we find the watcher associated with that window and stop it.

Listing 6.21 Setting up a Map to watch files: ./app/main.js

```
const openFiles = new Map();
```

As I mentioned earlier, we want to start watching a file path when it's opened and stop watching when either the window has been closed or the user opens a different file in the window. Let's set up two functions: `startWatchingFile()` and `stopWatchingFile()`.

Listing 6.22 Setting up a listener: ./app/main.js

```
const startWatchingFile = (targetWindow, file) => {
  stopWatchingFile(targetWindow);        // Closes the existing watcher if there is one.

  const watcher = fs.watchFile(file, (event) => {   // If the watcher fires a change event, rereads the file.
    if (event === 'change') {
      const content = fs.readFileSync(file);
      targetWindow.webContents.send('file-opened', file, content);   // Sends a message to the renderer process with the content of the file.
    }
  });

  openFiles.set(targetWindow, watcher);   // Tracks the watcher so we can stop it later.
};

const stopWatchingFile = (targetWindow) => {
  if (openFiles.has(targetWindow)) {      // Checks if we have a watcher running for this window.
    openFiles.get(targetWindow).stop();   // Stops the watcher.
    openFiles.delete(targetWindow);       // Deletes the watcher from the maps of open windows.
  }
};
```

In the listing, we start watching a given file path. If the watcher fires a "change" event, we send a message to the window alerting it to the fact that the file has changed. Lastly, add the window and the associated watcher to the `openFiles` Map, which allows us to find it later when it comes time to close the watcher. As an added precaution, let's close any existing watcher for that window before creating a new one. Doing so is helpful if the user opens a file window that was already watching a file.

Listing 6.23 Closing the watcher when the browser window closes: ./app/main.js

```
const createWindow = exports.createWindow = () => {
  let x, y;

  const currentWindow = BrowserWindow.getFocusedWindow();

  if (currentWindow) {
    const [ currentWindowX, currentWindowY ] = currentWindow.getPosition();
    x = currentWindowX + 10;
    y = currentWindowY + 10;
  }

  let newWindow = new BrowserWindow({ x, y, show: false });

  newWindow.loadFile('index.html');
```

```
  newWindow.once('ready-to-show', () => {
    newWindow.show();
  });

  newWindow.on('close', (event) => {
    if (newWindow.isDocumentEdited()) {
  // ...
    }
  });

  newWindow.on('closed', () => {
    windows.delete(newWindow);
    stopWatchingFile(newWindow);
    newWindow = null;
  });

  windows.add(newWindow);
  return newWindow;
};
```

When the window is closed, stops the watcher for the file associated with that window.

6.6 Prompting the user before discarding changes

Right now, the window's title reflects whether the user has made changes to the current document that haven't been saved. But what if the user tries to close the window? The changes are gone and unrecoverable. In the previous section, we added the ability to watch the currently active file path. If the file is changed by another application, Fire Sale overwrites the changes without warning. In both cases, this is unacceptable behavior for a desktop application. Users expect to be prompted if they are about to lose their work. In this section, we implement those safeguards.

In chapter 5, we set up a listener for the closed event, which is fired when the window has successfully been closed. Electron also supports a close event, which fires when the user attempts to close the window. If the user has unsaved changes, we can intervene and prompt the user to confirm that they—in fact—want to close the window and lose their changes.

Listing 6.24 Prompting the user if they try to close a window with unsaved changes: ./app/main.js

```
newWindow.on('close', (event) => {
  if (newWindow.isDocumentEdited()) {
    event.preventDefault();

    const result = dialog.showMessageBox(newWindow, {
      type: 'warning',
      title: 'Quit with Unsaved Changes?',
      message: 'Your changes will be lost if you do not save.',
      buttons: [
        'Quit Anyway',
```

Checks if the document has been edited. We set this in the renderer process on every keyup in the Markdown view by comparing the current content with the original content.

If the window has unsaved changes, prevents it from closing.

Prompts the user with a custom message box asking if they are sure they'd like to close the window and lose their changes. Saves their selection into "result".

Provides a list of button labels.

```
      'Cancel',
    ],
    defaultId: 0,
    cancelId: 1
   });

  if (result === 0) newWindow.destroy();
 }
});
```

Sets the first option as the default option if the user hits the Return key.

Sets the second button as the button selected if the user dismisses the message box.

If the user selects "Quit Anyway," forces the window to close.

In previous chapters, we used `dialog.showOpenDialog()` and `dialog.showSaveDialog()` for prompting the user to select a file. `dialog.showMessageBox()` is a general-purpose, customizable dialog box. You can provide a list of button labels to the buttons array. `dialog.showMessageBox()` returns the index of the button that the user selected. If the user selects the first button, `dialog.showMessageBox()` returns `0`. We can use the return value to figure out how to proceed in our application based on the user's preference. `dialog.showMessageBox()` also takes additional options that allow us to specify what the default action should be if the user clicks the Return button and what option should be returned if the user dismisses the dialog box.

In the previous example, we listen for the `close` event. If the window has unedited changes, we prompt the user. Based on the user's response, we either prevent the window from closing or purposely destroy the window.

We also need to safeguard against two other situations where the user could lose their changes. The first is if the user attempts to open another file in the same window when there are unsaved changes; the second is if another application changes the file. The major difference between these two functions is in the message shown to the user. Either way, if the user decides to move forward, then we load the file and replace the content in the UI. In an effort to avoid repeating ourselves, we'll move this process into its own function to use it in both places.

Listing 6.25 Refactoring the process of displaying a new file: ./app/renderer.js

```
const renderFile = (file, content) => {
  filePath = file;
  originalContent = content;

  markdownView.value = content;
  renderMarkdownToHtml(content);

  updateUserInterface(false);
};
```

With our new `renderFile()` function in place, we can set up two IPC listeners. When the user opens a new file (listing 6.26), we continue to use the `file-opened` channel. But if the file has been modified by another application (listing 6.27), we send a message over the `file-changed` channel instead. Based on from which channel we receive the message, we display a different message to the user.

Listing 6.26 Prompting the user when opening a new file if there are unsaved changes: ./app/renderer.js

```
ipcRenderer.on('file-opened', (event, file, content) => {
  if (currentWindow.isDocumentEdited()) {
    const result = remote.dialog.showMessageBox(currentWindow, {
      type: 'warning',
      title: 'Overwrite Current Unsaved Changes?',
      message: 'Opening a new file in this window will overwrite your unsaved
     changes. Open this file anyway?',
      buttons: [
        'Yes',
        'Cancel',
      ],
      defaultId: 0,
      cancelId: 1
    });

    if (result === 1) { return; }
  }

  renderFile(file, content);
});
```

Uses the remote module to trigger the dialog box from the main process.

If the user cancels, returns from the function early.

Sets the window to its unedited state because the user just opened a new file.

Listing 6.27 Prompting the user when a file changes: ./app/renderer.js

```
ipcRenderer.on('file-changed', (event, file, content) => {
  const result = remote.dialog.showMessageBox(currentWindow, {
    type: 'warning',
    title: 'Overwrite Current Unsaved Changes?',
    message: 'Another application has changed this file. Load changes?',
    buttons: [
      'Yes',
      'Cancel',
    ],
    defaultId: 0,
    cancelId: 1
  });

  renderFile(file, content);
});
```

In this situation, we don't care if the document has been edited. We want to prompt the user regardless.

The last step is to modify the `startWatchingFile()` function to send a message over the `file-changed` channel, instead of the `file-opened` channel, to trigger the correct message box.

Listing 6.28 Sending a message over the file-changed channel: ./app/main.js

```
const startWatchingFile = (targetWindow, file) => {
  stopWatchingFile(targetWindow);

  const watcher = fs.watch(file, (event) => {
    if (event === 'change') {
```

```
    const content = fs.readFileSync(file).toString();
    targetWindow.webContents.send('file-changed', file, content);
  }
});

openFiles.set(targetWindow, watcher);
};
```

Fires a different event if there has been a change to the current file

And with that, our application now supports drag-and-drop functionality, watches the filesystem for changes, adds files to the operating system's list of recently opened files, updates the window's title bar, sets a represented file on macOS, and alerts the user before discarding unsaved changes. The code for the application can be found at https://github.com/electron-in-action/firesale/tree/chapter-6, or the appendix.

Summary

- When implementing the ability to save a file, we must consider if this is a new or existing file and handle each scenario differently.
- When saving a new file, we can use `dialog.showSaveFileDialog()` to prompt the user to select a location to which to write the file.
- When saving an existing file, Fire Sale writes to the existing file's current location.
- By default, Electron windows display the contents of the HTML documents' `<title>` tag. The `setTitle()` method on all `BrowserWindow` instances allows users to update and customize a window's title based on the state of the application.
- Electron provides the ability to further customize windows in macOS.
  - We can set the "represented file" to a given path, and it is added to the menu bar. macOS allows users to drag the file as if they were dragging it from the Finder.
  - We can use the `setDocumentedEdited()` method on `BrowserWindow` instances to display a small dot in the window's close button that signifies to the user that they have unsaved changes.
- Electron provides the `app.addRecentDocument()` method, which appends a given file path to the operating system's list of recently opened documents. This works across all the supported platforms.
- When the user selects a file from the operating system's list of recently opened documents, Electron does not know how to handle this by default. We must provide a custom listener on the app object that handles `file-open` events.
- Electron provides several shortcuts to common locations where users typically want to save files. This is done under the hood, relieving us from the responsibility of customizing the default location for each supported operating system.
- In addition to the file selection dialogs provided by Electron, we can also use the HTML File API to support drag-and-drop actions from the user.
- Node provides the `fs.watch()` method, which allows us to watch currently open files and alerts us if they have been changed by other applications.

7 Building application and context menus

This chapter covers

- Creating menus using Electron's `Menu` and `MenuItem` modules
- Building menus from a template
- Defining custom menus for target operating systems
- Assigning common operating system roles to our menu items
- Making menu items with custom, application-specific functionality
- Creating custom context menus for different parts of your UI

In browser-based applications, developers have access only to the visible area of the application's window. They can't add controls to the browser's tool bar or menu bar. The entire UI for the application's functionality must be inside of the window. Developers also face limitations within the window. They can't modify the context menus that appear when the user right-clicks their UI. It can be a challenge to find a place for every option and command. Electron, on the other hand, enables developers to add functionality outside of the browser window, such as custom application and context menus that appear when the user right-clicks a component of the UI.

In this chapter, we explore how to create and configure these menus in Fire Sale. We'll replace the default menu provided by Electron with our own and walk through exposing common operating system functionality in our menus. We assign keyboard shortcuts to menu items to make them easy to trigger from anywhere in the application. With the basic menu functionality implemented, we then add in our own application-specific menu items—notably, the ability to open a Markdown file from the filesystem, display it in the left pane of our UI, and render its contents as HTML in the right pane. Finally, we create a custom context menu containing common text manipulation tasks (cut, copy, and paste, as shown in figure 7.1) whenever the user right-clicks the left pane.

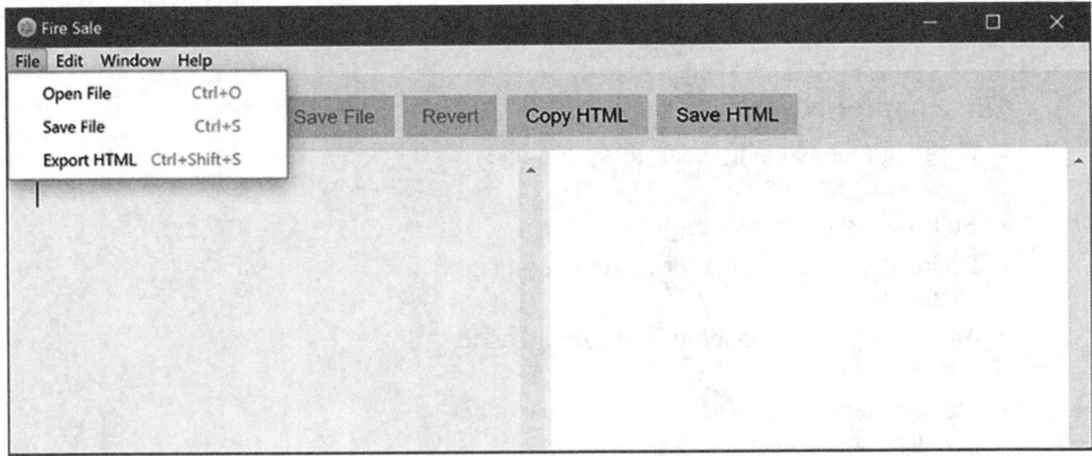

Figure 7.1 In this chapter, we build custom menu items that trigger some of the functionality found in the UI.

Throughout the previous few chapters, we've had a menu in Fire Sale. So why build a custom one now? Developers can overwrite Electron's default menu, but then they are responsible for building the menu from the ground up. Over the course of this chapter, we restore some of the basic functionality common to most desktop applications. After the foundation has been laid, we extend it with our own custom functionality. From our menu users can save the currently active file as well as export the HTML to its own file. In addition to being able to access this functionality from the application's menu, users can use keyboard shortcuts to trigger the menu items. In this chapter, we build a menu for Fire Sale that has the structure shown in figure 7.2.

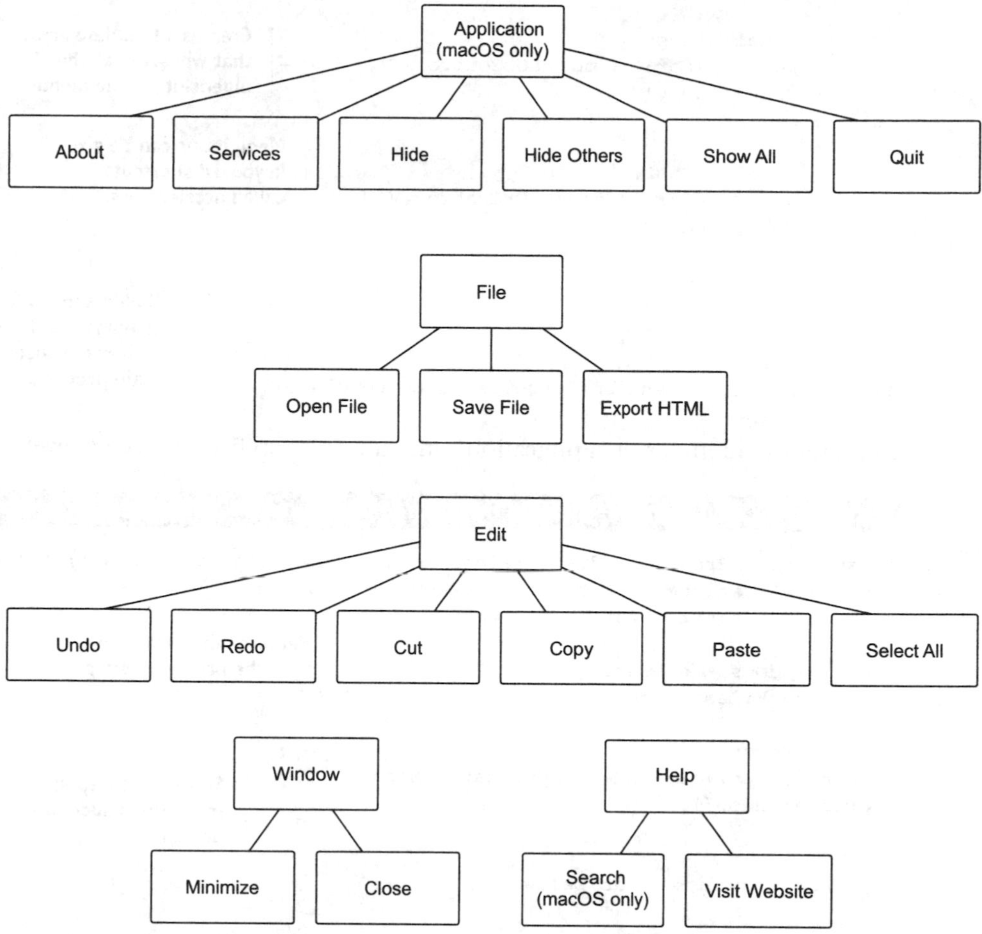

Figure 7.2 The structure of the application menu for Fire Sale

7.1 Replacing and replicating the default menu

To get started, make a new file called ./app/application-menu.js. This file will grow large by the end of the chapter, so we address that now by breaking it out into its own file. Let's begin by adding copy and paste back to the application menu.

Listing 7.1 Creating an Edit menu with copy and paste: ./app/application-menu.js

```
const { app, BrowserWindow, Menu, shell } = require('electron');
const mainProcess = require('./main');

const template = [
  {
    label: 'Edit',
    submenu: [
```

Requires the modules that we need as we build the application menu throughout this chapter

Creates a template array that will serve as the blueprint for the menu

```
      {
        label: 'Copy',
        accelerator: 'CommandOrControl+C',
        role: 'copy',
      },
      {
        label: 'Paste',
        accelerator: 'CommandOrControl+V',
        role: 'paste',
      },
    ]
  }
];

module.exports = Menu.buildFromTemplate(template);
```

Creates a template array that will serve as the blueprint for the menu

Menu items can be given keyboard shortcuts called accelerators.

Builds a menu from the template, and exports it so it can be used in the main process.

Next, set the menu as the application's menu when app fires the `ready` event.

Listing 7.2 Loading the menu in the main application file: ./app/main.js

```
const { app, BrowserWindow, dialog, Menu } = require('electron');
const applicationMenu = require('./application-menu');
const fs = require('fs');

const windows = new Set();
const openFiles = new Map();

app.on('ready', () => {
  Menu.setApplicationMenu(applicationMenu);
  createWindow();
});

// … Additional methods below …
```

Requires the Menu module from Electron

Requires the menu built in the previous listing

Sets it as the application menu upon successful launch

Electron includes the `Menu` and `MenuItem` modules for building menus. In theory, we could build a menu out of individual `MenuItems`, but this method can be tedious and error prone. As a convenience, `Menu` provides the `buildFromTemplate()` method that accepts an array of regular JavaScript objects. Internally, Electron creates the `MenuItems` based on the array you provided.

7.1.1 macOS and the case of the missing Edit menu

If you start the application in Windows, you should see an Edit menu with two menu items: Copy and Paste. This is to be expected. But if you're testing the application on macOS, you'll see something a bit different, as shown in figure 7.3.

In macOS, the menu is called Electron rather than Edit because the first menu on macOS is always the Application menu. To solve this issue in Electron, we need to shift the Edit menu—and all subsequent menu items in the future—down one spot, as shown in listing 7.3 and figure 7.4, to make room for the Application menu, which we implement later in this chapter.

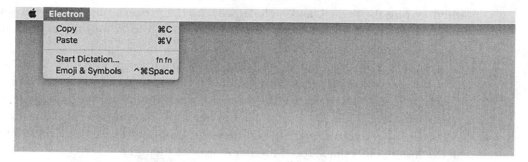

Figure 7.3 macOS takes the first menu item and uses it as the Application menu, which is not always the expected or intended behavior.

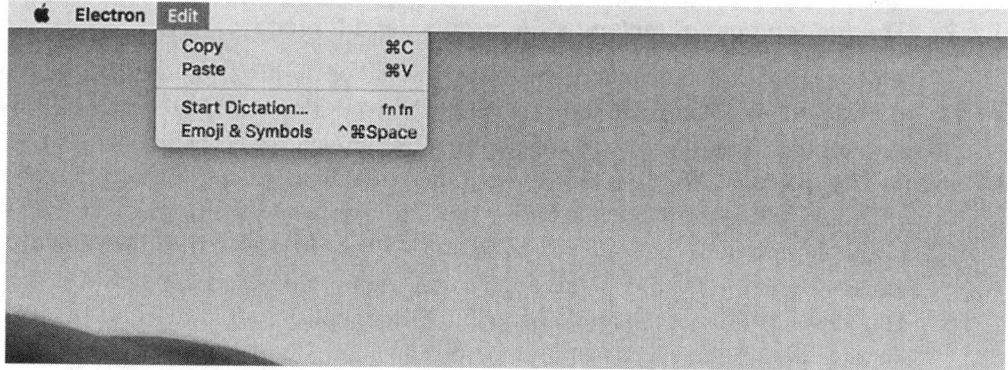

Figure 7.4 By shifting all of the menus down one position, the Edit menu renders correctly. Soon, we implement an Application menu that behaves like a native macOS application.

Listing 7.3 Prepending to the list of menu items in macOS: ./app/application-menu.js

```
const { app, BrowserWindow, Menu, shell } = require('electron');
const mainProcess = require('./main');

const template = [
  // ... Menu template from the last section. ...
];

if (process.platform === 'darwin') {
  const name = 'Fire Sale';
  template.unshift({ label: name });
}

module.exports = Menu.buildFromTemplate(template);
```

- `if (process.platform === 'darwin')` — Asks Node's process global what platform the application is running on. macOS reports that it is darwin. If this is the case, moves a new menu item to the beginning of the template array.
- `const name = 'Fire Sale';` — Gets the name of the application. This won't show up in the menu now but is useful down the road.

One of the great things about building applications with Electron is that developers can target macOS, Windows, and Linux with one codebase. The caveat is that the developer should consider the idiosyncrasies of each of the supported operating systems when writing the code. Luckily, Node provides the `process` object, which has several properties, methods, and events that provide introspection into the environment in which the application is running.

`process.platform` returns the name of the platform in which the application is currently executing. As of this writing, `process.platform` returns one of five strings: `darwin`, `freebsd`, `linux`, `sunos`, or `win32`. Darwin is the UNIX operating system upon which macOS is built. We can adjust our menu at runtime by checking if `process.platform` is equal to `darwin`. If it is, then the application is running on macOS and all the menu items should be shifted one place to the right.

For all of the extra work required to get menus in the correct order, you may have noticed in figure 7.4 that we were rewarded with dictation and emoji support without having to implement it just by having an Edit menu.

7.1.2 The hidden cost of replacing Electron's default menu

Electron provides a default menu, but it's an all or nothing affair. When we replace the menu, we lose all its original functionality. Not only do we lose a few menu items, we also lose their keyboard shortcuts. Try to use the Command-X keyboard shortcut on macOS, or Control-X on Windows and Linux, to cut text from the left pane. What about Command-A or Control-A on macOS or Windows, respectively, to select all the text? How about Command-Z or Control-Z to undo? Nothing happens. If you're on macOS, try to press Command-Q to quit the application. Again, nothing happens. We also lose the functionality to hide this application and other applications in macOS. On all operating systems, we lose the ability to undo and redo changes, minimize and close the window, and select all text in each field. All that's left is the ability to copy and paste, shown in figure 7.5—and that's only because it was added back in our custom menu.

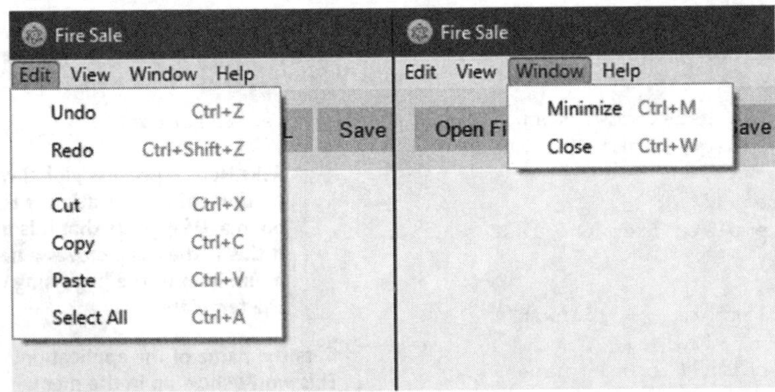

Figure 7.5 The Edit and Window menus as implemented in Electron's built-in menu

It's up to the developer to add these features back to the application. If we want to omit any of these features from our application, we can. Your first thought might be that re-implementing this functionality is a bit like reinventing the wheel. Luckily, Electron makes it easy to create menu items that perform common operating system tasks. When a new menu item is created, a number of options can be set on it. So far, we've been exposed to the `label` option and the `type` option, which we set to `separator` on the third menu item in each of the previous listings.

7.1.3 Implementing the Edit and Window menus

To get practice building menus in Electron, let's start by implementing the Edit and Window menus similar to how they were defined in Electron's default menu, as shown in figure 7.5.

Listing 7.4 Edit menu template: ./app/application-menu.js

```
const template = [
  {
    label: 'Edit',
    submenu: [
      {
        label: 'Undo',
        accelerator: 'CommandOrControl+Z',
        role: 'undo',
      },
      {
        label: 'Redo',
        accelerator: 'Shift+CommandOrControl+Z',
        role: 'redo',
      },
      { type: 'separator' },
      {
        label: 'Cut',
        accelerator: 'CommandOrControl+X',
        role: 'cut',
      },
      {
        label: 'Copy',
        accelerator: 'CommandOrControl+C',
        role: 'copy',
      },
      {
        label: 'Paste',
        accelerator: 'CommandOrControl+V',
        role: 'paste',
      },
      {
        label: 'Select All',
        accelerator: 'CommandOrControl+A',
        role: 'selectall',
      },
    ],
  },
```

```
  {
    label: 'Window',
    submenu: [
      {
        label: 'Minimize',
        accelerator: 'CommandOrControl+M',
        role: 'minimize',
      },
      {
        label: 'Close',
        accelerator: 'CommandOrControl+W',
        role: 'close',
      },
    ],
  },
];

if (process.platform === 'darwin') {
  const name = app.getName();
  template.unshift({ label: name });
}

module.exports = Menu.buildFromTemplate(template);
```

7.1.4 Defining menu item roles and keyboard shortcuts

One thing you may have noticed is that all of the menu items added so far have a special `role` property. This setting is important because functionality like copy and paste is hard to implement by hand. Menu items can have a `role`, which correlates to a built-in capability provided by the operating system to all applications. On Windows, Linux, and macOS, the `role` of a menu item can be set to any of the following:

- `undo`
- `redo`
- `cut`
- `copy`
- `paste`
- `selectall`
- `minimize`
- `close`

These roles overlap with much of the functionality we lost when we replaced the default menu with our own. Adding menu items with these roles restores the functionality to the menu but not the keyboard shortcuts that many users are accustomed to.

Electron provides an additional property called `accelerator` for defining a keyboard shortcut to trigger a menu item's action. When creating menu items, you can set the `accelerator` property to a string that follows a set of Electron-specific conventions. Listing 7.5 codes a menu item that adds the copy functionality.

Listing 7.5 Using roles and accelerators: ./app/application-menu.js

```
const { app, BrowserWindow, Menu, MenuItem, shell } = require('electron');

const copyMenuItem = new MenuItem({
  label: 'Copy',
  accelerator: 'CommandOrControl+C',
  role: 'copy'
});
```

On Windows and Linux, it's common to prefix keyboard shortcuts with the Control key. On macOS, it's common to use the Command key for a similar purpose. In addition to being unconventional, the Command key isn't available on Linux and Windows. Rather than needing to rely on `process.platform` along with conditional logic in our menu items, Electron provides the `CommandOrControl` shorthand. On macOS, this binds the keyboard shortcut to the Command key. On Windows and Linux, Electron uses the Control key instead. As additional shorthand, Electron provides `Cmd`, `Ctrl`, and `CmdOrCtrl`, which are aliased to `Command`, `Control`, and `CommandOrControl`, respectively.

7.1.5 Restoring the application menu on macOS

When Electron runs, it compiles the template into a collection of `MenuItems` and sets the application's menu accordingly. Keyboard shortcuts for common operations like copying and pasting are restored, and the application behaves as expected in Windows and Linux. In macOS, however, the application is still missing important functionality, not least of which is the ability to quit the application. Standard application menus in macOS have the structure shown in figure 7.6.

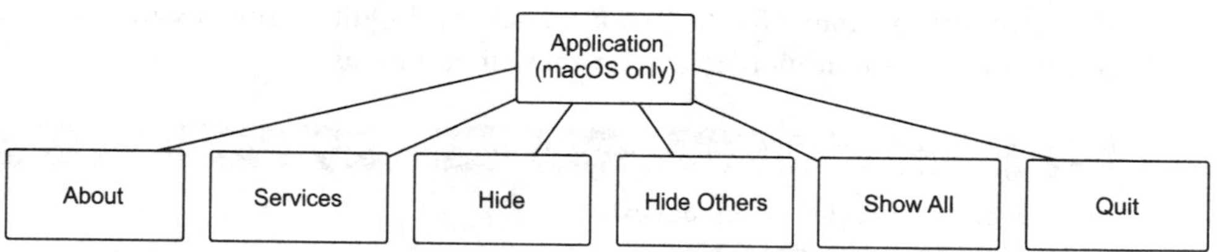

Figure 7.6 The structure of the application menu in macOS applications

When running on macOS, Electron provides an additional set of roles that make it easy to restore the application menu common to most Mac applications. These additional roles are

- `about`
- `hide`
- `hideothers`
- `unhide`
- `front`

- `window`
- `help`
- `services`

The default application menu provided by Electron has menu items for showing the application's About panel, exposing services provided by macOS, hiding the application, hiding all other applications, and quitting the application, as shown in figure 7.7.

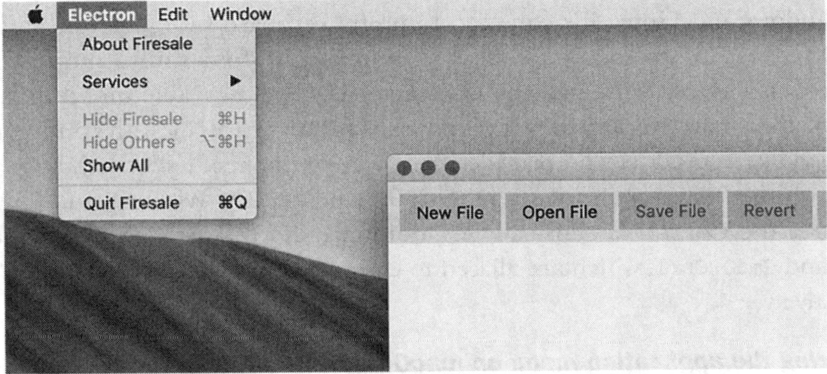

Figure 7.7 Menu items in the application menu use special `roles` in Electron that allow you to trigger operating system functionality without reinventing the wheel.

Implementing the application menu is similar to implementing the Edit and Window menus. `Command` is preferable over `CommandOrControl` for defining accelerators, because this menu appears only on macOS. In addition, we use template strings to get the application's name for the About, Hide, and Quit menus because it is customary to include the application's name in these menu items.

Listing 7.6 Application menu for macOS: ./app/application-menu.js

```
if (process.platform === 'darwin') {
  const name = 'Fire Sale';
  template.unshift({
    label: name,
    submenu: [
      {
        label: `About ${name}`,
        role: 'about',
      },
      { type: 'separator' },
      {
        label: 'Services',
        role: 'services',
        submenu: [],
      },
      { type: 'separator' },
```

```
        {
          label: `Hide ${name}`,
          accelerator: 'Command+H',
          role: 'hide',
        },
        {
          label: 'Hide Others',
          accelerator: 'Command+Alt+H',
          role: 'hideothers',
        },
        {
          label: 'Show All',
          role: 'unhide',
        },
        { type: 'separator' },
        {
          label: `Quit ${name}`,
          accelerator: 'Command+Q',
          click() { app.quit(); },
        },
      ],
    });
  }
```

There is no built-in role for quitting an application. Instead, we add a click method that is called whenever the menu item is clicked or keyboard shortcut activated.

Our application now has almost all of the functionality of a native application on macOS, but we still need to address a few subtle differences. On macOS, the Window menu has a few additional menu items—most notably Bring All to Front, which moves all of the windows of the application to the front of the stack. In addition, the macOS-exclusive `window` role adds the ability to close and minimize the current window from the Window menu, as well as a list of all of the application's windows, and the ability to bring them all to the front. This role is ignored on platforms that don't support it.

Listing 7.7 Combining the application, Edit, and Window menus: ./app/application-menu.js

```
const template = [
  {
    label: 'Edit',
    submenu: [
      // "Edit" menu shown in Listing 7.4
    ],
  },
  {
    label: 'Window',
    role: 'window',
    submenu: [
      // "Window" menu shown in Listing 7.4
    ],
  },
];

if (process.platform === 'darwin') {
  const name = app.getName();
  template.unshift({
```

The window role on the Window menu causes Electron to add a list of all open windows at the end of the menu when running in macOS.

```
    label: name,
    submenu: [
      // #Application menu shown in Listing 7.6
    ],
  });

  const windowMenu = template.find(item => item.label === 'Window');
  windowMenu.role = 'window';
  windowMenu.submenu.push(
    { type: 'separator' },
    {
      label: 'Bring All to Front',
      role: 'front',
    }
  );
}
```

The Array.prototype.find() method traverses our menu template and looks for the menu with the label of Window. If the order of the items ever changes, this approach is resilient to change.

Sets the menu's role to "window". This enables the display of a list of currently open windows as shown in figure 7.8.

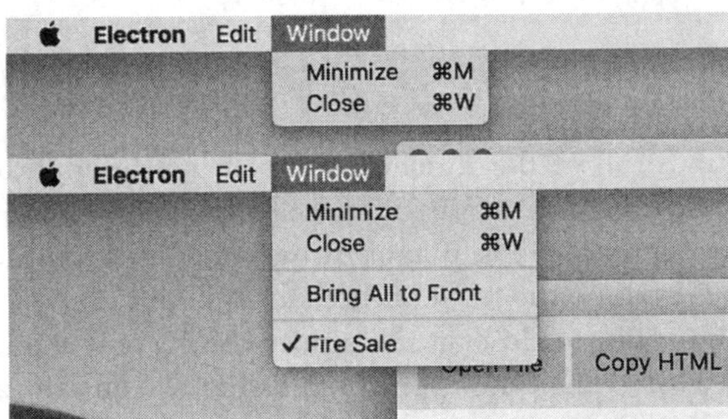

Figure 7.8 The Window menu in macOS allows you to see all of the windows currently open in the application.

7.1.6 Adding a Help menu

Adding a Help menu is a good practice regardless of platform, but there is an added benefit for doing so on macOS. Even if your application does not have any documentation or support yet, the built-in Help menu allows users to search the application to find menu items, as shown in figure 7.9. This works in most macOS applications and is useful for searching through deeply nested menus quickly. You can access the menu search by pressing Command-Shift-? at any time.

To add a Help menu to your application, such as the structure shown in figure 7.10, add an additional menu with the role of `help` and a submenu of additional menu items. You must provide an array as the submenu, as shown in listing 7.8, even if it's empty. For now, we can also add the ability to trigger the developer tools. Depending on the application, you might want to remove this feature before publishing the application. That said, popular applications such as Atom, Nylas Mail, and Visual Studio Code have chosen to leave it in.

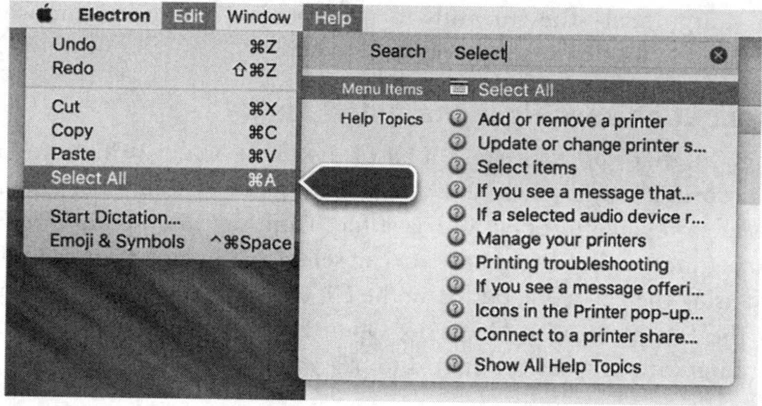

Figure 7.9 On macOS, the Help menu allows you to search for items in your menu.

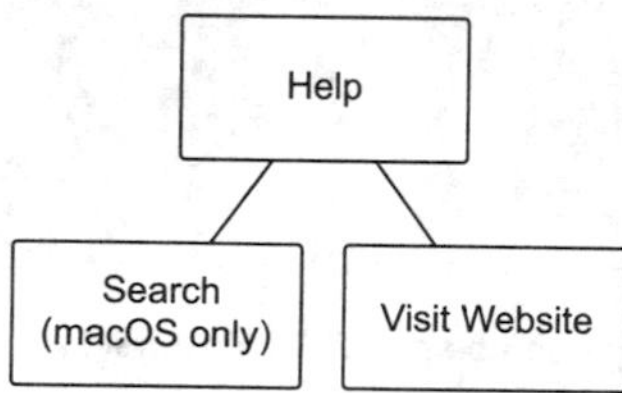

Figure 7.10 The structure of the Help menu that we build in listing 7.8.

Listing 7.8 Creating a Help menu: ./app/application-menu.js

```
const template = [
  // "Edit"  and "Window" menus defined in Listing 7.7
  {
    label: 'Help',
    role: 'help',
    submenu: [
      {
        label: 'Visit Website',
        click() { /* To be implemented */ }
      },
      {
        label: 'Toggle Developer Tools',
        click(item, focusedWindow) {
          if (focusedWindow) focusedWindow.webContents.toggleDevTools();
        }
      }
    ],
  }
];
```

Click methods can optionally take the menu item itself and the currently focused window as arguments.

The `click()` method can optionally take up to three arguments: the menu item itself, the currently focused `BrowserWindow` instance, and an event object. In listing 7.8, we use the second argument—the currently focused window—to determine which window we should tell to toggle the developer tools.

7.2 Adding application-specific menu functionality

Going through all that work to restore a lot of the functionality, which we originally got for free, is worth it only if we use it as a template to add custom functionality. Users typically expect to be able to open and save files from the File menu. Fire Sale currently lacks this functionality. Right now, we can select and open a Markdown file from the filesystem using the Open File button in the UI. Our next step, shown in figure 7.11, is to modify the File menu with New File, Open File, Save File, and Export HTML menu items along with keyboard shortcuts to trigger each action.

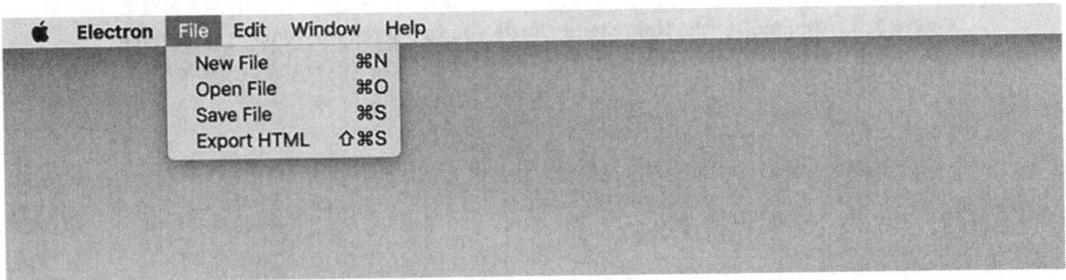

Figure 7.11 In this section, we will add a File menu with application-specific functionality.

When the user clicks the Open File menu item or presses the keyboard shortcut, the menu item triggers the same `openFile()` function from the main process that the button in the UI triggers. Clicking New File calls the `createWindow()` function from the main process. Let's start by adding a File menu to our template with each of the features shown in figure 7.11 as menu items to its `submenu` array.

In the case of saving or exporting a file, however, we need the current contents of the Markdown pane or the HTML pane, respectively. We'll also need the name of the currently open file if there is one because the main process doesn't have access to this information. Instead, we send a message to the currently focused window that it should gather this information for us and then trigger the same functionality it would if a user clicked on a button in the UI.

Listing 7.9 Custom menu functionality: ./app/application-menu.js

```
const template = [
  {
    label: 'File',
    submenu: [
      {
        label: 'New File',
        accelerator: 'CommandOrControl+N',
        click() {
          mainProcess.createWindow();
```

Tells the main process to create a new window when New File is selected

```
          }
        },
        {
          label: 'Open File',
          accelerator: 'CommandOrControl+O',
          click(item, focusedWindow) {
            mainProcess.getFileFromUser(focusedWindow);
          },
        },
        {
          label: 'Save File',
          accelerator: 'CommandOrControl+S',
          click(item, focusedWindow) {
            focusedWindow.webContents.send('save-markdown');
          },
        },
        {
          label: 'Export HTML',
          accelerator: 'Shift+CommandOrControl+S',
          click(item, focusedWindow) {
            focusedWindow.webContents.send('save-html');
          },
        },
      ],
    },
    // "Edit", "Window", and "Help" menus are defined here as well.
];
```

Prompts the user to select a new file to open in the current window

Sends a message to the currently focused window to save its Markdown

Sends a message to the currently focused window to export its HTML

Sending a message to the focused window is half the battle. We still need to configure the renderer process to listen for these messages and act accordingly. Let's set up an IPC listener to receive these messages and call our existing save and export functionality whenever a message is received.

Listing 7.10 Add IPC listeners to the renderer process: ./app/renderer.js

When a message is received on the save-markdown channel, sends a message back to the main process with the name of the currently open file—if any—and the text content from the DOM.

```
ipcRenderer.on('save-markdown', () => {
  mainProcess.saveMarkdown(currentWindow, filePath, markdownView.value);
});

ipcRenderer.on('save-html', () => {
  mainProcess.saveHtml(currentWindow, filePath, markdownView.value);
});
```

When a message is received on the save-html channel, sends a message back to the main process with the name of the currently open file and the rendered HTML.

7.2.1 Handling the case of having no focused window

In Windows and Linux, the application quits when all the windows are closed. On macOS the application remains running even when all the windows have been closed. A new window is opened when the icon is clicked, but in some cases, the user might select one of the three menu items we just implemented and the focused window is `undefined`. In chapter 9, we cover how to enable and disable menu items. For now, we take a simpler approach: open a new window if the user selects Open File, and display an error message if there is no content to save or export.

To display the error messages when a user tries to save or export a nonexistent file, we use `dialog.showErrorBox()`, which is similar to `dialog.showMessageBox()` but specializes in displaying error messages and doesn't have as many options for configuration.

Listing 7.11 Displaying an error when trying to save or export a file that doesn't exist: ./app/application-menu.js

```
const { app, dialog, Menu, MenuItem shell } = require('electron');    ◁ Requires Electron's dialog module
const mainProcess = require('./main');

const template = [
  {
    label: 'File',
    submenu: [
      {
        label: 'New File',
        accelerator: 'CommandOrControl+N',
        click() {
          mainProcess.createWindow();
        }
      },
      {
        label: 'Open File',
        accelerator: 'CommandOrControl+O',
        click(item, focusedWindow) {
          mainProcess.getFileFromUser(focusedWindow);
        },
      },
      {
        label: 'Save File',
        accelerator: 'CommandOrControl+S',
        click(item, focusedWindow) {
          if (!focusedWindow) {
            return dialog.showErrorBox(    ◁ Uses dialog.showErrorBox() to display an alert, and returns from the function early
              'Cannot Save or Export',
              'There is currently no active document to save or export.'
            );
          }
          focusedWindow.webContents.send('save-markdown');
        },
      },
      {
```

```
          label: 'Export HTML',
          accelerator: 'Shift+CommandOrControl+S',
          click(item, focusedWindow) {
            if (!focusedWindow) {
              return dialog.showErrorBox(
                'Cannot Save or Export',
                'There is currently no active document to save or export.'
              );
            }
            focusedWindow.webContents.send('save-html');
          },
        },
      ],
    },
```

Provides the same functionality if the user tries to export a nonexistent file

Things are not nearly as hopeless if the user selects Open File and there is no window available to receive the command. We simply make a new window, wait for it to be shown, and then trigger the File Selection dialog box as if the window had been there all along.

Listing 7.12 Creating a window when the user opens a new file if one does not exist: ./app/application-menu.js

```
const template = [
  {
    label: 'File',
    submenu: [
      {
        label: 'Open File',
        accelerator: 'CommandOrControl+O',
        click(item, focusedWindow) {
          if (focusedWindow) {
            return mainProcess.getFileFromUser(focusedWindow);
          }

          const newWindow = mainProcess.createWindow();

          newWindow.on('show', () => {
            mainProcess.getFileFromUser(newWindow);
          });
        },
      }, // "Save File" and "Export HTML" menus are defined here.
    ],
  }, // "Edit", "Window", and "Help" menus are defined here.
];
```

If focusedWindow is defined, uses the functionality we defined earlier in the chapter.

When the new window has been shown, prompts the user to select a file as if the window had been there all along.

If there is no focused-Window, creates one using the createWindow() function we created in the main process in chapter 5.

First, we check if there is a `focusedWindow`. If there is, we want to trigger the functionality that we implemented earlier and return from the function early. If there isn't a focused window, we need to create one. Luckily, we created a function in chapter 5 to assist us with this process. When the new window has finished initalizing, we use it as we would use any existing window. Our code is now resilient to this case, and we're ready to move on.

7.3 Building context menus

In the previous section, we defined a menu and set it as the application menu in the main process when the app module fired its "ready" event. Our application can only have one application menu at a time. We can, however, define additional menus in the renderer process, shown in figure 7.12, that spring into action when the user right-clicks (or does a two-finger click on certain computers) a part of the UI.

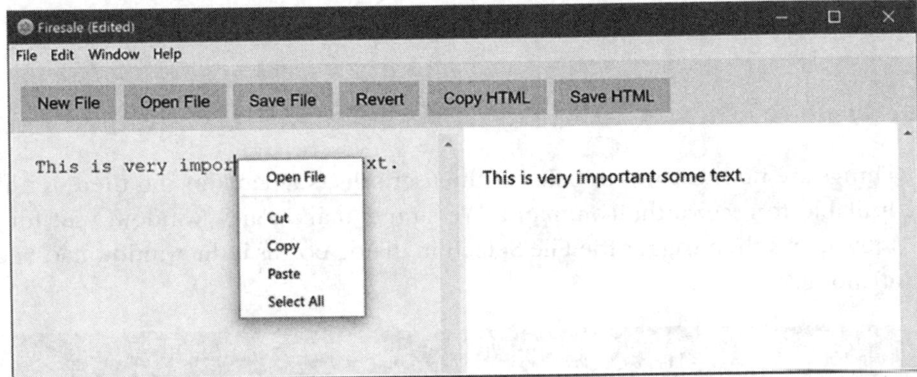

Figure 7.12 Electron allows developers to define custom context menus when the user right-clicks on a specific part of the DOM.

Next, we listen for `contextmenu` events in the left-hand markdown pane.

Listing 7.13 Listening for `contextmenu` events: ./app/renderer.js

```
markdownView.addEventListener('contextmenu', (event) => {
  event.preventDefault();
  alert('One day, a context menu will go here.');
});
```

Notice that the alert does not fire unless the user clicks the left pane. If you want a context menu that is triggered from anywhere within the application, listen on the `window` object instead of on a DOM node. The `Menu` module is not available from within the renderer process, but it can be accessed from the context of the main process using the `remote` module as shown in the following listing. Once imported, we can use `Menu.buildFromTemplate()` to construct a menu as shown in listing 7.15.

Listing 7.14 Creating a context menu: ./app/renderer.js

```
const { remote, ipcRenderer } = require('electron');
const { Menu } = remote;                                  // Requires the Menu module from the context of the main process via the remote module.
const path = require('path');
const mainProcess = remote.require('./main.js');
const currentWindow = remote.getCurrentWindow();
```

```
// Our existing renderer code…

const markdownContextMenu = Menu.buildFromTemplate([
  { label: 'Open File', click() { mainProcess.getFileFromUser(); } },
  { type: 'separator' },
  { label: 'Cut', role: 'cut' },
  { label: 'Copy', role: 'copy' },
  { label: 'Paste', role: 'paste' },
  { label: 'Select All', role: 'selectall' },
]);
```

To trigger this menu, replace the `contextmenu` event listener with a function that will call the `popup()` method on the newly created menu, shown here.

Listing 7.15 Triggering the context menu: ./app/renderer.js

```
markdownView.addEventListener('contextmenu', (event) => {
  event.preventDefault();
  markdownContextMenu.popup();
});
```

The `popup()` method takes four arguments: a `BrowserWindow`, `x`, `y`, and a `positioningItem`. All of these arguments are optional, and if they're omitted, then the context shows up in the current browser window directly under the mouse cursor, which is the behavior we expect in this context. With that code in place, we can now trigger a context menu in our Markdown pane. We add functionality to the context menu as well as additional context menus as we add more features to our application. The complete code for this chapter can be found at https://github.com/electron-in-action/firesale/tree/chapter-7 or in the appendix. Alternatively, you can clone from the GitHub repository at https://github.com/electron-in-action/firesale.git, check out the `chapter-7` branch, and run `npm install` to see it in action.

Summary

- Electron allows developers to build custom application and context menus.
- Electron provides the `Menu` and the `MenuItem` modules for building menus.
- `Menu.buildFromTemplate()` allows developers to build a menu out of an array of JavaScript objects instead of having to use the `MenuItem` constructor.
- Electron comes with a built-in application menu filled with sensible defaults. Overriding this menu means that we have to replace the built-in functionality.
- `process.platform` allows developers to detect what operating system their application is running in.
- macOS expects a special application menu as its first menu item.
- Electron provides roles for `MenuItems` allowing developers to easily implement common, operating system-level functionality.

- `MenuItems` have a `click()` method that defines their behavior when clicked by the user.
- `MenuItems` support an `accelerator` property that allow developers to define a keyboard shortcut to trigger its action.
- Electron supports a `contextmenu` event in the renderer process that fires whenever a user right-clicks the DOM.

8 Further operating system integration and dynamically enabling menu items

This chapter covers

- Showing files in the native operating system's filesystem manager
- Opening a file in the operating system's default application for that file type
- Modifying application and context menus dynamically
- Opening the URLs in the default browser instead of the application itself

In addition to creating custom application modules, opening isolated browser window processes, and accessing native file dialogs in Electron, we can use the `shell` module to interact with the operating system.

How does your application know your system's default browser for opening websites? If you want to open an image file in its default application, which application should you send it to?

Users of our applications typically set these preferences in the operating system itself. Instead of trying to figure out our user's settings, we're better off just asking the operating system for the answer. Electron provides the `shell` module to make this easy for us.

The `shell` module is relatively small compared to some of the other modules provided by Electron. It allows us to open a given file path in the operating system's file browser, send it to its default application, move it to the trash, trigger a system beep, and create shortcut links in Windows. The `shell` module made a brief appearance in chapter 2, when we used it to make sure that hyperlinks open in the user's web browser of choice instead of in the application itself, which also happens to be a web browser.

In this chapter, we take a subset of these features—opening a file's location in the file browser and sending a file to the operating system's default application—and implement them in multiple places in Fire Sale, as shown in figure 8.1. We add this functionality to Fire Sale's UI, to the context menu that opens when the user right-clicks the editor pane, and to the application's menu. Depending on the feature you're implementing in your application, all or a subset of these might be the right approach for your purposes. As we implement them in each of the three places throughout the chapter, I discuss the advantages and disadvantages of each approach. All the code from this chapter is available on GitHub in the `chapter-8` branch (https://github.com/ electron-in-action/firesale/tree/chapter-8).

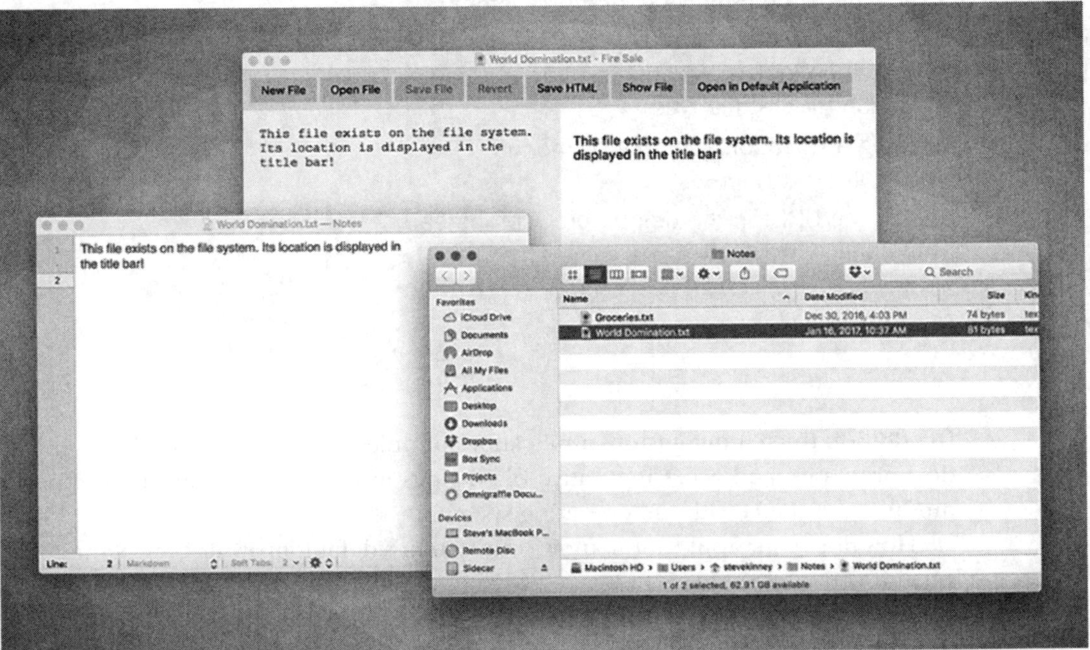

Figure 8.1 Electron allows us to integrate with the operating system to trigger the file browser to navigate to the location of a given file or to open a file path in the default application for that file type.

8.1 Using the shell module from the UI in the renderer process

In chapter 7, in learning how to implement custom menus, we added features to Fire Sale like we would in a traditional browser environment: by adding buttons to the DOM. The Electron `shell` module, which is available in the main process as well as the renderer process, can be triggered from buttons in the UI, from application and context menu items, through keystrokes, and more. But let's start with what we're good at: triggering functionality from the UI. The Show File and Open in Default Application buttons, shown in figure 8.2, have been in the UI since chapter 3. Now it's their turn to shine. When a file is opened or a new file is first saved to the filesystem, the buttons are enabled. When a user clicks the Show File button, the file browser opens so the user can navigate to the directory containing the currently open file. When the Open in Default Application button is selected, the operating system opens the file in the application that typically opens Markdown and text files on the user's computer.

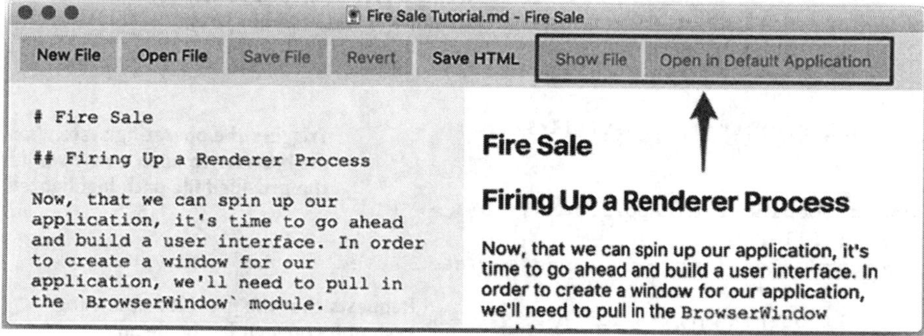

Figure 8.2 The Show File and the Open in Default Application buttons have been present since chapter 3. In this chapter, we'll use the Electron `shell` module to implement their functionality.

In the previous chapters, the Show File and Open in Default Application buttons have been disabled by default. Like the Save and Revert buttons implemented in a previous chapter, there are situations where the buttons should be enabled. With the Save and Revert buttons, this was whenever the original content of the file—or an empty string in the case of a new, unsaved file—differed from what was currently shown in the left editor pane. Thus, we listened for `keyup` events in the editor and compared the contents to evaluate if the buttons should be enabled. For Show File and Open in Default Application, we do not care so much whether they have been modified. What we want is a file path to either show or open, respectively.

Listing 8.1 Enabling the buttons when there is a file to show: ./app/renderer.js

```
const renderFile = (file, content) => {
  filePath = file;
  originalContent = content;
```

```
  markdownView.value = content;
  renderMarkdownToHtml(content);

  showFileButton.disabled = false;
  openInDefaultButton.disabled = false;

  updateUserInterface(false);
};
```

When a file path has been sent to the renderer process to be displayed, we activate the Show File and Open in Default buttons.

The Show File and Open in Default Editor buttons should be enabled whenever we are working with a file that is stored in the filesystem, not a new, unsaved file. Whenever the active file is changed, we update the `filePath` variable. After this variable has been set, enable the buttons.

Listing 8.2 Adding event listeners to the buttons: ./app/renderer.js

```
const showFile = () => {
  if (!filePath) {
  return alert('This file has not been saved to the filesystem.');
  }
  shell.showItemInFolder(filePath);
};

const openInDefaultApplication = () => {
  if (!filePath) {
  return alert('This file has not been saved to the filesystem.');
  }
  shell.openItem(filePath);
};

showFileButton.addEventListener('click', showFile);
openInDefaultButton.addEventListener('click', openInDefaultApplication);
```

It seems unlikely that a user could click a disabled button, but we guard against them seeing a cryptic error by showing a more helpful one and returning from the function.

Triggers the operating system's native file browser to open a new window with the provided file path highlighted.

Requests that the provided operating system be opened by the default application designated by the user.

When either button is clicked, we trigger the two functions declared earlier. By omitting the parentheses, we provide a reference to the function to be executed when the button is clicked instead of immediately invoking it.

Enabling the buttons is helpful, but it would be even better if the buttons did something. Whenever a button is clicked, it triggers the appropriate method from the `shell` module. You might notice that I decided to define the functions in constants instead of just passing anonymous functions to `addEventListener`. Later in this chapter, we call these functions from Fire Sale's application menu as well as from a context menu. These names allow me to reference the two functions later.

8.2 Using the shell module in the application menu

The first place we might consider adding this functionality is in the application menu, just below the menu items that allow the user to save and export files. In this section, we implement two new menu items, Show File and Open in Default Editor, as shown in figure 8.3, which exposes the file in its containing folder, and opens it in the application set as the default for Markdown files in the operating system, respectively.

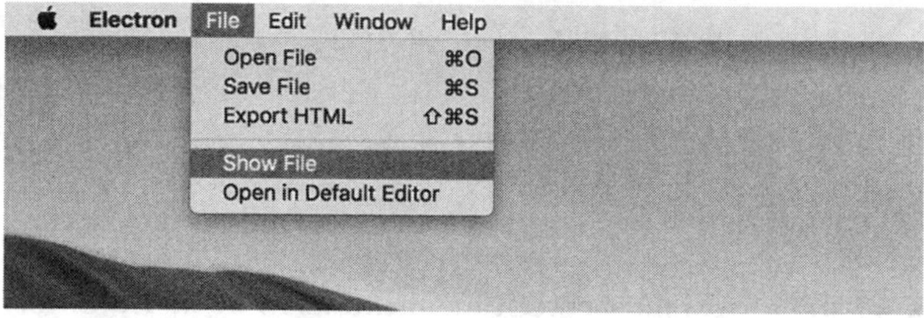

Figure 8.3 Menu items that work with the Electron shell module to communicate with the native operating system

You must add these two new menu items to the application menu template to appear when the application starts. What if no windows are open? In a perfect world, we would disable the menu items unless at least one window was open. But that's beyond the scope of this chapter, so we'll do the next best thing and display a useful error message to help the user see the error of their ways.

Listing 8.3 Adding additional menu items: ./app/application-menu

```
const { app, BrowserWindow, dialog, Menu, shell } = require('electron');
const mainProcess = require('./main');

const template = [
  {
    label: 'File',
    submenu: [
      //Additional submenu items above.
      { type: 'separator' },
      {
        label: 'Show File',
        accelerator: 'Shift+CommandOrControl+S',
        click(item, focusedWindow) {
          if (!focusedWindow) {
            return dialog.showErrorBox(
              'Cannot Show File\'s Location',
              'There is currently no active document show.'
            );
          }
          focusedWindow.webContents.send('show-file');
        },
      },
      {
        label: 'Open in Default Editor',
        accelerator: 'Shift+CommandOrControl+S',
        click(item, focusedWindow) {
          if (!focusedWindow) {
            return dialog.showErrorBox(
```

Adds Electron's shell module to the list of modules being required from the electron library.

Electron's menu templates allow us to easily define separators between other—more functional—menu items.

If there is no focused window, then we display an error to the user and return from the function.

If the user selects the Show File menu item, we send a message over the show-file channel via IPC to the frontmost window.

```
            'Cannot Open File in Default Editor',
            'There is currently no active document to open.'
          );
        }
        focusedWindow.webContents.send('open-in-default');
      },
    },
  ],
},
// Edit, Window, and Help menus defined here.
];
```

If the user selects the Open in Default Editor menu item, we send a message over the open-in-default channel via IPC to the front-most window.

In listing 8.3, we add a separator between the menu items we added in the previous chapter and the ones we're adding in this chapter. This separator is solely for aesthetic reasons and is not required for the menu to work properly. After the separator, we have added two new menu items: Show File and Open in Default Editor. Each window has a reference to the path of the file that is currently rendered in it. So, how do we know what file to show or open? We could devise a complicated system for figuring out which files were opened in which windows, or we could just send a message to the window over interprocess communication (IPC) and let the window figure it out for itself.

To get this working, we listen for IPC messages over the show-file and open-in-default channels. Luckily, we were smart enough earlier to name the functions responsible for handling these requests. This makes setting up the listeners easy.

Listing 8.4 Implementing IPC listeners for Show File and Open in Default applications: ./app/renderer.js

```
ipcRenderer.on('show-file', showFile);
ipcRenderer.on('open-in-default', openInDefaultApplication);
```

When the ipcRenderer receives a show-file event from the main process, triggers the showFile() function.

When the ipcRenderer receives a open-in-default event from the main process, triggers the openInDefaultApplication() function.

8.2.1 Additional features of the Electron shell module

The Electron `shell` module also allows developers to move a given file to the macOS Trash or the Windows Recycle Bin without concerning themselves with the finer points of how that works on each platform. It can also allow developers to trigger a system beep. On Windows, developers can create and read shortcut links as well.

8.3 Accessing the shell module from a context menu

You can also add these features to the context menu we originally added to the application in chapter 7. This menu appears when a user right-clicks the left editor pane, shown in figure 8.4. To implement this feature, we need to combine the two approaches from earlier in this chapter: we add menu items to the template, but

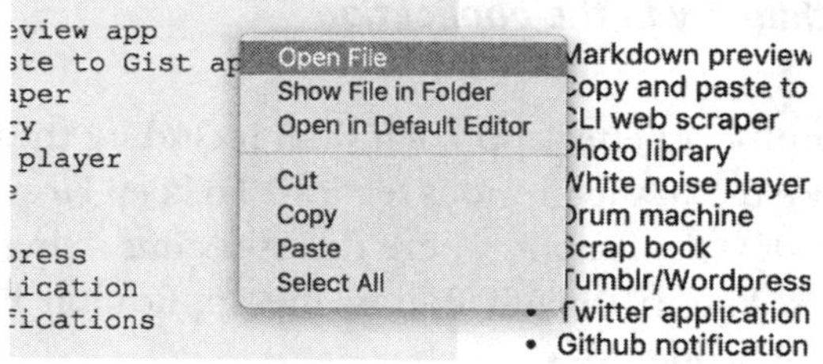

Figure 8.4 Accessing the `shell` module from context menus. Show File in Folder and Open in Default Editor are disabled when working on a new, unsaved file because unsaved files do not have a valid file path for the `shell` module's methods.

because we're in the renderer process already, we can call the functions directly—just as we did with the buttons in the UI—instead of having to send messages via IPC.

Listing 8.5 Adding `shell` module access to the context menu template: ./app/renderer.js

```
const { remote, ipcRenderer, shell } = require('electron');
const { Menu } = remote;
const path = require('path');
const mainProcess = remote.require('./main.js');
const currentWindow = remote.getCurrentWindow();

// Other renderer code from the previous chapters will remain here, but has
     been ommited for brevity…

const markdownContextMenu = Menu.buildFromTemplate([
  { label: 'Open File', click() { mainProcess.getFileFromUser(); } },
  {
    label: 'Show File in Folder',
    click: showFile
  },
  {
    label: 'Open in Default Editor',
    click: openInDefaultApplication
  },
  { type: 'separator' },
  { label: 'Cut', role: 'cut' },
  { label: 'Copy', role: 'copy' },
  { label: 'Paste', role: 'paste' },
  { label: 'Select All', role: 'selectall' },
]);
```

Add the shell module and other modules being required from Electron in the renderer process.

The syntax is a little different here because we're just pointing the click method to a reference of the showFile() function. When the user clicks the menu item, it is opened.

We take a similar approach with the Open in Default Editor button.

8.3.1 *Deciding between putting functionality in a menu or in the browser*

When is adding buttons to the UI a better choice than adding the same functionality to menu items in an application or context menu? It depends on the role that the feature plays in your application. Contextual menu items are obscure; a user may never think to right-click a given part of your application. If the feature you're implementing is essential to the application, it is better to put it in the UI. That said, there is only a limited amount of space to work with, and less used, but nice-to-have, functionality is a great fit for contextual menu items.

8.3.2 Deciding between putting functionality in the application or context menu

When would using a context menu be a better approach than including these menu items in the application menu as we did in the previous section? To keep Fire Sale simple, it was designed as a single-window application where the user edits a single file at a time. When a user selects Open File in Default Editor, the application implicitly knows which file because there is only one.

But what if we were building a photo-management application, and we wanted to add a feature where the user could right-click each of the photographs to show it in the Finder or Windows Explorer? This feature would be difficult to add to the application menu, because it would be hard to decipher exactly which photograph the user wanted to see in its containing folder. By using a context menu, we can easily determine which photograph the user right-clicks.

8.4 Disabling menu items when appropriate

Right now, Fire Sale shows an error message if the user selects a menu item that isn't available. It's better than crashing or throwing an indecipherable error message, but it's not going to win any awards for being a great user experience. What if we disable the context and application menu items that would otherwise throw an error if clicked? This way, it's clear to the user that this is not a valid action.

It is possible to mutate menus after they have been set, but it's tricky. Menu items are stored as arrays, and finding a given menu item involves traversing all the top-level menu items and their submenus. Most of the time, it's easier to either generate a new context menu based on the current state of the window just before displaying it to the user or to regenerate a new application menu when the state of the application has changed.

How we approach solving this problem depends on which menu we're working with. Context menus within a window are easier because we're working with only a single window and we're storing the `filePath` variable in the global scope. If there is a `filePath`, then we enable Show File in Folder and Open in Default. If `filePath` is `false`, then these menu items are disabled.

The application menu is a little trickier. In addition to Show File and Open in Default Application, we also have Save File and Export HTML, which can remain enabled if the file has not been saved to the filesystem but should be enabled only if there is at least one window open. See figure 8.5.

8.4.1 Dynamically enabling and disabling menu items in the context menu

Earlier in this chapter, we created a context menu from a template and then called its `popup()` method whenever a `contextmenu` DOM event is fired. To dynamically enable or disable the Show File and Open in Default menu items, as in figure 8.6, let's create a context menu each time the user right-clicks the Markdown view. We

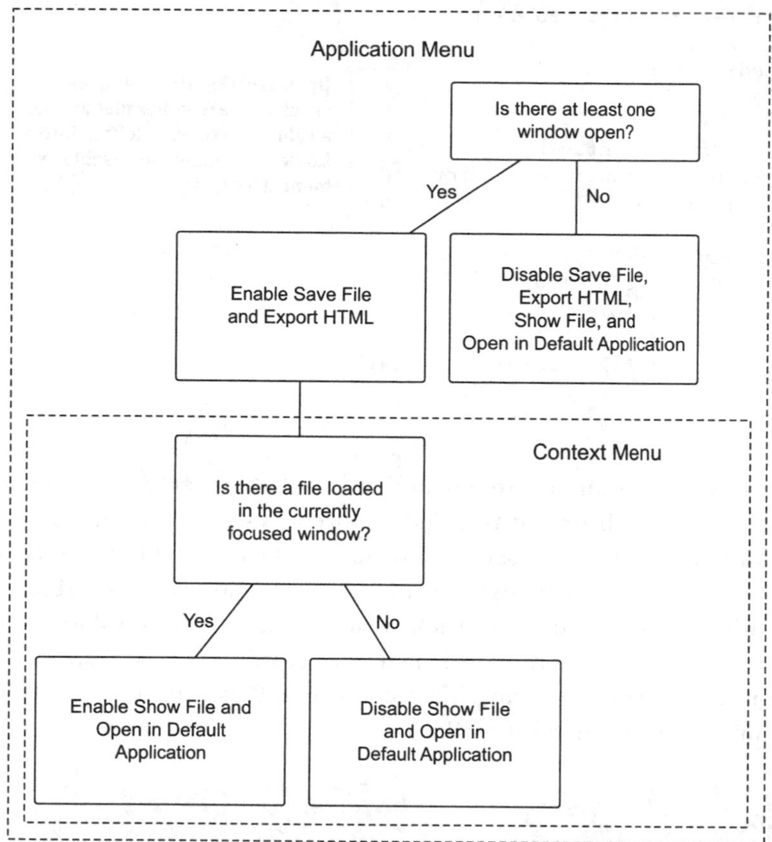

Figure 8.5 Certain menu items are either enabled or disabled depending on the state of the application. In this application, we have two menus: application and context. The application menu must track all the open windows, whereas the context menu should deal with only a subset of the same concerns because it can assume that at least one window is open.

enable these items based on whether there is a `filePath`. To accomplish this, we move the creation of the menu into a function, which allows us to re-create the menu each time it is called.

Listing 8.6 Creating a function to dynamically create context menus: ./app/renderer.js

In chapter 7, we made a single context menu that was shown every time the user right-clicked the Markdown view. In this chapter, we replace that menu with a function that creates a new context menu each time.

The return value of this function is a Menu object created using Electron's Menu.buildFromTemplate() function.

```
const createContextMenu = () => {
  return Menu.buildFromTemplate([
    { label: 'Open File', click() { mainProcess.getFileFromUser(); } },
    {
```

```
      label: 'Show File in Folder',
      click: showFile,
      enabled: !!filePath
    },
    {
      label: 'Open in Default',
      click: openInDefaultApplication,
      enabled: !!filePath
    },
    { type: 'separator' },
    { label: 'Cut', role: 'cut' },
    { label: 'Copy', role: 'copy' },
    { label: 'Paste', role: 'paste' },
    { label: 'Select All', role: 'selectall' },
  ]);
};
```

Upon creating the menu, we check to see whether filePath has a value. We coerce filePath into a Boolean to enable or disable the menu accordingly.

In the previous code sample, we created a `createContextMenu()` function that returns a new menu each time it is called. As it creates the Show File and Open in Default menu items, it checks to see if `filePath` can be coerced to `true` using the `!!` operator. The enabled property expects a Boolean—either `true` or `false`. If you're not familiar with this technique, it's a trick to take a truthy or falsey value and cocrce it into `true` or `false`, respectively. The `!` operator returns `false` for any truthy value, and `true` for any falsey value. Using it a second time flips it back, but this time to a Boolean primitive, as shown in listing 8.7.

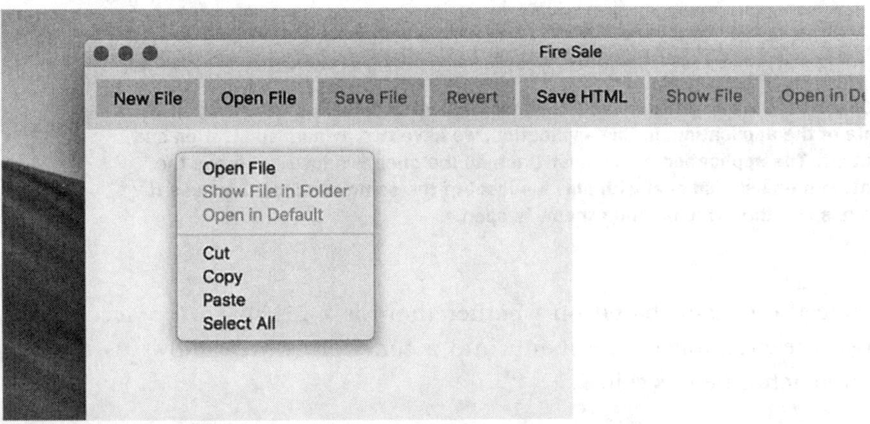

Figure 8.6 Show File in Folder and Open in Default is disabled if there is no file open.

Listing 8.7 Converting values into Booleans

```
null   // Null falsey in JavaScript.
!null  // Returns true.
!!null // Returns false.
```

```
'/Users/stevekinney/Notes/Groceries.txt'  // A file path
!/Users/stevekinney/Notes/Groceries.txt'  // Returns false.
!!/Users/stevekinney/Notes/Groceries.txt' // Returns true.
```

The next step is to modify our event listener to use the function we just created. Each time it generates a new menu, the function checks if `filePath` is truthy or falsey and enables Show File and Open in Default Application accordingly. The next step is to use this function to generate a new menu on the fly each time the user right-clicks the Markdown view of the application.

Listing 8.8 Creating a context menu each time a `contextmenu` event is fired: ./app/renderer.js

```
markdownView.addEventListener('contextmenu', (event) => {
  event.preventDefault();
  createContextMenu().popup();
});
```

Instead of using a preexisting menu, we call createContextMenu() to create a menu each time and then immediately call its popup() method.

With this change, the user gets a new menu each time they request one. If there is a file to show in the filesystem or open in another application, the respective menu items are enabled. If not, they are disabled. Now it's time to turn our attention to the—slightly trickier—application menu.

8.4.2 Dynamically enabling and disabling menu items in the application menu

The process of dynamically enabling menu items in the application menu shares some similarities with doing so in the context menu. We use the same approach of generating new menus and replacing the existing application menu but with a few catches: the application menu is shared across all windows. The first window might have a file loaded that we can show or open in another application, but the second one may not. On macOS, we might run into the scenario where there are no windows open. In this case, the Save File and Export HTML menu items should be disabled along with Show File and Open in Default Application, as shown in figure 8.7. Furthermore, our context menu could take advantage of the fact that `filePath` was in scope. The application menu lives in the main process and doesn't have access to this variable. See figures 8.8 and 8.9.

To implement this feature, we take the following approach. First we'll create a function that returns a new application menu based on the one we implemented in the previous chapter. Each time we create a new menu, we check if there are any windows and if the currently focused window is representing a file on the filesystem. With this in place, we'll modify the main process to generate a new application menu when

- The application fires its "ready" event
- A window is closed.
- A window gains focus (thereby becoming the new focused window).
- A file is opened.

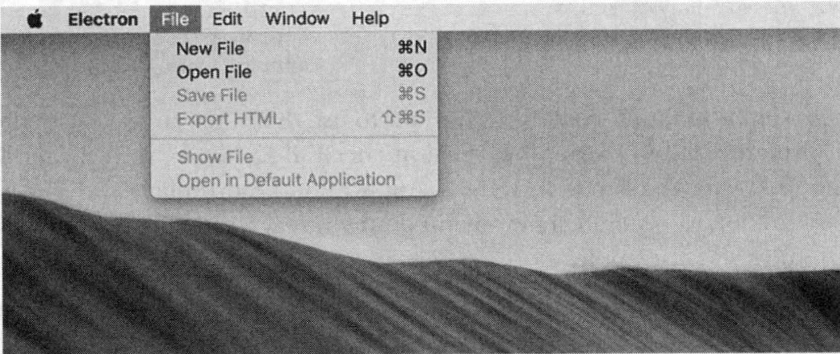

Figure 8.7 If there are no windows open, Save File, Export HTML, Show File, and Open in Default Application should be disabled.

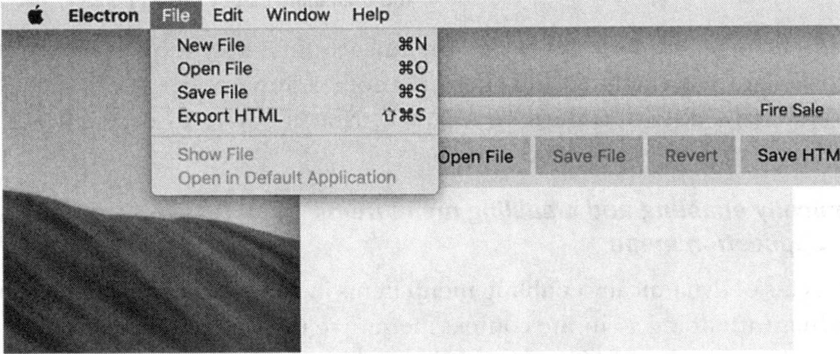

Figure 8.8 If there is a focused window, but the user is working on a file that has not yet been saved to the filesystem, then the Save File and Export HTML items should be enabled. The Show File and Open in Default Application menu items should not be, however, because there is no file location to show or open.

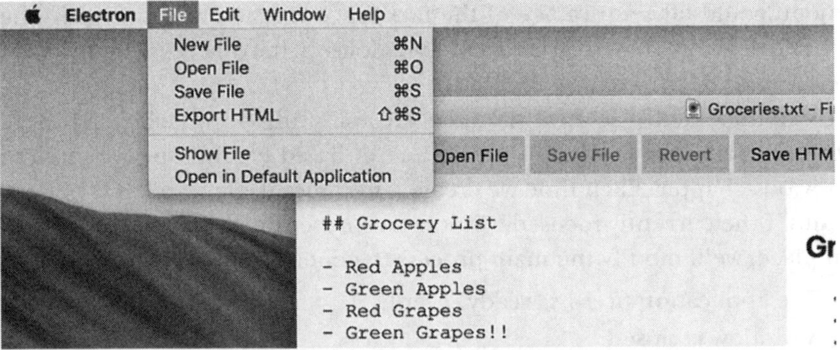

Figure 8.9 If the window is representing a file on the filesystem, all the menu items should be enabled.

Let's start by refactoring the template in application-menu.js to a function that will generate a menu and set it as the new application menu.

Listing 8.9 Generating a new application menu based on the application's menu: ./app/application-menu.js

```
const { app,
        BrowserWindow,
        dialog,
        Menu,
        shell
      } = require('electron');
const mainProcess = require('./main');

const createApplicationMenu = () => {
  const hasOneOrMoreWindows = !!BrowserWindow.getAllWindows().length;
  const focusedWindow = BrowserWindow.getFocusedWindow();
  const hasFilePath = !!(focusedWindow &&
     focusedWindow.getRepresentedFilename());

  const template = [
    {
      label: 'File',
      submenu: [
        {
          label: 'New File',
          accelerator: 'CommandOrControl+N',
          click() {
            mainProcess.createWindow();
          }
        },
        {
          label: 'Open File',
          accelerator: 'CommandOrControl+O',
          click(item, focusedWindow) {
            // Omitted for brevity...
          },
        },
        {
          label: 'Save File',
          accelerator: 'CommandOrControl+S',
          enabled: hasOneOrMoreWindows,
          click(item, focusedWindow) {
            // Omitted for brevity...
          },
        },
        {
          label: 'Export HTML',
          accelerator: 'Shift+CommandOrControl+S',
          enabled: hasOneOrMoreWindows,
          click(item, focusedWindow) {
            // Omitted for brevity...
          },
        },
```

We imported the BrowserWindow module because it has methods that are useful for reasoning about the windows in our application.

An easy way to see if any windows are open is to use BrowserWindow.getAllWindows(). If no windows are open, this array will be empty with a length of 0, which is falsey in JavaScript.

Gets the currently focused window (or null if there is no focused window).

If there is a focused window, we use its getRepresentedFile() method to get a reference to the current file path. If one exists, we'll set the hasFilePath Boolean.

The Save File and Export HTML menu items are set based on the hasOneOr-MoreWindows Boolean.

```
        { type: 'separator' },
        {
          label: 'Show File',
          enabled: hasFilePath,
          click(item, focusedWindow) {
            // Omitted for brevity…
          },
        },
        {
          label: 'Open in Default Application',
          enabled: hasFilePath,
          click(item, focusedWindow) {
            // Omitted for brevity…
          },
        },
      ],
    },
    // Additional Menus…
  ];

  // Additional Functionality…

  return Menu.setApplicationMenu(Menu.buildFromTemplate(template));
};

module.exports = createApplicationMenu;
```

The Show File and Open in Default Application menu items are set based on the hasFilePath Boolean.

Builds the menu from the template, and sets it as the application menu.

In chapter 7, we built the menu once when the application started and set it as the application menu as soon as it was ready. This approach still works, now that this module exports a function that creates the menu and sets it as the application menu. Along the way, it checks if there are any browser windows, and if there is a focused window, it checks whether that window has a represented file set, shown in listing 8.10. If you recall, we set the represented file in chapter 4 when opening a file. At the time, we did this to get the little file icon in the window's title bar in macOS. (Calling this method has no discernible visual effect on Windows or Linux.)

Listing 8.10 Setting the represented file: ./app/main.js

```
const openFile = exports.openFile = (targetWindow, file) => {
  const content = fs.readFileSync(file).toString();
  startWatchingFile(targetWindow, file);
  app.addRecentDocument(file);
  targetWindow.setRepresentedFilename(file);
  targetWindow.webContents.send('file-opened', file, content);
};
```

We set the represented file path when opening a file.

With these two pieces of information—the number of open windows and whether the focused window is representing a file path—we can toggle the menu items appropriately. The next step is to trigger this process whenever either of these two might have changed. Triggering events include when the application first launches, when a new window takes focus, when a window is closed (it could be the last window), and when the user opens a file. Whenever one of these events occurs, we re-create the application menu.

Listing 8.11 Generating a new application menu when state might have changed: ./app/main.js

```
const { app, BrowserWindow, dialog, Menu } = require('electron');
const createApplicationMenu = require('./application-menu');
const fs = require('fs');

const windows = new Set();
const openFiles = new Map();

app.on('ready', () => {
  createApplicationMenu();
  createWindow();
});

app.on('window-all-closed', () => {
  // Omitted for brevity...
});

app.on('activate', (event, hasVisibleWindows) => {
  if (!hasVisibleWindows) { createWindow(); }
});

const createWindow = exports.createWindow = () => {
  let x, y;

  const currentWindow = BrowserWindow.getFocusedWindow();

  if (currentWindow) {
    const [ currentWindowX, currentWindowY ] = currentWindow.getPosition();
    x = currentWindowX + 10;
    y = currentWindowY + 10;
  }

  let newWindow = new BrowserWindow({ x, y, show: false });

  newWindow.loadFile('index.html');

  newWindow.once('ready-to-show', () => {
    newWindow.show();
  });

  newWindow.on('focus', createApplicationMenu);

  newWindow.on('close', (event) => {
    // Omitted for brevity...
  });

  newWindow.on('closed', () => {
    windows.delete(newWindow);
    createApplicationMenu();
```

Updates the require statement to reflect the new function, createApplicationMenu, we're importing

Creates an application menu when the application is first launched and is ready

Creates a new application menu whenever a new window gains focus

Creates a new application whenever a window is closed

```
    newWindow = null;
  });

  windows.add(newWindow);
  return newWindow;
};

const getFileFromUser  = exports.getFileFromUser = (targetWindow) => {
  // Omitted for brevity...
};

const openFile = exports.openFile = (targetWindow, file) => {
  const content = fs.readFileSync(file).toString();
  startWatchingFile(targetWindow, file);
  app.addRecentDocument(file);
  targetWindow.setRepresentedFilename(file);
  targetWindow.webContents.send('file-opened', file, content);
  createApplicationMenu();
};

// Additional functions below...
```

Creates a new application menu whenever a file has been opened and the represented file has been set

With the ability to create application menus and replace the existing one, implementing this functionality in main.js is just a matter of invoking this function at the right time. With this in place, we've accomplished the feature that we set out to implement at the beginning of this section. The full code at the end of this chapter can be found in the appendix book or on GitHub at https://github.com/electron-in-action/firesale.

Summary

- The `shell` module enables the application to communicate with the operating system to show files in the file browser, open files in their default application, move files to the Trash or Recycling Bin (depending on the operating system), trigger a system beep, and create or read shortcut links in Windows.
- The `shell` module is available in the main process as well as the renderer processes. Thus, it can be used in the application menus, context menus, or in event listeners on UI elements.

9 Introducing the tray module

This chapter covers

- Building a simple application that lives in the menu bar on macOS or the system tray in Windows.
- Using Electron's `tray` module to create applications that live in the operating system's menu bar or system tray.
- Reading from and writing to the system clipboard.
- Registering global shortcuts that listen for specific keystrokes even when the application is not in use.
- Triggering native notifications in macOS and Windows 10.

For most of the first half of the book, we worked on Fire Sale. Although its initial feature set in chapter 3 could have conceivably been matched by a traditional, browser-based web application, we spent the subsequent chapters adding functionality outside the scope of what most browsers allow. In this chapter, we begin well outside the realm of where we expect to find web technologies: the macOS menu bar and Windows system tray. In the beginning, we won't have a renderer process or the DOM. By the end of this chapter, we explore how to create hidden renderer processes to access features not available to the main process. In the next chapter, we create a `BrowserWindow` to serve as the UI for our tray application.

With Fire Sale behind us, we'll embark on building a new application: Clipmaster, shown in figure 9.1. By the end of this chapter, we launch the application. It will have no dock, taskbar icon, or windows of its own. We activate it by pressing a keyboard shortcut that is globally available throughout the operating system. When the shortcut is triggered, Clipmaster reads from and records the contents of the user's clipboard. If the user selects a previously saved clipboard item from the menu, the app places it back onto the system clipboard for pasting in another application.

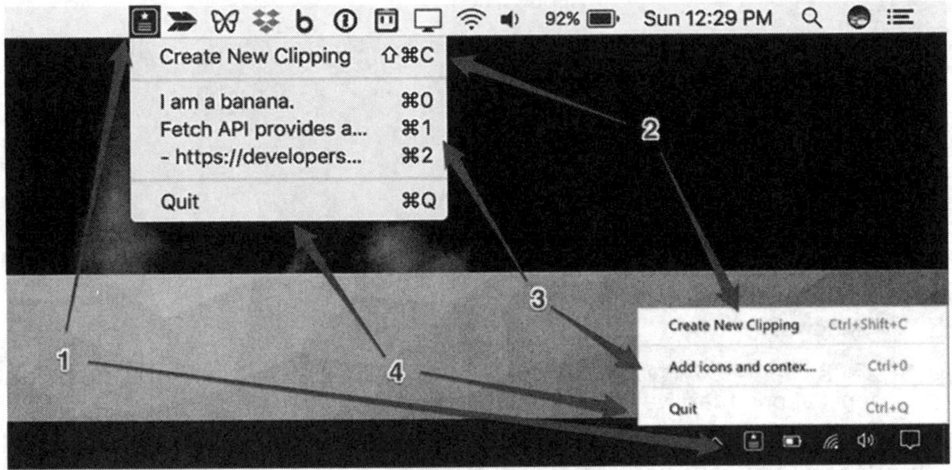

Figure 9.1 This is what the application looks like when completed. macOS is on the top, and Windows is on the bottom.

As shown in the figure, we need to implement the following:

- A menu bar or tray icon that is available from anywhere in the respective operating system.
- A menu item that reads from the clipboard and places its contents in a menu item.
- A list of menu items. When the user clicks one of the menu items in this section, Clipmaster writes the string of text back to the clipboard.
- A final menu item for quitting Clipmaster.

If you look closely, you'll notice that each of these items has a keyboard shortcut as well. In addition to these menu-based accelerators, we register global shortcuts with the operating system that allow the user to activate this menu or create a new clipping from anywhere.

The source code for Clipmaster is available at https://github.com/electron-in-action/clipmaster. I use the master branch as a boilerplate and starting point for the code in this chapter. There is also a branch called "completed-example" that contains the code shown at the end of this chapter. I show the code as we go along, and a completed version will be available at the end.

9.1 Getting started with Clipmaster

The folder structure for Clipmaster is roughly the same as we saw in Fire Sale with much of the code in the ./app directory. You might notice that there isn't a renderer.js or index.html. Those are added by the end of the chapter but aren't needed in the beginning. You may also notice a few small image files. Our application needs an icon if it's going to live in the tray or menu bar. macOS expects this icon to be a PNG file, and Electron automatically checks if there is a version of the image with the suffix "@2px" if it is running on a device with a retina screen. Windows accepts a PNG but works best with an ICO file. Unlike the built-in switch between high- and low-resolution versions based on the density of the display, we need to manually check which operating system the application is running on to select the best image.

To get started, clone the master branch, and run either `npm install` or `yarn install` to download the dependencies. After everything is installed, we can get started on building Clipmaster.

9.2 Creating an application with the tray module

To get the ball rolling, we can add our application to the system tray or menu bar with just one feature: the ability to click Quit and close the application (see figure 9.2). To accomplish this heroic task, we need help from Electron's `tray` module. You can think of the `tray` module as a peer to `BrowserWindow`. It's a constructor that—when instantiated—creates a system tray or menu bar item in much the same way that `BrowserWindow` creates a browser window.

Figure 9.2 In the first iteration, Clipmaster is nothing more than a small application that allows the user to immediately quit it. Don't worry: there is more functionality to come, and you'll have a fully functional application by the end of the chapter.

To do this, as you'll see in listing 9.1, we need to wait until the application is ready, create a `tray` instance, and provide it with an icon and a menu loaded up with the `Quit` command. When the application is ready, we create the menu and set it as the context

Figure 9.3 When the user hovers over the icon, they see the tooltip. This can be customized and changed based on the state of the application.

menu of the `tray` instance. In a fit of ambition, we also set a tooltip that will be shown when the user hovers over our proud new tray icon. See figure 9.3.

Listing 9.1 Creating a `tray` instance: ./app/main.js

```
const path = require('path');
const {
  app,
  Menu,
  Tray,
  } = require('electron');

let tray = null;

app.on('ready', () => {
  tray = new Tray(path.join(__dirname, '/Icon.png'));

  if (process.platform === 'win32') {
    tray.on('click', tray.popUpContextMenu);
  }

  const menu = Menu.buildFromTemplate([
    {
      label: 'Quit',
      click() { app.quit(); }
    }
  ]);

  tray.setToolTip('Clipmaster');
  tray.setContextMenu(menu);
});
```

- Declares a variable in the global scope that eventually stores a reference to the tray instance (`let tray = null;`)
- Creates a tray instance by calling the constructor with a path to an image (`tray = new Tray(...)`)
- On Windows, we register a click event listener to open the menu.
- Builds a menu in the same fashion that we built application and context menus in earlier chapters
- Optionally, defines a tooltip to be shown when the user hovers over the tray icon
- Takes the menu created and sets it as the menu that appears when the user clicks the icon in the menu or system tray in macOS and Windows, respectively.

As with the windows in Fire Sale, we declared the `tray` variable in the global scope to prevent it from being thrown out sometime after the event listener on the app's ready event has run to completion. Inside the event listener, we assign a new `tray` instance to the variable with a reference to the image we want to use as an icon.

If you recall from chapter 7, `Menu.buildFromTemplate()` is an abstraction that allows you to create complicated menu structures using objects and arrays. This menu isn't exactly complicated, but it's still easier than building a menu by instantiating `MenuItem` instances one at a time. At this point, the menu has one item with Quit as its label. When it's clicked—or later activated by a keystroke—it will tell Electron to quit the application. With the menu built, all that is left is to set it as the context menu for `tray`.

Windows treats the `tray` instances menu as a context menu. This means the menu shows up only if the icon is right-clicked. In listing 9.1, we also register a click event that triggers the menu if the application is running on Windows.

The application works, but if you fire it up on macOS, you can notice that it also shows up in the dock. Clicking it doesn't do anything, because the application doesn't have any browser windows to show. We could add functionality such as the ability to trigger the menu from the menu bar when the dock icon is clicked, but I vote that we hide the dock icon altogether.

Listing 9.2 Hiding the dock icon on macOS: ./app/main.js

```
app.on('ready', () => {
  if (app.dock) app.dock.hide();      <-- Hides the dock icon if running on macOS.

  // ...
}
```

The line of code checks if the app has a dock object, which it does if it's running on macOS. If so, then Electron tells the dock icon to hide itself. This approach is interesting because it leaves the developer room to hide or show the dock icon at will, depending on what mode their application is in or the user's preference. In our case, we hide it when the application launches and never show it again.

9.2.1 Using the correct icon for macOS and Windows

macOS and Windows prefer different file types for icons. Their UIs each work better with a different color. By default, the menu bar on macOS is white and works better with dark icons whereas Windows 10 has a dark task bar and works better with white icons. Windows prefers ICO files, and macOS uses PNG files. To solve this issue, Node checks the platform it's running on and gets the appropriate icon based on the platform. Electron does such a good job of providing a consistent cross-platform experience that this is one of the few times in this book that we find ourselves doing something like this.

Listing 9.3 Conditionally choosing an icon based on the platform: ./app/main.js

```
const getIcon = () => {                                              <--
  if (process.platform === 'win32') return 'icon-light@2x.ico';
  return 'icon-dark.png';
};
                                        The getIcon() function checks
                                        the platform the application is
app.on('ready', () => {                 running on and returns the
  if (app.dock) app.dock.hide();        appropriate filename.
```

```
  tray = new Tray(path.join(__dirname, getIcon()));
  // … More code below …
});
```

When creating a new tray instance, use getIcon() to get the correct filename.

If we're on Windows, it gives us the filename of the light ICO icon. Otherwise, it gives us the filename of the dark PNG icon. When the application is ready, we use the new `getIcon()` function instead of the string we had hard-coded originally.

9.2.2 *Supporting dark mode in macOS*

Earlier, I said that the macOS menu bar is white by default. In macOS El Capitan and later, users can turn on dark mode, which inverts the color of the menu bar and dock. In this case, we would want to use a PNG file like we would normally for macOS, but we also want to use the light versions like we would with the transparent black system tray in Windows 10, as shown in listing 9.4 and figure 9.4.

Figure 9.4 If the macOS menu bar is in dark mode, we'll use the inverted icon.

Listing 9.4 Supporting dark mode on macOS: ./app/main.js

```
const path = require('path');
const {
  app,
  Menu,
  Tray,
  systemPreferences,
} = require('electron');

let tray = null;

const getIcon = () => {
  if (process.platform === 'win32') return 'icon-light.ico';
  if (systemPreferences.isDarkMode()) return 'icon-light.png';
  return 'icon-dark.png';
};
```

Imports the systemPreferences module from Electron

Uses the systemPreferences.isDarkMode() to detect if macOS is in dark mode

Electron makes this easy using the `systemPreferences` module, which conveniently has a method called `isDarkMode()` that returns a Boolean. I leave it as an exercise to the reader to determine under which conditions it returns `true` or `false`.

9.2.3 *Reading from the clipboard and storing clippings*

This application is supposed to store clippings, and we have many ways we could go about doing this. In chapter 11, we look at using an SQLite database to store clippings.

But for now, let's start with the easiest possible solution: storing them in memory. This approach is easy because it allows us to use a built-in JavaScript data structure, but it has the disadvantage of being cleared away whenever the user quits the application.

To ship this feature, we need to create an array to hold our clippings. We also need to create a function that reads from the clipboard and adds the contents to the array, as well as a way for the user to trigger this function. Finally, we want to update the menu with the clippings we stored and allow users to select one to be added back to the clipboard. See figures 9.5 and 9.6.

Figure 9.5 The application with its two basic commands on macOS

Figure 9.6 In addition to being able to quit the application, users need a way to add a clipping to the application. Here the application is shown in the Windows tray.

We update the menu whenever the user saves a new clipping. As we discussed in chapter 7, it's possible to traverse and mutate the menu after it is created, but it's often easier and more efficient to completely replace it. To facilitate this, we move the code to create the context menu into its own function that we can call whenever we need to update the menu.

Listing 9.5 Storing clippings in memory using an array: ./app/main.js

```
const path = require('path');
const {
  app,
  Menu,
  Tray,
  systemPreferences,
} = require('electron');

const clippings = [];        // Declares an empty array to store clippings
let tray = null;
```

```
const getIcon = () => {
  if (process.platform === 'win32') return 'icon-light.ico';
  if (systemPreferences.isDarkMode()) return 'icon-light.png';
  return 'icon-dark.png';
};

app.on('ready', () => {
  if (app.dock) app.dock.hide();

  tray = new Tray(path.join(__dirname, getIcon()));

  if (process.platform === 'win32') {
    tray.on('click', tray.popUpContextMenu);
  }

  updateMenu();

  tray.setToolTip('Clipmaster');
});

const updateMenu = () => {
  const menu = Menu.buildFromTemplate([
    {
      label: 'Create New Clipping',
      click() { null; }
    },
    { type: 'separator' },
    ...clippings.map((clipping, index) => ({ label: clipping })),
    { type: 'separator' },
    {
      label: 'Quit',
      click() { app.quit(); },
    }
  ]);

  tray.setContextMenu(menu);
};
```

Updates the menu immediately when the application starts to build it for the first time

Eventually, we implement the ability to add clippings to the array.

Each time updateMenu() is called, we map through the array of clippings and render them as simple menu items.

tray.setContextMenu() has been moved into updateMenu() to replace the menu whenever the list of clippings has been modified.

We start by creating a simple array called `clippings` with a global scope that stores clippings and is accessed throughout our application. Next, we create a function called `updateMenu()` to generate a new menu and set it as the context menu for the `tray` instance. `updateMenu()` takes the contents of the clippings array, maps it into objects that can be turned into `MenuItem` instances, and then uses the ECMAScript 2015 spread operator to include them as siblings with Create New Clipping and Quit-menu items.

We added a menu item with the label Create New Clipping (see figure 9.7), but if you look closely, you'll notice that we haven't yet added any functionality. To get it working, we need to figure out a way to access the operating system's native clipboard. Once we can do that, we can update this function to read from the clipboard and push its contents into the array of clippings and then call `updateMenu()` to re-render it.

9.3 Reading from and writing to the clipboard

At this point, it should come as no surprise that Electron provides a module that makes it easy to access the operating system's clipboard on Linux, macOS, and Windows. It should come as even less of a surprise that this module is conveniently called `clipboard`.

The `clipboard` module is available in the main process as well as in the renderer process, and it has several useful methods for reading images, rich text, HTML, bookmarks, and other formats. For now, let's keep it simple and stick to working with strings of plain text. Figure 9.7 shows our application with a single clipping.

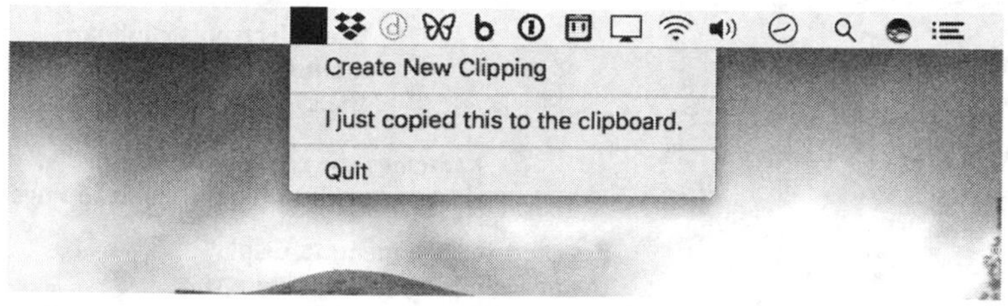

Figure 9.7 When clippings are added to the array, the menu is updated with a new menu item with the clipping's content as the label.

To get the Create New Clipping menu item to work, we want to create a function that we can call that reads from the clipboard and adds it to the `clippings` array. In the spirit of simplicity and clarity, we call this function `addClipping()`.

Listing 9.6 Adding a clipping to the array when the menu item is clicked: ./app/main.js

```
const path = require('path');
const {
  app,
  clipboard,          <-- Pulls in the clipboard module from Electron
  Menu,
  Tray,
  systemPreferences
} = require('electron');

const clippings = [];
let tray = null;

app.on('ready', () => {
  // ...
});

const updateMenu = () => {
  const menu = Menu.buildFromTemplate([
    {
      label: 'Create New Clipping',
      click() { addClipping(); },     <-- When a user clicks the Create New Clipping menu item, calls the addClipping() function
```

```
      accelerator: 'CommandOrControl+Shift+C'
    },
    { type: 'separator' },
    ...clippings.map((clipping, index) => ({ label: clipping })),
    { type: 'separator' },
    {
      label: 'Quit',
      click() { app.quit(); },
      accelerator: 'CommandOrControl+Q'
    }
  ]);

  tray.setContextMenu(menu);
};

const addClipping = () => {
  const clipping = clipboard.readText();
  clippings.push(clipping);
  updateMenu();
  return clipping;
};
```

Adds an accelerator for the Create New Clipping menu item. This is available when the menu is active.

Adds an accelerator for the Quit menu item. This is available when the menu is active.

Uses Electron's clipboard module to read text from the system clipboard

Pushes the text read from the clipboard into the array of clippings

Regenerates the menu to display the new clipping as a menu item

To do anything with the Electron's clipboard module, we need to include it like every other module from Electron. With the module included, `addClipping()` can read text from the clipboard and push it onto the array. With a new clipping in the array, the next logical step is to update the menu and display the new contents to the user as shown in figure 9.7.

9.3.1 *Writing to the clipboard*

With this feature in place, we can read from the clipboard and save the text snippets in our application, but we haven't yet written the functionality to take one of the saved clippings and write it back to the clipboard. As it stands, our application is a scrapbook of the clippings we've saved in the past.

Writing to the clipboard isn't much different from reading from it. So, let's up the ante and assign keyboard shortcuts to the menu items associated with the clippings, as shown in figure 9.8 and in listing 9.7. When a user presses the keystroke, the respective clipping is written to the clipboard.

Figure 9.8 The application now has keyboard shortcuts.

Listing 9.7 Listing out the clippings as menu items: ./app/main.js

```
const path = require('path');
const {
  app,
  clipboard,
  Menu,
  Tray,
  systemPreferences
} = require('electron');

const clippings = [];
let tray = null;

app.on('ready', () => {
  // ...
});

const updateMenu = () => {
  const menu = Menu.buildFromTemplate([
    {
      label: 'Create New Clipping',
      click() { addClipping(); },
      accelerator: 'CommandOrControl+Shift+C'
    },
    { type: 'separator' },
    ...clippings.map(createClippingMenuItem),
    { type: 'separator' },
    {
      label: 'Quit',
      click() { app.quit(); },
      accelerator: 'CommandOrControl+Q'
    }
  ]);

  tray.setContextMenu(menu);
};

const addClipping = () => {
  // ...
};

const createClippingMenuItem = (clipping, index) => {
  return {
    label: clipping,
    click() { clipboard.writeText(clipping); },
    accelerator: `CommandOrControl+${index}`
  };
};
```

Uses the createClippingMenu() in place of the anonymous function we were using previously when mapping over the array of clippings.

Creates a function called createClippingMenuItem()

When a user clicks on a given clipping, writes it to the clipboard. The correct clipping is wrapped inside of a closure.

Assigns the menu item an accelerator based on its index inside of the clippings array

Mapping the strings into menu items inside of the array with an anonymous function was a short-term solution at best. Now that we're adding click methods and accelerators to each menu item, it makes sense to break out this process into its own function. `createClippingMenuItem()` takes the first two arguments passed by `Array.prototype.map()` to its callback function: the item currently being iterated over and its index. We use this index to determine which accelerator to assign to it.

9.3.2 Handling edge cases

With this in place, the user can now write a clipping back to the clipboard with a keystroke. That's great, but what happens if the user copies a big string of text? Eventually the operating system will trim stuff down, as shown in figure 9.9, but we need to step in and do better.

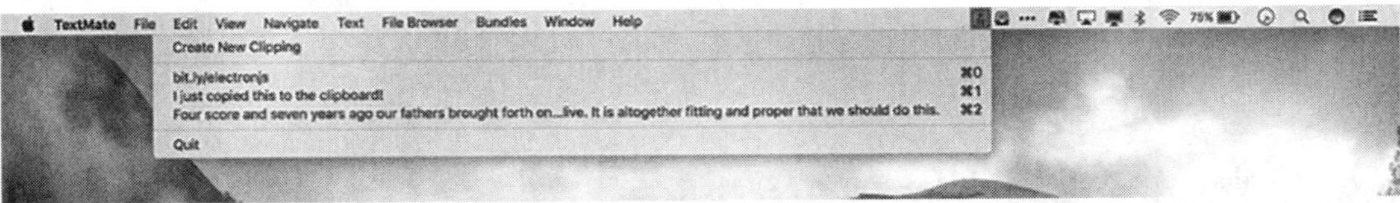

Figure 9.9 The operating system will eventually truncate long menu item labels, but even this is a bit unwieldy.

When we iterate over the clippings to create menu items, we check if it is over 20 characters long. If it is, slice off the first 20 characters, add an ellipsis, and use that as the label. Figure 9.10 shows an example of a shortened menu item name and listing 9.8 gives the code for truncating the labels. This truncation has no effect on the clipping itself. If the user selects the clipping, its full text is written back to the clipboard. If the clipping is less than than 20 characters, use it as the label without modification.

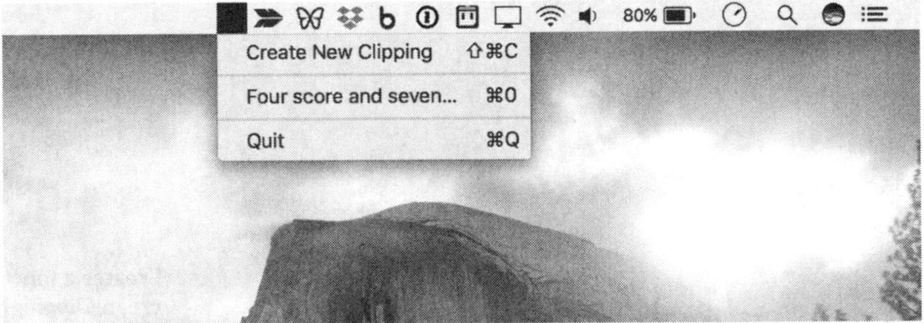

Figure 9.10 Clipping menu item labels are now capped at 20 characters. You can adjust this to your liking, or create a setting to allow users to control the length.

Listing 9.8 Truncating menu item labels: ./main/app.js

```
const createClippingMenuItem = (clipping, index) => {
  return {
    label: clipping.length > 20
      ? clipping.slice(0, 20) + '…'
```

```
        : clipping,
    click() { clipboard.writeText(clipping); },
    accelerator: `CommandOrControl+${index}`
  };
};
```

If the length of the clipping is longer than 20 characters, slices off the first 20 characters and adds an ellipsis.

I chose 20 as an arbitrary number. You can choose another number if you prefer. In a larger application, it might make sense to allow the user to express their preference and use that number instead.

What if a user accidentally added a clipping that is already stored in our array? To get around this, we check if the array includes the current clipping. If it does, then return early to short-circuit the function. Another option would be to use a set instead of an array, which is the approach we took with managing unique windows in Fire Sale. This method works for preventing duplicates, but sets do not have a `map()` method, so we would need to come up with another method for turning the clippings into menu items.

Listing 9.9 Preventing duplicate clippings: ./app/main.js

```
const addClipping = () => {
  const clipping = clipboard.readText();
  if (clippings.includes(clipping)) return;
  clippings.push(clipping);
  updateMenu();
  return clipping;
};
```

Checks if the clippings array already contains the current clippings. If so, returns early from the function.

`Array.prototype.push()` adds items to the end of the array, so the first clipping added always is assigned Command-0 or Control-0 as an accelerator. `Array.prototype.unshift()` adds the new item to the beginning of the array. This means that the most recently saved clipping is accessible with Command-0 or Control-0, the second most recently saved clipping is accessible with Command-1 or Control-1, and so on.

Listing 9.10 Adding clippings to the beginning of the array: ./main.js

```
const addClipping = () => {
  const clipping = clipboard.readText();
  if (clippings.includes(clipping)) return;
  clippings.unshift(clipping);
  updateMenu();
  return clipping;
};
```

Unshift adds an element to the beginning of an array.

If the user falls in love with our application, it could get fairly long. Therefore, it makes sense to limit the number of clippings in the menu. I chose to limit it to 10 items because we're assigning keyboard shortcuts based on the array indices, and there is no "11" key on most keyboards.

Listing 9.11 Displaying only the first 10 clippings: ./app/main.js

```
const menu = Menu.buildFromTemplate([
  {
    label: 'Create New Clipping',
    click() { addClipping(); },
    accelerator: 'CommandOrControl+Shift+C'
  },
  { type: 'separator' },
  ...clippings.slice(0, 10).map(createClippingMenuItem),   <-- Displays only the first 10 items of an array by using Array.prototype.slice()
  { type: 'separator' },
  {
    label: 'Quit',
    click() { app.quit(); },
    accelerator: 'CommandOrControl+Q'
  }
]);
```

These shortcuts have a limitation—they work only when we are actively working with the menu. This means the user would have to mouse over to the menu bar or system tray icon and click it. After that action they can use one of the keyboard shortcuts provided. This is slightly useful, but not as useful as if the shortcuts were globally available.

9.4 Registering global shortcuts

All the accelerators we've used so far have worked only when the application is actively being used. By using the `globalShortcut` module, Electron also allows us to register global shortcuts with the operating system that can be activated even when the application is in the background. We'll register two global shortcuts for Clipmaster: one to trigger the menu to appear, and another to save the contents of the clipboard to Clipmaster without needing to trigger the menu at all.

Listing 9.12 Registering a global shortcut: ./app/main.js

```
const path = require('path');
const {
  app,
  clipboard,
  globalShortcut,      <-- Requires the globalShortcut module from Electron
  Menu,
  Tray,
  systemPreferences
} = require('electron');

const clippings = [];
let tray = null;

app.on('ready', () => {
  if (app.dock) app.dock.hide();

  tray = new Tray(path.join(__dirname, '/Icon.png'));
```

```
  if (process.platform === 'win32') {
    tray.on('click', tray.popUpContextMenu);
  }

  const activationShortcut = globalShortcut.register(
    'CommandOrControl+Option+C',
    () => { tray.popUpContextMenu(); }
  );

  if (!activationShortcut) {
    console.error('Global activation shortcut failed to register');
  }

  const newClippingShortcut = globalShortcut.register(
    'CommandOrControl+Shift+Option+C',
    () => { addClipping(); }
  );

  if (!newClippingShortcut) {
   console.error('Global new clipping shortcut failed to register');
  }

  updateMenu();

  tray.setToolTip('Clipmaster');
});

const updateMenu = () => {
  // ...
};

const addClipping = () => {
  // ...
};

const createClippingMenuItem = (clipping, index) => {
  // ...
};
```

Passes a string defining the accelerator and an anonymous function that should be invoked whenever the accelerator is pressed

If registration fails, Electron does not throw an error. Instead, it returns undefined. In this line, we check if the activationShortcut is defined.

We register a second shortcut to add a clipping to the array.

If either shortcut fails, we log the issue with console.error. In a more robust application, you might show the user that there was an issue or implement a fallback.

The first thing we need to do is require the `globalShortcut` module from Electron. After we have the module, we can use its `register()` method, which takes two arguments: an accelerator, and a function to call when it has been activated. If the global shortcut is already taken, Electron returns `null` instead of throwing an error, which—if uncaught—could take down the entire application. In this case, we log a message to the console informing us that the registration has failed. In a more robust application, you could prompt the user to select a new shortcut or fallback to a second choice.

This functionality behaves slightly differently on macOS and Windows. On macOS the menu appears in the same manner as it would if the user clicked it. On Windows, however, the menu appears beneath the cursor, as shown in figure 9.11, instead of above the system tray icon as you might expect.

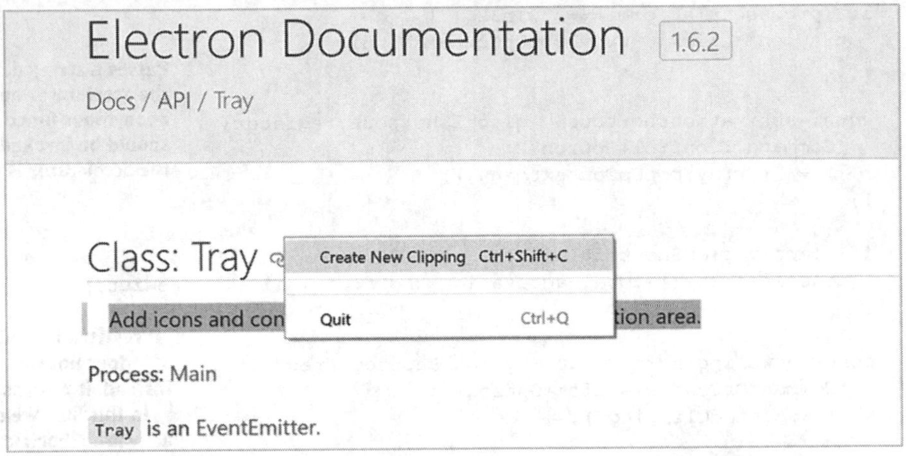

Figure 9.11 On Windows, the menu appears beneath the cursor when triggered with the global shortcut.

9.4.1 *Checking registrations and unregistering global shortcuts*

Electron's `globalShortcut` module also provides other useful methods for working with shortcuts. `globalShortcut.isRegistered()` returns a Boolean that is `true` if the application has already registered the shortcut; otherwise, it returns `false`. However, it also returns `false` if another application has registered that shortcut.

In Clipmaster, you've chosen to hard-code our global shortcuts, but you may choose to create a UI that allows users to set their own keyboard shortcuts. If a user decides to switch shortcuts for a given command, we want to unregister the old shortcut with `globalShortcut.unregister()` after we've successfully registered the new one. We can also unregister all global shortcuts using the conveniently named `globalShortcut.unregisterAll()` method.

9.5 *Displaying notifications*

With our global shortcuts in place, users can save new clippings from anywhere with a touch of a few buttons. But how does the user know when they've successfully saved a clipping? Not only does our application not have much of a UI to begin with, it isn't being shown when they activate it using a global shortcut. One solution would be to show a native system notification, such as that shown in figures 9.12 and 9.13.

Support for notifications

Notifications work out of the box on macOS and Windows 10. They also work with the most common Linux desktop environment. Things get a bit tricky when working with older versions of Windows. This is beyond the scope of this book, but it is covered in the official documentation: http://mng.bz/nJRO.

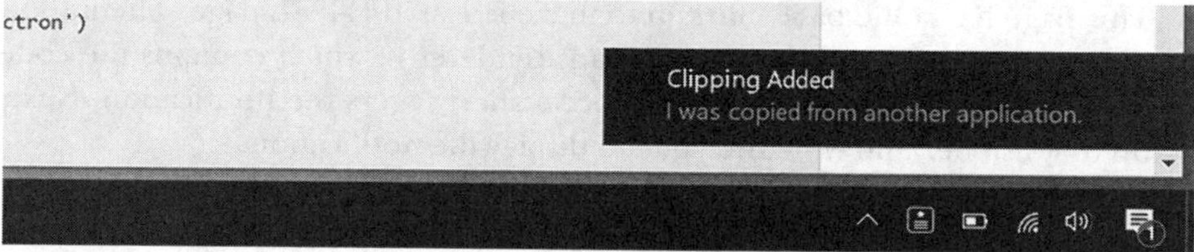

Figure 9.12 A notification in Windows 10

Figure 9.13 A notification in macOS

This is the solution that we're going with, but it's not without its complications. Electron applications can create notifications using Chromium's Notification API. As a web API, Notifications are available only in the renderer process and not in the main process.

To deliver this feature, we need to create a hidden `BrowserWindow` instance. When the user saves a new clipping using the global shortcut, we send a message via IPC to the renderer process. When the renderer process receives this message, it triggers the notification.

Let's start by making an invisible process and then send messages to it and let it trigger the notifications. If you recall from Fire Sale, `BrowserWindow` instances can load HTML, which in turn can load JavaScript like a traditional web page would. The first thing we need is a bare minimum HTML page.

Listing 9.13 Setting up a simple HTML document: ./app/index.html

```
<!DOCTYPE html>
<html lang="en">

<head>
  <meta charset="UTF-8">
  <meta name="viewport" content="width=device-width,initial-scale=1">
  <title>Clipmaster</title>
</head>

<body></body>

<script>
  require('./renderer');      <- The purpose of this HTML file
</script>                        is to load the JavaScript for
                                 the renderer process.

</html>
```

This page has some basic markup to make it a valid HTML page. The important part is that it contains a script tag that loads renderer.js, which contains the code that listens for messages from the main process and triggers the notification. Next, let's set up that listener and write the code to display the notification.

Listing 9.14 Listening for messages and displaying notifications: ./app/renderer.js

```
const { ipcRenderer } = require('electron');

ipcRenderer.on('show-notification', (event, title, body) => {
  const myNotification = new Notification(title, { body });
});
```

Notifications are part of Chromium's built-in APIs and are not specific to Electron. It takes two arguments: a string for the title, and an object of additional parameters. In this example, we're providing a body using ES2015's enhanced object literal syntax. This is equivalent to { body: body }.

We pull in the `ipcRenderer` module and begin listening for notifications on the appropriately named `show-notification` channel. This listener expects three arguments in addition to the event object that is included by default: a title and body for the notification, as well as a function detailing what to do if the user clicks the notification. If no function is provided, `onClick` is an empty function by default.

With the code for our renderer process in place, we need to run it when the application starts. In Fire Sale, we created `BrowserWindow` instances that started out hidden and then were displayed when the content has been loaded. In Clipmaster, there isn't any content to display, so we never show the window itself. Include this code snippet inside the app.on ready block.

Listing 9.15 Launching the hidden browser window: ./app/main.js

```
const {
  // . . .
  BrowserWindow,
  // . . .
} = requre('electron');

browserWindow = new BrowserWindow({
  show: false
 });

browserWindow.load.URL(`file://{$_dirname}/index.html`);
```

Even though the window is not shown, we can load the HTML page we created earlier to execute the code and set up our listener. Now when we add a clipping, we send a message to the renderer process to have it show a notification.

Listing 9.16 Sending a message to the renderer process: ./app/main.js

```
constnewClippingShortcut=globalShortcut.register(
  'CommandOrControl+Shift+Option+C',
```

```
  () => {
    constclipping=addClipping();
    if (clipping) {
      browserWindow.webContents.send(
        'show-notification',
        'Clipping Added',
        clipping,
      );
    }
  },
);
```

addClipping() returns the string of the clipping that was added to the array.

If there was a clipping saved, we send a notification to the renderer process, which triggers the notification.

When a clipping has been added, a message is sent to the renderer process. Before sending the message, we check if `addClipping()` returned a value. If you recall, if the list of clippings already contains the new clipping, then the function returns early with a value of `undefined`. This conditional prevents the message from being sent if no new clipping was saved. I leave it as an exercise to the reader to display a useful notification informing the user that the clipping already exists.

9.6 Switching menu bar icons when pressed in macOS

On macOS, our menu bar icon doesn't behave the same way as its peers. The expected behavior is that the icon's colors are inverted when the menu is activated. Luckily, Electron makes it easy to implement this feature. See figure 9.14.

Figure 9.14 macOS can use an alternate icon when the menu bar application is clicked. In this example, we used an inverted version of the icon to match the rest of the menu bar icons.

The `tray` module has a method called `setPressedImage()`. On Windows, this method is ignored. On macOS it allows us to provide the path to a second image file. When the menu bar icon is clicked, Electron swaps out the primary image for this second image. The code in this listing belongs immediately after the statement that sets `tray`, which also invokes `getIcon()`.

Listing 9.17 Setting an alternate icon for when icon is pressed: ./app/main.js

```
tray.setPressedImage(path.join(__dirname, 'icon-light.png'));
```

You may be asking, "What about dark mode?" It turns out that the default behavior in macOS is not to invert the icons when they're pressed in dark mode. As a result, you do not need to implement any additional logic to handle that situation.

9.7 Completed code

The code for Clipmaster, in line with the features in this chapter, has been implemented as follows: Listing 9.18 shows the code for the main process and listing 9.19 shows the code for the renderer process. You can also find this code on the `completed-example` branch of the repository you cloned at the beginning of this chapter (http://mng.bz/xJ98).

Listing 9.18 Clipmaster's completed main process: ./app/main.js

```
const path = require('path');
const {
  app,
  BrowserWindow,
  clipboard,
  globalShortcut,
  Menu,
  Tray,
  systemPreferences,
} = require('electron');

const clippings = [];
let tray = null;
let browserWindow = null;

const getIcon = () => {
  if (process.platform === 'win32') return 'icon-light@2x.ico';
  if (systemPreferences.isDarkMode()) return 'icon-light.png';
  return 'icon-dark.png';
};

app.on('ready', () => {
  if (app.dock) app.dock.hide();

  tray = new Tray(path.join(__dirname, getIcon()));
  tray.setPressedImage(path.join(__dirname, 'icon-light.png'));

  if (process.platform === 'win32') {
    tray.on('click', tray.popUpContextMenu);
  }

  browserWindow = new BrowserWindow({
    show: false,
  });

  browserWindow.loadURL(`file://${__dirname}/index.html`);

  const activationShortcut = globalShortcut.register(
    'CommandOrControl+Option+C',
    () => {
      tray.popUpContextMenu();
    },
  );
```

```
  if (!activationShortcut)
    console.error('Global activation shortcut failed to regiester');

  const newClippingShortcut = globalShortcut.register(
    'CommandOrControl+Shift+Option+C',
    () => {
      const clipping = addClipping();
      if (clipping) {
        browserWindow.webContents.send(
          'show-notification',
          'Clipping Added',
          clipping,
        );
      }
    },
  );

  if (!newClippingShortcut)
    console.error('Global new clipping shortcut failed to regiester');

  updateMenu();

  tray.setToolTip('Clipmaster');
});

const updateMenu = () => {
  const menu = Menu.buildFromTemplate([
    {
      label: 'Create New Clipping',
      click() {
        addClipping();
      },
      accelerator: 'CommandOrControl+Shift+C',
    },
    { type: 'separator' },
    ...clippings.slice(0, 10).map(createClippingMenuItem),
    { type: 'separator' },
    {
      label: 'Quit',
      click() {
        app.quit();
      },
      accelerator: 'CommandOrControl+Q',
    },
  ]);

  tray.setContextMenu(menu);
};

const addClipping = () => {
  const clipping = clipboard.readText();
  if (clippings.includes(clipping)) return;
  clippings.unshift(clipping);
  updateMenu();
```

```
  return clipping;
};

const createClippingMenuItem = (clipping, index) => {
  return {
    label: clipping.length > 20 ? clipping.slice(0, 20) + '…' : clipping,
    click() {
      clipboard.writeText(clipping);
    },
    accelerator: `CommandOrControl+${index}`,
  };
};
```

Listing 9.19 Clipmaster's completed renderer process: ./app/renderer.js

```
const { ipcRenderer } = require('electron');

ipcRenderer.on('show-notification', (event, title, body, onClick = () => { })
    => {
  const myNotification = new Notification(title, { body });

  myNotification.onclick = onClick;
});
```

Summary

- The `clipboard` module provides several ways to read and write content to and from the clipboard.
- The `globalShortcut` module allows Electron applications to register listeners for keyboard shortcuts.
- Renderer processes can be used as background threads and don't always need to be shown.
- Chromium's Notification API allows us to trigger native notifications on macOS and Windows 10.

10 Building applications with the menubar library

This chapter covers

- Creating an application with the `menubar` library
- Sending HTTP requests with the `request` library
- Creating clickable notifications
- Adding secondary menus to `tray` instances

In the previous chapter, we created an application that lived in the menu bar on macOS or the system tray on Windows. Out of the box, Electron's `tray` module allows you to set a menu to display when the user clicks the tray icon. This is the same type of menu used in the application and context menus that we built in Fire Sale. This menu also has the same limitations: it is limited to text, is hard to modify, and provides limited functionality.

Being able to build applications that live in the system tray or menu bar allows us to build entire classes of applications that we couldn't build in the browser. It's unfortunate that we have these restrictions, but—luckily—we can work around them. In this chapter, we explore a clever way to get around the limitations of the `tray` module using a third-party library conveniently called `menubar`.

`menubar` is an abstraction built on a set of core Electron modules that we've used previously in the book. A high-level explanation is that it creates an empty tray module. When the user clicks the icon, menubar shows a frameless, correctly positioned BrowserWindow instance beneath the icon, which creates the illusion that it's attached to the icon. menubar also provides a cute cat icon by default.

In this chapter, we'll rebuild Clipmaster from the ground up into a completely new application. This time it has a much more pleasant UI, shown in figure 10.1, compared to its predecessor. We add the ability to remove a clipping from the list or publish it to the web using an example API so that it can be shared publicly. Finally, we add some interactivity to our notifications and global shortcuts to trigger the application's functionality using predetermined keystrokes.

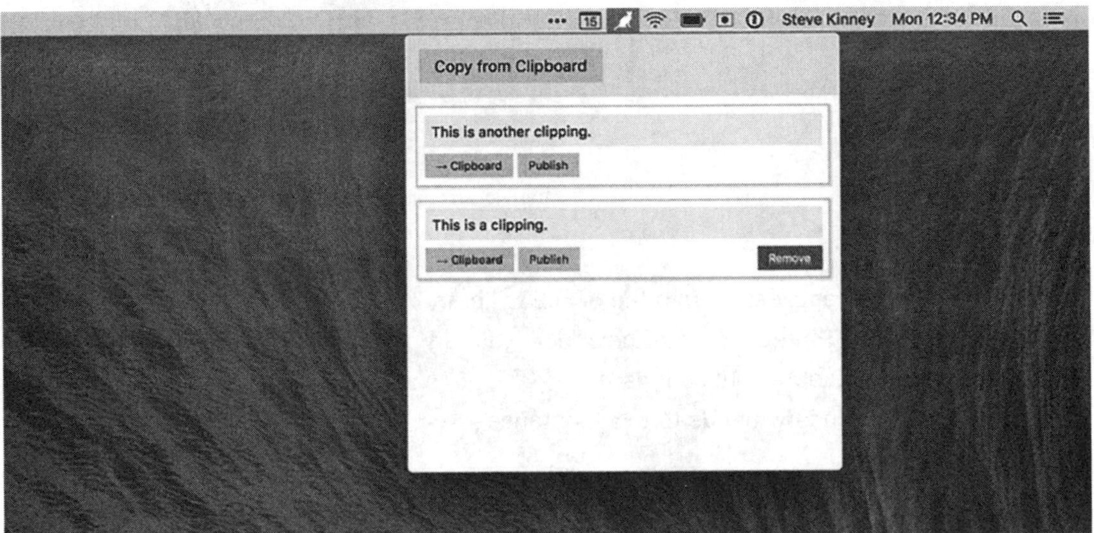

Figure 10.1 This is what the application will look like at the end of the chapter.

10.1 Starting an application with menubar

The menubar library provides a function that allows you to create new menu bar applications. It uses the app module to control the lifecycle of the application, an instance from the tray module to create the icon in the operating system's menu bar or system tray, and a BrowserWindow instance for displaying the UI (as shown in figure 10.2). menubar uses another third-party library called electron-positioner to correctly position the BrowserWindow instance under the icon. It also provides methods for hiding and showing the window programmatically.

A boilerplate for Clipmaster 9000 is available on Github (https://github.com/electron-in-action/clipmaster-9000). You can start on the master branch and code along or check out the completed-example branch to see the code in its state at the end of the chapter.

Listing 10.1 Getting started with menubar: ./app/main.js

```
const Menubar = require('menubar');

const menubar = Menubar();

menubar.on('ready', () => {
  console.log('Application is ready.');
});
```

Instead of requiring the app module from Electron, we create an instance of menubar.

menubar wraps up several common Electron modules. It fires its ready event when the app module fires its ready event.

In listing 10.1, we don't require the app module from Electron. `menubar` does that for us when we call the function and create the instance. You can also see that we're listening for the `ready` event on `menubar` instead of `app`. `menubar`'s event is waiting on getting everything else set up, in addition to listening to the `app`'s `ready` event.

Figure 10.2 By default, `menubar` creates a browser window but does not load an HTML document into it.

You can start the simple application using the `npm start` command. If all goes well, you should see a message in your terminal as well as a small cat in either your menu bar or system tray, depending on which platform the application is running on. If you click the icon, you see an empty browser window. `menubar` created a `BrowserWindow` instance on our behalf, but it did not load an HTML document into the window.

To get a UI in that window, we need to do a few things shown in the listing 10.2. First, we need to create an HTML document with some basic markup. Second, we need to define a CSS to style the UI. Third, we need the HTML document to load the code for our UI from renderer.js.

Listing 10.2 The markup for the UI: ./app/index.html

```
<!DOCTYPE html>
<html>
  <head>
    <meta charset="UTF-8">
    <meta name="viewport" content="width=device-width,initial-scale=1">
    <meta http-equiv="Content-Security-Policy"
          content="
            default-src 'self';
            script-src 'self' 'unsafe-inline';
            connect-src https://cliphub.glitch.com/*
          "
    >
    <!--
      Change the URL in the line above if you fork the back end server.
    -->
    <title>Clipmaster 9000</title>
    <link rel="stylesheet" href="style.css" type="text/css">
  </head>
  <body>
    <div class="container">
      <section class="controls">
        <button id="copy-from-clipboard">Copy from Clipboard</button>
      </section>

      <section class="content">
        <div id="clippings-list"></div>
      </section>
    </div>
    <script>
      require('./renderer');
    </script>
  </body>
</html>
```

This element contains the Copy from Clipboard button, as seen in figure 10.1.

This element contains all the clippings that the user has saved using the application.

Requires the JavaScript for the renderer process.

I included the stylesheet in the repository, but let's highlight some of the interesting bits next. I use one or two Electron-specific techniques in the CSS to give the application a more native feel; renderer.js starts out completely empty, but we add to it as the chapter goes on.

Listing 10.3 Styling for the UI: ./app/style.css

```
// ...Omitted for brevity...

body > div {
  height: 100%;
  overflow: scroll;
  -webkit-overflow-scrolling: touch;
}
```

To give Clipmaster 9000 the feel of a native application on macOS, we turn on momentum scrolling. You can read more about this on CSS Tricks (http://mng.bz/i82A).

```
.container {
  position: absolute;
  top: 0;
  bottom: 0;
  left: 0;
  right: 0;
  overflow: auto;
}

textarea, input, div, button { outline: none; }

// ...Omitted for brevity...

.clipping-text::-webkit-scrollbar {
  display: none;
}

.clipping-controls {
  margin-top: 0.5em;
}

// ...Omitted for brevity...
```

We don't want to show a scroll bar that might appear on top of the shadow of a clipping.

With these files in place, we now have the foundation for building our application. menubar does not create a window immediately. Instead, it creates a `BrowserWindow` instance the first time the user clicks the icon and triggers the window. This behavior comes back to bite us later in the chapter when we try to manipulate the DOM before it has been loaded, but let's follow the happy path for now by listening for an event that is fired after the window has been created and subsequently loading the HTML in the newly created window.

Listing 10.4 Loading the HTML page after a window has been created: ./app/main.js

```
menubar.on('after-create-window', () => {
  menubar.window.loadURL(`file://${__dirname}/index.html`);
});
```

The after-create-window event is fired after a window has been created. By default, menubar does not create a window when it first loads. It instead waits until the menu bar or tray icon is clicked and needs to show a window.

Your application at this stage should look like figure 10.3. At this point, the button should not work, because we have not written any JavaScript for the frontend.

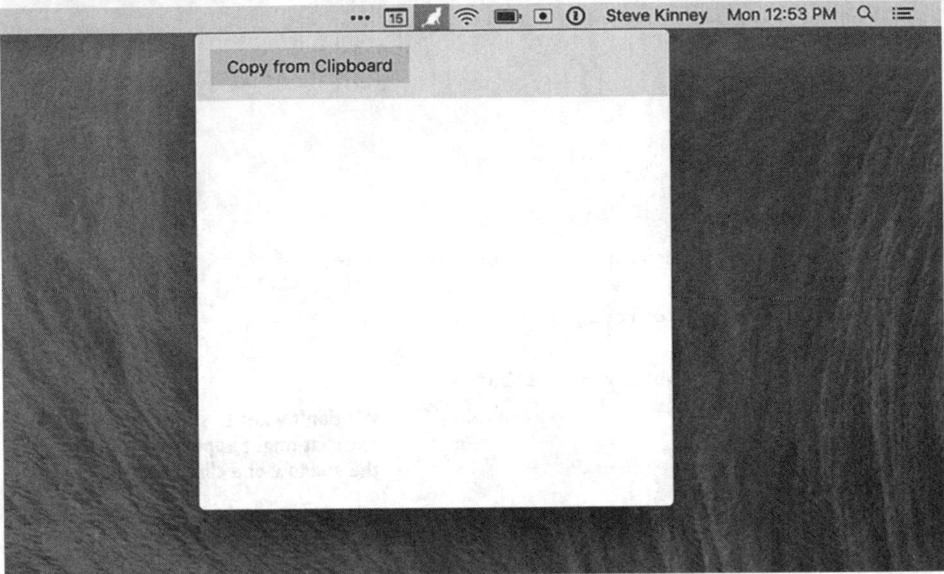

Figure 10.3 The basic UI for Clipmaster 9000 is in place.

10.2 Adding clippings to the UI

We have a UI for our application, but it doesn't do anything yet. Just like in chapter 9, we first want to allow the user to add clippings to the application. This is slightly more complicated than it was in the previous chapter because we must generate DOM nodes for the clipping. We need to add this new node to the node in our Markup that contains the list of clippings. Finally, we need to add an event listener to the button to call the two methods we just described. Let's start by querying and caching two of the selectors that we use frequently as we move through the chapter.

Listing 10.5 Querying for and caching frequently used selectors: ./app/renderer.js

```
const clippingsList = document.getElementById('clippings-list');
const copyFromClipboardButton = document.getElementById(
  'copy-from-clipboard'
);
```

Creating the element is straightforward, with one important catch. In listing 10.6, we create an article element and add the `.clippings-list-item` class to it so that it's styled appropriately. Next, we set its inner content. We query for the node in charge of displaying the text of the clipping and set its inner text accordingly. Finally, we return our new element so that it can be added to the DOM.

Listing 10.6 Creating an element for the UI based on the clipping's text: ./app/renderer.js

```
const createClippingElement = (clippingText) => {
  const clippingElement = document.createElement('article');    // Creates a new element for the clipping

  clippingElement.classList.add('clippings-list-item');

  clippingElement.innerHTML = `                                  // Sets the inner HTML of the new element
    <div class="clipping-text" disabled="true"></div>
    <div class="clipping-controls">
      <button class="copy-clipping">&rarr; Clipboard</button>
      <button class="publish-clipping">Publish</button>
      <button class="remove-clipping">Remove</button>
    </div>
  `;

  clippingElement.querySelector('.clipping-text').innerText = clippingText;
  // Finds the node where the clipping text should go, and sets its content to the text of the clipping

  return clippingElement;    // Returns the new element
};
```

You might be wondering why I didn't use interpolation with the template literal when setting the inner HTML of the element. We're not setting the content of the new element using `innerHTML`, because it does not escape the input and render it as HTML. If a user had copied HTML to the clipboard, it would render the Markup, which is not what we want. Instead we use `innerText` to set the content of that node, which escapes any HTML and renders it as the user might expect.

We can now take an arbitrary string of text and return the element needed for the UI. The next step is to get the text to feed this function, take the result, and add it to the page.

Listing 10.7 Reading from clipboard and adding a clipping to list: ./app/renderer.js

```
const { clipboard } = require('electron');    // Requires the clipboard module from Electron

const addClippingToList = () => {
  const clippingText = clipboard.readText();    // Uses Electron's clipboard module to read text from the clipboard
  const clippingElement = createClippingElement(clippingText);    // Creates a DOM node to display the clipping in the UI
  clippingsList.prepend(clippingElement);    // Adds it to the top of the list of clippings in the UI
};

copyFromClipboardButton.addEventListener('click', addClippingToList);
// Triggers addClippingToList() whenever the user clicks the Copy from Clipboard button in the UI.
```

Reading from the system's clipboard is as easy as requiring the `clipboard` module from Electron and calling its `readText()` method. With the clipping text, we create the element and then add it to the top of the list of clippings. Last, we add an event listener to the Copy from Clipboard button that triggers this entire process.

10.3 Working with clippings in the application

Users can now save clippings to Clipmaster 9000, but that is only half the battle. What if they want to write the contents of a clipping back to the clipboard? Technically, because this new version of the application has a UI, they could select the text and copy it again, but we can do better than that. In addition, Clipmaster 9000 will be an improvement over the old version by letting users remove clippings they no longer want to store and publish them on the web to share publicly if they desire.

10.3.1 Preventing memory leaks using event delegation

The most obvious approach to implementing the functionality described in the previous section would be to add an event listener to each button that calls the appropriate function. When creating a new element for each clipping using `createClippingElement()`, we could add these event listeners.

The problem here is that if a user removes a clipping, we also need to remove these event listeners. Failing to do so would cause a memory leak, because the event listener and the DOM element would still reference each other. It's much easier to take advantage of the fact that events bubble up the DOM.

If you click a button, the browser checks that element for any event listeners for a click event. Next it checks that element's parent. It will continue this process until it gets to the top of the DOM tree. By adding an event listener to the `clippingsList`, we can catch an event that originated for a particular clipping. Because the list itself will never be removed from the DOM, we don't need to worry about removing event listeners whenever a clipping is removed from the UI.

All event objects in the DOM come with a `target` property, which contains a reference to the element that triggered the event. We look at this to figure out which button was clicked on which clipping and then take the appropriate action.

Listing 10.8 Setting up an event listener for each clipping's buttons: ./app/renderer.js

```
clippingsList.addEventListener('click', (event) => {
  const hasClass = className =>
  event.target.classList.contains(className);

  if (hasClass('remove-clipping')) console.log('Remove clipping');
  if (hasClass('copy-clipping')) console.log('Copy clipping');
  if (hasClass('publish-clipping')) console.log('Publish clipping');
});
```

Adds an event listener to the list of clippings. Click events from individual clippings bubble up the list.

Creates a helper function that determines whether the target element has a given class.

Right now, we're going to determine what kind of button was clicked and log an appropriate message to the console. The functionality will be added as the chapter progresses.

We check the element for three different classes, so it makes sense to create a small helper method called `hasClass()` to aid in this process. Based on the class, we need to call different functions. We haven't written those functions yet, so we'll simply log to the console for now to confirm that everything works as it should.

10.3.2 Removing a clipping

To remove a clipping, we navigate up to its grandparent, which is the element for the entire clipping.

Listing 10.9 Removing a clipping from the DOM: ./app/renderer.js

```
const removeClipping = (target) => {
  target.parentNode.parentNode.remove();
};
```

Removes the entire clipping from the DOM. This effectively removes it from memory as well.

When we have a reference to the element for the clipping, removing it from the page is as simple as calling the element's `remove()` method.

Listing 10.10 Configuring the event listener to remove clippings: ./app/renderer.js

```
clippingsList.addEventListener('click', (event) => {
  const hasClass = className => event.target.classList.contains(className);

  if (hasClass('remove-clipping')) removeClipping(event.target);
  if (hasClass('copy-clipping')) console.log('Copy clipping');
  if (hasClass('publish-clipping')) console.log('Publish clipping');
});
```

Replaces the log with the new function to remove the clipping.

Instead of logging to the console whenever the user clicks a clipping's Remove button, we call `removeClipping()` and pass it a reference to the button. That works, but we can do a little bit better. Looking ahead, it's safe to assume that we'll need to get either a reference to the clipping element or its text. It makes sense to pull these out into their own functions.

Listing 10.11 Setting up helper methods for working with clippings: ./app/renderer.js

```
const getButtonParent = ({ target }) => {
  return target.parentNode.parentNode;
};

const getClippingText = (clippingListItem) => {
  return clippingListItem.querySelector('.clipping-text').innerText;
};
```

Creates an abstraction to navigate to the DOM node that contains the entire clipping.

Creates an abstraction for traversing the clipping and finding the text that was originally saved by the user.

`getButtonParent()` can navigate to the parent from any of the three buttons. Although simple, this function is useful in case we ever update the Markup. You don't want to have to change the code for traversing up the DOM from a button to the clipping element three times. From the parent, we need to get the text of the clipping because we're effectively using the DOM as our data store. Luckily, traversing down the DOM is easier than traversing up, and `getClippingText()` can take advantage of the `querySelector()` method. We can now use this method in our event listener.

Listing 10.12 Configuring the event listener to display the clipping's text: ./app/renderer.js

```
clippingsList.addEventListener('click', (event) => {
  const hasClass = className =>
    event.target.classList.contains(className);

  const clippingListItem = getButtonParent(event);

  if (hasClass('remove-clipping')) removeClipping(clippingListItem);
  if (hasClass('copy-clipping')) console.log('Copy clipping',
➥ getClippingText(clippingListItem));
  if (hasClass('publish-clipping')) console.log('Publish clipping',
➥ getClippingText(clippingListItem));;
});
```

Gets the containing DOM node at the very beginning instead of within each function

Passes the clipping element to removeClipping() instead of the event

In the previous listing, we immediately get a reference to the clipping element because we'll need it in every case. Now that getting the clipping text is easy, let's update our console logs to include the clipping text as well to verify that we've implemented this functionality correctly. `removeClipping()` can now get a lot simpler as well. It's arguable that we don't need a function for this at all, but it's conceivable that we might want to add more functionality later. As a result, it makes sense to leave it for now.

Listing 10.13 Refactoring the `removeClipping()` function: ./app/renderer.js

```
const removeClipping = (target) => {
  target.remove();
};
```

Refactors the removeClipping() function to use the element instead of the event's target node.

10.3.3 Writing to the clipboard

Not only did we implement the ability to write to the clipboard in the previous chapter, we've already laid a lot of the groundwork in this chapter to make implementing this feature easy. The first thing that we need is a function that handles writing the text of the clipping to the clipboard.

Listing 10.14 Creating a function to write a clipping to the clipboard: ./app/renderer.js

```
const writeToClipboard = (clippingText) => {
  clipboard.writeText(clippingText);
};
```

Creates a function that takes care of writing text to the clipboard. This is simple now, but we add more to it later in the chapter.

We add more to this function later in the chapter, so it makes sense to keep it as a function instead of just adding inline in our event listener. The next step is to replace the console log in the event listener with this new function and pass the function the text of the clipping that was selected by the user.

Listing 10.15 Adding `writeToClipboard()` to the event listener: ./app/renderer.js

```
clippingsList.addEventListener('click', event => {
  const hasClass = className => event.target.classList.contains(className);

  const clippingListItem = getButtonParent(event);

  if (hasClass('remove-clipping')) removeClipping(clippingListItem);
  if (hasClass('copy-clipping'))
    writeToClipboard(getClippingText(clippingListItem));
  if (hasClass('publish-clipping'))
    console.log('Publish Clipping', getClippingText(clippingListItem));
});
```

Sets the Write to Clipboard button to call our new functionality

10.4 Publishing clippings

We now have the core functionality that any self-respecting application that calls itself Clipmaster 9000 would need to do its job. It's time to start going for extra credit. Let's implement the ability to publish clippings to an example API, as shown in figure 10.4.

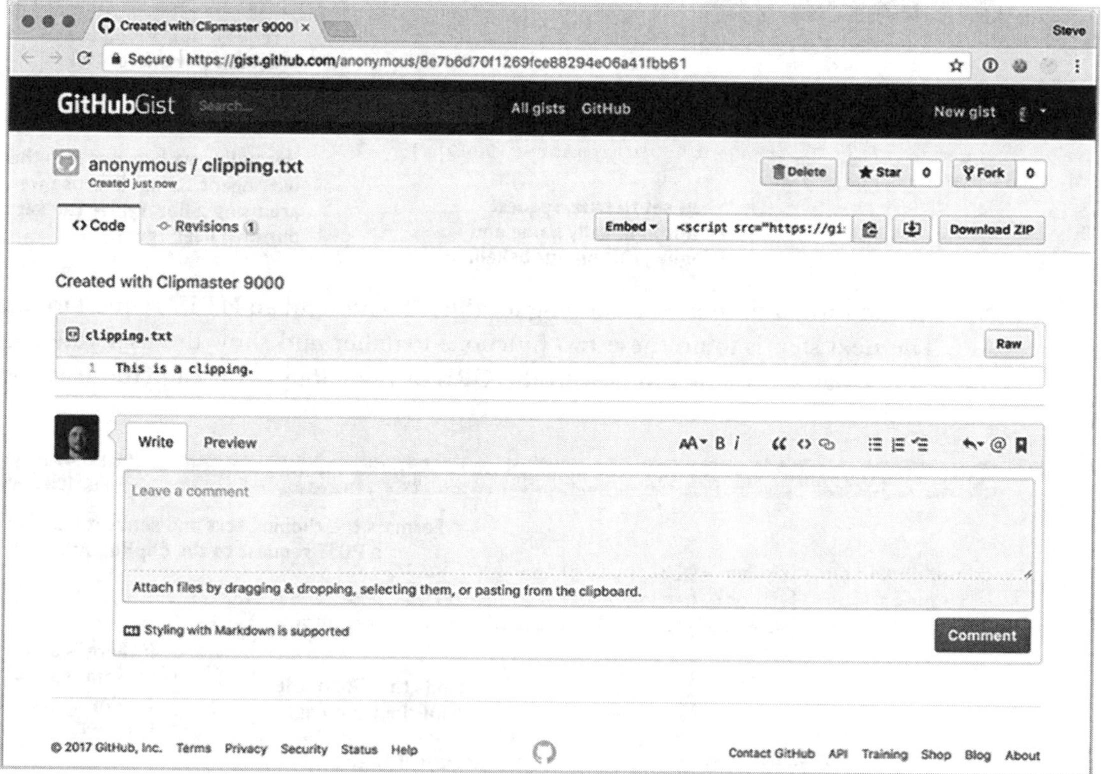

Figure 10.4 A published clipping on the ClipHub service

We cannot do this in a browser for the same security reasons we discussed in chapter 2. In addition, we use a Node library that would not normally work in the browser to send our requests to the API.

In the name of focus, we'll take a few shortcuts. This is a deliberatively simple API—it stores the clippings in memory. All of the clippings will be cleared out periodically. The source code for the server can be found at https://glitch.com/~cliphub.

10.4.1 Setting up request

`request` is another popular, well-named library that makes it easy to perform HTTP requests to remote servers. `request` allows us to set defaults for every request that it makes. For this application, we send all our requests to the same API endpoint, so it makes sense to set that as a default. We will also create a custom user agent string that will differentiate Clipmaster from an ordinary browser.

In this section, we set up `request` to make requests to the ClipHub API, format our clippings so that the ClipHub API will accept those requests, and then set up our UI to make the requests.

Listing 10.16 Requiring and configuring default parameters for `request`: ./app/renderer.js

```
const request = require('request').defaults({
  url: 'https://cliphub.glitch.me/clippings',
  headers: { 'User-Agent': 'Clipmaster 9000' },
  json: true,
});
```

- request allows you to set default parameters for every HTTP request
- Normally, the browser sets the user agent string. Because we are using a library, we can set our own user agent.
- When set to true, request will automatically parse and stringify JSON on our behalf.

Now we can format the text of a clipping for the API and send an HTTP request to the API. The next step is to tie these two functions together and show the user whether the request was successful, along with the URL of the clipping on ClipHub if it was successful.

Listing 10.17 Creating a function to publish a clipping to ClipHub's API: ./app/renderer.js

```
const publishClipping = (clipping) => {
  request.post({ json: { clipping } }), (error, response, body) => {
    if (error) { return alert(JSON.parse(error).message); }

    const url = body.url;

    alert(url);
    clipboard.writeText(url);
  });
};
```

- Formats the clipping text and sends it via a POST request to the ClipHub API.
- If there is an error for some reason, we display an alert to the user.
- Finds the URL of the published clipping.
- Displays it to the user via an alert.
- Writes it to the clipboard.

`request.post()` sends a POST request to a URL. We set the default URL earlier, so there is no need to specify it now. `request.post()` takes two arguments: the data we want to send and a callback that is invoked when we hear back from the server. `request` passes three arguments to the callback: an error object in the event the request is not successful, the full HTTP response, and the body of the response. If the request was successful, `error` is `null`.

If the request is successful, we get the `url` property, which contains the URL for our new published clipping. For now, we use an alert to display the URL. We also write it to the clipboard so that the user can paste it into the address bar of their favorite web browser. With the code for this feature in place, the last thing to do is call it when the user clicks the Publish button on a clipping.

Listing 10.18 Adding `publishClipping()` to the event listener: ./app/renderer.js

```
clippingsList.addEventListener('click', (event) => {
  const hasClass = className => event.target.classList.contains(className);

     const clippingListItem = getButtonParent(event);

  if (hasClass('remove-clipping')) removeClipping(clippingListItem);
  if (hasClass('copy-clipping'))
     writeToClipboard(getClippingText(clippingListItem));
  if (hasClass('publish-clipping'))
     publishClipping(getClippingText(clippingListItem));
});
```

Correctly sets up the Publish Clipping button.

In this listing, we used a technique similar to writing the clipping's text to the clipboard. The only difference is that we swap out `writeToClipboard()` in favor of `publishClipping()`.

10.5 Displaying notifications and registering global shortcuts

We let the user know that something has happened in Clipmaster in various ways. We silently write to the clipboard without informing the user as to whether the action ended in success. When publishing we use an alert that locks up the application until the user dismisses it.

Later in this chapter, we implement global shortcuts that allow the user to trigger the application's functionality without having it open. In this situation, having useful notifications is even more important. Displaying these notifications is simple because we do all the heavy lifting in the renderer process and don't have to worry about IPC. With that in mind, we look at how to add event handlers to our notifications to add functionality that wasn't present in the previous chapter.

Let's start by tackling the alert that pops up whenever the user publishes a clipping. In its place, we display one of two notifications, shown in listing 10.19: that an error occurred with the message received from the server, or that the request was successful with the URL of the newly published clipping on ClipHub. If the request was successful, we add an event handler to the notification that opens ClipHub in their default browser when the user clicks the notification.

Listing 10.19 Setting up notifications when publishing a clipping: ./app/renderer.js

```
const { clipboard, shell } = require('electron');

// Code omitted for clarity…

const publishClipping = (clippingText) => {
  request.post({ json: { clipping } }), (error, response, body) => {
    if (error) {
      return new Notification('Error Publishing Your Clipping', {
        body: JSON.parse(error).message
      });
    }

    const url = body.url;
    const notification = new Notification(
      'Your Clipping Has Been Published',
      { body: `Click to open ${url} in your browser.` }
    );

    notification.onclick = () => { shell.openExternal(url); };

    clipboard.writeText(url);
  };
};
```

Creates a notification in the event there is an error

Creates a notification when the clipping is successfully published

If the user clicks the notification, takes them to the published clipping.

To open a URL in the user's default browser, we need to pull in the `shell` module from Electron. We'll set the `onclick` method of the notification to an anonymous function that is triggered when the user clicks the notification.

10.5.1 Registering global shortcuts

Asking the user to take their hand off the keyboard and navigate to a small icon in the menu bar or system tray isn't always optimal. They're likely typing when they want to create a clipping, and they want the convenience of having a key combination that they can press from anywhere in the operating system to trigger a command inside Clipmaster 9000.

If you remember from the previous chapter, we must register global shortcuts in the main process. In chapter 9, we implemented most of the application's functionality in the main process, and we could call functions directly. In this chapter, the opposite is true, and we need to set up some IPC. In the following listing, let's start by registering a shortcut to create a new clipping. We start by having it log to the console for now. In the next step, we implement its functionality.

Listing 10.20 Setting up a simple global shortcut: ./app/main.js

```
const { globalShortcut } = require('electron');        ◁— Requires the
const Menubar = require('menubar');                        globalShortcut
                                                           module from Electron
const menubar = Menubar();

menubar.on('ready', function() {
  console.log('Application is ready.');

  const createClipping = globalShortcut.register('CommandOrControl+!', ()
    ➥ => {
    console.log('This will eventually trigger creating a new clipping.');
  });                                                    ◁— Creates a global
                                                            shortcut that
  if (!createClipping) {                                    eventually creates
    console.error('Registration failed', 'createClipping');  a new function
  }                                                 ◁— If registering the
});                                                    global shortcut fails,
                                                       logs an error to the
menubar.on('after-create-window', () => {              console
  menubar.window.loadURL(`file://${__dirname}/index.html`);
});
```

This is similar to what we did in the previous chapter. The important difference is that we're storing all the clippings in the DOM in the renderer process. As a result, we need to communicate with the renderer process to create the clipping. In Fire Sale, we kept a reference to each window that we created. `menubar` created a browser window on our behalf and stored it in its `window` property. Let's update our global shortcut to send a message to the renderer process whenever the user presses the keystroke to create a new shortcut. We can also register shortcuts for writing clippings back to the clipboard and publishing them to ClipHub.

Listing 10.21 Setting up global shortcuts with IPC: ./app/main.js

```
const createClipping = globalShortcut.register('CommandOrControl+!', () => {
  menubar.window.webContents.send('create-new-clipping');
});

const writeClipping = globalShortcut.register('CmdOrCtrl+Alt+@', () => {
  menubar.window.webContents.send('write-to-clipboard');
});

const publishClipping = globalShortcut.register('CmdOrCtrl+Alt+#', () => {
  menubar.window.webContents.send('publish-clipping');
});

if (!createClipping) {
  console.error('Registration failed', 'createClipping');
}
```

```
  if (!writeClipping) {
    console.error('Registration failed', 'writeClipping');
  }

  if (!publishClipping) {
    console.error('Registration failed', 'publishClipping');
  }
```

Each shortcut is sending a message on a different channel. In this case, we send no additional information to the renderer process because the process reads from the clipboard. The next step is to configure the renderer process to receive the messages sent from the main process. The user may not have the application open when they press the keystroke, so we add notifications where appropriate.

Listing 10.22 Setting up IPC listeners in the renderer process: ./app/renderer.js

```
const { clipboard, ipcRenderer, shell } = require('electron');

ipcRenderer.on('create-new-clipping', () => {
  addClippingToList();
  new Notification('Clipping Added', {
    body: `${clipboard.readText()}`
  });
});

ipcRenderer.on('write-to-clipboard', () => {
  const clipping = clippingsList.firstChild;
  writeToClipboard(getClippingText(clipping));
});

ipcRenderer.on('publish-clipping', () => {
  const clipping = clippingsList.firstChild;
  publishClipping(getClippingText(clipping));
});
```

- Pulls in the ipcRenderer module from Electron (first line)
- If an IPC message comes across on the create-new-clipping channel, calls the function that is called when a user clicks the Copy to Clipboard button. (addClippingToList)
- After adding the clipping, displays a notification because the user does not have the UI open and may not know that it was added successfully. (new Notification)
- Previously, we knew what clipping the user wanted based on the button they clicked. In this case, we don't know, so we grab the first one on the list. (const clipping = clippingsList.firstChild)
- Writes that clipping to the clipboard. (writeToClipboard)
- The process of publishing the clipping is similar to writing it to the clipboard: Find the first one, and pass it to the function. (publishClipping)

In chapter 9, we stored all the clippings in an array in the main process. In this chapter, we're using the DOM as our temporary data store. If the user clicks the button to write to the clipboard or publish the clipping, we know which clipping, based on the button clicked. But how do we find the appropriate clipping when the user activates a global shortcut? In the previous listing, we traverse to the first child of the clippings list and call one of the functions we wrote earlier in the chapter with that element.

10.5.2 Solving for the edge case that occurs if the window has never been shown

You might have noticed a bug when implementing the last feature. If you start your application and immediately press one of your new global shortcuts, you get an error, shown in figure 10.5, that reads "TypeError: Cannot read property `'webContents'` of undefined." If you look at the previous listing, you'll notice that we're attempting to access the `webContents` property on `menubar.window`, which is apparently `undefined`. Click the cat icon to open the window and try the shortcut again. It should work this time.

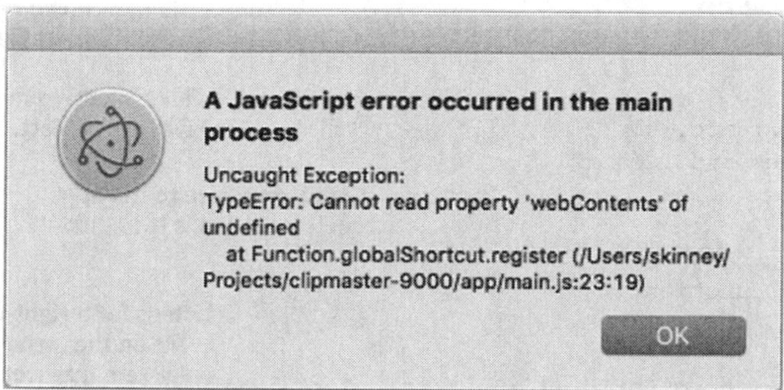
A JavaScript error occurred in the main process
Uncaught Exception:
TypeError: Cannot read property 'webContents' of undefined
at Function.globalShortcut.register (/Users/skinney/Projects/clipmaster-9000/app/main.js:23:19)
OK

Figure 10.5 If you try to use one of your global shortcuts before the window is opened for the first time, you see this error.

So why does it suddenly work? `menubar` lazily loads the window the first time it is needed. To prevent this error, we must tell `menubar` to immediately load the window when it starts up. We also want it to load our HTML page, which—in turn—loads renderer.js, which sets up our IPC listeners.

Listing 10.23 Preloading window and contents on start-up: ./app/main.js

```
const menubar = Menubar({
  preloadWindow: true,
  index: `file://${__dirname}/index.html`,
});
```

Sets the preloadWindow option to true to load the UI, even if it has never been requested.

Specifies the HTML document that should be preloaded.

Previously, we were invoking the `Menubar()` function with no arguments. In listing 10.23, we modified the function call and passed in a configuration object. We preload the window before the first time the user clicks on the menu bar or tray icon and we load in our HTML page as soon as `menubar` loads the window.

10.6 Adding a secondary menu

In Fire Sale, I boasted that one of the great things about building applications in Electron is that we could use application and context menus to provide functionality without needing to find a place for it in the UI. In the previous chapter, we could have created additional submenus if necessary. But what about Clipmaster 9000? It turns out that the `tray` module allows us to display a secondary menu when the user right-clicks the icon. Let's create a simple menu that allows users to quit the application. We accomplish this in three steps: create the menu using `Menu.buildFromTemplate()`, add an event handler for right-clicks on `menubar.tray`, and pop up the menu when the user right-clicks the icon.

Listing 10.24 Creating a secondary menu: ./app/main.js

```
const { globalShortcut, Menu } = require('electron');     <-- Requires the menu module from Electron.

const secondaryMenu = Menu.buildFromTemplate([     <-- Builds a menu from a JavaScript object.
  {
    label: 'Quit',
    click() { menubar.app.quit(); },     <-- Gets a reference to the app module, and tells it to quit.
    accelerator: 'CommandOrControl+Q'
  },
]);

menubar.on('ready', function () {
  console.log('Application is ready.');

  menubar.tray.on('right-click', () => {     <-- Listens for a right-click event on the menu bar or system tray icon.
    menubar.tray.popUpContextMenu(secondaryMenu);     <-- Triggers a pop-up menu.
  });

  // Omitted for brevity…
});
```

With this small change, we create an entire secondary interface to the application. This would be a great place for user preferences and other advanced options that don't have a good place in the main UI of the application.

The first phase of Clipmaster 9000 is now complete. You can find the complete code in the appendix or on the completed-example branch of this repository (http://mng.bz/UE9).

Summary

- `menubar` is a third-party library that is a high-level abstraction around core Electron modules and another third-party library called `electron-positioner`.
- `menubar` creates a browser window and positions it directly below the menu bar icon (on macOS) or above the tray icon (on Windows).
- Event delegation is a technique that allows you to add an event listener to a parent node and wait for the event to bubble up rather than manually adding and removing listeners from child nodes to prevent memory leaks.
- `request` is a library for Node.js that allows you to make HTTP requests to external URLs.
- We can define Notifications' `onclick` method to allow custom behavior when a user clicks a notification.
- `menubar`'s browser window instance can be preloaded when the application starts.
- A secondary menu can be added to the `tray` instance to provide additional functionality.

11 Using transpilers and frameworks

This chapter covers

- Setting up `electron-compile` to transpile CoffeeScript, TypeScript, and upcoming JavaScript features (using Babel) without a build step in an Electron application.
- Using `electron-compile` to transpile Less, Sass, and Stylus to CSS and Jade to HTML.
- Building a simple Electron application using React, Sass, and Jade.
- Setting up live reload, which reloads the browser window whenever the code in the renderer process has been changed.

In the chapters leading up to this one, we've been writing all of our UIs using vanilla JavaScript and CSS. This was intentional—this is a book on Electron, after all. It's not a book on client-side frameworks. That said, it's impossible to ignore that modern web developers use a wide variety of languages, frameworks, and tools to build the increasingly complex UIs that users have come to expect from the web.

In this chapter, I'll show you how to set up Electron to work with an assortment of web languages. With that covered, we build a small application using three languages: React (using JSX and upcoming JavaScript features that are not yet supported by Node or Chromium), Sass, and Jade. It's not a requirement that you've used React or any of the other languages. In fact, if you're an expert in any of them, you might notice that we kept them deliberately simple and omit things like `PropTypes`. I chose React, Sass, and Jade because they hit the sweet spot of being popular and relatively approachable for developers unfamiliar with them. Though this book is not on React, Sass, or Jade, it is titled *Electron in Action* so we we're going to learn by doing. We use this application in the next chapter when we hook up real, persistent data stores to the application. A branch of this application is ready for you to use if you are already familiar with React or don't have a strong desire to learn it. That said, do not miss section 11.5 where I cover how to enable live reloading using `electron-compile`.

In this chapter, we build an application called Jetsetter, shown in figure 11.1. This application solves a problem that I've been having. I've been traveling a lot recently to speak at JavaScript conferences, and the only thing worse than showing up to the conference venue without the right adapter is showing up at the hotel without enough socks for the week. In the past, I've tried to use a to-do list to track everything I needed to pack. But to-do list applications aren't really built for this purpose, and I find it tedious to check and uncheck all the tasks when I'm packing for the next trip. Hence, Jetsetter was born.

You can find the source code for Jetsetter at https://github.com/electron-in-action/jetsetter. We start with the `master` branch as the foundation of the application as we go through this chapter, but you can also find a completed version on the branch named `completed-example`. To get started, clone the repository, and install the dependencies.

Figure 11.1 In this chapter, we build an application to track what we need to pack for an upcoming trip.

We build an application that allows the user to add items and mark them as either packed or unpacked. A button at the bottom of the UI allows the user to mark everything as unpacked again when they're getting ready for the next trip. The version we are building in this chapter has a fatal flaw: it doesn't save the list of items anywhere. This means that whenever you close the application, all your new items are lost. Chapter 12 addresses this issue by showing how to persist data in several different ways, from in-browser storage to directly accessing databases from the UI.

11.1 Introducing electron-compile

Despite all the languages that developers use to build web applications these days, the browser understands only three of them: HTML, CSS, and JavaScript. Some minor exceptions have existed over the years—Google's Dartium, which was a build of Chromium that ran Dart alongside JavaScript, and Netscape Navigator's short-lived support of JavaScript Stylesheets come to mind—but, for the most part, this situation has been true for as long as the web has been around.

In addition to compiling from alternative languages into JavaScript, it has become fashionable to compile JavaScript into JavaScript. Tools such as Babel allow developers to use the latest and greatest—and in some cases, upcoming—features of the language and then compile them down into more verbose versions that older browsers support. We're not concerned with older browsers when building Electron applications because we're shipping our own modern versions of Chromium and Node, but Babel plugins are available for upcoming language features and alternative syntaxes like JSX or Flow, the former of which we use in this chapter.

Typically, developers write in their language of choice and then use a build tool to compile their code into JavaScript, CSS, or HTML for the browser. This process is commonly called *transpilation* because we're compiling one language into another instead of into byte code or assembly. We could certainly do that in this chapter, but it requires running a separate process to compile our code. We'd have to wait for that process to finish before refreshing the Electron application's browser window to see the changes.

More importantly, the process is not much different for Electron applications than it is for traditional web applications and certainly doesn't warrant an entire chapter in this book. And so, it is with great pleasure that I get to introduce you to `electron-compile`.

`electron-compile` enables Electron to use alternative languages in addition to the ones supported by Chromium and Node, as illustrated in figure 11.2. They are transpiled on the fly and without the need for an additional build process.

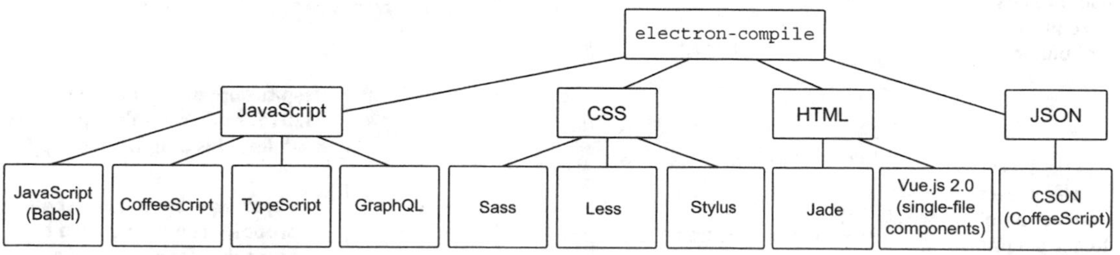

Figure 11.2 **`electron-compile` supports a wide variety of languages.**

As you can see in figure 11.2, `electron-compile` supports a healthy number of languages. Getting started with `electron-compile` is suspiciously easy. In the package.json file of the application, you'll find the important dependency `electron` as well as `electron-prebuilt-compile`, which is a version of Electron that has been configured with `electron-compile`.

`electron-compile` determines the language by looking at the file extension. If you load a file with a .coffee extension, it automatically transpiles it using CoffeeScript. The same goes for TypeScript with the .ts extension and so on. All files with a .js extension will be transpiled using Babel. By default, Babel doesn't do anything, so it has no effect on your JavaScript files unless you intentionally configure it to, which I cover in the next section.

For now, if you run `npm start`, the application starts as you'd expect, but it now has full support for `electron-compile`. If your needs are simple, then this is all that you must do. In the next section, we configure `electron-compile` to support JSX and other upcoming features to JavaScript as well as support source maps in development.

11.2 Laying the application's foundation

In this chapter, we use JavaScript with a few additional features and support for JSX—an HTML-like syntax that makes it easier to define React components. As such, we need to configure Babel to support these features. When the application starts, `electron-compile` looks to a file called .compilerc for any additional configuration beyond the default. I've included this file for you in the repository you cloned earlier in this chapter, but let's look at it in this listing.

Listing 11.1 Configuring Babel for use with electron-compile: ./.compilerc

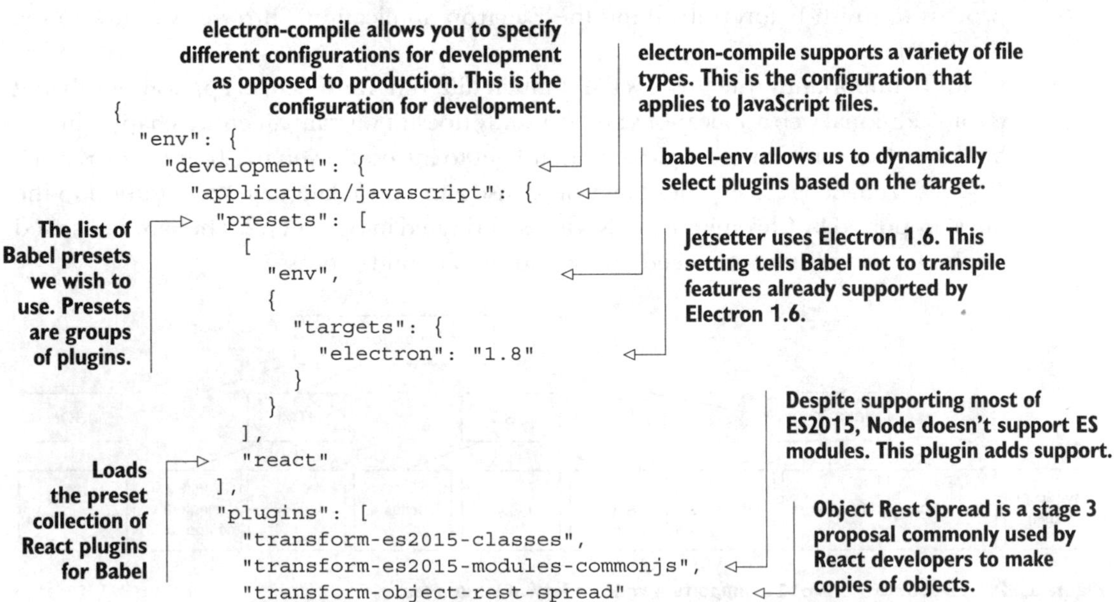


```
{
  "env": {
    "development": {
      "application/javascript": {
        "presets": [
          [
            "env",
            {
              "targets": {
                "electron": "1.8"
              }
            }
          ],
          "react"
        ],
        "plugins": [
          "transform-es2015-classes",
          "transform-es2015-modules-commonjs",
          "transform-object-rest-spread"
```

```
      ],
      "sourceMaps": "inline"
    },
    "text/jade": {
      "pretty": true
    }
  },
  "production": {
    "application/javascript": {
      "presets": [
        [
          "env",
          {
            "targets": {
              "electron": "1.8"
            }
          }
        ],
        "react"
      ],
      "plugins": [
        "transform-es2015-classes",
        "transform-es2015-modules-commonjs",
        "transform-object-rest-spread"
      ],
      "sourceMaps": "none"
    }
  }
}
}
```

Source maps allow developers to see the untranspiled source in their developer tools.

By default, Jade formats its output without any spaces or new lines. This setting generates more human-readable output.

In production, we instruct electron-compile not to include source maps or format Jade's output.

At first glance, this configuration file can be overwhelming, but there is a beauty to it. First, `electron-compile` allows us to maintain two separate configuration sets: one for development, and one for production. We chose to omit source maps and not format the HTML generated by Jade for production. Source maps are a convenience for developers.

When we are using transpilation, the code we write is not the code that is being executed by the browser. This inherently makes sense because that's the whole point of using transpilation, but the catch is that it can be hard to debug code that has been compiled. An error on line 36 of the code in the output may be on line 12 of the code you wrote. Source maps allow Chromium to map the output to the input and show you where that error is in the code you wrote. Generating source maps can take time, so they are generally omitted from production versions of the application.

`electron-compile` doesn't configure the transpilation process itself. It simply passes on those options to the tool doing the actual transpilation. Under the development key, we have two additional keys: `text/jade` and `application/javascript`. These options are passed to Jade and Babel, respectively. Any options listed under an `application/coffeescript` are passed to the CoffeeScript compiler.

Within the options being passed to Babel, we see that we're using both plugins and presets. Presets are just groups of plugins. The `react` preset includes all the presets related to React, such as the ability to parse and transform JSX. Many other presets are available on npm, but `babel-preset-env` is a bit of a special beast. It maintains a list of commonly used plugins and the browsers—Electron is included among these—that already have built-in support and do not require a plugin. This allows Babel to intelligently skip transpiling features that are already natively supported by Electron.

In addition to the presets, we include a few other plugins. Node.js does not currently support the ES modules, so I included a plugin that will convert the ES module syntax into the CommonJS module syntax that we've been using thus far in this book. We also add support for an upcoming language feature called Object Rest Spread, which is popular with React developers and used to clone objects to avoid mutation.

> **What's with the support for ECMAScript classes?**
>
> You may have noticed that I've included a plugin for ECMAScript classes, which are already supported in both Node and Chromium, so this plugin is not required. At the time of this writing, a bug with hot module reloading in React requires that this plugin be included. I mention this because if you try to apply the concepts from this chapter in the future, you may also run into this bug (https://github.com/gaearon/react-hot-loader/issues/313). This bug has been open for just over a year and a half, so you may run into it and lose the better part of your afternoon, like I did.

With `electron-compile` configured, let's look at the foundation of the application. Instead of an HTML file, we use Jade as the markup language. This file is relatively simple, because React handles most of the heavy lifting for the UI. Replace index.html with index.jade, and add the following content.

Listing 11.2 The renderer process's HTML file written in Jade: ./app/index.jade

```
doctype html
html(lang='en')
  head
    title Jetsetter
    meta(charset='UTF-8')
    meta(name='viewport', content='width=device-width, initial-scale=1')
    meta(
      http-equiv="Content-Security-Policy",
      content="default-src 'self'; script-src 'self' 'unsafe-inline'"
    )
    link(rel='stylesheet', href='style.scss')
  body
    #application
      .loading Loading...
    script.
      require('./renderer');
```

Jade was officially renamed Pug a while back due to a trademark dispute, but it is still referred to as Jade by `electron-compile`, so I do the same for the remainder of this chapter. We also write our stylesheet in Sass, a feature-rich alternative to CSS. Rename style.css to style.scss, and update the content as follows.

Listing 11.3 Application styles using Sass: ./app/style.scss

```
$accent-color: rgb(243,46,91);

html {
  box-sizing: border-box;
}

body, input {
  font: caption;
}

input {
  padding: 0.5em;
  border: 1px solid $accent-color;
  background-color: lighten($accent-color, 30);
}

button, .button, input[type="submit"] {
  background-color: $accent-color;
  border: 1px solid darken($accent-color, 10);
  color: white;
  padding: 0.5em;
  &:hover {
    background-color: lighten($accent-color, 10);
  }
  &:active {
    background-color: lighten($accent-color, 5);
  }
  &.full-width {
    width: 100%;
    margin: 1em 0;
  }
}

.NewItem {
  display: flex;
}

.NewItem-input {
  width: 100%;
}
```

Sass supports variables.

Sass includes many helper functions for working with colors. The first argument is the color. The second argument is the amount you wish to adjust the color.

Sass allows you to nest selectors. This is the equivalent to writing each of the selectors with the addition of the :hover pseudo-selector.

Sass supports a wide range of features—many of which I won't discuss in this chapter. In the previous example, I used a variable to set the main color of the buttons and input fields and used built-in helper functions such as `lighten()` and `darken()` to adjust the color for different parts of the UI.

With the markup and styling in place, we can set up our main and renderer processes. The main process is deliberately simpler than it has been in previous chapters because it's not the focus.

Listing 11.4 The main process for Jetsetter: ./app/main.js

```
import { app, BrowserWindow } from 'electron';

let mainWindow;

app.on('ready', () => {
  mainWindow = new BrowserWindow({
    width: 300,
    height: 600,
    minWidth: 300,
    minHeight: 300,
    show: false
  });
  mainWindow.loadFile('index.jade');
  mainWindow.once('ready-to-show', () => {
    mainWindow.show();
  });
});
```

electron-compile allows us to use nonstandard file extensions (annotates `mainWindow.loadFile('index.jade');`)

Notice that we can use files with extensions that are not normally supported in the browser. `electron-compile` transpiles this to an HTML file on the fly, and Chromium is none the wiser. If you look again at listing 11.2, you notice that we requested a stylesheet named style.scss instead of style.css. The .scss extension is used by Sass, and `electron-compile` transpiles it using Sass before handing the CSS off to Chromium. The last piece of the puzzle is to set up the renderer process.

Listing 11.5 A simple component using JSX and React: ./app/renderer.js

```
import React from 'react';
import { render } from 'react-dom';

const Application = () => {
  return (
    <div>
      <h1>Hello world!</h1>
      <button className="full-width">
        This button does not do anything.
      </button>
    </div>
  );
};

render(<Application />, document.getElementById('application'));
```

Requires the React library.

Pulls in the render() method from the ReactDOM library.

Creates an Application component with some placeholder content.

Renders the Application component into the DOM node with the ID of "application."

If this is your first time seeing React, you might be surprised to see HTML in your JavaScript. This syntax is known as JSX (JavaScript with XML). It's a convenient way of describing the markup that a React component should create. Babel transpiles this code into traditional JavaScript to be read by the browser. The actual JavaScript looks like this listing.

Listing 11.6 The Application component after transpilation

```
const Application = () => {
  return React.createElement(
    "div",
    null,
    React.createElement(
      "h1",
      null,
      "Hello world!"
    ),
    React.createElement(
      "button",
      { className: "full-width" },
      "This button does not do anything."
    )
  );
};
```

Listing 11.5 is a bit easier on the eyes than listing 11.6—especially as the application begins to grow. We didn't need to set up a build chain using webpack or Gulp. `electron-compile` takes care of configuring Babel based on the options we specify in .compilerc. If you fire up the application using `npm start`, you should see a slightly taller version of figure 11.3.

Figure 11.3 The foundation of our application using React, Sass, and Jade.

11.3 Building the UI in React

Our `Application` component is the starting point for Jetsetter's UI. Jetsetter has four main parts: a form for adding new items, a list of all the items that still need to be packed, a list of all the items that have been packed, and a button for returning all of the items marked as packed to the unpacked list.

The two lists are pretty much the same, so they use the same component, but each list also has a subcomponent for every item on the list. In addition to modifying `Application` to be a bit more useful, we need to create three more components: `Item`, `Items`, and `NewItem`. The Mark All as Unpacked button can use a standard `<button>` element. The hierarchy of the components is laid out in figure 11.4.

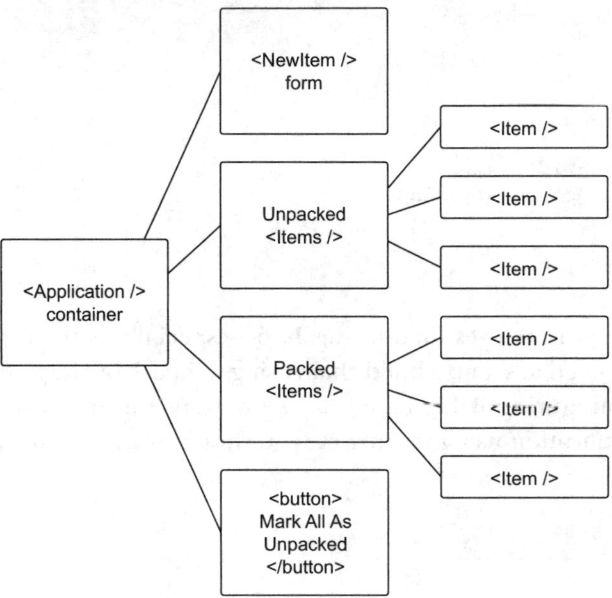

Figure 11.4 Jetsetter is broken into small components as illustrated here.

11.3.1 The Application component

Our pleasant greeting to the world and useless button serve admirably as proof that `electron-compile` processed our JavaScript, but we need to swap it out with something a bit more functional. We haven't built our `NewItem` form, `Items` list, or individual `Item` components yet, but we lay the groundwork now for managing the state of our application and getting the bones in place. By the end of this section, our application will look like figure 11.5.

The first version of our `Application` component was what's known as a stateless functional component. It was a function and, when called, returned a value. It couldn't maintain any UI state. In this chapter, the `Application` component maintains the master list of all the items being tracked in Jetsetter. Like with Clipmaster, we use a simple array in memory to track the list. In chapter 12, we'll replace this array with a persistent data store so that we don't lose our list every time we quit the application.

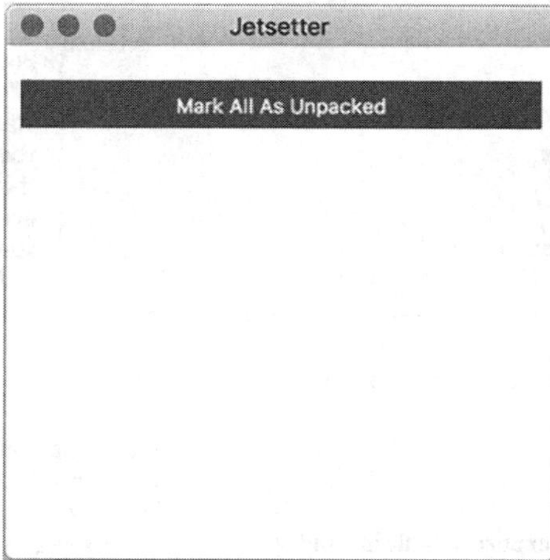

Figure 11.5 The Application component without items

The `Application` component tracks the items in Jetsetter, adds new items to that list, and marks them as either packed or unpacked. We add these features as we need them. Let's start by initializing the component with a list of items and adding placeholder methods for adding and marking the items. We also set up a foundation for the UI as shown in figure 11.1. You'll find a file for the `Application` component in the ./app/components directory.

Listing 11.7 `Application` component foundation: ./app/components/Application.js

```
import React, { Component } from 'react';

class Application extends Component {
  constructor(props) {
    super(props);
    this.state = {
      items: [{ value: 'Pants', id: Date.now(), packed: false }]
    };

    this.addItem = this.addItem.bind(this);
    this.markAsPacked = this.markAsPacked.bind(this);
    this.markAllAsUnpacked = this.markAllAsUnpacked.bind(this);
  }

  addItem(item) {} // To be implemented…

  markAsPacked(item) {} // To be implemented…

  markAllAsUnpacked() {} // To be implemented…
```

- The Application component is a subclass of React's component class.
- In addition to importing React, we import its Component class.
- The constructor() method is called when the component is first initialized.
- When the component is initialized, we set its state to include an array of items with one item in it.
- Each of the actions happens on the event loop, which means that they lose context of this component. Binding the methods to the current instance of the Application component is a common pattern in React.

```
  render() {
    const { items } = this.state;
    const unpackedItems = items.filter(item => !item.packed);
    const packedItems = items.filter(item => item.packed);

    return (
      <div className="Application">
        {/* To be implented: <NewItem /> */}
        {/* To be implented: <Items title="Unpacked Items" /> */}
        {/* To be implented: <Items title="Packed Items" /> */}
        <button
          className="full-width" onClick={this.markAllAsUnpacked}
        >
          Mark All As Unpacked
        </button>
      </div>
    );
  }
}

export default Application;
```

Pulls the list of items off the component's state. Alternatively, you could use this.state.items everywhere that you see items in the code that follows.

Filters the list to find all the items that are not marked as packed.

Filters the list to find all the items that are marked as packed.

React components use className, instead of class, because class is a reserved word in JavaScript.

export default is similar to module.exports in CommonJS modules, which is what we used in previous chapters.

Components that inherit from React's `Component` class can have methods and hold onto state. In the previous listing, we initialize the state to have an array of items. For now, we put an important article of clothing in there. In chapter 12, we'll fetch this item from persistent storage when the application launches. We also follow a common React pattern of binding the methods to the new instance when it's initialized. This ensures that the methods are bound to the correct `this` when they are called later. We put in empty placeholders for `addItem()`, `markAsPacked()`, and `markAllAsUnpacked()` for now. We fill these in as we move through the chapter.

When it's time to render the component to the DOM, we separate the complete list of items into smaller lists of packed and unpacked items. We haven't built the rest of the components needed to render the UI, so we include placeholders for now. We are, however, able to place the Mark All as Unpacked button at the bottom of the page. The last thing we need to do is replace that placeholder `Application` component in ./app/renderer.js with the real—if incomplete—thing.

Listing 11.8 Mounting the new `Application` component onto the DOM: ./app/renderer.js

```
import React from 'react';
import { render } from 'react-dom';
import Application from './components/Application';

render(<Application />, document.getElementById('application'));
```

Imports the new Application component.

11.3.2 Displaying the lists of items

An application that tracks your packed and unpacked items isn't much good if it can't display those items to you. In this section, we implement the two lists, as well as the ability to toggle an item between its packed and unpacked states. This capability requires creating components for individual items and for the lists of items. With the ability to mark items as packed or unpacked in place, we also go the extra mile and connect the Mark All as Unpacked button to the list of items. At the end of this section, the application looks like figure 11.6.

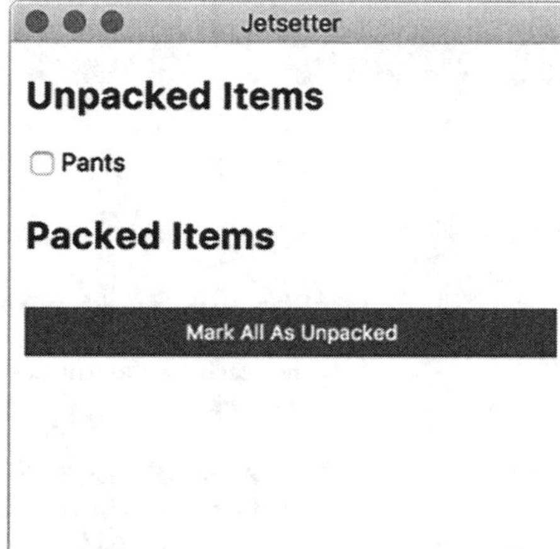

Figure 11.6 The application now includes lists of packed and unpacked items.

INDIVIDUAL ITEMS

The `Application` component is doing the hard work of tracking all of the items loaded into Jetsetter. The individual `Item` just needs to be told what it should display and given a function to be called in the event that a user clicks its check box.

Listing 11.9 Individual `Item` component: ./app/components/Item.js

```
import React from 'react';

const Item = (({ packed, id, value, onCheckOff }) => {
  return (
    <article className="Item">
      <label>
        <input type="checkbox" checked={packed} onChange={onCheckOff} />
        {value}
      </label>
    </article>
  );
});

export default Item;
```

This functional component expects four properties and stores them as local variables inside of the function.

The function passed to the input as the onChange property is called whenever checkbox is clicked.

The individual `Item` component is relatively straightforward. It's a container with a check box and a label. Surrounding the input in the `<label>` tag allows the user to click the label in addition to the check box to check or uncheck the box. React triggers the function passed to `onChange()` whenever the check box is checked or unchecked.

This functionality eventually becomes the Application component's markAsPacked() method.

Having individual items is well and good, but they need a container. In the following listing we create a simple component that accepts a list of items along with what to do if one of them is clicked. It returns a <section> with each item as a child. It also takes a title property to help us differentiate between the packed and unpacked lists.

Listing 11.10 Item list component: ./app/components/Items.js

```
import React from 'react';
import Item from './Item';

const Items = ({ title, items, onCheckOff }) => {
  return (
    <section className="Items">
      <h2>{ title }</h2>
      {items.map(item => (
        <Item
          key={item.id}
          onCheckOff={() => onCheckOff(item)}

          {...item}
        />
      ))}
    </section>
  );
};

export default Items;
```

When working with an array of components, React requires that each component has a unique key.

Passes the specific item that should be checked off to onCheckOff()

The spread operator passes all the item's properties to the component.

The Items component takes the title property for itself and then creates a set of Item components based on the array of items it was provided and passes the onCheckoff() function it was given to each of them with a reference to the specific item. We now have the UI elements we need. It's time to hook them up to the Application component.

The Items component knows how to work with the individual Item components, so we only need to bring the Items component into the Application component. We do need to implement markAsPacked() and markAllAsUnpacked().

Listing 11.11 Item and Items in the Application component: ./app/components/Application.js

```
import React, { Component } from 'react';
import Items from './Items';

class Application extends Component {
  constructor(props) {
    // Omitted for brevity...
  }

  addItem(item) {} // To be implemented...
```

Imports the Items component

```
  markAsPacked(item) {
    const otherItems = this.state.items.filter(
      other => other.id !== item.id
    );
    const updatedItem = { ...item, packed: !item.packed };
    this.setState({ items: [updatedItem, ...otherItems] });
  }

  markAllAsUnpacked() {
    const items = this.state.items.map(item => ({ ...item, packed: false }));
    this.setState({ items });
  }

  render() {
    const { items } = this.state;
    const unpackedItems = items.filter(item => !item.packed);
    const packedItems = items.filter(item => item.packed);

    return (
      <div className="Application">
        <Items
          title="Unpacked Items"
          items={unpackedItems}
          onCheckOff={this.markAsPacked}
        />
        <Items
          title="Packed Items"
          items={packedItems}
          onCheckOff={this.markAsPacked}
        />
        <button
          className="button full-width"
          onClick={this.markAllAsUnpacked}
        >
          Mark All As Unpacked
        </button>
      </div>
    );
  }
}

export default Application;
```

Creates a new array of all the items that are not the one we're looking for

Uses the object rest spread operator to make a clone of the object replacing the packed key with its opposite.

Replaces the items in the component's state with the item and all the other items

Makes a new array of items with copies of the existing items with their packed property set to false.

Replaces the items in state with the new array of items we just made.

Uses the new Items component to display the unpacked items.

Uses the new Items component to display the packed items.

Calls the markAllAsUnpacked() method when the Mark All as Unpacked button is clicked.

We start by bringing in the `Items` component that we created in the previous section. We use it twice in the `render()` method: once for packed items, and once for the unpacked items. We pass each instance its respective list of items along with a title and the `markAsPacked()` method, which will eventually be passed down to the individual components.

The trickier part lies in the `markAsPacked()` and `markAllAsPacked()` methods. Both are modifying and updating the array of items being passed to the two lists. A core tenant of building React actions is that we try not to mutate objects and arrays;

instead, we create new ones. It is easier for React's virtual DOM diffing algorithm to see that it's working with a totally new object, as opposed to a new version of an existing object that has been subtly changed.

In `markAsPacked()`, we start with a list of all of the items we're not working with and put them aside. We then make a copy of the item passed to the method. We keep everything the same but override the `packed` key with its opposite. If it was `true`, now it's `false`; if it was `false`, now it's `true`. We then update the state of the component with a new array containing our new item mixed in with all the items we put aside earlier.

In `markAllAsPacked()`, we create an array of items by mapping over the existing items and replacing their `packed` key with a value of `false`. The Mark All as Unpacked button should set the item back to unpacked, regardless. With these methods in place, you should be able to mark "Pants" as either packed or unpacked. This application benefits from the fact that we hard-coded an item into the initial state of the application, but it's high time we gave users the ability to add their own items to Jetsetter.

11.4 Adding new items

Our next step is to create the `NewItem` component and connect it to the application's state. Unlike `Item` and `Items`, `NewItem` needs to hold on to its own piece of state: the contents of the input field. At the end of this section, the application will look like figure 11.7.

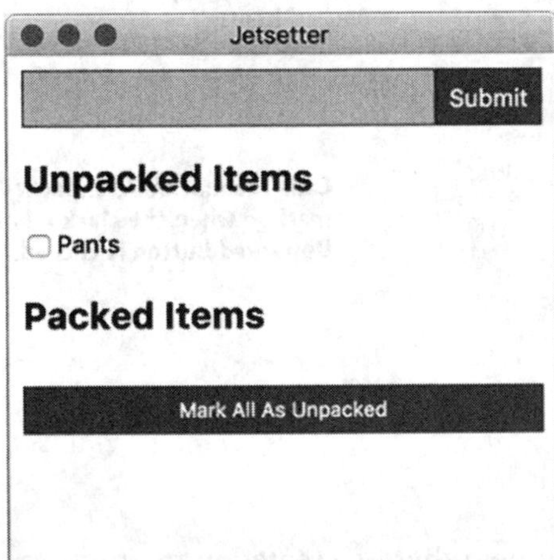

Figure 11.7 The application can now add a new item in addition to "Pants."

`NewItem` is another stateful component. It needs to track the value of the input field to correctly name the new item that it creates when the user submits the form. It updates its internal state to reflect the value whenever the user types into the input field. This change itself is represented in the input field, creating a virtuous cycle.

Listing 11.12 Adding a `NewItem`: ./app/components/NewItem.js

```
import React, { Component } from 'react';

class NewItem extends Component {
  constructor(props) {
    super(props);
    this.state = {
      value: ''
    };

    this.handleChange = this.handleChange.bind(this);
    this.handleSubmit = this.handleSubmit.bind(this);
  }

  handleChange(event) {
    const { value } = event.target;
    this.setState({ value });
  }

  handleSubmit(event) {
    const { onSubmit } = this.props;
    const { value } = this.state;

    event.preventDefault();
    onSubmit({ value, packed: false, id: Date.now() });
    this.setState({ value: '' });
  }

  render() {
    const { value } = this.state;

    return (
      <form className="NewItem" onSubmit={this.handleSubmit}>
        <input
          className="NewItem-input"
          type="text"
          value={value}
          onChange={this.handleChange}
        />
        <input className="NewItem-submit button" type="submit" />
      </form>
    );
  }
}

NewItem.defaultProps = {
  onSubmit: () => {}
};

export default NewItem;
```

Annotations:

- Sets the initial state of the input field as an empty string
- Binds the handleChange() method so that it has a reference to the component when invoked from the event queue
- Binds the handleSubmit() method so that it has a reference to the component when invoked from the event queue
- Updates the state of the component based on the value of the input field.
- event.target is the DOM node that triggered the event. In this case, that is the input field. We pull the value from the input field.
- We pass in a function dictating what to do when the user clicks submit (or presses the return key) from the Application as a prop to this component.
- Pulls the current value of the input field from the component's state.
- Passes an object representing the new item using the current UNIX timestamp as a plausibly unique identifier.
- Resets the value of the input to an empty string to make it easy for the user to enter another item.
- Triggers the handleSubmit() method when the user submits the form.
- Uses the current value in state when the user submits the form.
- Updates the value in state whenever the user makes a change to the input field.
- Sets the default value of onSubmit() to an empty function so that we don't accidentally trigger "undefined is not a function" as an error if it's omitted.

The user typing in the input field triggers the function passed in as its `onChange` prop. We're using the aptly named `handleChange()` method for this purpose. `onChange` passes in a representation of the DOM event to `handleChange()`. `event.target` is the input field's DOM node. We ask for its value as we did with the text area in Fire Sale. With this value, we update the state of the component, which also updates the value of the input as shown in the UI.

In React, components do not typically know about their parents. `NewItem` cannot talk to `Application` directly. Instead, `Application` passes in a function as a prop to `NewItem`. `NewItem` uses this function when the user submits the form. We haven't written this function yet, but—when we do—it simply adds the new item to `Application`'s array of items, which—as of right now—contains only a lonely pair of pants.

When the user submits the form, the function passed in as its `onSubmit` prop is called. Again, we are good at naming things and opted to name this method `handleSubmit()`. On form submission, create an item and pass it in to the method passed in as the `NewItem`'s `onSubmit` prop. The `Application` component will pass one of its methods to `NewItem` as its `onSubmit` prop. `NewItem`, in turn, passes it as the `onSubmit` prop to the form that it creates. Once the form is submitted, we replace the value in state with an empty string—allowing the user to enter another item.

`NewItem` currently lives in a vacuum. It theoretically works, but it needs to be added to the `Application` component before we can effectively use it. Our next step is to add it to the UI and pass it a function that adds it to `Application`'s list of items. We do this here.

Listing 11.13 `NewItem` in the `Application` component: ./app/components/application.js

```
import React, { Component } from 'react';
import NewItem from './NewItem';
import Items from './Items';

class Application extends Component {
  constructor(props) {
      // Omitted for brevity…
  }

  addItem(item) {
    this.setState({ items: [item, ...this.state.items] });
  }

  markAsPacked(item) {
      // Omitted for brevity…
  }

  markAllAsUnpacked() {
      // Omitted for brevity…
  }

  render() {
    const { items } = this.state;
```

addItem() sets the state to a new array consisting of all of the existing items along with the item passed in as an argument.

```
    const unpackedItems = items.filter(item => !item.packed);
    const packedItems = items.filter(item => item.packed);

    return (
      <div className="Application">
        <NewItem onSubmit={this.addItem} />
        <Items
          title="Unpacked Items"
          items={unpackedItems}
          onCheckOff={this.markAsPacked}
        />
        <Items
          title="Packed Items"
          items={packedItems}
          onCheckOff={this.markAsPacked}
        />
        <button
          className="button full-width"
          onClick={this.markAllAsUnpacked}
        >
          Mark All As Unpacked
        </button>
      </div>
    );
  }
}

export default Application;
```

We add the NewItem component to the Application component and pass it the addItem() method as its onSubmit prop.

With the `NewItem` component added to the `Application` component, you should now be able to create additional items, toggle them between the unpacked and packed lists, and move all items to the unpacked list.

11.5 Live reload and hot module reloading

Throughout this book, we've developed muscle memory by pressing Command-R or Control-R to refresh the renderer process after changes on macOS and Windows/Linux, respectively. It can get a bit tedious, however, to switch back and forth between your text editor and your application every time you make a relatively small change.

`electron-compile` can trigger a reload whenever the file is changed on disk. This means that when you save the file in your text editor, it instantly reloads the open renderer processes—allowing you to see your changes immediately. `electron-compile` also supports hot module reloading in React, which takes live reloading one step further by swapping modules that have been updated on the fly without reloading the page itself. In this section, we look at implementing each of these approaches.

11.5.1 Enabling live reload

Until this point, `electron-compile` has *just worked.* We used `electron-compile-prebuilt` in place of `electron` in our package.json, did some minimal—and optional—configuration, and we were off to the races. `electron-compile` can also be required like any other module. The module provides an `enableLiveReload()` method that does what it says on the tin.

Listing 11.14 Enabling live reload: ./app/main.js

```
import { app, BrowserWindow } from 'electron';
import { enableLiveReload } from 'electron-compile';    // Pulls in the enableLiveReload() function from the electron-compile module

enableLiveReload();    // Invokes the function before the application is ready to enable live reloading

let mainWindow;

app.on('ready', () => {
  // Omitted for brevity...
});
```

When we call the `enableLiveReload()` function before the application has started, `electron-compile` sets up an IPC connection that listens for filesystem changes and sends a message to the renderer process, requesting that it reload whenever it detects a change.

11.5.2 Setting up hot module reloading

`enableLiveReload()` is framework-agnostic and works even in simple applications like Fire Sale and Clipmaster 9000. `enableLiveReload()` also supports hot module reloading with React applications. The first step is to let `enableLiveReload()` know that we prefer it to use hot module reloading as an alternative to refreshing the entire page.

Listing 11.15 Setting up hot module reloading: ./app/main.js

```
import { app, BrowserWindow } from 'electron';
import { enableLiveReload } from 'electron-compile';

enableLiveReload({ strategy: 'react-hmr' });    // Passes enableLiveReload() an object that tells it to use hot module reloading

let mainWindow;

app.on('ready', () => {
  // Omitted for brevity...
});
```

With `enableLiveReload()` configured to use hot module reloading, it no longer refreshes the page when you change a file. But hot module reloading doesn't work, either. Bummer. We're effectively back at square one. We have a little more work to do.

If you're using TypeScript, you can skip this next step. But we haven't been using TypeScript in this chapter, so it's on us to let Babel know that we are using hot module reloading. We add it to the list of plugins in .compilerc. We won't add it as a plugin in production, because we'll likely not be changing files often on our users' machines.

Listing 11.16 Adding Babel support for hot module reloading: ./.compilerc

```
{
  "env": {
    "development": {
      "application/javascript": {
        // Omitted for brevity...
        "plugins": [
          "react-hot-loader/babel",          <- Adds react-hot-loader/babel
          // Additional plugins here...         to the list of Babel plugins
        ],
        "sourceMaps": "inline"
      },
      "text/jade": {
        "pretty": true
      }
    },
    "production": {
      // Omitted for brevity...
    }
}
```

We're not out of the woods yet—there is one other change that we need to make: our application needs to be wrapped in a container component that listens for the changes and passes those changes to our `Application` component. The good news is that we don't have to write this component ourselves; we only have to require it from the `react-hot-loader` module.

Listing 11.17 Using `AppContainer` to subscribe to updates: ./app/renderer.js

```
import React from 'react';
import { render } from 'react-dom';
import { AppContainer } from 'react-hot-loader';

const renderApplication = () => {     <- Wraps our initial render method in a function that we can call repeatedly
  const { default: Application } = require('./components/Application');     <- Requires a fresh version of the Application, which requires all the other modules in our application when rendering
  render(
    <AppContainer>
      <Application />
    </AppContainer>,
    document.getElementById('application')
  );
};

renderApplication();     <- Renders the application as we would normally when the application starts for the first time

if (module.hot) { module.hot.accept(renderApplication); }     <- If hot module reloading is enabled, renders the application again whenever we receive a message that the components have changed.
```

We have a few moving pieces. In our original implementation, we pull in the `Application` component and render it when the renderer process starts. This method is standard practice when building React applications and not specific to the fact that we're doing all of this inside of Electron. But if we are going to take advantage of hot module reloading, we need to make some adjustments. We need to move the act of rendering the application into a function that we can call repeatedly. We name this function `renderApplication()` and call it when the renderer process is first evaluated. This function mimics the existing functionality before we implemented the changes described earlier.

When rendering the application, we need a fresh version of the `Application` component because it may have changed. As of this writing, ECMAScript's module imports can be used only at the top level, so we have to fall back on the CommonJS `require()` function to pull in the `Application` component. We wrap `Application` in `react-hot-loader`'s `AppContainer` component, which lets it know about changes to the filesystem, and mounts it to the same DOM node that we did at the beginning of the chapter.

With all of this in place, hot module reloading should be enabled and you can see the changes to your modules in real time. If the mix of the CommonJS `require()` and ECMAScript `import` statements make you feel weird inside, you do have some options. An upcoming change to the specification allows for a second version of `import()` that can asynchronously fetch modules using a promise-based API. Listing 11.19 shows how to implement this. We used `export default` in ./components/Application.js, so we need to destructure the `default` property of the object passed to the promise and name it `Application`.

Listing 11.18 Using `import()` to asynchronously load dependencies: ./app/renderer.js

```
const renderApplication = () => {
  import('./components/Application').then(
    ({ default: Application }) => {
      render(
        <AppContainer>
          <Application />
        </AppContainer>,
        document.getElementById('application'),
      );
    }
  );
};
```

import() returns a promise with the contents of the module.

Both Node and Chromium support the upcoming `async/await` syntax that allows for a more traditional, synchronous syntax when using promised-based APIs. You can use this without Babel and `electron-compile`, because it is natively supported by Node and the browser.

Listing 11.19 Using `async/await` to asynchronously load dependencies: ./app/renderer.js

```
const renderApplication = async () => {
  const { default: Application } = await import('./components/Application');
  render(
    <AppContainer>
      <Application />
    </AppContainer>,
    document.getElementById('application')
  );
};
```

Both refactors are completely optional and exist mostly to illustrate the fact that Electron supports cutting-edge syntax out of the box and that `electron-compile` makes it easy to use Babel to add support for future features of the JavaScript language.

Summary

- `electron-compile` allows developers to use an assortment of languages that compile to HTML, JavaScript, and CSS such as Jade, TypeScript, CoffeeScript, Sass, and Less.
- `electron-prebuilt-compile` is a version of the Electron binary with `electron-compile` installed.
- Many languages can be used without configuration, but `electron-compile` also supports a .compilerc file that allows developers to configure each language.
- `electron-compile` can be configured to compile JSX using Babel.
- `electron-compile` can automatically detect which transpiler to use based on the file extension.
- Electron applications using `electron-compile` can use live reloading to automatically refresh all open browser windows.
- `electron-compile`'s live reloading feature also supports hot module reloading in React applications

12 Persisting user data and using native Node.js modules

This chapter covers

- Using Node.js modules built with C++ in your main and renderer processes
- Getting the correct versions of your dependencies for Electron's version of Node
- Using SQLite and IndexedDB databases to persist data
- Storing user-specific application data in the operating system's designated location

In chapter 11, we built a small application to track items we needed to pack between trips. By the end of the chapter, we got the UI working, but the application still had a fatal flaw: it lost all of its data whenever the page refreshed. That's a bit of a deal killer for an application that is allegedly supposed to help you remember things. Fire Sale was working with files stored on disk, so it wasn't an issue, but Clipmaster and Clipmaster 9000 had this problem as well. All clippings were lost whenever a user quit the application, or we refreshed the page in development.

In this chapter, we solve this problem once and for all. Data is persisted between page loads and remains available even if the user quits the application and restarts their computer. For good measure, we solve this problem two ways: we create a local SQLite database and a browser-based IndexedDB storage. Along the way, we also cover some interesting implementation details: Where do we store data on a per-user basis? How do we build compiled modules for Electron's version of Node if it differs from the version installed on our computers? How does working with an SQL database like SQLite differ from a NoSQL database like IndexedDB?

Removing items wasn't particularly important in chapter 11 when we couldn't hold on to data, but it certainly is now. By the end of this chapter, we'll have an application that looks suspiciously similar to what we had at the beginning but with a few major differences: The data is persisted to disk and users can remove items from the list and remove all items that haven't been packed.

12.1 Storing data in an SQLite database

The first approach that we take is storing our data in an SQLite database. This approach is commonly used by traditional native applications, particularly on macOS and iOS. SQLite is a good choice because the database is stored in a file and doesn't require the user to have MySQL or PostgreSQL installed on their system.

If you're a recovering database administrator, I'll give you fair warning: I'm not going to optimize every query, and some techniques might be a little wasteful. I'm optimizing for clarity of the code over performance. We know that—in this case—we're working with a very small data set.

If you're coming from a frontend, web development background, you may not have thought to use an SQLite database in your application. You've typically sent HTTP requests to a server or used a browser-based solution like IndexedDB, WebSQL, or LocalStorage. The reason that SQLite databases aren't used frequently in traditional web applications is because they can't be. We don't have access to the filesystem from the browser. Also, we can't use what I'm going to refer to as native modules for the duration of this chapter.

What is a *native module*? Many libraries—like Lodash or Moment.js—are written purely in JavaScript. Both the browser and Node can execute JavaScript, so these modules can be used in either context. Some libraries—like jQuery—are tightly coupled with the DOM and therefore work only in the browser context. Native modules typically wrap a C or C++ library in JavaScript. The C or C++ component of the library must be compiled for the operating system in which the library will be used. SQLite—and most other database drivers—have libraries written in C or C++. The `sqlite3` modules on npm wrap this library in JavaScript bindings so that we can use it from within our Node applications. Not only does the browser not have access to the filesystem, it also can't run platform-specific C and C++ code. Some projects like Emscripten compile C code to run on the JavaScript virtual machine, but that is far beyond the scope of this book.

As we've discussed throughout the book, Electron applications combine a Chromium browser runtime with a Node runtime, so we can use native modules in our applications. We start by setting up an SQLite database, creating a table for our items, and connecting the UI to read from and write to the database—directly from the renderer process.

12.1.1 Using the right versions with electron-rebuild

When we install a native module in Node, it is compiled against the current version of the V8 engine used by Node. Upgrading versions of Node typically results in having to recompile all the native modules used by the application. Electron ships with its own Node runtime, which may or may not be the same version as the Node running on your computer when you run `npm install` or `yarn install`. This mismatch can cause problems when you attempt to use native modules with an Electron application.

Lucky for us, the community has been kind enough to provide us with a solution called `electron-rebuild`, which rebuilds native modules against the version of Node used by Electron as opposed to the version installed on the filesystem. You can install `electron-rebuild` via npm using `npm install electron-rebuild --save-dev`. It can then be triggered by using `$(npm bin)/electron-rebuild` on macOS or `.\node_modules\.bin\electron-rebuild.cmd` on Windows.

I prefer not to be burdened by having to remember to call it every time I install a dependency. Instead, I recommend using a `postinstall` hook in your package.json, which will run after every install.

Listing 12.1 Adding a `postinstall` hook: /package.json

```
{
  "name": "jetsetter",
  "version": "1.0.0",
  "description": "An application for keeping track of the things you need
➥ to pack.",
  "main": "app/main.js",
  "scripts": {
    "start": "electron .",
    "test": "echo \"Error: no test specified\" && exit 1",
    "postinstall": "electron-rebuild"
  },
  // Additional configuration omitted for brevity.
}
```

The postinstall script is called after each run of npm install.

By default, npm checks for a pre– or postscript before running any script. When you run `npm test`, it first tries to run `pretest`, then `test`, followed by `posttest`. I've found this trick incredibly helpful across a wide variety of projects over the years.

12.1.2 Setting up SQLite and Knex.js

In this chapter, we're using a helpful library called Knex.js to make working with SQL in Node a bit easier. It acts as our interface between our application code and the underlying SQLite queries. This is set up for you in the `chapter-12-beginning` branch on the Jetsetter repository. If you want to build off your implementation from chapter 11, you can install these dependencies using `npm install sqlite3 knex`.

Before we can integrate SQLite into our application, we have to do some initial setup. As I mentioned earlier, SQLite stores data in a file so we need to figure out where we're going to store this file. We start with a simple but flawed solution for now. Later in the chapter, I'll revisit the best place to store user data, but for now let's focus on getting our application working.

Listing 12.2 Setting up an SQLite database: ./app/database.js

```
import 'sqlite3';                       <- Pulls in the SQLite library
import knex from 'knex';

const database = knex({                 Tells Knex.js that we're intending
  client: 'sqlite3',                 <- to use it with an SQLite database
  connection: {
    filename: './db.sqlite'          <- Specifies the location where the
  },                                    SQLite database should be created
  useNullAsDefault: true             <- Configures Knex.js to use NULL whenever a
});                                     value for a particular column isn't provided.

export default database;             <- Exports the configured database.
```

We need to include the `sqlite3` library so it's loaded into the application when Knex goes looking for it, as well as let Knex know that we'll be using SQLite as our database for this application.

Calling this property `connection` is a bit of a misnomer here. If we were connecting to a MySQL server, this name would be fine, but as I mentioned, SQLite uses a file stored on disk, so we put the name of the location where we want to store the file here. I've called it db.sqlite for now. We revisit this later.

What's with that `useNullAsDefault` option? Knex.js isn't a library specifically for SQLite. Rather, it works with PostgreSQL, MySQL, MSSQL, and Oracle databases. Many of these support default values for columns in the database. SQLite doesn't, and Knex displays a warning if we don't turn on this option, which causes Knex.js to opt for `NULL` instead of attempting to use a default value.

This isn't enough to get us all the way there. We created the database, but we still haven't configured it with a table to store our items. When the application starts, we check if there's a table for storing items. If there isn't, then we create the table.

Listing 12.3 Creating a table to store items: ./app/database.js

```
import 'sqlite3';

const database = require('knex')(//…);

database.schema.hasTable('items').then(exists => {     <- Checks if the database already has an items table
  if (!exists) {                                        <- Moves forward only if the items table doesn't exist
    return database.schema.createTable('items', t => {  <- Creates the items table
      t.increments('id').primary();                     <- Creates an id column to serve as the primary key and auto-increments it
      t.string('value', 100);                           <- Sets the value column to a string with a width of 100 characters
```

```
      t.boolean('packed');        <-- Sets the packed
    });                               column to store a
  }                                   Boolean type
});

export default database;
```

Knex.js uses a promise-based API. The check for the table returns a promise that is fulfilled with a Boolean based on whether it does in fact exist. All of our queries in the next section are based on promises. The data in Jetsetter is deliberately simple, and our schema reflects that. SQLite creates a unique ID and auto-increments the ID on each new item added to the database. We also store the item's name as a string in the value column and a Boolean that represents whether the item has been packed.

12.1.3 Hooking the database into React

In a traditional web application, if we want to put something into an SQLite database, we'd likely have to send AJAX requests to a server, which would interact with the database. This means that we'd probably also implement some kind of authentication as well as authorization to make sure that users couldn't read or edit another user's data. In an Electron application, we can talk directly to the database from our client code.

At the top level, we pull in the configured database we just created and pass it to the `Application` component as a prop—React-speak for "property"—which has access to the database inside of its methods.

Listing 12.4 Passing the database into the application component: ./app/renderer.js

```
import React from 'react';
import { render } from 'react-dom';
import { AppContainer } from 'react-hot-loader';
import database from './database';      <-- Requires the database we created in ./app/database.js.

const renderApplication = async () => {
  const { default: Application } = await import('./components/Application');
  render(
    <AppContainer>
      <Application database={database} />      <-- Passes it into the Application as a property.
    </AppContainer>,
    document.getElementById('application')
  );
};

renderApplication();

if (module.hot) { module.hot.accept(renderApplication); }
```

Now comes the fun part. Previously, we stored the state of the application in the `Application` component. Every time the application is reloaded, that state is replaced. Every time the user quits the application, the state is gone for good. In the next few examples, we replace this behavior with reading from and writing to the database.

This process contains a few pieces. When the `Application` component starts for the first time, it reads all of the items from the database and loads them into its internal state. It also does this whenever it has reason to believe that the data has changed, which allows us to have one source of truth: the database. Depending on your needs, you may decide you want to approach your data storage strategy differently, but this method works for us in Jetsetter.

When a user creates a new item, we add it to the database. When they check off an item, we update it in the database by flipping the "packed" Boolean to its opposite. When the user selects Mark All as Unpacked, we—unsurprisingly—select all of the items for the database and set their "packed" property to `false`.

As I mentioned at the beginning of the chapter, we're adding the ability to remove an item from the database. This capability wasn't important back when we lost everything on every reload, but it's necessary now. In addition, we add a button to remove all of the unpacked items from the database.

12.1.4 Fetching all of the items from the database

We continue using `this.state` to hold a list of the items most recently fetched from the database. But instead of hard-coding a pair of pants into this list, we add a method that fetches all of the items from the database and then updates this list. We also call this method whenever the component starts for the first time.

Listing 12.5 Fetching items from the database: ./app/components/Application.js

```
class Application extends Component {
  constructor(props) {
    super(props);

    this.state = {
      items: []          <- Sets the initial state of the component to an empty array
    };

    this.fetchItems = this.fetchItems.bind(this);   <- Binds the fetching function so that it has access to the correct context
    this.addItem = this.addItem.bind(this);
    this.markAsPacked = this.markAsPacked.bind(this);
    this.markAllAsUnpacked = this.markAllAsUnpacked.bind(this);
  }

  componentDidMount() {
    this.fetchItems();     <- Fetches the items from the database as soon as the component starts
  }

  fetchItems() {          <- Queries the database for a list of items
    this.props
      .database('items')
      .select()
      .then(items => this.setState({ items }))   <- Updates the array of items stored in state
      .catch(console.error);
  }
```

```
  addItem(item) { … }
  markAsPacked(item) { … }
  markAllAsUnpacked() { … }

  render() { … }
}

export default Application;
```

We don't want to get any errors about trying to map or iterate over an undefined value, so we set the component's initial state to an empty array. In the previous example, we take the database instance that was passed into the `Application` component as a property and ask for its items table, which we set up earlier. The `.select()` method selects all of the rows from that table—which are all of the items in our case—and returns a promise. If everything is successful, we can use `.then()` to take the results from the `.select()` method and work with those rows.

We start with the list of items being an empty array. `this.fetchItems()` queries the database and returns a promise. When this promise resolves, we swap out items being stored in the component's state with the items we received from the database. React is smart enough to figure out what this means in terms of changing the UI on our behalf. We don't need to worry about that.

Because `this.fetchItems()` does its work asynchronously, we need to bind it to the context of the component as we did with `this.addItem()`, `this.markAsPacked()`, and `this.markAllAsPacked()`. Finally, we need to call `this.fetchItems()` to load the initial state. We do this once the component has started, which immediately updates the state of the component.

12.1.5 Adding items to the database

The functionality we implemented is impressive. We're connecting directly to the database from the UI. This isn't something we've been able to do in traditional web applications. But it doesn't seem to feel that impressive just yet, because there isn't anything in the database to show. It's only an empty list at the moment. We could put mock data in there, but let's cut to the chase and implement the ability to add new items to the database.

If you recall from chapter 11, we passed a function from the `Application` component to the `NewItem` component. When a user clicks the Submit button, the `NewItem` component took the contents of its input field and passed it into the function provided by the `Application` component, which—in turn—pushed it onto the end of the array of items stored in state.

We're going to leave much of this functionality in place with one notable exception: instead of pushing the item onto the end of the array stored in the `Application` component's state, we `insert` it into the database and then trigger `this.fetchItems()` to reload all of the items now in the database. We start by rewriting `this.addItem()` in the `Application` component to use the database instead of an in-memory array.

Listing 12.6 Implementing the ability to add items to the database: ./app/components/Application.js

```
class Application extends Component {
  constructor(props) { … }
  componentDidMount() { … }
  fetchItems() { … }

  addItem(item) {
    this.props
      .database('items')
      .insert(item)
      .then(this.fetchItems);
  }

  markAsPacked(item) { … }
  markAllAsUnpacked() { … }

  render() { … }
}

export default Application;
```

- `.insert(item)`: Inserts the item into the database.
- `.then(this.fetchItems)`: When inserting the item into the database has completed, refetches all of the items.

Accessing the items table in the database is the same as it is for fetching all of the items. The main difference is that we use the `insert()` method to add the new item from the `NewItem` component to the database. When that has successfully completed, we call `this.fetchItems()`, which gets the most up-to-date list of items and subsequently updates the state of the UI.

We can add items to the database and see them in the UI, but we have a subtle problem. React is particular about having unique keys for every item. We engaged in a less-than-optimal hack by using the current date as an integer for the unique key. This worked, but I didn't feel good about it at the time, and I certainly don't feel good about it now, considering we have a database that tracks and auto-increments unique IDs. Let's remove our trick for manually creating unique IDs.

Listing 12.7 Letting the database handle incrementing the ID: ./app/components/NewItem.js

```
class NewItem extends Component {
  constructor(props) { … }
  handleChange(event) { … }

  handleSubmit(event) {
    const { onSubmit } = this.props;
    const { value } = this.state;

    event.preventDefault();
    onSubmit({ value, packed: false });
    this.setState({ value: '' });
  }
```

- `onSubmit({ value, packed: false });`: Removes the property that sets an ID on our new item

```
  render() { … }
}
```

It might be difficult at first to notice the change, but we just engaged in one of my favorite activities as a software engineer: deleting code. Previously, we passed in three properties: `value`, `packed`, and `id`. By omitting our own ID, SQLite creates one on our behalf, thus eliminating our need to rely on weird tricks involving the time-space continuum.

12.1.6 Updating items in the database

Most applications that work with data implement the four basic CRUD operations: create, read, update, and delete. We're able to read all of the items from the database, and we just implemented the ability to create new items. We're halfway there. Our next step is to be able to update existing items.

The UI of our application provides two ways to update the state of an item in the database: Users can check or uncheck the check box input associated with the item. Users can click the Mark All as Unpacked button to manipulate all of the items in the database. We need two, slightly different approaches for each case.

Let's start with the case where we want to update a single item in the database. To accomplish this, we need to perform two operations: find the particular item we want to update and then update it.

Listing 12.8 Marking items as packed: ./app/components/Application.js

```
class Application extends Component {
  constructor(props) { // … }
  componentDidMount() { // … }
  fetchItems() { // … }
  addItem(item) { // … }

  markAsPacked(item) {
    this.props
      .database('items')
      .where('id', '=', item.id)        // Finds the item with the correct ID
      .update({
        packed: !item.packed            // Updates the packed column of the item to the opposite of its current state
      })
      .then(this.fetchItems)
      .catch(console.error);
  }

  markAllAsUnpacked() { // … }

  render() { // … }
}

export default Application;
```

We find all of the items where the value in the `id` column matches the ID of the item in the UI that was just clicked. Hint: Only one of these exists. We then use the update() method to update the packed column to the opposite of whatever the item is in the UI. If this action is successful, we get all of the items—including our newly updated item—and refresh the UI. If something goes wrong, we log that error to the console for debugging purposes. A more robust application would either implement a fallback here or—at the very least—display some kind of notification alerting the user to the fact that their change couldn't be completed successfully.

We can now change the status of one item, but what about all of them? The answer lies somewhere between the implementation of this.fetchItems() and this.markAsPacked(). With this.markAsPacked(), we found the item with an ID that matched the one we're looking for and then updated it. With this.fetchItems(), we used select() to get all of the items. To implement this.markAllAsPacked(), we get all of the items in the entire set.

Listing 12.9 Marking all items as packed: ./app/components/Application.js

```
class Application extends Component {
  constructor(props) { // … }
  componentDidMount() { // … }
  fetchItems() { // … }
  addItem(item) { // … }
  markAsPacked(item) { // … }

  markAllAsUnpacked() {
    this.props
      .database('items')
      .select()                  <-- Selects all of the items from the database
      .update({
        packed: false            <-- Updates all of the items by setting their packed column to false.
      })
      .then(this.fetchItems)
      .catch(console.error);
  }

  render() { // … }
}

export default Application;
```

As I mentioned before, this implementation roughly combines two of our previous approaches. Selecting all of the items from the database allows you to make changes in bulk using SQL. This case is also true for the .where() method that we used when updating a single item. It just happened to be that when you query based on a unique identifier, you—hopefully—end up with only one record. this.markAllAsPacked() could be changed to use .where() to find all of the items where packed was set to true. I leave this as an exercise to the reader because I'm going to discuss it in the next section.

12.1.7 Deleting items

When our application lost all of its data on every reload, we didn't have a lot of users clamoring for the ability to remove items. But now we're in a place where we've implemented persistent storage. Maybe you've decided that you don't need to travel with your selfie stick anymore, and you'd like to remove it from the list.

We now implement two features: the ability to remove an individual item, and the ability to remove all items that weren't packed, which might include our selfie stick, Furby, and ugly sweater. We need UI elements for this as well, but let's start with the database piece of this.

Listing 12.10 Deleting items: ./app/components/Application.js

```
class Application extends Component {
  constructor(props) {
    super(props);

    // Omitted for brevity...

    this.deleteItem = this.deleteItem.bind(this);
    this.deleteUnpackedItems = this.deleteUnpackedItems.bind(this);

  }

  componentDidMount() { ... }
  fetchItems() { ... }
  addItem(item) { ... }
  markAsPacked(item) { ... }
  markAllAsUnpacked() { ... }

  deleteItem(item) {
    this.props
      .database('items')
      .where('id', item.id)
      .delete()
      .then(this.fetchItems)
      .catch(console.error);
  }

  deleteUnpackedItems() {
    this.props
      .database('items')
      .where('packed', false)
      .delete()
      .then(this.fetchItems)
      .catch(console.error);
  }

  render() { ... }
}

export default Application;
```

Annotations:
- Binds the context for the this.deleteItem() method
- Binds the context for the this.deleteUnpackedItems() method
- Finds the item that matches the ID of the item selected from the UI
- Uses the delete() method to remove the item from the database
- Finds all of the items where the packed property is set to false

Careful readers can see I used a slightly different syntax here than `this.markAsPacked()`. When you're trying to match based on equality, you can use this shorthand where you provide the name of the column and the value you're trying to match. In the previous example, we provided an operator. This method is powerful because we could filter using more sophisticated logic. In `this.deleteUnpackedItems()`, we are using the `where()` method to find all of the items where the `packed` property is set to `false`.

This is all well and good, but it's somewhat difficult to know if they work because we don't have any UI to trigger these methods. This is suspiciously similar to how we set the check boxes to toggle items between their packed and unpacked states, but that was an entire chapter ago. Let's review the process.

We pass the `this.deleteItem()` method to each of the lists. Each list, in turn, passes this method to the items on the list. We add a check box **X** button to each item. When a user clicks the **X** button, we pass a reference to the specific item to `this.deleteItem()` that was passed down from the `Application` component. These additions give us everything we need to trigger the method we implemented moments ago. We also add a Remove Unpacked Items button beneath the Mark All as Unpacked button. This button is a lot simpler as it doesn't need to pass that method along.

Listing 12.11 Passing in delete methods: ./app/components/Application.js

```
class Application extends Component {
  constructor(props) { … }

componentDidMount() { … }
  fetchItems() { … }
  addItem(item) { … }
  markAsPacked(item) { … }
  markAllAsUnpacked() { … }
  deleteItem(item) { … }
  deleteUnpackedItems() { … }

  render() {
    const { items } = this.state;
    const unpackedItems = items.filter(item => !item.packed);
    const packedItems = items.filter(item => item.packed);

    return (
      <div className="Application">
        <NewItem onSubmit={this.addItem} />
        <Items
          title="Unpacked Items"
          items={unpackedItems}
          onCheckOff={this.markAsPacked}
          onDelete={this.deleteItem}        <- Passes this.deleteItem() to the Unpacked Items
        />
        <Items
          title="Packed Items"
          items={packedItems}
```

```
          onCheckOff={this.markAsPacked}
          onDelete={this.deleteItem}        <-- Passes this.deleteItem() to the Packed Items
        />
        <button
          className="button full-width"
          onClick={this.markAllAsUnpacked}>
          Mark All As Unpacked
        </button>
        <button
          className="button full-width secondary"
          onClick={this.deleteUnpackedItems}>   <-- Adds a button to trigger this.deleteUnpackedItems().
          Remove Unpacked Items
        </button>
      </div>
    );
  }
}

export default Application;
```

The Remove Unpacked Items button should be fully functional at this point. But we still need to keep passing `this.deleteItem()` along. The next step is to receive it as the `onDelete` property in the `Items` component, which powers the Packed Items and Unpacked Items, and then pass it down to each individual item with a reference to the specific item.

Listing 12.12 The `Items` component: ./app/components/Items.js

```
const Items = ({ title, items, onCheckOff, onDelete }) => {
  return (
    <section className="Items">
      <h2>{ title }</h2>
      {items.map(item => (
        <Item
          key={item.id}
          onCheckOff={() => onCheckOff(item)}
          onDelete={() => onDelete(item)}
          {...item}
        />
      ))}
    </section>
  );
};

export default Items;
```

There isn't a lot that's new here. I included it for the sake of completeness. We're almost there, and the next step is to add the button to the individual item. This button should have a click event that triggers the `this.deleteItem()` method that was passed in from the `Application` component as the `onDelete()` command.

Listing 12.13 The `Item` component: ./app/component/Item.js

```
const Item = (({ packed, id, value, onCheckOff, onDelete }) => {
  return (
    <article className="Item">
      <label>
        <input type="checkbox" checked={packed} onChange={onCheckOff} />
        {value}
      </label>
      <button className="delete" onClick={onDelete}>?</button>
    </article>
  );
});
```

Pulls in the onDelete() property using object destructuring

Adds the button and set its click event handler to the onDelete() function passed in from the parent

With this last piece, the delete functionality is now in place. We have implemented the ability to create, read, update, and delete items from the database. If the user quits Jetsetter, restarts their computer, and then restarts the application, their items will be in the same state as when they left them. Maybe.

12.1.8 Storing the database in the right place

For the sake of expediency, I had you place the application in the root of the project directory. But this isn't normally where user-specific data goes. As it stands, this database is shared by all users on a given computer, which is certainly confusing.

On one hand, operating systems have solved this problem for us. Users have designated places where their particular data should be stored. But, each operating system solves this problem in a slightly different way. Luckily, we aren't concerned about this because Electron protects us. The Electron `app` module exposes a method called `getPath()`, which figures out the operating system–specific path for a common location. We're going to look for the userData path, but you can see a full list of the paths available at (https://electron.atom.io/docs/api/app/ #appgetpathname).

Listing 12.14 Storing the database in the appropriate location: ./app/database.js

```
import * as path from 'path';
import { app } from 'electron';

const database = knex({
  client: 'sqlite3',
  connection: {
    filename: path.join(
      app.getPath('userData'),
      'jetsetter-items.sqlite'
    )
  },
  useNullAsDefault: true
});
```

Uses Electron's built-in API for finding the correct path for user data depending on the operating system

Gives the database a unique name in development

I tend to give files stored outside of the project unique names to avoid the chance of colliding with another project on my machine. Before branding, all Electron applications are called "Electron." If I give things a unique name, it won't matter much in the event they happen to end up in the same folder under the hood.

12.2 IndexedDB

You can store data in an Electron application in many ways. We discussed SQLite earlier, but you could just as easily use a NoSQL database such as LevelDB. You could even just use a JSON file that you write to and read from.

If managing files and recompiling dependencies seems like a bit much for your application, you can opt for browser-based storage. In chapter 2, we used `localStorage` to track our bookmarks. `localStorage` is great, but it has some limitations: everything must be stored as a large JSON object of strings. We must parse and resave the object every time we want to read or write to `localStorage`.

Before we start using IndexedDB, we should cover some terminology. SQL databases contain tables of rows and columns. They're a lot like incredibly powerful, interconnected spreadsheets. NoSQL databases are typically key-value stores—much like a giant JavaScript object. When working with IndexedDB, you create stores of data, which contain a series of keys. Each key points to an object. IndexedDB differs from SQLite in that keys and values can be any valid JavaScript type—including objects, arrays, maps, and sets.

All interactions with IndexedDB are asynchronous, which makes sense. Natively, however, IndexedDB uses events to handle asynchrony, which can be confusing to read and understand. Luckily, Jake Archibald—a developer advocate at Google—has done the yeoman's work of wrapping the event-based API with a promise-based API called `idb`. The abstraction is lightweight and doesn't hide any of the inner workings of IndexedDB. It's what I personally recommend, and after you're comfortable with a promise-based API, it's easier to wrap your head around than the event-based one. You normally don't need a library to use IndexedDB, but you do need to import `idb` if you'd like to use the promise-based API.

12.2.1 Creating a store with IndexedDB

In this example, we start by opening the jetsetter database. The name of this database is completely arbitrary. You could name it eggplant-parmigiana, if that is more appealing to you. We also passed the number 1, which represents the version of our database. Version 1 is a good place to start. (There's no schema like SQLite!)

Listing 12.15 Setting up a store in IndexedDB: ./app/database.js

```
import idb from 'idb';

const database = idb.open('jetsetter', 1, upgradeDb => {      ◁ Opens up version 1 of the jetsetter database
  upgradeDb.createObjectStore('items', {                      ◁ Creates a store for the items in the application
```

```
    keyPath: 'id',
    autoIncrement: true
  });
});
```

We'll use the id property of the objects to serve as the key.

Tells IndexedDB to take care of autoincrementing the id key on our behalf

Versioning is important in that in web applications, each user stores their IndexedDB locally in their browser. If you change the way your code works, it could corrupt the user's data if they are using an old version of the database.

Having a version number allows you to bump up that number whenever you make a change to how your database works. In that event, you'd be able to migrate the data to be compatible with the changes you've made before any other application code accesses the database. We stick with one version of the database in this chapter because our data is very simple.

Typically, you have one database. This is similar to the fact that most smaller and medium-sized, server-side web applications have just one database that they work with in a given environment (e.g., production). But you may have many stores. Think of stores like tables in an SQL database. In this application, we have only one store for items, but you could have a store for people, locations, or any other model in your application.

We created a store called items, which is a reasonable name for a place where we are going to store all of our items. We also passed two options: we set the `keyPath` to `id` and `autoIncrement` to `true`. What does this mean? It means that if we pass in an item with an `id` property, it uses that property as the key. If we don't, then it adds one to the object and sets it as the key, incrementing the number each time so that the key is unique.

12.2.2 Getting data from IndexedDB

We cheated a bit when we implemented SQLite by using Knex.js to eliminate a lot of the tedium. `idb` is an abstraction over IndexedDB, but it's more lightweight than Knex.js. This means we have to do a bit more of the manual labor ourselves. There are libraries like localForage (https://github.com/localForage/localForage) that provide higher-level abstractions over IndexedDB, but let's stick with `idb` and create our own abstraction.

Here is the approach we take: in ./app/database.js, we create an object with methods to get all of the items from IndexedDB, create new items, update existing items, and delete items. We then use these methods in the `Application` component, replacing the calls to SQLite as we go. Let's start by writing a method to get all of the items from the database.

Listing 12.16 Getting all of the items from IndexedDB: ./app/database.js

```
export default {
  getAll() {
    return database.then(db => {
      return db.transaction('items')
               .objectStore('items')
               .getAll();
    });
  },
```

Accesses the database

Starts a transaction and declares that you'll be working with the items store.

Accesses the items store

Gets all of the items from the store

```
  add(item) { },
  update(item) { },
  markAllAsUnpacked() { },
  delete(item) { },
  deleteUnpackedItems() { }
};
```

I began by exporting an object with all of the methods that we need to match the functionality of SQLite. Most of those methods are empty right now, but we fill them in as we go through the chapter. I did, however, implement the `getAll()` method.

We start by accessing the database, similar to what we did with Knex.js and SQLite. Next, we start a transaction. Transactions prevent multiple changes to the database from occurring at the same time. If something blows up in a transaction, all of the changes made in the transaction are reverted. This practice protects data from corruption. All interactions with IndexedDB must be wrapped in a transaction. Once inside our transaction, we access the items store and get all of the items from it.

12.2.3 Writing data to IndexedDB

Getting all of the items from IndexedDB isn't particularly helpful if there aren't any items in the store to begin with. Let's implement the ability to add an item to the database. This procedure is similar to reading from the database with a few important distinctions. When reading from the database, the transaction is complete when we finish reading. Modifying the database is a little more complicated. As a result, we need to be more explicit about when a transaction has completed. We also need to let IndexedDB know that we intend to write to the database. After that, it's a matter of adding the item to the database and then calling the transaction complete.

Listing 12.17 Adding an item to IndexedDB: ./app/database.js

```
export default {
  getAll() { … },
  add(item) {
    return database.then(db => {
      const tx = db.transaction('items', 'readwrite');
      tx.objectStore('items').add(item);
      return tx.complete;
    });
  },
  update(item) { },
  markAllAsUnpacked() { },
  delete(item) { },
  deleteUnpackedItems() { }
};
```

Creates a new read/write transaction with the items store

Accesses the items store, and adds the item to the database

Returns the completed transaction

When we fetched all of the items, we chained the promises together neatly. If this code looks a bit more complicated, don't worry—it's similar. We need to return the transaction promise we created on the first line, so we store it in a variable. Inside of the transaction, we add the item passed as an argument to the items store. If we had other work to do, we could do it here. Finally, we return a promise that resolves when the transaction has been completed.

Listing 12.18 Updating an item in IndexedDB: ./app/database.js

```
export default {
  getAll() { … },
  add(item) { … },
  update(item) {
    return database.then(db => {
      const tx = db.transaction('items', 'readwrite');
      tx.objectStore('items').put(item);
      return tx.complete;
    });
  },
  markAllAsUnpacked() { },
  delete(item) { },
  deleteUnpackedItems() { }
};
```

Updating an item in the database is similar to adding a new item to the database except we use the `put()` method instead of the `add()` method. Updating all of them, however, is a little more involved. First, we need to get all of the items from the database. Then we change the `packed` status of each of them to `false`. Finally, we create a transaction where we update each item in the database.

Listing 12.19 Marking all items as packed: ./app/database.js

```
export default {
  getAll() { … },
  add(item) { … },
  update(item) { … },
  markAllAsUnpacked() {
    return this.getAll()
      .then(items => items.map(item => ({ ...item, packed: false })))
      .then(items => {
        return database.then(db => {
          const tx = db.transaction('items', 'readwrite');
          for (const item of items) {
            tx.objectStore('items').put(item);
          }
          return tx.complete;
        });
      });
  },
  delete(item) { },
  deleteUnpackedItems() { }
};
```

Gets all of the items from the database

Sets the packed status of each item to false

Creates a transaction for updating the items in the database

Iterates over all of the items

Updates the item in the database

Completes the transaction

If a single update fails, the entire transaction fails, and all of the items return to their original state. The advantage of using transactions is that it ensures you can't end up in a state where half of your data has been updated and half remains unchanged. Transactions are an all-or-nothing affair.

Deleting items from the database is virtually the same as updating them. We use the IndexedDB `delete()` method instead of `update()`. If you want to be clever, you could probably provide an abstraction over the shared pieces of these implementations, but my job as your author is to be clear rather than clever.

Listing 12.20 Removing an item from IndexedDB: ./app/database.js

```
export default {
  getAll() { … },
  add(item) { … },
  update(item) { … },
  markAllAsUnpacked() { … },
  delete(item) {
    return database.then(db => {
      const tx = db.transaction('items', 'readwrite');
      tx.objectStore('items').delete(item.id);
      return tx.complete;
    });
  },
  deleteUnpackedItems() { }
};
```

Uses the delete method to remove an item from the database

When we implemented `markAllAsUnpacked()`, we mapped over all of the items, regardless of their status. In implementing `deleteUnpackedItems()`, we need to be more careful. Our job is to delete only those that have their `packed` property set to `false`.

Listing 12.21 Deleting all unpacked items from IndexedDB: ./app/database.js

```
export default {
  getAll() { … },
  add(item) { … },
  update(item) { … },
  markAllAsUnpacked() { … },
  delete(item) { … },
  deleteUnpackedItems() {
    return this.getAll()
      .then(items => items.filter(item => !item.packed))
      .then(items => {
        return database.then(db => {
          const tx = db.transaction('items', 'readwrite');
          for (const item of items) {
            tx.objectStore('items').delete(item.id);
          }
          return tx.complete;
        });
      });
  }
};
```

Filters out all of the items that have been packed, and returns an array of items that remain unpacked.

Deletes each of those items

Unlike SQLite, IndexedDB doesn't provide support for querying the database, which makes a certain amount of sense considering it is a NoSQL database. When working with NoSQL databases, you can take some interesting approaches, such as storing your data in multiple places with different indices for quick retrieval, but that is a bit outside the scope of this book.

We're opting for the simplest approach—and one that is a perfect fit for our data set, which is to simply fetch all of the items from the database and find only the ones that meet our criteria. Again, we do this in a transaction. If deleting any of these items fails, the database returns to the state that it was in before we triggered this method.

12.2.4 Connecting the database to the UI

With this last method in place, we need to connect all of the new database methods to the UI. By building the database methods in the previous section, we've made transitioning from the SQLite implementation to one based on IndexedDB relatively painless. The main difference is that we aren't querying for items in the database.

Listing 12.22 Updating the `Application` component to use IndexedDB: ./app/components/Application.js

```
fetchItems() {
  this.props
    .database
    .getAll()
    .then(items => this.setState({ items }))
    .catch(console.error);
}

addItem(item) {
  this.props.database.add(item).then(this.fetchItems);
}

deleteItem(item) {
  this.props
    .database
    .delete(item)
    .then(this.fetchItems)
    .catch(console.error);
}

markAsPacked(item) {
  const updatedItem = { ...item, packed: !item.packed };
  this.props
    .database
    .update(updatedItem)
    .then(this.fetchItems)
    .catch(console.error);
}

markAllAsUnpacked() {
  this.props
```

```
      .database
      .markAllAsUnpacked()
      .then(this.fetchItems)
      .catch(console.error);
  }

  deleteUnpackedItems() {
    this.props
      .database
      .deleteUnpackedItems()
      .then(this.fetchItems)
      .catch(console.error);
  }
```

Summary

- Compiled dependencies work only with the version of the V8 engine used by Node that they were compiled against.
- The version of Node on your system may differ from the version of Node bundled with Electron.
- Normally, when you install dependencies using `npm install` or `yarn install`, the dependencies are built against the system version of Node—not that of Electron.
- `electron-rebuild` goes through your installed dependencies and rebuilds them for the version of Node packaged with Electron.
- User data should be stored in the appropriate place on the filesystem. This differs between filesystems, but Electron provides a helpful abstraction called `app.getPath()` that can determine the correct path on your behalf.
- SQLite is a common choice for native applications because it stores data in a file instead of requiring that a database server be installed and running.
- IndexedDB is a popular browser-based option for storing user data on the client. It is a NoSQL database provided by Chromium.

13 Testing applications with Spectron

This chapter covers

- Using Spectron to test Electron applications
- Understanding the relationship among Spectron, WebdriverIO, and Selenium WebDriver
- Controlling Electron APIs within integration tests

At this point in the book, we've built a number of Electron applications. Testing these applications to make sure that they work as expected has been something of a manual process. Make a change, start the application, and click around to ensure that everything works. This is fine for small applications, but this method can become tedious in larger applications. What if a change in the code in one part of the application breaks some functionality elsewhere?

In these situations, it's helpful to automate the tests. Let the computer do the boring, repetitive work, while you focus on the features that bring value to your customers. That sounds great, but how do we do that? In a traditional web application, you might point something like Selenium WebDriver to your website, make some assertions as to how the site should behave, and then have it click around and confirm that everything works as expected.

That's great, but we have a few problems: our Electron applications don't have web addresses per se, but they do support APIs that give us unprecedented access to the underlying operating systems, which are typically not supported by web browsers. At this point, it shouldn't surprise you that this tricky problem has an easy solution. The Electron team supports a project called Spectron, which allows developers to write integration tests for our Electron applications.

In this chapter, we write integration tests for a special version of Clipmaster 9000 that does not live in the menu bar, as shown in figure 13.1. We test all the core functionality and learn a few tricks along the way. To get started, you need to add Spectron and a test runner to your package.json. I've opted to use Mocha in an attempt to stay consistent with the official documentation, but you could use Jest, Karma, Jasmine, or any other test runner that makes you happy. I've included this in the example repository (http://mng.bz/UxHY), but if you're working on your own, you can run `npm install --save-dev spectron mocha`.

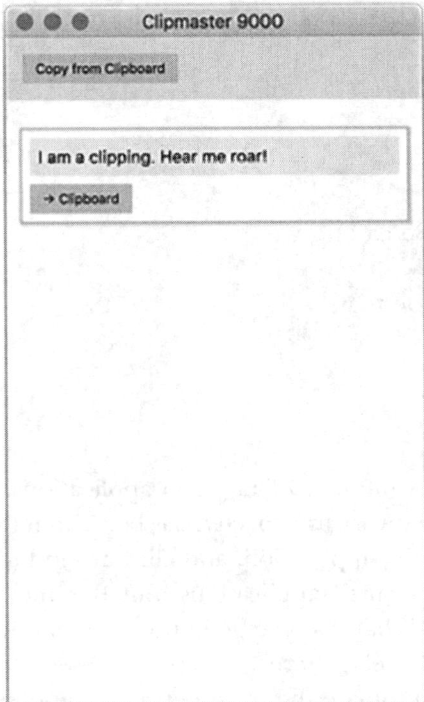

Figure 13.1 A simplified version of Clipmaster 9000 that does not live in the menu bar.

First, it's important to understand the relationship among Spectron, WebdriverIO, and Selenium WebDriver because we use methods from more than one of them in a given test. Let's start at the bottom and work our way up. Selenium WebDriver allows developers to write tests that control a web browser so they can test their applications from a user's perspective—as opposed to unit tests, which exercise a given piece of code in isolation. Selenium WebDriver is a language-agnostic library and is typically wrapped by a library that gives it native API bindings for a given programming language.

Enter WebdriverIO, which wraps Selenium WebDriver with a pleasant JavaScript API and makes it easy to use from within Node.js—or an Electron application, in our case. But as I pointed out in the beginning of this chapter, Electron applications have some major differences from traditional web applications, as well as a lot of additional power and functionality. Spectron wraps WebdriverIO, as shown in figure 13.2, and allows us to access this functionality in an environment custom-tailored for Electron applications.

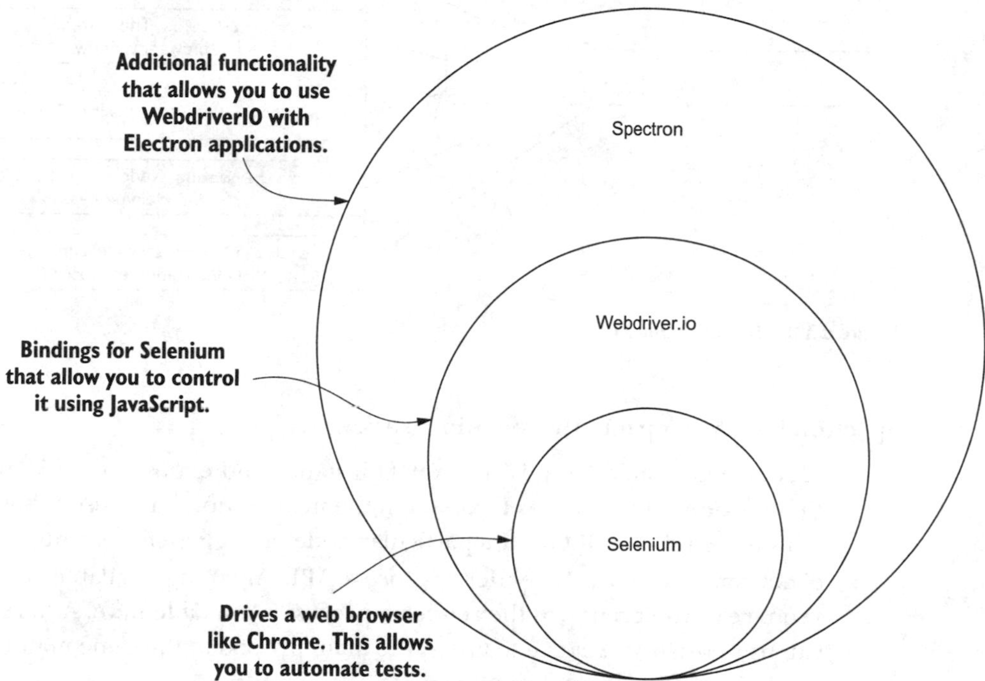

Figure 13.2 Spectron is a wrapper around WebdriverIO, which—in turn—is a wrapper around Selenium WebDriver.

We won't need to touch Selenium WebDriver in this chapter. WebdriverIO takes care of controlling Selenium WebDriver on our behalf. We douse methods from both Spectron and WebdriverIO. In practice, you don't really have to think about the line between the two, but some of Spectron's methods delegate to WebdriverIO. Where this ends up being important is when it comes time to look up the documentation for a given method. I'll make sure to point out when we're delegating to WebdriverIO, as opposed to using a method that belongs to Spectron itself.

13.1 Introducing Spectron

Spectron makes it easy to start our application and control its UI from our test suite. The primary way to use Spectron is to create an `Application` instance. This object includes a number of child objects that allow us to access different parts of our application, as shown in figure 13.2

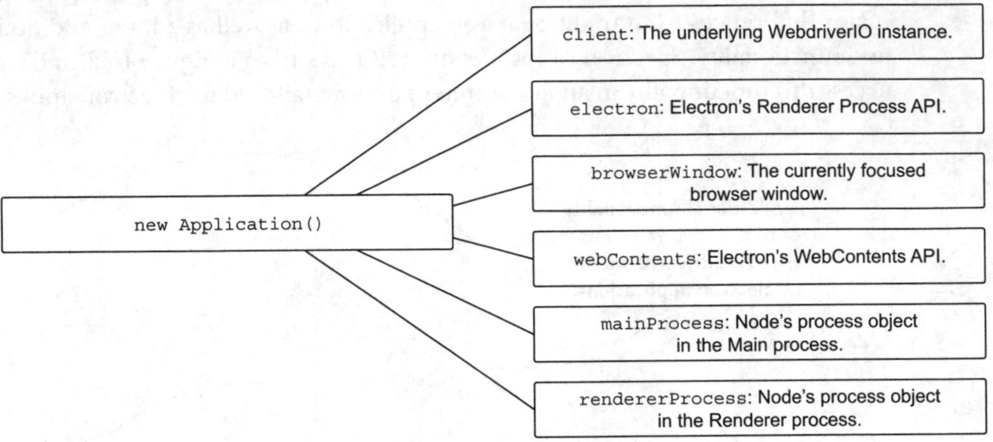

Figure 13.3 The Spectron API

Spectron is broken up into the following parts:

1. `client` is the underlying WebdriverIO instance and exposes all of its methods. (This is only partly true, as I explain in the next section.) You use this when you want to search the DOM for a particular node or trigger click events.
2. `electron` is Electron's renderer process API. Anything available when using `require('electron')` in the renderer process is available here. As a result, you can use `electron.remote` to access the main process in the same manner as you would in the renderer process.
3. `browserWindow` is a convenient alias to access the currently focused browser window in your application. It's equivalent to `electron.remote.getCurrentWindow()`. In addition, `browserWindow.capturePage()` is useful when you want to take a screenshot of the currently active browser window and save it to the desktop. This can be useful when you're trying to diagnose why your tests are failing.
4. `webContents` is an alias to Electron's `webContents` API, which is useful for getting information about, or controlling the browser that is executing, your application. It is an alias for `electron.remote.getCurrentWebContents()`. Throughout this book, we've used this API to load an HTML page into a newly created `BrowserWindow` instance or to toggle the developer tools. The API provides access to browser functionality like the forward and back buttons, printing the page, setting the zoom level, and reloading the page. It emits events as the browser loads that can be useful for testing. It also provides the `webContents.savePage()` method, which allows you to save the currently loaded page as an

HTML file on your filesystem for further inspection if your tests are not behaving as expected.

5 `mainProcess` is an alias to Node's process global in the main process. It is equivalent to `electron.remote.process`. It's important to note that `mainProcess` is not an alias to Electron's main process API, but it can be accessed using `electron.remote`. `mainProcess` is useful if you need to access the environment variables or the arguments passed to Electron when it was started.

6 `rendererProcess` is similar to `mainProcess` and provides access to the renderer process's `global.process` object. Again, this can be useful for reading environment variables. If you need Electron's renderer process APIs, use `electron` instead.

The first two properties of the `Application` instance provide deep access to the browser's APIs as well as Electron's own APIs. With this combination, we have deep, programmatic insight into and control over almost all of the inner workings of our application at any time. This access makes testing Electron applications easy once you get the hang of it. The `browserWindow`, `webContents`, `mainProcess`, and `rendererProcess` properties provide convenient aliases to the first two properties.

13.2 Getting comfortable with Spectron and WebdriverIO

In the previous section, I mentioned that I was fibbing I bit when I said that the `client` property delegated to WebdriverIO. That statement is technically true—but it isn't the whole truth. `client` also has additional, Electron-specific methods, shown in figure 13.4, to make your testing experience even more pleasant.

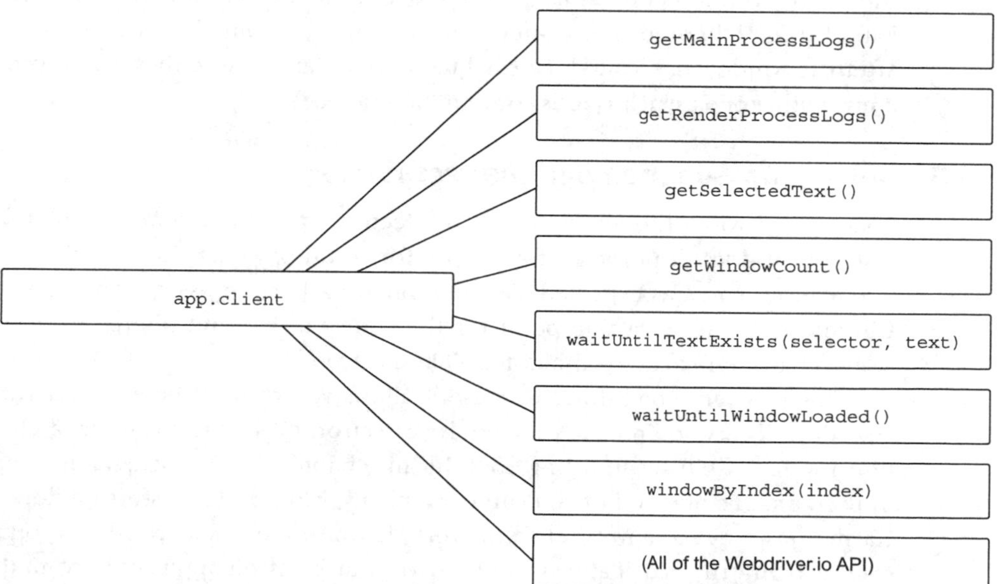

Figure 13.4 Spectron adds a number of utility methods to the WebdriverIO API. This is an exploded view of the client in figure 13.3.

Some of the methods look familiar if you've written integration tests in the past. Methods like `getSelectedText()`, for example, consider that your application might have multiple windows—something that isn't possible in a traditional web application. Others are unique to testing Electron applications. I introduce you to these methods now as a reference. We use many of them in the sections that follow.

`getMainProcessLogs()` and `getRenderProcessLogs()` return a promise that resolves to an array of messages that have been logged to the respective console. As soon as either method is called, it clears the messages from the console. This means that subsequent calls contain only messages that have been logged to the console since the last time the method was called.

`getWindowCount()` returns a promise that resolves to an integer that—unsurprisingly—represents the number of windows currently open in the application. This value might be useful if you are writing tests for an application like Fire Sale, which has a button allowing users to open another window. `app.browserWindow` references the currently focused window. `app.client.windowByIndex()` allows you to focus on an alternate window instead.

`waituUntilWindowLoaded()` takes a given number of milliseconds as an argument and returns a promise. If the window loads in the allotted time, the promise resolves. Otherwise the promise is rejected. This method allows you to delay execution of your tests until you've confirmed that the window has actually loaded.

`waitUntilTextExists()` takes three arguments: a selector, a string of text, and an optional number of milliseconds to wait before giving up. It returns a promise that resolves when the selector contains the text, Alternatively, it rejects if the 5 seconds or the provided number of milliseconds pass and the text has not appeared. This setting is useful for UI components where the content may come in asynchronously shortly after the window has loaded. Normal tests would fail because they would run immediately, before the asynchronous content has loaded.

13.3 Setting up Spectron and the test runner

Spectron provides the ability to start an Electron application and control it from your tests, but it doesn't provide a framework for running your tests or verifying that your application works as expected. As mentioned earlier, we use a simplified version of Clipmaster 9000. A starting point for the code can be found here at https://github.com/electron-in-action/clipmaster-9000-spectron.

This is a very good thing because it allows you to use whatever test runner and assertion library you prefer. Just require Spectron in your test runner of choice, configuring it as we'll see in listing 13.2. In this chapter, I use Mocha along with Node's built-in `assert` library, but you can certainly use Chai and an assertion library or Jest, Karma, Jasmine, or any other framework, if you prefer. Spectron is not opinionated on this front. Instead, it allows you to drive your Electron application from the framework of your choice.

I've already included Mocha as one of the development dependencies for the example project. As I mentioned earlier, if you're working on your own application and following along, you can run `npm install --save-dev spectron mocha` from the command line to install both Spectron and Mocha. This will install the `mocha` command line tool into your node_modules directory, which can be run by typing `./node_modules/.bin/mocha`. This can be tedious. It would be much easier to assign it to be run using `npm test`. So, let's add it to our project's scripts in our package.json. (This should already be set up for you if you've cloned the repository from GitHub.)

Listing 13.1 Setting up Mocha as a test script: ./package.json

```
"scripts": {
  "start": "electron .",
  "test": "mocha"          <-- Sets npm test to run the locally installed version of Mocha
}
```

Now whenever we run `npm test`, Jest runs our test suite by looking for all files with a *.test.js suffix. You can also use this suffix for any unit tests that you want to write—Mocha runs those as well. In a larger application, you might create a folder for all of your tests or include them alongside your implementation files. For the sake of simplicity, I'm going to use a single file called test.js to hold all of the tests for our application.

Let's begin by examining the boilerplate provided in the repository to start our application before each test and stop the application after the individual test has run. This gives us a fresh instance of the application for each test, which eliminates the need to clean up any of the side effects and leftover state from previous tests.

Listing 13.2 Writing up Spectron with the test runner: ./test/spec.js

```
const assert = require('assert');          <-- Requires Node's built-in assertion library
const path = require('path');              <-- Brings in Node's helper utility for working with file paths
const Application = require('spectron').Application;   <-- Pulls in Spectron's application driver
const electronPath = require('electron');  <-- Requires Electron. This will give us access to a locally installed development version of Electron.

const app = new Application({
  path: electronPath,                      <-- Tells Spectron's application to use the locally installed development version of Electron
  args: [path.join(__dirname, '..')],      <-- Points to the root directory of the application itself as a starting point for the application
});

describe('Clipmaster 9000', function () {
  this.timeout(10000);                     <-- Increases Mocha's default timeout because launching the application can take a while

  beforeEach(() => {
    return app.start();                    <-- Starts the application before each test
  });
```

```
  afterEach(() => {
    if (app && app.isRunning()) {
      return app.stop();                    <-- Stops the application
    }                                           after each test
  });
});
```

The first thing we need is the location of the Electron application that we want to test. Theoretically, you could point Spectron to any of the Electron-based applications on your computer and control them programmatically, but I leave that as a devious exercise for the reader. I'm going to be a boring rule follower and get the path to the locally installed version of Electron that we pulled down from npm when we installed our dependencies using `npm install`.

We want access to a variable holding the instance of our application in each of our tests, so we declare it in the `describe()` block. Before each test, we create an application instance and assign it to the `app` variable. The `new Application()` constructor takes the path of the Electron binary, as well as the location of the directory where we would normally type `npm start`. This should be the directory that contains the package.json, which references the JavaScript file containing the code for the main process. After the instance has been created, we start the application. We're now ready to test—despite the fact that we haven't written a test case just yet. But imagine that we had a test and it has run. We check that there is a value assigned to the `app` variable and the application is still running. (It may have crashed.) If both of those cases are true, then we stop the application and move onto the next test case, where we go through this process again.

13.4 Writing asynchronous tests using Spectron

We've talked about our testing tools. We've set them up. Now let's sit down and write some tests. Over the course of the chapter, we'll check that Clipmaster

- Shows an initial window when it starts
- Displays "Clipmaster 9000" as the title
- Doesn't have the Developer Tools open when it starts
- Has a button with the text Copy from Clipboard
- Doesn't have any clippings displayed in the UI when the application starts
- Contains one clipping when the Copy from Clipboard button has been pressed a single time
- Successfully removes a clipping when a clipping's Remove button has been clicked
- Has the correct text when a new clipping is created
- Writes the text of the clipping to the clipboard when the Copy button is clicked

We'll start with a simple test: start the application, and confirm that this special version of Clipmaster 9000 creates a single browser window. Spectron and WebdriverIO use an asynchronous, promise-based API for controlling Electron and the web application within. Most methods return promises, which can be chained. As I've mentioned repeatedly throughout this book, Electron provides us with a modern version of Node and Chromium. We frequently have the latest and greatest browser and language features at our disposal. This includes the `async/await` syntax for working with asynchronous APIs in a way that's as easy to wrap our head around as synchronous code. With this syntax, you don't have to worry about passing around callbacks or chaining promises.

As shown in listing 13.3, we use the `async` keyword before the arrow function to denote that we'll be using the `async/await` syntax in this function. The `await` keyword pauses until `app.client.getWindowCount()` has resolved and then assigns the result to the `count` variable. After this is done, we expect the count to equal one. Mocha expects asynchronous tests to return a promise when they're done, so you need to make sure that you prefix your expectation with the `return` keyword. Your author failed to do that on multiple occasions when writing this chapter before his first cup of coffee. He paid dearly for that oversight with his time and sanity.

Listing 13.3 Writing a test to count the number of windows: ./test/spec.js

```
it('shows an initial window', async () => {
  const count = await app.client.getWindowCount();
  return assert.equal(count, 1);
});
```

The application has started; get a count of all of the windows.

Verify that this version of Clipmaster creates only one window.

This test is simple, and a traditional implementation using promises would not look that much different, but more involved tests require longer promise chains that might become tedious to write or confusing to reason about at best.

13.4.1 Waiting for the window to load

In many tests, you have to wait for the window to load the HTML, CSS, and JavaScript before you can continue testing the application. Electron loads the HTML quickly, but it's not instantaneous. We frequently use the `app.client.waitUntilWindowLoaded()` method described earlier to wait until the application has fully loaded before moving forward. Let's write a test confirming that the window's title is the name of the application.

Listing 13.4 Writing a test to verify the window title: ./test/spec.js

```
it('has the correct title', async () => {
  const title = await app.client.waitUntilWindowLoaded().getTitle();
  return assert.equal(title, 'Clipmaster 9000');
});
```

After the window has loaded, gets the title of that window

Verifies that the title of the window is what we expect

Many of Spectron's methods are chainable, with each subsequent method in the chain being called after the promise returned from the previous method has resolved. In the previous example, we wait for the window to finish loading and then get the title of the window and store it in the title variable; after that asynchronous operation is complete, we can verify that the window's title is what we expect it to be.

13.4.2 Testing Electron BrowserWindow APIs

Traditionally, integration-testing tools like Selenium and WebdriverIO point a browser to a webpage and interact with it. They typically don't have much more access to the internals of the browser itself like we do as developers. Electron allows developers to programmatically open the developer tools when the window first loads. That said, it would be bad if we accidentally forgot to remove this code and shipped this to users. Let's write a test that verifies that developer tools are not opened when the application is loaded.

Listing 13.5 Testing that the developer tools are not open: ./test/spec.js

```
it('does not have the developer tools open', async () => {
  const devToolsAreOpen = await app.client
    .waitUntilWindowLoaded()
    .browserWindow.isDevToolsOpened();
  return assert.equal(devToolsAreOpen, false);
});
```

Gets a reference to the browser window instance

Checks to see if the developer tools are open

Verifies that the developer tools are not open

The `isDevToolsOpened()` method is available on all `BrowserWindow` instances. When the application has loaded, we get the current browser window and ask it whether it has the developer tools open. We expect this to be `false`. If it is `true`, the test will fail.

13.4.3 Traversing and testing the DOM with Spectron

In addition to testing Electron APIs, we almost definitely want to test the UI of our application like we would a traditional application. Let's start with a simple example where we search the page for a particular element and verify that it has the copy that we expect.

Listing 13.6 Testing the content of the Copy from Clipboard button: ./test/spec.js

```
it('has a button with the text "Copy from Clipboard"', async () => {
  const buttonText = await app.client
  .getText('#copy-from-clipboard');
  return assert.equal(buttonText, 'Copy from Clipboard');
});
```

Uses the WebdriverIO API to get the text from a DOM node on the page

The `getText()` method is provided by WebdriverIO as opposed to Spectron. It accepts a selector as an argument, finds the first node that matches that selector, and returns a promise that resolves to the text content of that node. Finally, we confirm that the text is what we expect it to be.

This works, but what about more complicated traversal? When the application starts, the clippings list is empty—remember this was before we knew how to persist data in our Electron applications. Each time the user clicks that Copy from Clipboard button, a new clipping should be added to the page. How might we go about testing these scenarios? Let's start with the first case: when the application starts, there should not be any clippings on the page.

Listing 13.7 Testing the initial state of the UI: ./test/spec.js

```
it('should not have clippings when it starts up', async () => {
  await app.client.waitUntilWindowLoaded();
  const clippings = await app.client.$$('.clippings-list-item');
return assert.equal(clippings.length, 0);
});
```

Waits until the window has loaded its content

Uses WebdriverIO's API to find all the clipping list items on the page

Verifies that, by default, there are no clipping list items

Webdriver exposes `$` and `$$` methods, which are aliased to `document.querySelector` and `document.querySelectorAll`, respectively. We use `$$` to select all of the clipping list items on the page, which returns a `NodeList` object. Ideally, there are no clipping list items on the page and the length of that `NodeList` is `0`.

So far we've inspected and verified the state of the application when it starts—an important task but typically only a small portion of the tests we write for a given application. We've confirmed that there are no clippings on the page when the application starts. It stands to reason that when the user adds a clipping, it should be added to the UI. We already know how to check for the number of elements matching a given selector on a page. But how do you add a clipping? You click the Copy from Clipboard button. We need to figure out how to program WebdriverIO to click on a particular element on a page.

Listing 13.8 Testing a click interaction: ./test/spec.js

```
it('should have one clipping when the "Copy from Clipboard" button has been
    pressed', async () => {
  await app.client.waitUntilWindowLoaded();
  await app.client.click('#copy-from-clipboard');
  const clippings = await app.client.$$('.clippings-list-item');
return assert.equal(clippings.length, 1);
});
```

Finds all of the clippings on the page

Triggers a click event on the Copy from Clipboard button

Verifies that there is one clipping now

Lucky for us, `app.client` provides a `click()` method that does exactly what you might expect: it triggers a click event on a node that matches the selector provided. When we click the Copy from Clipboard button, we expect that a clipping is added to the page. The prior test verifies that there is one clipping on the page after the Copy from Clipboard button has been clicked.

What about the flip side? If you recall, clippings can also be removed from the UI. But there is a catch—the Remove button appears only when the user's cursor is hovering over the clipping. We can't simply query for the Remove button, because it's not on the page yet. Instead, we need to take control of the cursor and move it over the clipping to have the Remove button appear.

Listing 13.9 Moving the cursor in a test: ./test/spec.js

```
it('should successfully remove a clipping', async () => {
  await app.client.waitUntilWindowLoaded();
  await app.client
    .click('#copy-from-clipboard')
    .moveToObject('.clippings-list-item')
    .click('.remove-clipping');
  const clippings = await app.client.$$('.clippings-list-item');
  return assert.equal(clippings.length, 0);
});
```

Moves the cursor to the clipping to trigger the Remove button to appear

Clicks the Remove button

Verifies that the clipping is no longer on the page

After clicking the Copy from Clipboard button, we use the `moveToObject()` method to move the cursor over the new clipping, which causes the Remove button to appear. We click Remove and then verify that the clipping is no longer on the page.

> **But Steve, I see a deprecation warning whenever I run this test!**
>
> Seeing a warning is normal, unfortunately. When you run the test in listing 13.9, you see a deprecation warning related to `moveTo` because of an incompatibility with recent versions of Firefox—an issue that doesn't concern us. The problem is that although `moveTo` has been deprecated, there isn't a replacement at the time of this writing. A number of open issues exist on GitHub about this. A good example can be found at https://github.com/webdriverio/webdriverio/issues/2076. You're not the only one seeing—and being frustrated by—these warnings.
>
> To suppress these warnings, you can configure WebdriverIO's options when creating your Spectron application as follows:
>
> ```
> const app = new Application({
>   path: electronPath,
>   args: [path.join(__dirname, '..')],
>   webdriverOptions: {
>     deprecationWarnings: false
>   }
> });
> ```

13.4.4 Controlling Electron's APIs with Spectron

At this point, we have tested that we can add and remove clippings from the page, but we still have a major blind spot: we have no idea whether the clipping is displaying the correct text. If you were able to squint at the application during the previous tests, you might have noticed that the clipping that was added contained whatever was on our clipboard at the time. This will be tricky because our tests should be isolated from the outside world.

What we need to do is use Electron's `clipboard` module to write text to the clipboard and then verify that the provided text is, in fact, what is displayed in the UI. Luckily, Spectron gives us access to all of Electron's APIs. This means we can manipulate what is currently on the clipboard as part of the test and confirm that it is what's found in the UI when the clipping is added to the page.

Listing 13.10 Accessing Electron APIs in a test: ./test/spec.js

```
it('should have the correct text in a new clipping', async () => {
  await app.client.waitUntilWindowLoaded();
  await app.electron.clipboard.writeText('Vegan Ham');
  await app.client.click('#copy-from-clipboard');
  const clippingText = await app.client.getText('.clipping-text');
return assert.equal(clippingText, 'Vegan Ham');
});
```

- Accesses Electron's API to write text to the system's clipboard
- Gets the text of the new clipping that was created
- Verifies that the new clipping contains the content of the clipboard

The `clipboard` module is available in both the main and renderer processes, so there is no need to use `electron.remote`. Before clicking the Copy from Clipboard button, we write text to the clipboard. We then click the button and verify that the clipping's text is exactly what we wrote to the clipboard.

This covers half of Clipmaster 9000's functionality. The flip side of the coin is that the user should be able to copy the clipping back to the clipboard when the clipping's → Clipboard button is clicked. To test this, we need to build on the work we did in the previous test. After clicking the Copy from Clipboard button and adding it to the page, we change the clipboard's content to something else, then click the → Clipboard button, read from the clipboard, and verify that it is back to the original text that we added to Clipmaster 9000.

Listing 13.11 Testing that the application writes to the clipboard: ./test/spec.js

```
it('should write the clipping text to the clipboard', async () => {
  await app.client.waitUntilWindowLoaded();
  await app.electron.clipboard.writeText('Vegan Ham');
  await app.client.click('#copy-from-clipboard');
  await app.electron.clipboard.writeText('Something different');
  await app.client.click('.copy-clipping');
  const clipboardText = await app.electron.clipboard.readText();
return assert.equal(clipboardText, 'Vegan Ham');
});
```

- Writes text to the clipboard using Electron's API
- Clicks the Copy from Clipboard button
- Writes some other text to the clipboard
- Clicks the button that should allegedly copy the text back to the clipboard
- Reads the text from the clipboard
- Verifies that the text is now the content of the clipping and not the text we manually wrote to the clipboard in our test

With this final test in place, we can verify that all of the UI elements work and behave as expected. We were able to use a combination of WebdriverIO and Electron APIs to test the application from multiple angles. The code as it stands at the end of this chapter can be found on the `completed-example` branch of the repository.

Summary

- Spectron is an officially supported library for testing Electron applications.
- Spectron wraps WebdriverIO, which provides Selenium with Node.js bindings.
- All of Electron's APIs are available in Spectron.
- Spectron does not provide its own test running or assertion library. Instead, it allows you to choose which one you want to use.
- Electron supports `async/await` syntax, which greatly simplifies writing asynchronous code.

Part 3

Deploying Electron applications

In part 2, we built a number of applications, but each shared a common flaw: our users would need to navigate to the appropriate directory using the command line and have Node.js installed to start the application. This isn't exactly ideal. As I'm sure you've guessed, things don't have to be this way. That's not the way I started Slack this morning. Part 3 covers the intricacies of packaging and distributing our wonderful applications.

Chapter 14 directly takes on the problem I illustrated in the previous paragraph by introducing us to two different ways to package our applications for distribution. We'll create standalone versions of Fire Sale and Jetsetter in the process. In chapter 15, I'll address a fear that may or may not have crossed your mind: how do we know if our application is working as intended once we release it into the wild? We'll wire up Fire Sale with Electron's built-in crash reporter. We'll also set up a simple server to receive and keep track of crash reports. Full-on crashes are not the only issue our users might come across. We'll also build our own ability to capture uncaught exceptions and report them to our server as well. This is above and beyond what Electron gives us out of the box, but, ultimately, it is fairly simple to implement.

Chapter 16 discusses how to get your application prepped and ready for the Mac App Store. You, by no means, have to go down this route, but it does solve some of the problems that you might come across if you decide that you'd like to get rich off of your Electron applications.

14 Building applications for deployment

This chapter covers

- Packaging your application for distribution
- Setting a custom name and icon for your packaged application
- Easily packaging applications containing transpiled code using Electron Forge
- Building source code in Electron archives (asar)

Throughout this book, we've built several applications. We've started each of them the same way: open the terminal, navigate to the directory, and launch the application using npm. If you've downloaded any of my completed applications, then it's likely that you went to the project on GitHub, cloned the repository, and installed its dependencies. This is all a bit tedious and—frankly—an unacceptable experience for our users. Our Electron applications should behave like any other desktop application. Users should be able to navigate to a website, download the application, and double-click its icon to launch the application. No terminal. No installing dependencies. No cloning repositories.

In this chapter, we take an application that we built earlier in this book—Fire Sale—and build it as a desktop application using a third-party library called Electron

Packager. You can find the repository on GitHub at https://github.com/electron-in-action/firesale. We'll start by checking out a branch conveniently called `chapter-14-beginning`. This is roughly where we left off in chapter 8.

We start by setting up Electron Packager. We use command-line flags to customize things like the output directory and set up npm scripts that allow us to build for multiple platforms at once—although I'll explain why this might be ill-advised. Next, we add a custom icon for Fire Sale. Finally, we discuss Electron's asar archive format and add it to our build process.

After building Fire Sale with Electron Packager, we build Jetsetter using an alternative called Electron Forge. Where Electron Packager is simple, low-level, and a great way to understand what's happening without getting too deep into the weeds, Forge contains more bells and whistles. I chose it for Jetsetter because we're using `electron-compile` to transform JSX to vanilla JavaScript. Electron Forge is also great for laying the foundation for a new Electron application. In the name of learning and getting our hands dirty, I chose not to use Electron Forge, but you may want to consider it when starting your next Electron application. This chapter covers how to transition an Electron application that wasn't originally created with Electron Forge.

By the end of this short chapter, we'll have an executable Electron application that doesn't need to be started from the command line and can be used by someone who does not have Node installed on their computer. Chapters 15 and 16 go deeper and discuss how to properly package your application for macOS and Windows.

14.1 Introducing Electron Packager

Electron Packager is an abstraction around the numerous steps required to develop an application and package it for distribution. In development, we've downloaded a prebuilt version of Electron for our platform (macOS, Windows, or Linux) and processor architecture (32- or 64-bit). We don't necessarily know what platform and architecture our users are using, and they won't build it themselves. It's our responsibility to build a version of the application for each platform and architecture combination we plan to support. Electron Packager is here to help us with that endeavor.

14.1.1 Setting up Electron Packager

You can install Electron Packager globally using `npm install electron-packager -g` or `yarn global add electron-packager`. I prefer to install it locally on the individual project because then each project specifies its own version of Electron Packager. I added it to the `devDependencies` in the project's package.json. If you've cloned the repository and installed the dependencies, you should be good to go.

We begin by adding a `build` script to package.json. In this chapter, we start with a deliberately simple configuration and build on top of it as we go along, refining this build script along the way.

Listing 14.1 Adding a build script: ./package.json

```
{
  // ...Omitted...
  "scripts": {
    "start": "electron .",
    "build": "electron-packager .",
    "test": "echo \"Error: no test specified\" && exit 1"
  },
  // ...Omitted...
}
```

Adds a simple build script to package.json

With our build script in place, it's time to start Electron Packager. You can run the build script using `npm run build`, which runs the local version of `electron-packager` installed in the `node_modules` directory. When the build is finished, you should see an additional directory with the name of the application along with the platform and architecture you're currently using, as shown in figure 14.1. As I write this, I'm using a 64-bit Mac and the directory is called `firesale-darwin-x64`.

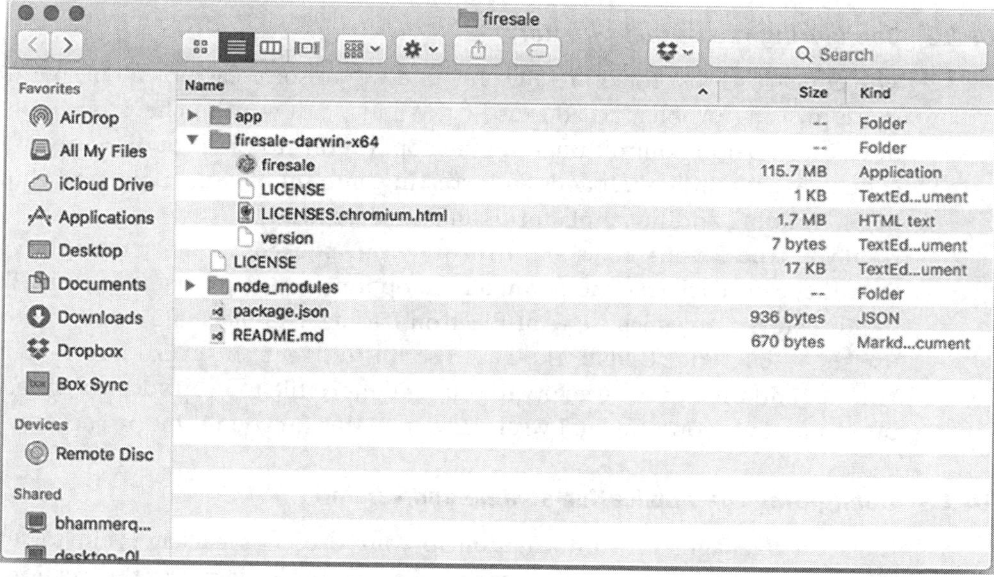

Figure 14.1 By default Electron Packager places builds inside the project's root. This can be problematic because we typically do not want to commit our built application into source control.

The `firesale-darwin-x64` directory contains the desktop application named firesale along with the license and a small text file containing the version. Double-click the application to open it like any other application. If you need to prove it to yourself, feel free to drag the application to another directory and launch it from there.

The output of Electron Packager on Windows is a bit more verbose. On macOS applications are effectively folders that hide much of this complexity from us. In chapter 15, we'll cover how to make an installer for Windows that hides this complexity from our users.

This was fast and simple, but there is still a lot left to be desired. The filename isn't capitalized, we're still using the stock Electron icon, and we've built a version for only our current architecture and platform, among other issues.

> **A quick word on dependencies**
>
> By default, Electron Packager includes all of the dependencies in your `node_modules` directory that are listed in your package.json. It does omit dependencies listed under `devDependencies` in your package.json. This is not an issue that we run into with any of the applications in the book, but it is something you might encounter in your adventures. You can deal with this in two ways: move the dependency from `devDependencies` to `dependencies` or pass the `--no-prune flag` to Electron Packager.

14.1.2 Configuring the output directory

The concerns I just listed are all valid, and we do solve each of them, but we have a more pressing problem to address first. We may not want to check our built applications into version control. Building the applications to the root directory of the project makes that difficult. It adds an increasing amount of visual noise and clutter as we begin building additional platforms and architectures.

If you type `./node_modules/.bin/electron-packager --help` from the command line, Electron Packager shows you all the options and flags that it accepts. To specify the directory into which we want Electron Packager to place our applications, we can use the `--out` flag. Update the `build` script to `electron-packager . --out=build`. You can add the `build` directory to your .gitignore file to keep your compiled applications out of version control. I've already done this for you in this project.

14.1.3 Configuring the application's name and version

Electron Packager uses information in your project's package.json to set certain parameters during the build process. For example, it reads the version field to determine what version of the application this is. It used the name field to set the name of the application as well. But, this has some limitations. You can't use spaces or capitalization in the name field in a package.json. Luckily, a package.json is only a text file, and npm ignores any properties it doesn't understand. This is a good place to store additional information that might be meaningful to Electron Packager. We know that we'd like to change the name of the application, as shown in figure 14.2.

Listing 14.2 Customizing the applications name and version: ./package.json

```
{
  "name": "firesale",
  "version": "1.0.0",
  "description": "Completed code from [Electron in
     Action](http://bit.ly/electronjs).",
  "productName": "Fire Sale",
  // …Additional properties omitted…
}
```

Electron Packager uses the productName field, if it is present, as the name of the application instead of the name, which cannot include spaces or capitalization.

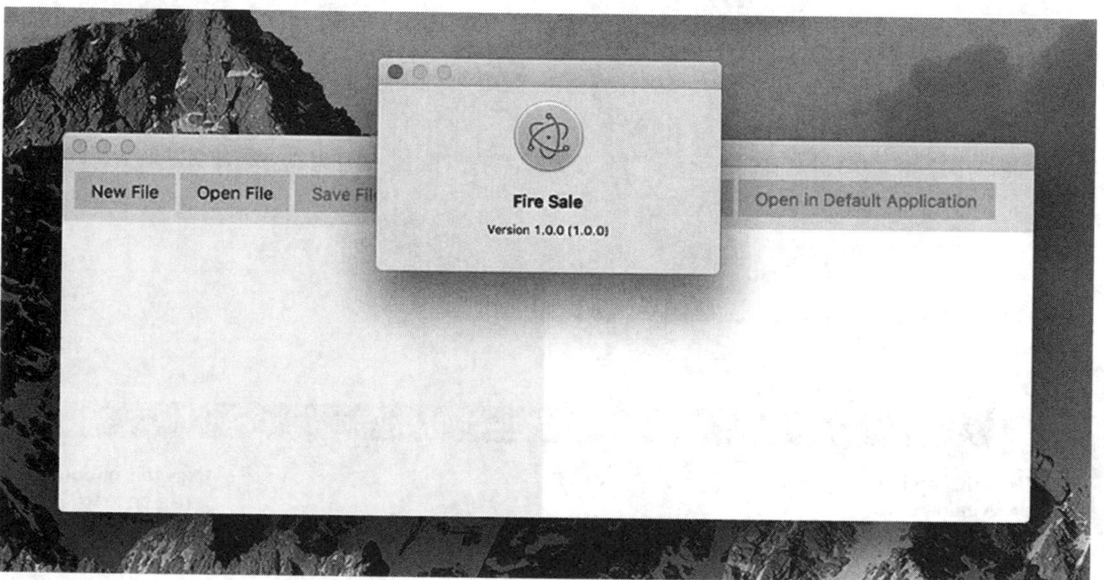

Figure 14.2 With the productName set, our application has the correct name after it is built.

14.1.4 Updating the application icon

I like Electron's logo. It's done well by us throughout this book. But if every application built on top of Electron used the same logo, it would be hard to tell one application from another. Let's replace the logo with our own.

As we saw in chapter 9, different operating systems have different preferences regarding the file format of its icons. At this point, we're building for our own operating system, so we'll make a choice based on which one we're using, as shown in figure 14.3. Later in the chapter, we add some nuance to guide Electron Packager in selecting the correct icon for a given platform.

macOS supports .icns files. Windows supports .ico files. Linux supports .png files. For now, pass the appropriate file to the `--icon` flag based on your current operating system as shown in listing 14.3.

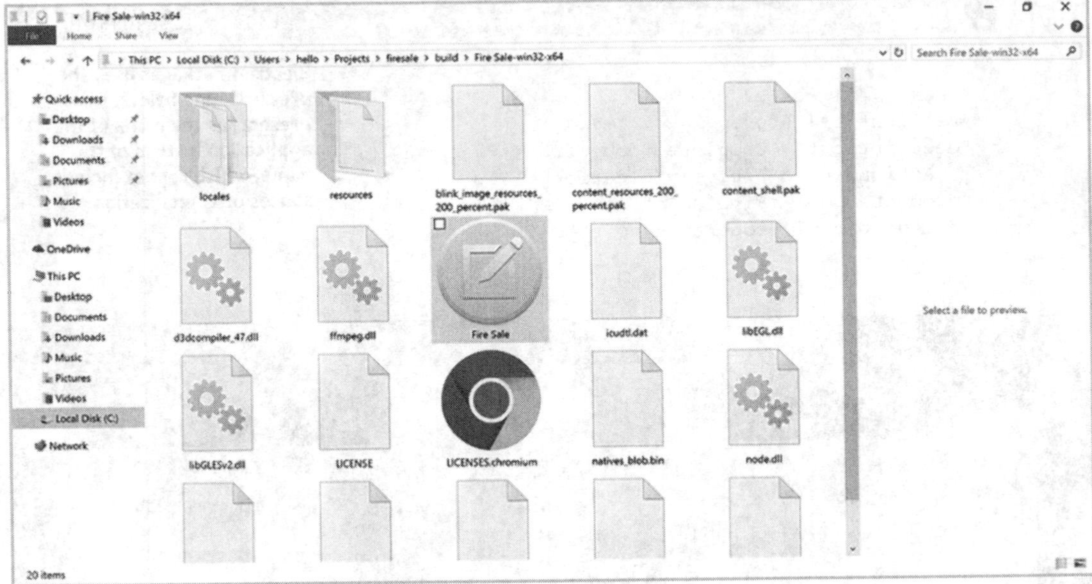

Figure 14.3 Hey, look! We have a custom icon now!

Listing 14.3 Building the application with a custom icon: ./package.json

```
electron-packager . --overwrite --out=build --icon=icons/Icon.icns
electron-packager . --overwrite --out=build --icon=icons/Icon.ico
electron-packager . --overwrite --out=build --icon=icons/Icon.png
```

- Line 1: Uses this option on macOS
- Line 2: Uses this option on Windows
- Line 3: Uses this option on Linux

14.1.5 Building for multiple operating systems

Electron Packager supports the `--all` flag, which creates five builds of the application: 64-bit macOS, 32- and 64-bit Windows, and 32- and 64-bit Linux. Later in this chapter we discuss why this isn't always possible. Although the `--all` flag provides a simple way to create builds for each platform, in the previous section we created different icons for each platform. As a result, we want to pass different options to Electron Packager on the platform.

Listing 14.4 Building for multiple platforms: ./package.json

```
{
    // …Omitted…
  "scripts": {
    "start": "electron .",
    "build": "npm run build-mac && npm run build-win
```

```
➥ && npm run build-linux",
    "build-mac": "electron-packager . --platform=darwin
➥ --out=build --icons=icons/Icon.icns --overwrite",
    "build-win": "electron-packager . --platform=win32
➥ --out=build --icons=icons/Icon.ico --overwrite",
    "build-linux": "electron-packager . --platform=linux
➥ --out=build --icons=icons/Icon.png --overwrite",
    "test": "echo \"Error: no test specified\" && exit 1"
  },
    // ...Omitted...
}
```

Builds the application for macOS

Builds the application for Windows

Builds the application for Linux

The build script calls each of the three subsequent build scripts.

If you're using macOS, you can build Windows binaries if you have Wine installed as well as binaries for Linux. Wine is a utility for running Windows applications on Linux and macOS that can be downloaded from www.winehq.org. On Windows, you cannot create symlinks for macOS and cannot build applications as a result. In chapters 15 and 16, we discuss code signing on macOS, which can be done only on a Mac.

14.2 Using asar

Electron applications are like traditional web applications in that all our code is hidden in plain sight. In a web application a user might right-click and select View Source or open the Developer Tools. In our Electron application, a curious user could open the application bundle and navigate to our source code, as shown in figure 14.4.

If you're using Windows, you can see a folder called resources in the same directory as the application. If you're using macOS, right-click Fire Sale and select Show

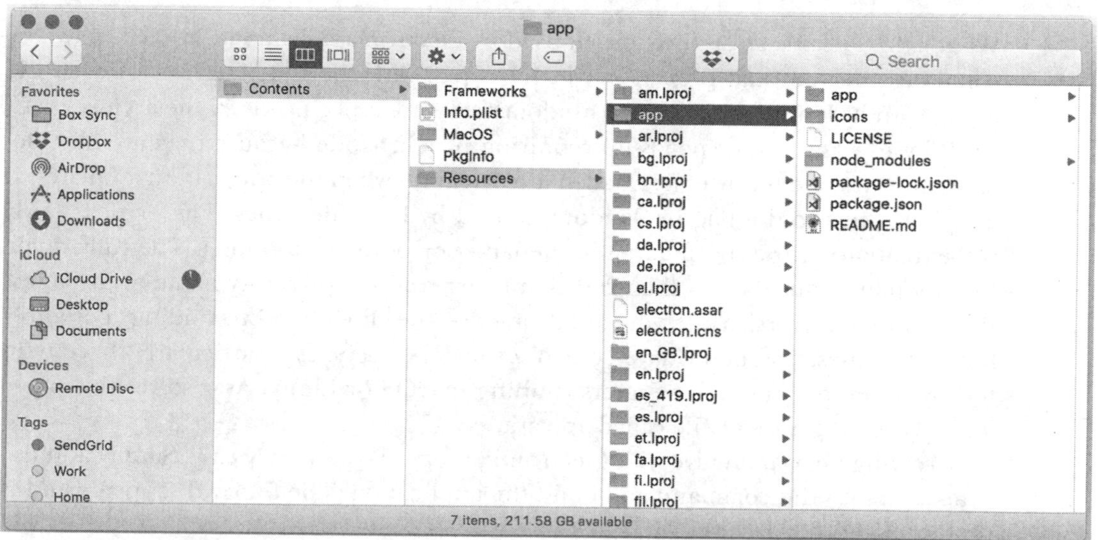

Figure 14.4 The application's source code is located within the application itself.

Package Contents. Next, you see a folder called Contents. Navigate into the Contents directory and then into Resources. Inside this folder are many folders. The one we're interested in is called app. Open this folder and you find all of Fire Sale's source code.

Your next impulse might be to run the same experiment on a popular Electron application such as Slack, Atom, or Visual Studio Code. But you won't find a folder containing the application's source code. Instead, you'll see a file with an unfamiliar file extension called app.asar, as shown in figure 14.5.

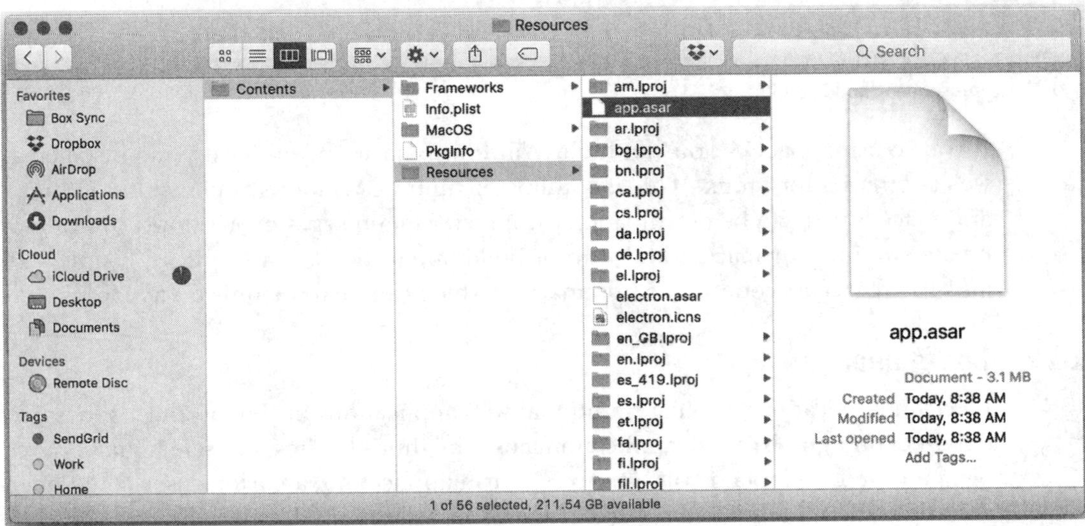

Figure 14.5 The application wrapped in an asar archive.

What's this? *Asar* is an archive format used by Electron applications. It effectively concatenates the files and prepends a JSON object with the start location of each file along with its length, which allows random access to a specific file in the archive.

Why use asar? Asar speeds up requiring files in Node because they are all colocated in the same file, which is loaded into memory when the application launches. It also helps us avoid a bug in Windows caused by long filenames. The error is fairly self-explanatory: the specified path, filename, or both are too long. The fully qualified filename must be less than 260 characters, and the directory name must be less than 248 characters. While you could practice the discipline of avoiding incredibly long filenames, you don't have control over dependencies—particularly those written by developers using computers running macOS or Linux. Asar solves this problem by creating a single file called app.asar.

Creating an asar archive with Electron Packager is incredibly easy. Simply add the `--asar` flag to the command and build the application. The folder disappears and is replaced with the archive.

Listing 14.5 Building for multiple platforms with asar: ./package.json

```
{
    // ...Omitted...
  "scripts": {
    "start": "electron .",
    "build": "npm run build-mac && npm run build-win && npm run build-linux",
    "build-mac": "electron-packager . --platform=darwin
➥ --out=build --icons=icons/Icon.icns --asar --overwrite",
    "build-win": "electron-packager . --platform=win32
➥ --out=build --icons=icons/Icon.ico --asar --overwrite",
    "build-linux": "electron-packager . --platform=linux
➥ --out=build --icons=icons/Icon.png --asar --overwrite",
    "test": "echo \"Error: no test specified\" && exit 1"
  },
    // ...Omitted...
}
```

Adds the --asar flag to the build script for macOS

Adds the --asar flag to the build script for Windows

Adds the --asar flag to the build script for Linux

Asar is not a way to secure or conceal your source code. The asar module on npm allows anyone to extract the folder structure from the archive. Alternatively, opening the archive in a text editor shows you that asar doesn't do anything in the way of obfuscation. If you wanted to peek at the source code of an Electron application, globally install the asar binary, navigate to the application's app.asar, and extract the folder structure.

Electron does not offer a way to hide or encrypt your HTML, CSS, and JavaScript code. If this is a business requirement for you, you might want to consider writing the sensitive parts of your application in a compiled language, like C++ with Node bindings. To the same end, there is nothing stopping you from cracking open your favorite Electron application—Slack, for example—and checking out some of the approaches used in producing for Electron applications.

> **Using asar in your Electron applications**
>
> Electron patches the Node APIs for reading from and writing to the filesystem to support asar automatically. This means you can treat an asar archive as if it were the original folder structure. If you need to use the unpatched version of Node's built-in `fs` module, you can use Electron's built-in `original-fs` module.

We have successfully set up packaging for Fire Sale. You can find the code for Fire Sale in the `chapter-14-ending` branch (http://mng.bz/vI4g). This setup works for a simple application like Fire Sale, but what about an application that has code that needs to be transpiled? Yes, you could set up some Gulp tasks or some other kind of build step that takes place before packaging, but at this point in the book, it shouldn't surprise you that the Electron community has already solved this problem for you. In the next section, we'll look at using Electron Forge to build and package Jetsetter, which requires a compile step before packaging.

14.3 Electron Forge

Electron Forge (https://github.com/electron-userland/electron-forge) is an abstraction around `electron-compile`, `electron-rebuild`, Electron Packager, and other popular third-party Electron libraries. Electron Forge lays the foundation for a brand-new Electron application using one of several different blueprints. It can also import existing applications. We use Electron Forge with the Jetsetter app from chapters 11 and 12 because it relies on `electron-compile` and `electron-rebuild`. Using these with tools like Electron Packager is certainly not impossible, but it's tedious compared to how easy the process is with Electron Forge, which has built-in support for `electron-compile` and `electron-rebuild`.

You'll start from the `chapter-14-beginning` branch, which can be found on GitHub (http://mng.bz/MdLb). You can also reference the completed example on the `chapter-14-ending` branch (http://mng.bz/mzhH).

> **A quick note on third-party dependencies**
>
> The trouble with publishing a book is that, sometimes, libraries change. In this section, we're working at the intersection of a few different libraries: Electron, `electron-precompile`, Electron Forge, React, and others. The cross-compatibility of all of these libraries fills your author with a sense of existential dread. If you have any trouble with the code printed in this section, I encourage you to visit the repository on GitHub, which should work with the most recent versions of the libraries involved.

Out of the box, Electron Forge also handles many of the concerns around distributing your application that we'll cover in chapters 15 and 16. It can take care of publishing your application to Amazon S3, GitHub Releases, or your own custom server. As I stated earlier, we've opted to do a lot of the work by hand in the name of understanding how Electron works, but I highly recommend considering Electron Forge for your next application. In this section, we cover how to convert an application that was not originally created with Electron Forge in mind to one that is ready and able to take advantage of Electron Forge.

We first need to complete a few steps: install the `electron-forge` binary, convert Jetsetter to an Electron Forge application, and run the `build` command. Electron Forge uses Yarn, an alternative to npm, for installing and managing packages. You need to install it if you haven't already. Visit the official documentation (https://yarnpkg.com/en/docs/install) for up-to-date instructions and to learn how to install it on your operating system.

After you install Yarn on your system, run `yarn global add electron-forge`. This installs the command-line tool that allows you to create Electron Forge applications, as well as converts existing Electron applications for use with Electron Forge.

14.3.1 Importing an Electron application into Electron Forge

When we built Jetsetter in chapter 11, we had not yet discussed Electron Forge. It follows that Jetsetter is not an Electron Forge application. Luckily, it's easy to convert it to one. From inside the `jetsetter` directory, run `electron-forge import`. At this point, you are asked a series of questions about how you'd like the script to proceed. Answer the questions as follows:

1 WARNING: We will now attempt to import `"/Users/<username>/Projects/jetsetter"`. This will involve modifying some files, are you sure you want to continue? *Yes.*
2 Do you want us to change the `"main"` attribute of your package.json? If you are currently using Babel and pointing to a `"build"` directory say yes. *No.*
3 Do you want us to update the `"start"` script to instead call the electron-forge task `"electron-forge start"`? *Yes.*
4 Do you want us to update the `"package"` script to instead call the electron-forge task `"electron-forge package"`? *Yes.*
5 Do you want us to update the `"make"` script to instead call the electron-forge task `"electron-forge make"`? *Yes.*

The first question is asking your permission to modify your application's package .json file. This is necessary. Answering no aborts the process. The second question does not apply to us. Jetsetter uses Electron Compile to transpile JavaScript, Sass, and other languages on the fly. If we were instead using a task runner such as Gulp, Grunt, or webpack to transpile our source code into another directory, we would answer yes to this question.

The final three questions are asking if we'd like to use Electron Forge to start our application in development, package the application as we did earlier in this chapter to Fire Sale, and build a distributable—which we'll cover in the next chapter. Because this is why we're importing the application to begin with, we'll answer yes to each of these questions.

14.3.2 Building the application with Electron Forge

As I mentioned earlier, Electron Forge is an abstraction around several helpful libraries in the Electron ecosystem. It exists to make common tasks easier. Building your application is as simple as running `yarn run package`. This drives Electron Packager through many of the steps we covered earlier in this chapter with Fire Sale.

Electron Forge passes parameters to Electron Packager. It calls the output directory `out` instead of `build`. Electron Packager pulls modules from your `node_modules` directory and installs them into your application. As of this writing, there is an issue where the modules were not moved properly. This issue appears with the current version of npm and may be alleviated by the time you read these words. In the meantime, I found that it was easy to work around this issue by using Yarn instead of npm.

Electron Forge adds a few fields to your package.json, so finds the field titled `electronPackagerConfig`, and modify it to match this listing.

Listing 14.6 Using Yarn as your package manager: ./package.json

```
"electronPackagerConfig": {
  "packageManager": "yarn"
}
```

With this code in place, run `yarn run package`. Your application should build successfully. See figure 14.6. You may have noticed that Electron Forge adds a few other configuration fields to package.json. As I mentioned earlier, Electron Forge also assists with creating installers and publishing your application to the web. We cover those features in the upcoming chapters.

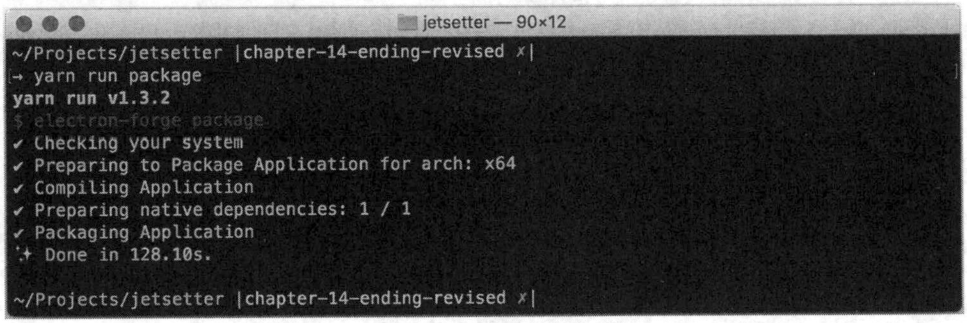

```
jetsetter — 90×12
~/Projects/jetsetter |chapter-14-ending-revised ✗|
→ yarn run package
yarn run v1.3.2
$ electron-forge package
✔ Checking your system
✔ Preparing to Package Application for arch: x64
✔ Compiling Application
✔ Preparing native dependencies: 1 / 1
✔ Packaging Application
✨ Done in 128.10s.

~/Projects/jetsetter |chapter-14-ending-revised ✗|
```

Figure 14.6 Packaging an application with Electron Forge

With Electron Forge, everything is set up on your behalf. At this point, you probably fall into one of two categories: you're either amazed by how much simpler Forge is compared to Packager, or you're bewildered by all of the black magic. Those reactions are both fair and underscore some of the trade-offs made along the spectrum between convention and configuration. My hope is that by trying both, you'll have a sense of which you prefer for your own applications.

Summary

- Electron Packager automates the otherwise manual and error-prone process of packaging an Electron application for distribution.
- The application should be packaged on each of the target platforms to which you wish to distribute.
- Setting the `productName` key in the package.json instructs Electron Packager to use a custom name that supports spaces and capitalization.
- Electron Packager accepts an `--icon` flag and allows you to define a custom icon for your application.

- Asar is an archive format used by Electron applications that concatenates files and allows random access to a specific file in the archive.
- Electron Forge can be used as a boilerplate for new Electron projects. It can also be used to facilitate building applications that rely on `electron-compile`.

15 Releasing and updating applications

This chapter covers

- Sending crash reports from Electron
- Sending reports of uncaught exceptions from Electron
- Creating a server to collect crash and exception reports
- Automatically pushing application updates to users

You've built your application, and you're ready to distribute it to the world. You've prepared your announcement, and your cursor is hovering over the Publish button when—all of a sudden—your mind begins to race with some very important questions: What if it doesn't work on all platforms as you expected? What if there is a bug you haven't encountered yet? What if you need to push out a new version of the application to your users?

These concerns are all valid. The good news is that Electron has you covered on each front. In this chapter, we cover how to collect crash reports and—in the event you receive an unexpectedly large number of them—how to push an update to all of the users that currently have the application installed on their system.

15.1 Collecting crash reports

Despite how good your skills as a developer are, your application is going to have bugs. Some users report them, but many others suffer in silence. Even among the users who report bugs, it can be difficult to determine how common a given issue is among your user base as a whole. Crash reporting is critical for discovering what types of problems occur and at what frequency your users are experiencing them.

Though it is certainly a relief that Electron includes support for crash reporting, it's surprising. As we've covered throughout this book, Electron is built on top of Chromium, and crash reporting is certainly something that the Chromium team deals with in their project. To stand on the shoulder of giants, however, we need to set up the crash reporter in our Electron application, as well as deploy a simple server to collect these crash reports for later analysis.

In this chapter, we implement crash reporting and auto-updating into Fire Sale, which is the application we began getting ready for deployment in chapter 14. We begin working on the `chapter-15-beginning` branch, found at https://github.com/electron-in-action/firesale.

We tackle the following:

- Configuring Electron's built-in ability to send a crash report when the application—umm—crashes unexpectedly. The crash reporter is triggered when the application goes down completely.
- Setting up a naively simple server to receive and collect the crash reports sent from versions of our application out in the wild.
- Configuring our application to listen for uncaught exceptions that occur at runtime. This code is our own handiwork and not something provided by Electron out of the box. This functionality is triggered when smaller errors occur that necessarily result in a complete failure of the application itself.
- Updating our server to receive those error reports as well.

15.1.1 Setting up the crash reporter

Under the hood, Electron uses one of two crash-reporting systems: on macOS, the Chrome team's Crashpad reporting engine; on Windows and Linux, an older engine known as Breakpad. These options impact how we implement crash reporting in Electron. The main difference is that Breakpad crash reporting needs to be set up only in the main process, whereas Crashpad must be started in the main and renderer processes.

Yes, you could copy and paste the code from the main process into each of the renderer processes. (We're lucky to have only one in Fire Sale.) But that means you'd have to remember to be diligent enough to change it in multiple places in the event you needed to update the configuration. Personally, I'd prefer to spend a few extra moments of effort now for a lifetime of laziness. Let's set up a single function that we can use in both places.

Listing 15.1 Creating a file to configure and start up the Crash Reporter: ./app/crash-reporter.js

```
const { crashReporter } = require('electron');

const host = 'http://localhost:3000/';

const config = {
  productName: 'Fire Sale',
  companyName: 'Electron in Action',
  submitURL: host + 'crashreports',
  uploadToServer: true,
};

crashReporter.start(config);

console.log('[INFO] Crash reporting started.', crashReporter);

module.exports = crashReporter;
```

The URL where the crash reports are sent via an HTTP POST request.

Indicates that you want the crash results to be sent to the server

Starts the Crashpad or Breakpad crash reporter using the configuration options passed in

We set up a reusable module for starting up the crash reporter, but you can change the value of any of those options. Particularly, we need to change `submitURL` because it is both unlikely that our users happen to be running a server on that port and ultimately unhelpful to us if they're collecting crash reports locally and never sending them to us.

The code by itself does not start the crash-reporting engine unless it is pulled into the main and renderer processes. We start by pulling it into the main process.

Listing 15.2 Starting the crash reporter in the main process: ./app/main.js

```
const { app, BrowserWindow, dialog, Menu } = require('electron');
const createApplicationMenu = require('./application-menu');
const fs = require('fs');

require('./crash-reporter');

const windows = new Set();
const openFiles = new Map();

// The rest of the main process code…
```

We require crash-reporter.js, which will start it up.

This method is effectively enough to implement the ability to send crash reports on Windows and Linux. We can verify that the code inside the crash reporter has executed by checking the terminal for the message we logged to the console in listing 15.1 when the application starts, as shown in figure 15.1.

As I mentioned earlier, we need to do one more—arguably simple—step to get crash reporting working on macOS: execute the same code in the renderer process.

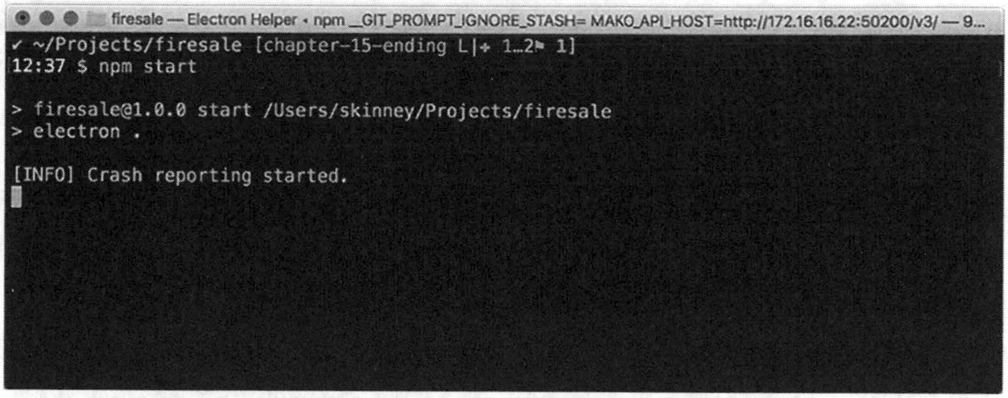

```
firesale — Electron Helper ◂ npm _GIT_PROMPT_IGNORE_STASH= MAKO_API_HOST=http://172.16.16.22:50200/v3/ — 9...
✓ ~/Projects/firesale [chapter-15-ending L|✚ 1…2⚑ 1]
12:37 $ npm start

> firesale@1.0.0 start /Users/skinney/Projects/firesale
> electron .

[INFO] Crash reporting started.
```

Figure 15.1 The console message verifies that the code inside crash-reporter.js has executed.

Listing 15.3 Starting the crash reporter in the renderer process: ./app/renderer.js

```
const { remote, ipcRenderer, shell } = require('electron');
const { Menu } = remote;
const path = require('path');
const mainProcess = remote.require('./main.js');
const currentWindow = remote.getCurrentWindow();

require('./crash-reporter');
```

Starts the crash reporter in the renderer process

We can verify that the crash reporter has started by opening the Developer Tools in the Fire Sale UI and confirming that the console message has been logged correctly, as seen in figure 15.2.

15.1.2 Setting up a server to receive crash reports

We can send crash reports—but where? We can trigger a crash by typing `process.crash()` into the Developer Tools in the renderer process. As shown in figures 15.3 and 15.4, doing so results in the following: the page crashing, the Developer Tools locking up, and the main process logging an error.

The immediate issue that we need to solve is the error in our terminal. The exact contents of the error varies by operating system, but the gist is that the crash reporter cannot connect to the server. This makes sense, because we haven't yet set up a server.

Depending on your application, you may already be using an API server. If so, I'd recommend adding an endpoint for receiving POST requests from your application. That said, Fire Sale has not had the need for an API server, and I'm going to work under the assumption that we don't have one. For those of you that do, I suspect what follows is still helpful because it illustrates what kind of payload you can expect when a crash is reported.

As described in listing 15.4, let's create a simple server for capturing and recording crash reports. The code can be found on GitHub at http://mng.bz/k6eT.

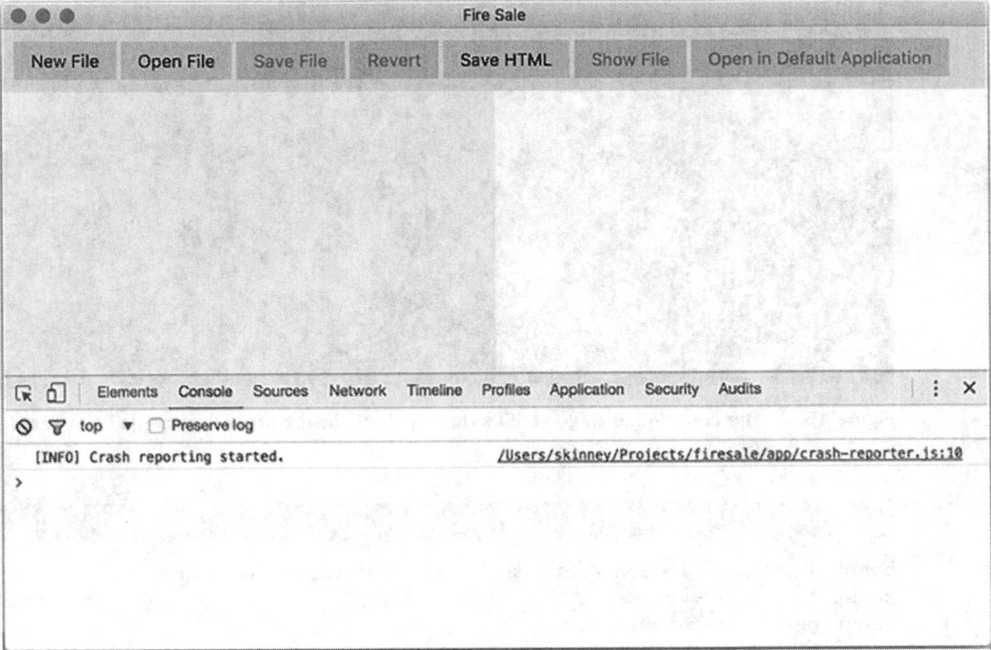

Figure 15.2 Verify that the crash reporter code has been executed by checking the console.

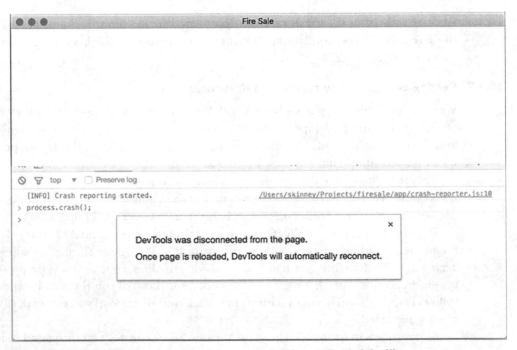

Figure 15.3 Triggering a crash in the render process requires a reload of the UI.

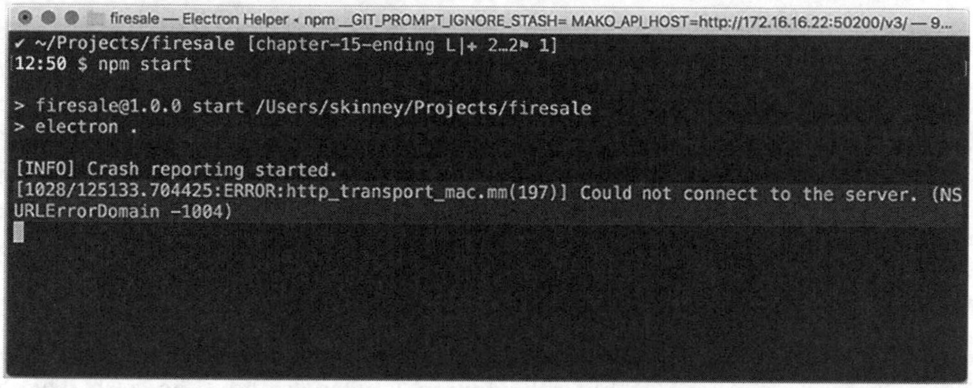

```
firesale — Electron Helper ◂ npm _GIT_PROMPT_IGNORE_STASH= MAKO_API_HOST=http://172.16.16.22:50200/v3/ — 9...
✓ ~/Projects/firesale [chapter-15-ending L|+ 2…2⚑ 1]
12:50 $ npm start

> firesale@1.0.0 start /Users/skinney/Projects/firesale
> electron .

[INFO] Crash reporting started.
[1028/125133.704425:ERROR:http_transport_mac.mm(197)] Could not connect to the server. (NS
URLErrorDomain -1004)
```

Figure 15.4 Electron attempts to send the crash report but cannot find the server.

Listing 15.4 Creating a simple crash reporting server

```
const express = require('express');
const multer = require('multer');
const bodyParser = require('body-parser');
const uuid = require('uuid');
const writeFile = require('write-file');
const path = require('path');
const http = require('http');

const app = express();
const server = http.createServer(app);

app.use(bodyParser.urlencoded({ extended: false }));

const crashesPath = path.join(__dirname, 'crashes');

const upload = multer({
  dest: crashesPath,
}).single('upload_file_minidump');

app.post('/crashreports', upload, (request, response) => {
  const body = {
    ...request.body,
    filename: request.file.filename,
    date: new Date(),
  };
  const filePath = `${request.file.path}.json`;
  const report = JSON.stringify(body);

  writeFile(filePath, report, error => {
    if (error) return console.error('Error Saving', report);
    console.log('Crash Saved', filePath, report);
  });
```

Express is a simple web server library for Node.js.

The bodyParser library is middleware for Express to work with the body of HTTP requests.

Multer allows us to receive multipart files (such as the crash report mini-dumps generated by Electron).

Adds the filename of the mini-dump and the current time to the JSON in the request body

Writes the file to the filesystem

```
  response.end();
});

server.listen(3000, () => {
  console.log('Crash report server running on Port 3000.');
});
```

If you clone the library from GitHub, install the dependencies, and run `npm start`. You should have a server ready and able to collect crash reports running on http://localhost:3000, which is exactly where we pointed the Electron crash reporter in listing 15.1.

Each crash report creates two files in the ./crashes directory: a mini-dump from Chromium and a JSON file with additional metadata about the crash. The JSON file contains useful data about the version of your application that crashed and the platform that it was running on.

Listing 15.5 An example of the JSON metadata from a crash report

```
{
  "_companyName": "Electron in Action",
  "_productName": "Fire Sale",
  "_version": "1.0.0",
  "guid": "46cecb8f-f2de-4159-a235-dc8713f8393f",
  "platform": "darwin",
  "process_type": "renderer",
  "prod": "Electron",
  "ver": "2.0.4",
  "filename": "a51d2ca2e13cad25cea6c2bd15ae4d4d"
}
```

The platform that the crash occurred on.

The process type that the crash occurred on.

The version of Electron currently in use.

The name of the file where the mini-dump is located.

When a crash is reported, the server saves two files to the /crashes directory: a51d2ca2e13cad25cea6c2bd15ae4d4d and a51d2ca2e13cad25cea6c2bd15ae4d4d.json. The former is a dump from Chromium of everything that was happening when the application crashed. This file is in a binary format and cannot be opened in a text editor.

The easiest way to parse this file is to use the `minidump` library from the Electron team. You can install this globally using `npm install -g minidump`. After you install it, you have the `minidump_stackwalk` command-line tool at your disposal and can use `minidump_stackwalk <name of mini-dump file>` to read the contents of the dump. Alternatively, you can use this tool programmatically on your crash-report server as outlined in the tool's documentation (www.npmjs.com/package/minidump).

15.1.3 Reporting uncaught exceptions

Electron's built-in crash reporter is good at what it claims to do on the box—reporting crashes. But in my experience, general bugs and minor errors are much more common than outright crashes. It would be great if we could collect these errors as well, to have better insight into where the rough edges of our application are and exactly how to fix them.

Unfortunately, this is not a tool that is already built into Electron. The good news is that this feature is relatively easy to implement given the knowledge we've already gained throughout the course of this book.

To implement this feature, we have to listen for any uncaught exceptions. The syntax for this is slightly different between the main and renderer processes, but the implementation is the same, as shown in the following listing. When an uncaught exception occurs, send an HTTP POST request to our crash server, which will then log the error to a JSON file.

Listing 15.6 Updating the crash reporter to report uncaught exceptions: ./app/crash-reporter.js

```
const { crashReporter } = require('electron');
const request = require('request');
const manifest = require('../package.json');

const host = 'http://localhost:3000/';

const config = {
  productName: 'Fire Sale',
  companyName: 'Electron in Action',
  submitURL: host + 'crashreports',
  uploadToServer: true,
};

crashReporter.start(config);

const sendUncaughtException = error => {
  const { productName, companyName } = config;
  request.post(host + 'uncaughtexceptions', {
    form: {
      _productName: productName,
      _companyName: companyName,
      _version: manifest.version,
      platform: process.platform,
      process_type: process.type,
      ver: process.versions.electron,
      error: {
        name: error.name,
        message: error.message,
           stack: error.stack,
      },
    },
  });
};

if (process.type === 'browser') {
  process.on('uncaughtException', sendUncaughtException);
} else {
```

Sets up a function to report uncaught exceptions

Sends an HTTP POST request to the crash server we created earlier

Sends information about the error that was fired

Checks if we're running in the main or renderer process

If the error occurred in the main process, uses Node's uncaughtException event

```
  window.addEventListener('error', sendUncaughtException);
}

console.log('[INFO] Crash reporting started.', crashReporter);

module.exports = crashReporter;
```

If the error occurred in the renderer process, adds an event listener to the global object

Any time an error is fired and it bubbles up to the window object without being handled, a report is sent to our server. But just as last time, our server has not been set up yet to handle this report. We need to add another route to log this error.

Listing 15.7 Setting up a server route to receive reports of uncaught exceptions

```
const express = require('express');
const multer = require('multer');
const bodyParser = require('body-parser');
const uuid = require('uuid');
const writeFile = require('write-file');
const path = require('path');
const http = require('http');

const app = express();
const server = http.createServer(app);

app.use(bodyParser.urlencoded({ extended: false }));

const crashesPath = path.join(__dirname, 'crashes');
const exceptionsPath = path.join(__dirname, 'uncaughtexceptions');

const upload = multer({
  dest: crashesPath,
}).single('upload_file_minidump');

app.post('/crashreports', upload, (request, response) => {
  // ...
});

app.post('/uncaughtexceptions', (request, response) => {
  const filePath = path.join(exceptionsPath, `${uuid()}.json`);
  const report = JSON.stringify({
    ...request.body,
    date: new Date()
  });

  writeFile(filePath, report, error => {
    if (error) return console.error('Error Saving', report);
    console.log('Exception Saved', filePath, report);
  });

  response.end();
});
```

Adds a path on the filesystem for storing uncaught exception reports

Uses the UUID module to create a unique identifier for the crash report

Adds the date to the crash report

Writes the report to the filesystem

```
server.listen(3000, () => {
  console.log('Crash report server running on Port 3000.');
});
```

15.2 Signing your applications

In chapter 14, we packaged our application so that users don't need to have Node installed or be familiar with the command line to start it up. In the previous section, we added crash and exception reporting to be confident that we'll be notified in the event our application does not work as intended. Our next step is to sign our application so that our users can be certain that they're getting the real thing and not a cheap substitute.

This process differs on macOS and Windows, so let's walk through each platform separately. Although some of the steps for macOS seem repetitive when we package Fire Sale for the Mac App Store in chapter 16, myriad subtle differences exist.

Before we get into the nitty-gritty of code signing our applications, I'll take a moment to explain what code signing is. The internet is a wild place. You can think of code signing as a tamper-proof seal around your application. Signing our applications allows users to be confident that it both came from you and that no one modified it or otherwise tampered with it along the way. On top of being a generally good idea, macOS and Windows prefer that users work with signed applications and present a series of warnings if they attempt to open an unsigned application. Depending on their settings, users may not be able to open unsigned applications at all.

15.2.1 Signing applications for macOS

You need a few prerequisites in place to sign a macOS application. First, you must be a registered member of the Apple Developer Program (https://developer.apple.com/programs/). Second, you must have Xcode installed. This can be downloaded from the Mac App Store or from Apple's Developer site (https://developer.apple.com/xcode/download/). In addition to having Xcode installed, you also need to have the Xcode command-line tools installed. To set these up, type `xcode-select -install` from the command line, and follow all of the subsequent prompts.

Creating Certificates

To sign your application, you need to create certificates either through iTunes Connect or from within Xcode. We spend an uncomfortable amount of time in iTunes Connect in chapter 16, so we'll do it in Xcode this time.

We generate two certificates: a "Developer ID Application" and a "Developer ID Installer" certificate. To create these certificates

1. Open Xcode
2. Select Preferences from the Xcode menu (as shown in figure 15.5)
3. Select the Accounts tab
4. Select your team
5. Click the Manage Certificates button (as shown in figure 15.6)

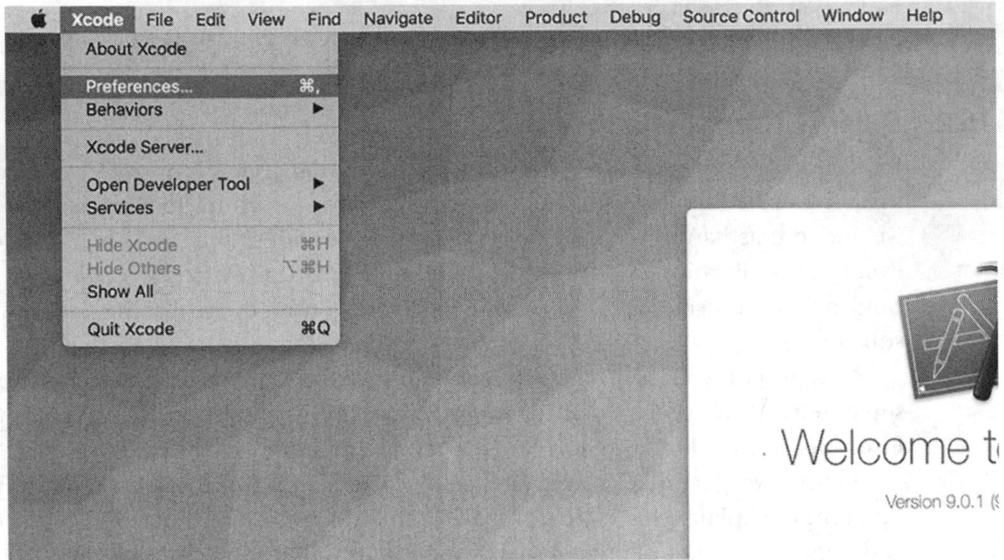

Figure 15.5 Select Preferences from the Application menu.

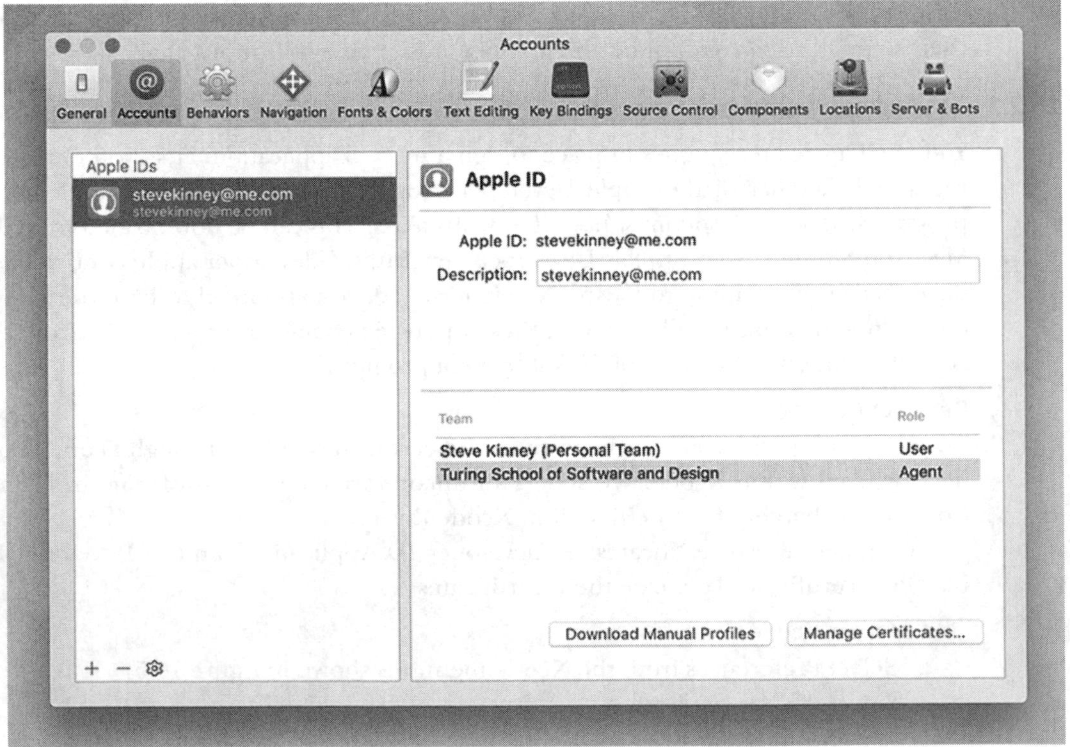

Figure 15.6 Select your team from the Accounts tab, and click Manage Certificates.

6 Click the + button in the lower-left corner
7 Choose Developer ID Application from the drop-down menu (shown in figure 15.7)
8 Repeat this process with Developer ID Installer

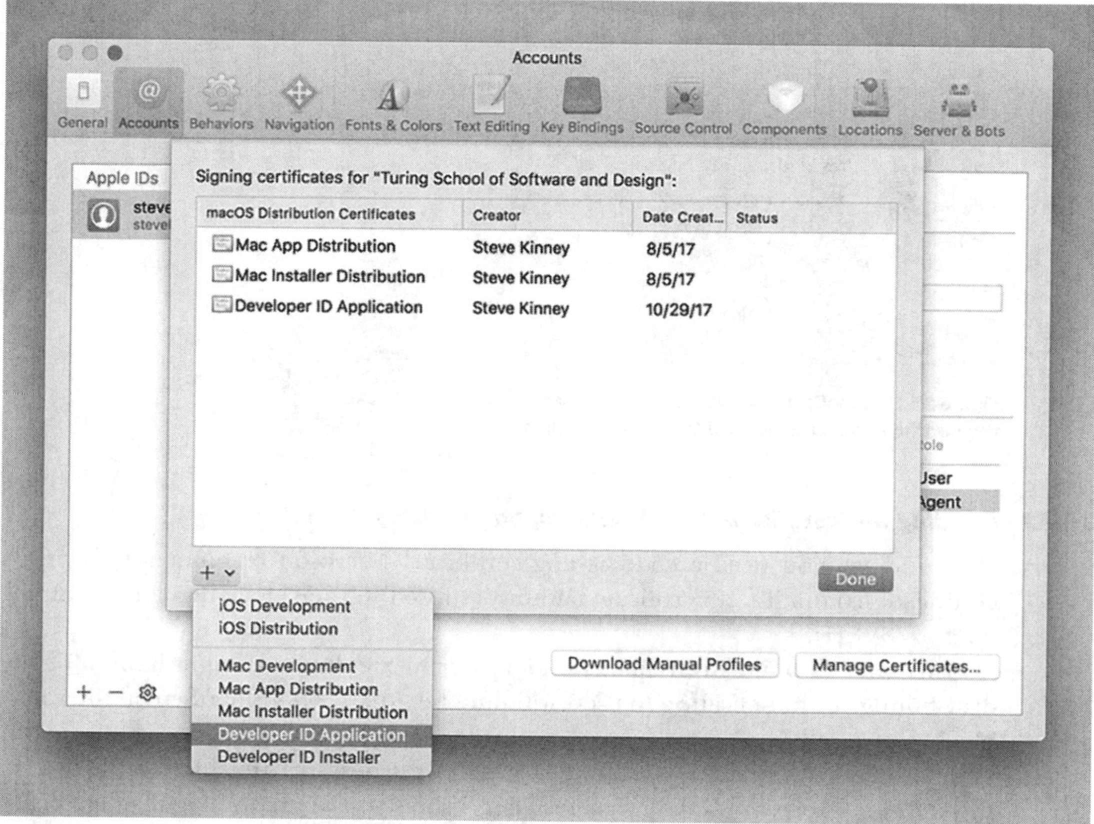

Figure 15.7 Select Developer ID Application and Developer ID Installer from the drop-down menu.

Xcode automatically adds these certificates to your Keychain. Electron Packager looks these up when it comes time to package your application and sign it. First, we need to modify the packaging script in our `package.json`.

Listing 15.8 Updated Mac packaging script: ./package.json

```
"build-mac": "electron-packager . --platform=darwin
➥--out=build --icon=./icons/Icon.icns --asar -overwrite
➥--app-bundle-id=\"net.stevekinney.firesale\"
➥--app-version=\"1.0.0\" --build-version=\"1.0.100\" --osx-sign",
```

This line is getting a bit long, and we begin to break it out a bit in chapter 16, but for now, we add a few important new arguments to the existing script: `--app-bundle-id`, `--app-version`, `--build-version`, and `--osx-sign`.

When running `npm run build-mac`, you are prompted for your password multiple times, as shown in figure 15.8, because Electron Packager accesses your keychain to use the certificates to sign your application.

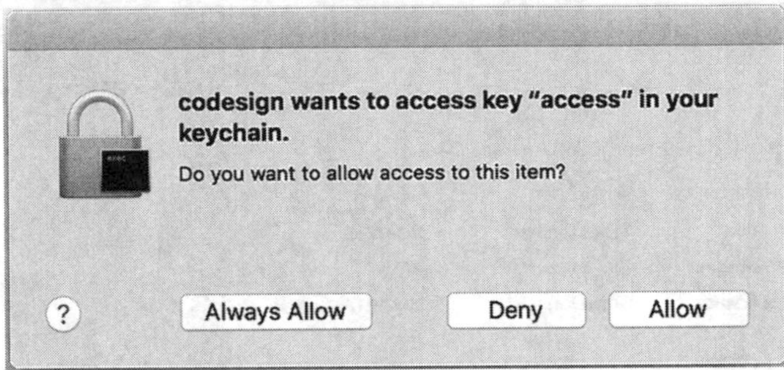

Figure 15.8 macOS's codesign utility accesses your keychain to use the certificates you generated to sign the application.

15.2.2 Building an installer and code signing on Windows

On Windows, you need a code-signing certificate. Microsoft recommends buying a certificate from a list of certificate authorities listed in their documentation (http://mng.bz/3VEH).

You can still build an installer without a certificate, but you might have difficulty distributing your application to users without one. Microsoft's SmartScreen filter may block your application from being downloaded, and many antivirus programs might mislabel your application as malware. For the purposes of this chapter, as we go through the process of building an installer, I show you where to plug in your certificate, should you move forward and decide to purchase one.

The Electron team maintains a helpful library for building installers on Windows. You can install this tool using `npm install --save-dev electron-winstaller`. We create a new folder called scripts and make a file called scripts/windows.js to store the configuration for our Windows installer. Add the content in listing 15.9 to the file we just created.

Listing 15.9 Windows installer configuration: ./scripts/windows.js

```
const { createWindowsInstaller } = require('electron-winstaller');
const path = require('path');

const iconPath = path.resolve(__dirname, '../icons/Icon.ico');
```

Imports the function to create a Windows installer

Locates the path to the icons for the application

```
const result = createWindowsInstaller({
  title: 'Fire Sale',
  authors: 'Steve Kinney',
  appDirectory: path.resolve(
    __dirname,
    '../build/Fire Sale-win32-x64'
  ),
  outputDirectory: path.resolve(
    __dirname,
    '../build/Fire Sale-win32-x64-installer'
  ),
  icon: iconPath,
  setupIcon: iconPath,
  name: 'FireSale',
  setupExe: 'FireSaleSetup.exe',
  setupMsi: 'FireSaleSetup.msi',
});

result
  .then(() => console.log('Success'))
  .catch(error => console.error('Failed', error));
```

Creates an installer. This returns a promise.

Locates the packaged application that you first built in chapter 14.

Specifies the directory where you would like the installer to be generated

Sets the icon for the application itself

Sets the icon for the installer packager. I've opted to use the same icon.

If the installer was created successfully, the promise resolves.

If an error occurred and the promise fails, log the error to the console.

If you have your certificates handy, you can add them to the configuration object. `certificateFile` should point to the path where the certificate is located. This process is similar to how we locate the `iconPath`. `certificatePassword` is the password for the certificate. Do not store the password in version control—particularly if your application is or ever will be open source.

SETTING UP SQUIRREL EVENTS

If you get really excited and double-click the FireSaleSetup executable, you may notice that things are a little strange. You see a loading GIF followed by the application immediately opening. It didn't add a shortcut to the desktop, or any other way of getting back to the application.

Uninstalling the application adds its own set of oddities. When you click the button in the Add and Remove Programs settings panel, you see the application open again before it finally uninstalls. We need to address this.

The Windows installer is set up with the Squirrel.Windows framework. When you start the application for the first time, or when it is being uninstalled, has been updated, or finds an available update, Squirrel passes an argument to your application. Luckily, working with Squirrel on Windows can range from incredibly simple to very easy. Let's start with the incredibly simple way, and then I'll show you what's happening under the hood.

The easiest way to get started is to delegate the work to someone else by installing `electron-squirrel-startup` using `npm install electron-squirrel-startup`. After you install this package, add the code from this listing to your ./app/main.js.

Listing 15.10 Setting up Squirrel events in the main process: ./app/main.js

```
const { app, BrowserWindow, dialog, Menu } = require('electron');
const createApplicationMenu = require('./application-menu');
const fs = require('fs');

require('./crash-reporter');

if(require('electron-squirrel-startup')) return;    <-- If the function in electron-squirrel-startup returns true, exits the main process.

// ...
```

With that simple change, all the oddities we encountered when working with `FireSaleSetup.exe` are squared away. So, what's happening in this module? The module is open source and can be found on GitHub (https://github.com/mongodb-js/electron-squirrel-startup), but it's a small file, and for the sake of completeness I list it here as well.

Listing 15.11 electron-squirrel-startup

```
var path = require('path');
var spawn = require('child_process').spawn;
var debug = require('debug')('electron-squirrel-startup');
var app = require('electron').app;

var run = function(args, done) {
  var updateExe = path.resolve(    <-- Gets the path of the Squirrel updater
    path.dirname(process.execPath), '..', 'Update.exe'
  );
  debug('Spawning `%s` with args `%s`', updateExe, args);
  spawn(updateExe, args, {
    detached: true
  }).on('close', done);
};

var check = function() {
  if (process.platform === 'win32') {    <-- Does any of the following, only if the application is running on Windows
    var cmd = process.argv[1];    <-- Gets the first argument passed from the command line
    debug('processing squirrel command `%s`', cmd);
    var target = path.basename(process.execPath);

    if (cmd === '--squirrel-install' || cmd === '--squirrel-updated') {    <-- Checks if the application is being run as an installer or updater
      run(['--createShortcut=' + target + ''], app.quit);    <-- Creates an application shortcut on the desktop, and quits
      return true;    <-- Returns true, which fulfills the conditional in the main process
    }
    if (cmd === '--squirrel-uninstall') {    <-- Checks if the application is being uninstalled
      run(['--removeShortcut=' + target + ''], app.quit);    <-- Removes the shortcut from the desktop, and quits the application
      return true;
    }
    if (cmd === '--squirrel-obsolete') {
      app.quit();
      return true;
```

```
    }
  }
  return false;
};
```

If none of the cases are true, returns false.

```
module.exports = check();
```

If Squirrel did anything, it returns `true`. Recall in ./app/main.js that we used a conditional and if `require('electron-squirrel-startup')` returned `true`, we ended the main process early. This allows us to tap into the Squirrel framework when necessary and not start the application when we're installing or uninstalling it. You can also see that on installation and uninstallation, Squirrel creates and removes the desktop shortcut as needed.

15.3 Automatically updating applications

Whether you've completed a hot new feature that you want everyone to have or you're trying to correct a critical bug that you found after implementing the crash and error report, the ability to push out updates to your users is important.

We tend to take this capability for granted as web developers. Whenever we deploy a new application to the web, we can reasonably expect that users are getting the latest and greatest version of it. But that's not necessarily true when we're building desktop applications. We can tell users about it, but there is no guarantee that they're going to take the time to download it.

Browsers used to suffer from this problem. New JavaScript language and web platform features would be released, but you couldn't use them because users typically did not update their browsers on a regular basis. Today, modern browsers like Chrome and Firefox push out new versions to users every six weeks or so. The update is automatically downloaded, and the next time the user starts the browser, the new one is swapped in without them having to think about the tedious process of upgrading.

It shouldn't be a surprise at this point to hear that Electron provides a mechanism for us to do this with our applications—with some exceptions. As of this writing, this feature is limited to macOS and Windows. There is currently no support for auto-updating Electron applications on Linux.

15.3.1 Setting up automatic updates in Electron

Like crash reporting, implementing automatic updates has two sides: your application and a server to host releases of your application. We get into the details momentarily, but let's talk about how this works at a high level first. After you've configured the `autoUpdater` module, it pings your release server every time the application starts. If the server responds with an HTTP 204 response, then Electron knows that it is running the latest version of the application. If there is a new version, the server returns an HTTP 200 JSON-formatted response with the URL of the new release.

You may have your own server for hosting releases. That's perfectly fine. If you do not, we create a simple server to get you off the ground and demonstrate auto-updating in action. But this is not meant to be prescriptive. As long as you have a server that responds with the correct HTTP status codes and payload if there is a new release, Electron does not have strong opinions on the implementation details, and we won't either, for the time being.

To get this working, we check if we're using a production version of the application. If so, we send a request to the server asking for the most recent version of the application. If a new version exists, ask the user if they are interested in updating. When they agree, tell the autoUpdater module to quit the application and install the new version on our behalf.

Listing 15.12 Implementing Electron's autoUpdater: ./app/auto-updater.js

```
const { app, autoUpdater, dialog, BrowserWindow } = require('electron');

const isDevelopment = app.getPath('exe').indexOf('electron') !== -1;

const baseUrl = 'https://firesale-releases.glitch.me';

const platform = process.platform;
const currentVersion = app.getVersion();

const releaseFeed =
    `${baseUrl}/releases/${platform}?currentVersion=${currentVersion}`;

if (isDevelopment) {
  console.info('[AutoUpdater]', 'In Developement Mode. Skipping…');
} else {
  console.info('[AutoUpdater]', `Setting release feed to ${releaseFeed}.`);
  autoUpdater.setFeedURL(releaseFeed);
}

autoUpdater.addListener('update-available', () => {
    dialog.showMessageBox({
    type: 'question',
    buttons: ['Install & Relaunch', 'Not Now'],
    defaultId: 0,
    message: `${app.getName()} has been updated!`,
    detail: 'An update has been downloaded and can be installed now.'
  }, response => {
    if (response === 0) {
      setTimeout(() => {
        app.removeAllListeners('window-all-closed');
        BrowserWindow.getAllWindows().forEach(win => win.close());
        autoUpdater.quitAndInstall();
```

Annotations:
- Gets the current OS on which application is running (platform)
- Checks if we're running this Electron application in development (isDevelopment)
- Stores the base URL of the server where you host releases (baseUrl)
- Gets the current version of the application (currentVersion)
- Creates the path from which to request an update, based on the OS and application version (releaseFeed)
- If the application is in development mode, does not check for an update . . .
- . . . otherwise, sets the feed of the autoUpdater to the URL you just created.
- If an update is available, performs the action provided
- Removes the event listener for the windows-all-closed event
- Closes all of the windows
- Quits the application, and installs the update

```
        }, 0);
      }
    });
  });

module.exports = autoUpdater;
```

On macOS, autoUpdater fails if the application has not been code signed. When we're developing the application, we use a version that has not been signed. These two facts are in direct opposition. The best course of action is not to fetch an update if we're in development. This outcome also makes sense, because we're likely working on the next version of the application, as opposed to the most recently released version.

You can implement this in a few ways. You could, for example, try to set the feed URL and then catch the error if the application hasn't been code signed. Based purely on aesthetic reasons, this is not something I like to do. Electron does not have an API to let us know whether we're in development, but when we are in development, we're using a version of Electron buried inside of our node_modules directory. In my case, it's located at ./node_modules/electron/dist/Electron.app/Contents/MacOS/Electron. In production it is located in the application bundle itself. I've taken advantage of this fun fact to determine whether the application is in development.

If it's not in development, then we create a URL to look for updates based on the platform on which the application is running. This URL can technically be anything you want. You don't have to follow my example, if your setup is different than the one we write together next.

We tell the autoUpdater module to send a request to the URL provided and ask if there are any updates. If there are, then the updates-available event runs. We've set up a listener for that event. If an update is available, we ask the user if they would like to update to the latest and greatest version of Fire Sale. If they agree, then we take a series of steps to gracefully transition them to the new version.

First, I remove the event listener that we set up in ./app/main.js that prevents the application from quitting if all of the windows are closed on macOS. Next, we iterate through the windows and close them. We do this to prompt the user to save any changes made to the file. Finally, we call autoUpdater.quitAndInstall(), which—unsuprisingly—closes the application and installs the newly downloaded update. Squirrel takes care of all of this on our behalf.

15.3.2 Setting up a server for automatic updates

As with the crash reporter, we set up a deliberately simple server for notifying your users of updates. A more robust example might use a database to store the most recent version along with release notes and more. You could store your application bundles on S3, but going through the process of creating a full-featured web server is outside the scope of this book.

As I mentioned earlier, our server must fulfill a simple contract to play nicely with Electron's autoUpdater module. If the application matches the latest release, the server should return a response with a 204 status code. If an update is available, the servers should return a JSON object that has a `url` property with the URL to the new application as its value.

I've hosted the server (https://firesale-releases.glitch.me/) and its code (https://glitch.com/edit/#!/firesale-releases) on Glitch, where you can remix it for your own purposes. Glitch also hosts the application, so we can use it in Fire Sale to pull down an update. I encourage you to visit the link to the previous code for the most recent version, but I include an annotated version here as well.

Listing 15.13 Setting up the release server

```
const express = require('express');
const fs = require('fs');
const path = require('path');
const app = express();

app.use(express.static('public'));

const latestRelease = '1.2.0';

app.get("/", (request, response) => {
  response.sendFile(__dirname + '/views/index.html');
});

app.get('/releases/:platform', (request, response) => {
  const { platform } = request.params;
  const { currentVersion } = request.query;

  if (currentVersion === latestRelease) {
    response.status(204);
    return response.end();
  }

  if (platform === 'darwin') {
    return response.json({
      url: …
    });
  }

  if (platform === 'win32') {
    return response.json({
      url: …
    });
  }

  if (platform === 'linux') {
    return response.json({
      url: …
    });
  }

  response.status(404).end();
});
```

Annotations:

- This is the most recent release of Fire Sale. (`const latestRelease = '1.2.0';`)
- Sets up a route that listens for GET requests on a specific platform with an optional version passed in (`app.get('/releases/:platform', …)`)
- Pulls the OS platform from the URL parameters (`const { platform } = request.params;`)
- Pulls the current version from a query parameter
- Checks if the current version equals the latest version referenced earlier
- If it matches, returns an HTTP 204 status code (`response.status(204);`)
- If the platform is macOS, returns a payload with the URL to the newest bundle for macOS (`if (platform === 'darwin')`)
- If the platform is Windows, returns a payload with the URL to the newest bundle for Windows (`if (platform === 'win32')`)
- If the platform is Linux, returns a payload with the URL to the newest bundle for Linux (`if (platform === 'linux')`)

```
const listener = app.listen(process.env.PORT, () => {
  console.log('Your app is listening on port ' + listener.address().port);
});
```

I started by storing a reference to the most recent version of Fire Sale in a variable. Next, I set up a dynamic route. If you recall, Fire Sale requests updates based on the platform on which it's running. Versions running on macOS, Windows, and Linux request updates from /releases/darwin, /releases/win32, and /releases/linux, respectively. We also check if the version number is included as a query parameter.

If the current version and the latest release match, then we respond with a 204 status code to let the application know that it is currently running the most recent version. If they do not match, we assume that an update is available. We then check which platform the user requested and send them the URL for the appropriate flavor of the latest release of Fire Sale, a shown in figure 15.9.

If you've used the code I provided for the `autoUpdater` and pointed it at https://firesale-releases.glitch.me/, then you should be notified about a very important update to Fire Sale.

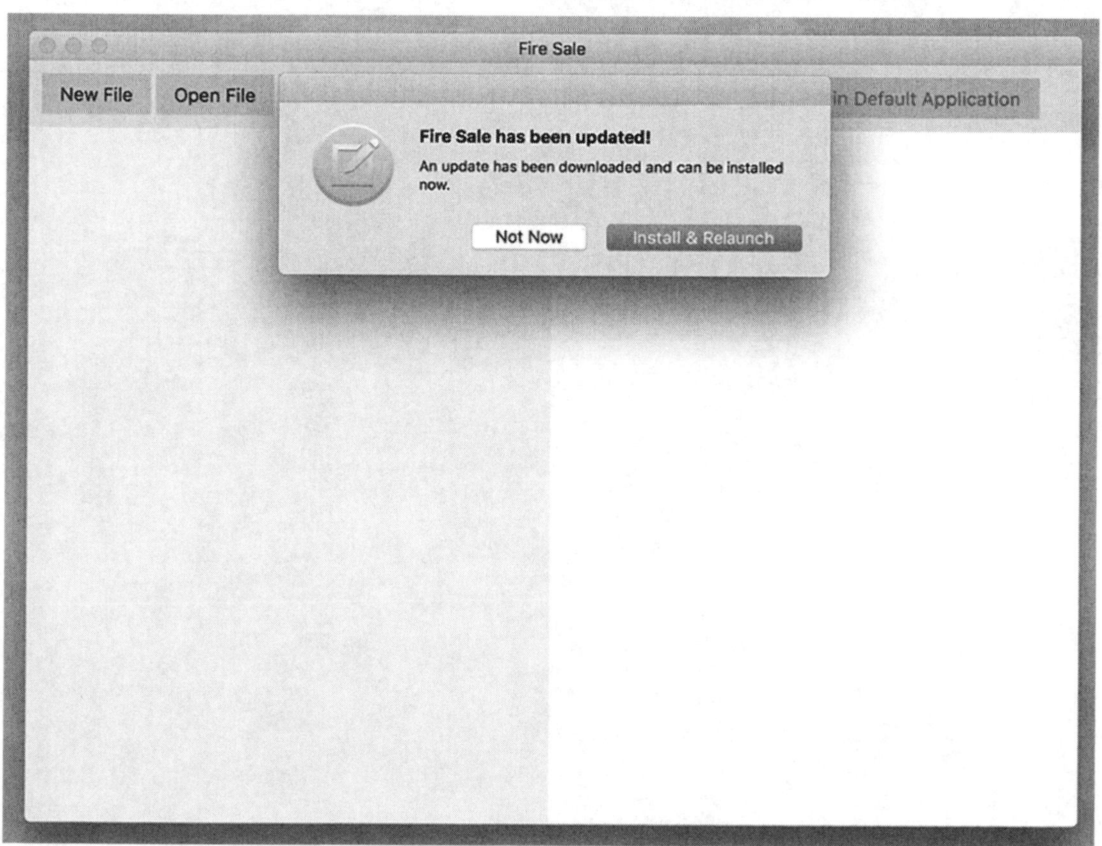

Figure 15.9 Fire Sale automatically notifies users when a new version is available on the server.

Summary

- Electron includes built-in modules for handling crash reports and automatic updates.
- The crash report sends reports in a mini-dump format when the application outright crashes.
- Uncaught exceptions can also be monitored and reported to a server for additional insight.
- Applications should be code signed to verify that they have not been tampered with.
  - On macOS, code-signing certificates can be generated from Xcode.
  - On Windows, developers can purchase certificates from a certificate authority.
- Windows installers can be easily created using the `electron-winstaller` and `electron-squirrel-startup` packages on npm.
- Electron's `autoUpdater` module checks for updates on start up.
- `autoUpdater` uses the open source Squirrel framework under the hood to manage installation and updates.

16 Distributing your application through the Mac App Store

This chapter covers

- Packing your application for the Mac App Store
- Creating certificates and signing your application
- Uploading your application to iTunes Connect

In the previous chapter, we built two of our projects from earlier in the book. This eliminated the need for our users to install Node.js and use the command line to start one of our applications. In this chapter, we discuss strategies for distributing an application built with Electron.

16.1 Submitting your application to the Mac App Store

Distributing your application through the Mac App Store has a few distinct advantages. First, you can easily charge money for your application if you're interested in going down that road. Second, the Mac App Store handles application updates on your behalf. The disadvantages are that enrolling in Apple's Developer Program isn't free and—should you decided to charge for your application—Apple takes a 30% cut of the sale price of your application.

Submitting your application to the Mac App Store takes many steps beyond simply packaging your application—as we did in chapter 14. You must also create security certificates and sign your application to ensure that users are receiving an official version of it. Signing your application is good practice in general, and this chapter is worth reading, even if you do not intend to submit your application to the Mac App Store. The process of signing and uploading your application is primarily performed through native and web-based UIs provided by Apple. As a result, this chapter is highly visual.

Before you can submit an application to the Mac App Store, you must have Xcode installed on your Mac, and you need to sign up for the Apple Developer Program. Xcode, which is available on the Mac App Store, is a large application, so start that download first before enrolling in the developer program. To do this, visit https://developer.apple.com/programs/, and enroll in the program as either an individual or an organization.

16.1.1 Signing the application

Code signing is a technology that allows you to certify that your application is, in fact, created by you and not some imposter. When a user first installs your application, the operating system tracks the certificate you included. Only you can generate this certificate, which means if it changes, the new version of the application could be from a malicious attacker.

We need two certificates: one for the application itself, and one for the installer we upload to the Mac App Store—which we create later in this chapter. To create these certificates, open the Keychain Access application, shown in figure 16.1, located in the /Applications/Utilities directory. This application is included in macOS and should be available even if you haven't installed Xcode yet.

> **Other uses of Keychain Access**
>
> As you might be able to guess from the name, Keychain Access does more than just generate certificates for signing applications. It is where macOS stores all of your saved passwords and certificates. It also stores all of the passwords for wireless networks that you've asked it to remember. If you ever need to look up a password, you can do so using Keychain Access.

With the application open, navigate to the Keychain Access application menu, then select Certificate Assistant, followed by Request a Certification From a Certificate Authority, as shown in figure 16.1. This action triggers a dialog box, shown in figure 16.2, where you can add additional information about the certificate to be generated.

Make sure you select Saved to Disk when creating the certificate. After you click Continue, you are prompted to save a file with the name CertificateSigningRequest .certSigningRequest. Where you choose to save the file is up to you—it doesn't make a difference as long as you can find it again later.

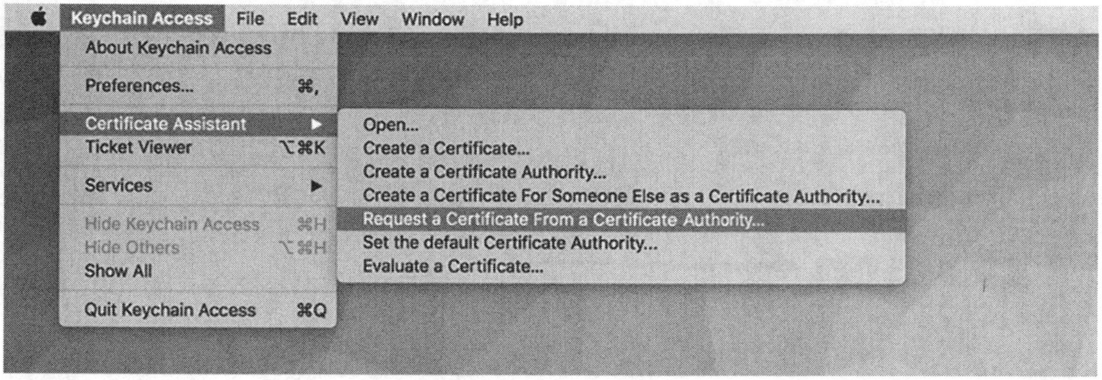

Figure 16.1 Request a certificate using Keychain Access.

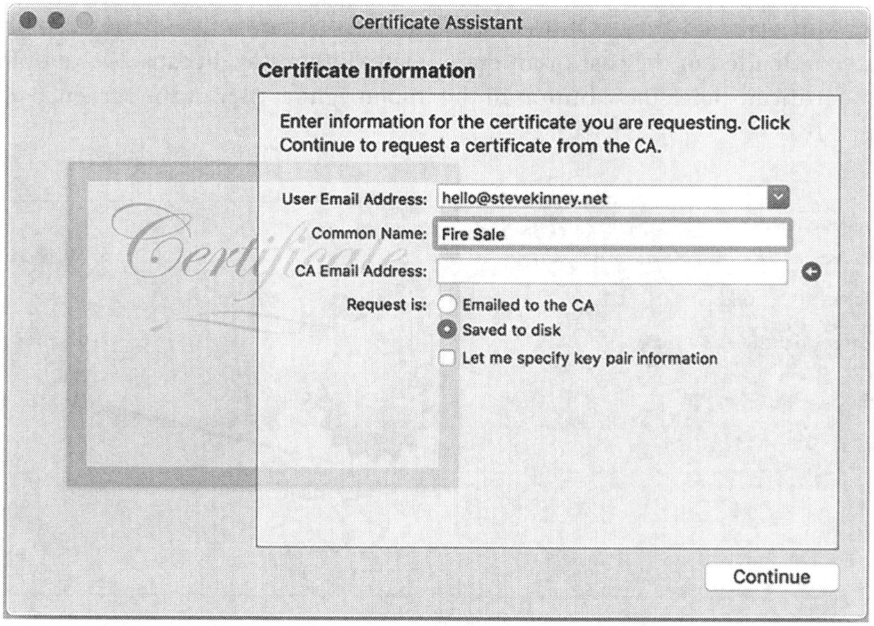

Figure 16.2 Enter information for your application signing certificate request.

When you have a certificate, you need to let Apple know about it. Visit the Apple Developer Program Member Center (https://developer.apple.com/account), and select Certificates, IDs, and Profiles from the left-hand sidebar. By default, the page for managing iOS certificates opens. Select macOS as the target platform, as shown in figure 16.3.

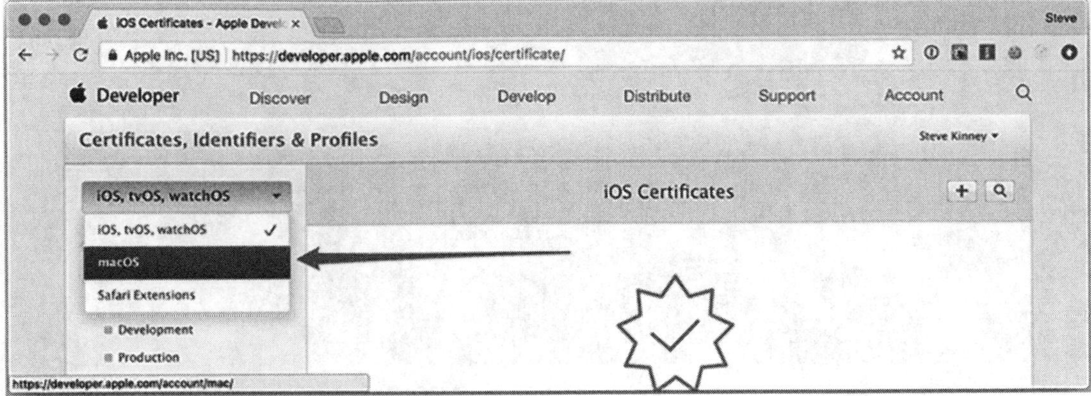

Figure 16.3 Select macOS as the target platform.

After you switched from iOS to macOS, you see either a list of the certificates that you've uploaded in the past or an empty state. Either way, because we're uploading a new certificate, click the + button in the upper-right corner of the screen, as shown in figure 16.4.

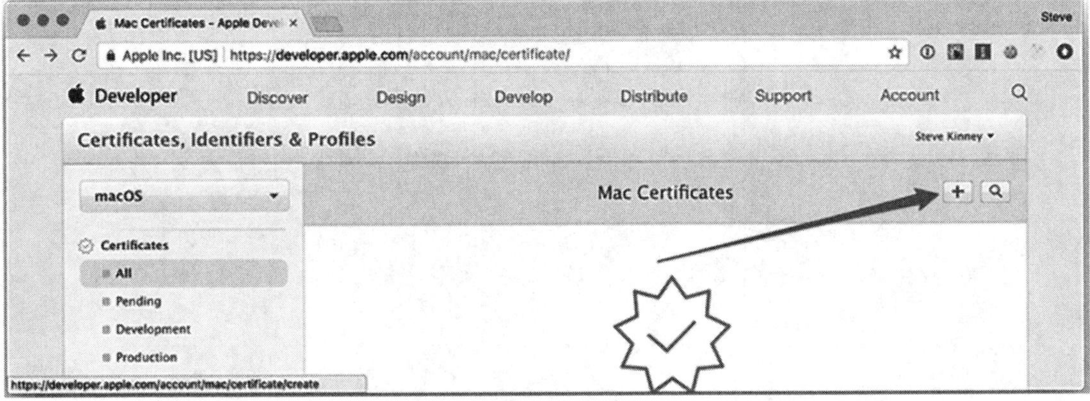

Figure 16.4 Add the certificate request you generated earlier.

The certificate can be used for a variety of purposes. In addition to signing your application, certificates can be used to sign server-generated push messages, which you may have seen on mobile platforms to inform users that something has happened in an application that is not currently open.

This is outside of the scope of this book and a topic for another day. As you may have guessed, we want to create a production-ready Mac App Store version of Fire Sale and need a Mac App Store certificate to do that. Scroll past the development options along the top, and select Mac App Store, as shown in figure 16.5.

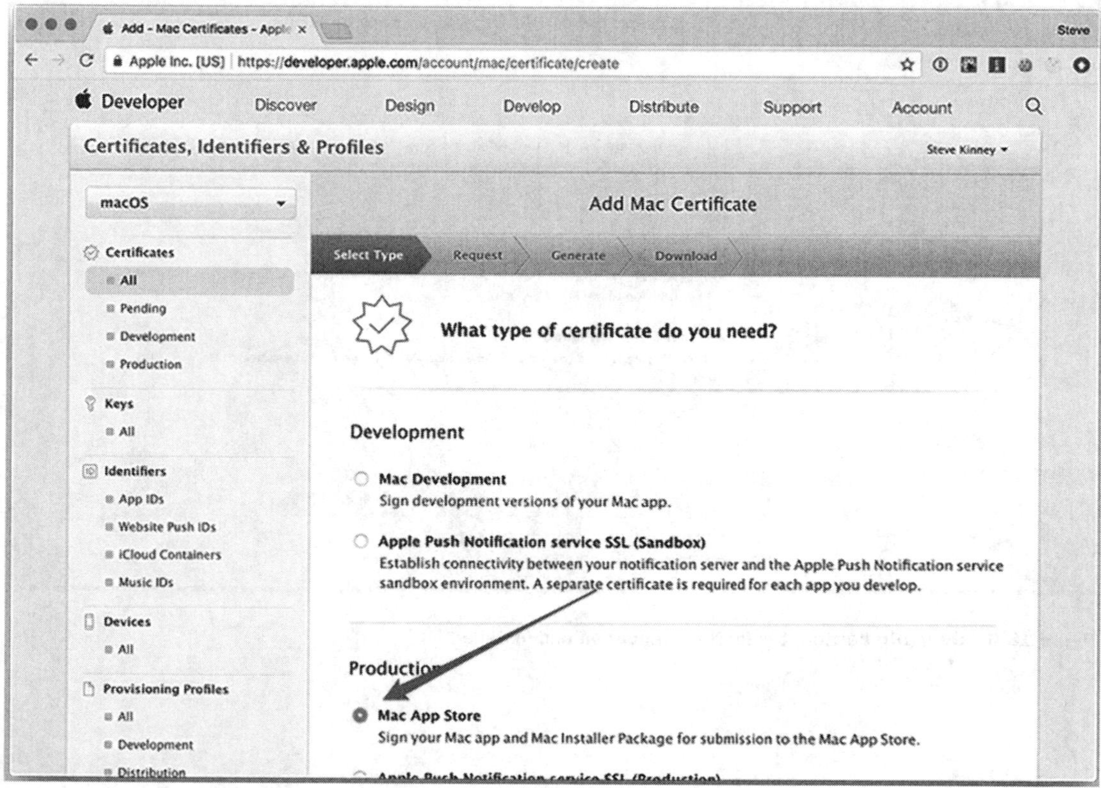

Figure 16.5 Select Mac App Store as the type of certificate that you're requesting.

Figures 16.6 through 16.8 show that I am creating a Mac App Distribution certificate. In practice however, you need to go through these steps twice—once with Mac App Distribution selected and once with Mac Installer Distribution selected. The process is exactly the same for both, and you receive two certificates at the end. The only difference is which radio button you choose at the very beginning of the process.

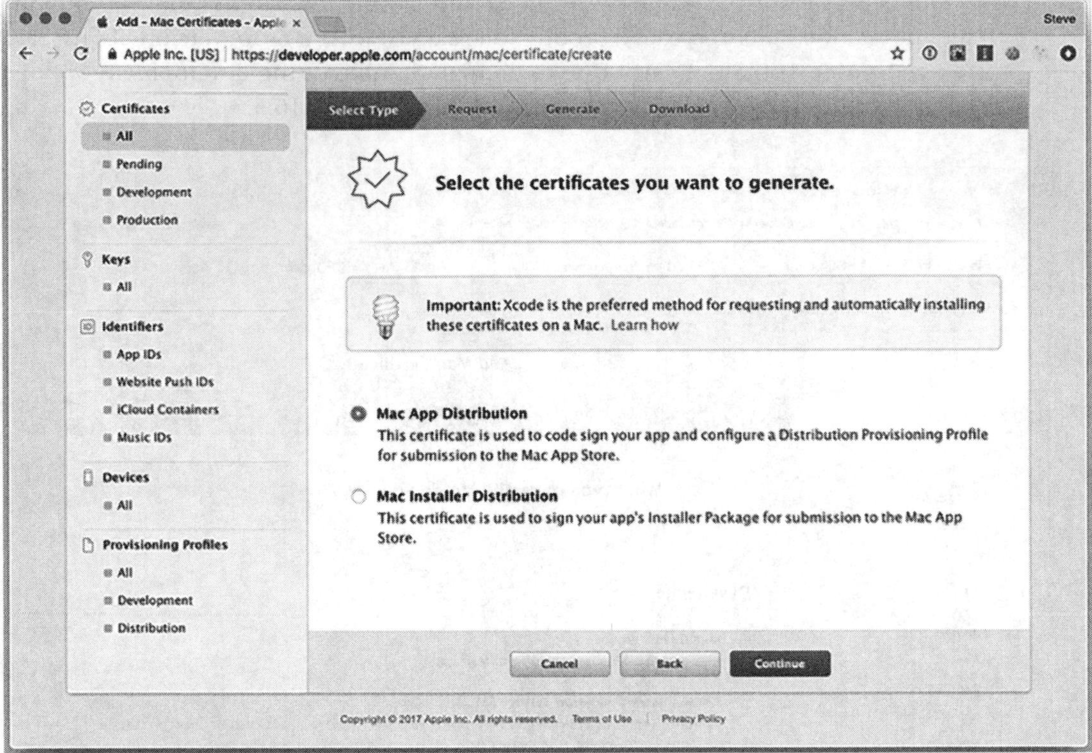

Figure 16.6 Generate certificates for the application and installer.

Earlier in the chapter, we created a file with the extension certSigningRequest. We use this file to request certificates from Apple, which are signed by the Apple Worldwide Developer Relations Certification Authority. When you sign an application, you use a key that can be generated only with a private key stored locally on your computer. It's important that you are careful with this private key. It's the only way to sign an application that matches the public key, and anyone with access to your private key can sign applications on your behalf.

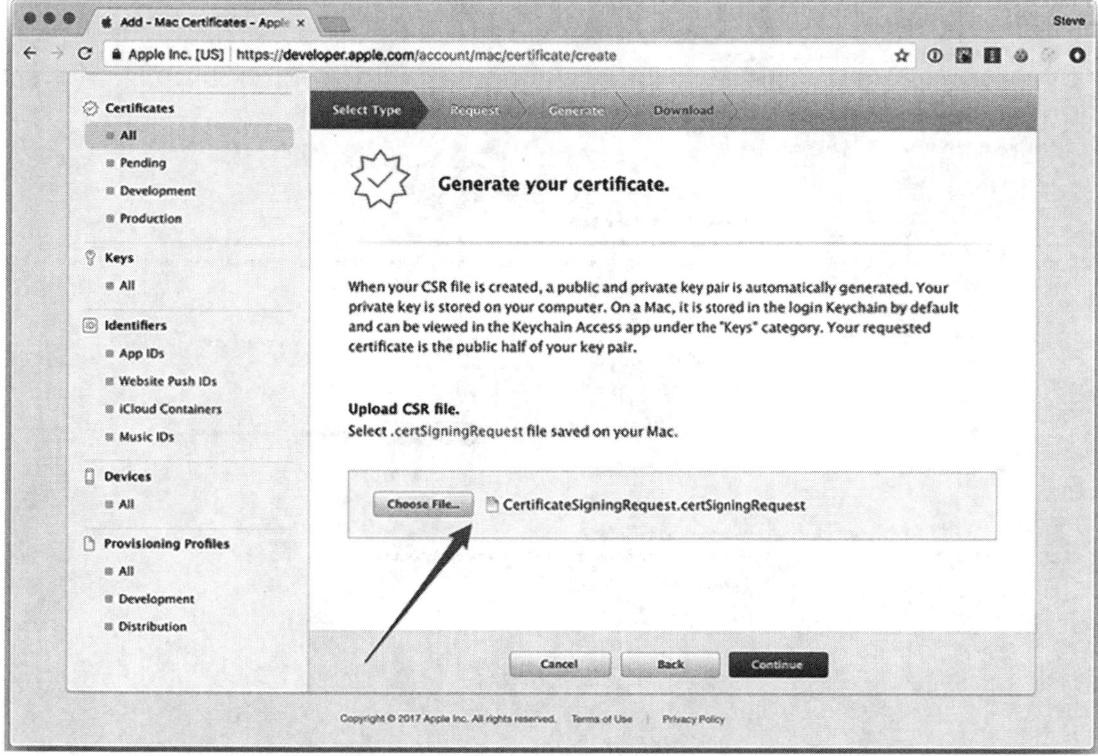

Figure 16.7 Upload the certificate signing request file you created earlier.

When prompted, upload the certificate-signing request that you generated in Keychain Access. Apple signs the certificate and prompts you to download it, as shown in figure 16.8. After downloading the certificate, you can double-click it to add to Keychain Access automatically.

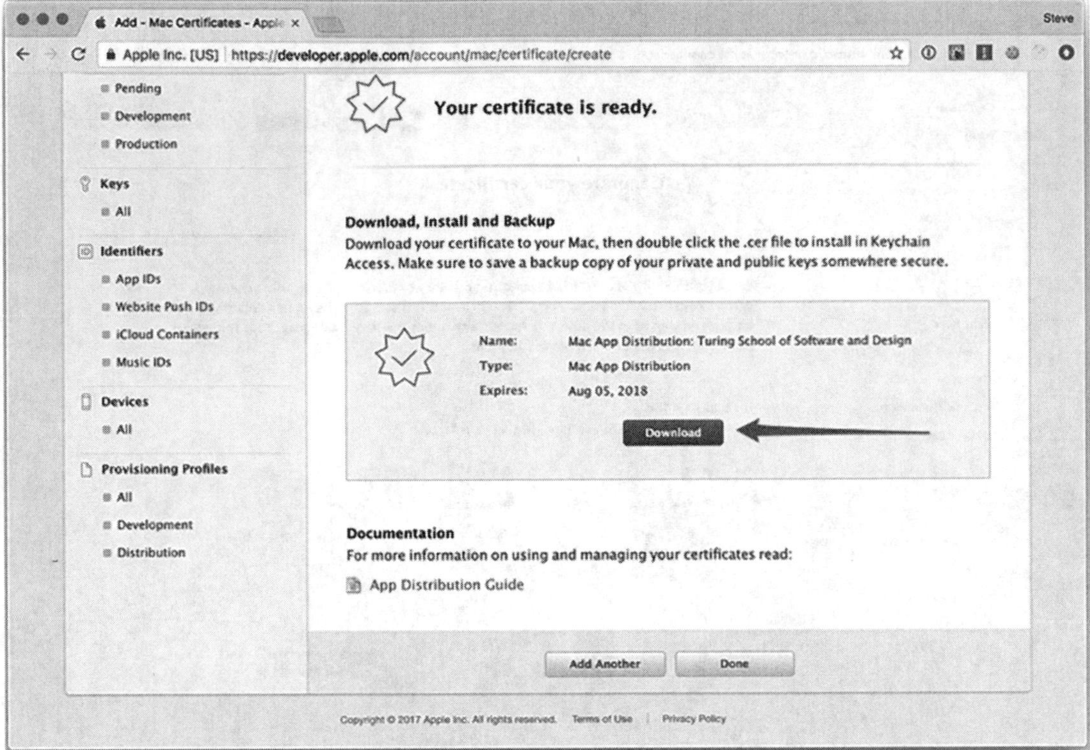

Figure 16.8 Download your completed certificate.

When you complete this process for both Mac App Distribution and Mac Installer Distribution certificates, you should see both certificates inside Keychain Access, as shown in figure 16.9. Congratulations—you're now ready to sign your application and begin getting it ready for submission to the Mac App Store. In the next section, we begin the process of registering the application with Apple and providing the metadata required to be listed in the App Store.

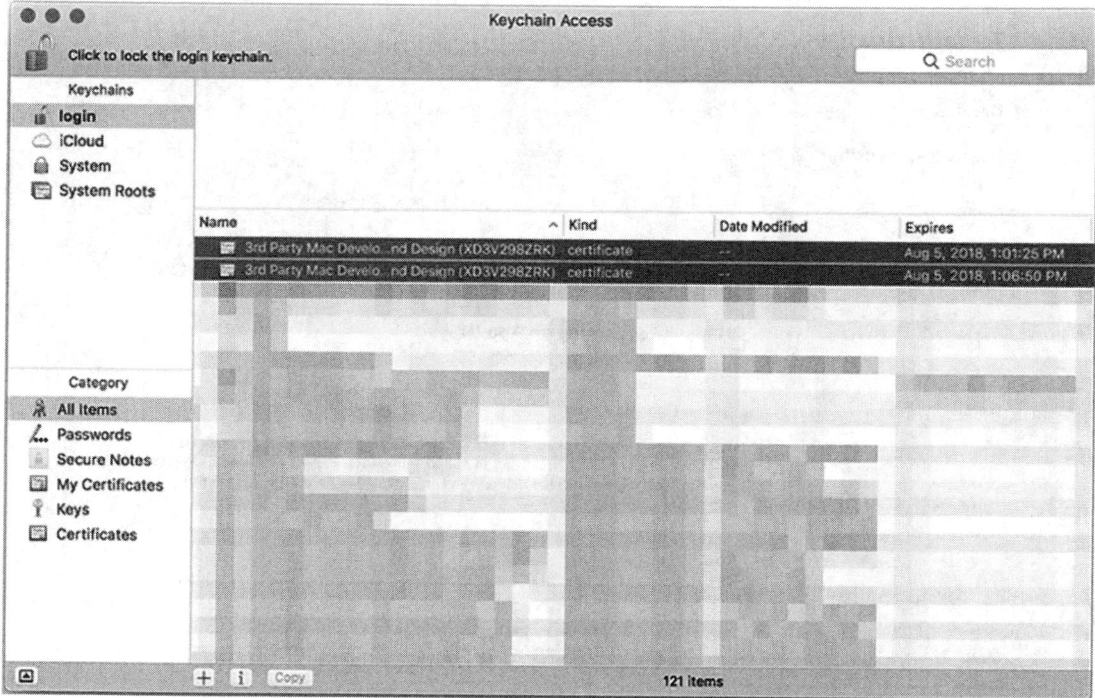

Figure 16.9 The application and installer certificates listed in Keychain Access.

16.1.2 Registering your application with the Mac App Store

With your certificates in place, you must register the application itself with Apple before you can upload your application binary. Even if you have no intention of distributing an application through the Mac App Store, signing your application and registering it with Apple is a good practice. Unsigned applications trigger those intimidating gatekeeper errors that Apple displays when a user tries to open an unsigned application inside modern versions of macOS. In addition, depending on a user's settings, they may not be allowed to open unsigned applications at all. Inside the Certificates, Identifiers, and Profiles section, select App ID from the sidebar on the left, as shown in Figure 16.10.

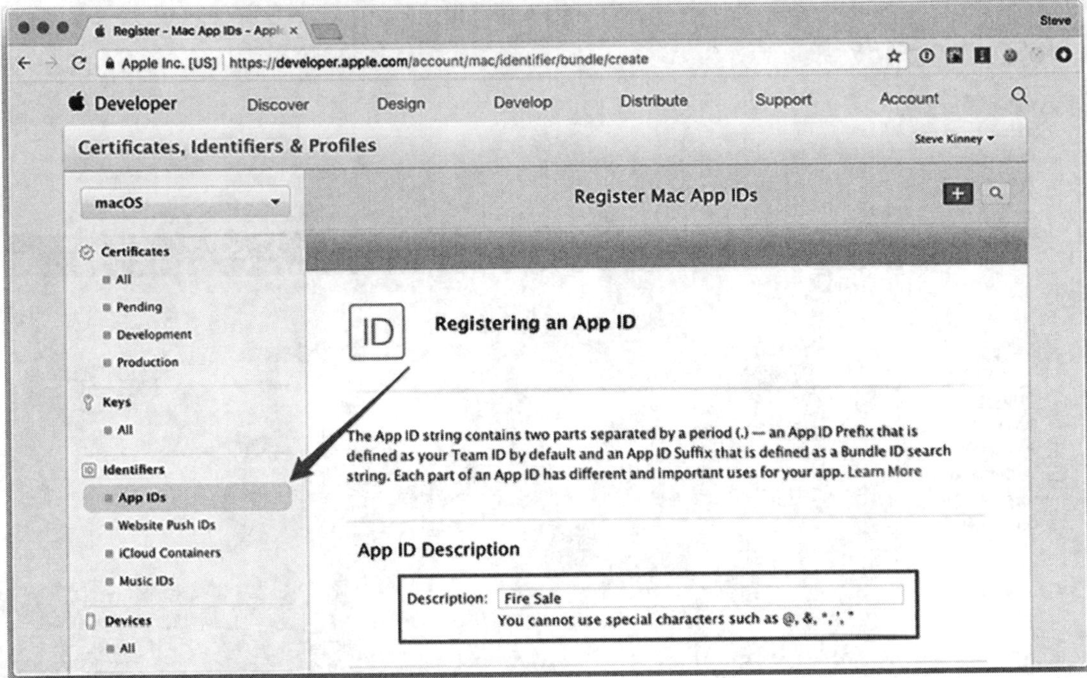

Figure 16.10 Register your App ID.

An App ID is a unique identifier for your application. Creating an App ID consists of three steps. The first is to give it an App ID description. This is a colloquial name for the application and is generally what users see as the title of your application when viewing it in the App Store.

The second is a list of services that your application requests access to, such as sending push notifications, displaying maps, or saving or retrieving files from iCloud. Fire Sale does not use any of these, so we'll stick with the defaults. Third, you create an App ID Suffix, which is the truly unique identifier for your application. It's a lot like a backward web domain. In this case, I used net.stevekinney.firesale as opposed to firesale.stevekinney.net, which is something you might expect to find on the web.

16.1.3 Adding the application to iTunes Connect

You're not out of the woods yet. Your next step is to add the application to iTunes Connect (https://itunesconnect.apple.com/), which represents the application's listing in the Mac App Store. From here, you can add a description of your application, screenshots, and more. A word of caution: I won't cover every aspect of uploading screenshots and things along those lines, but I will tell you that Apple takes this seriously and will reject your application if you fail to include all of the necessary information—including a link to a valid webpage where users can find support for your application.

Once inside iTunes Connect, click the My Apps icon in the upper-left corner, shown in figure 16.11. In this section, you see either a list of your existing applications or an empty state if this is your first application. Click the + button in the upper-left side of the window, and select New Mac App, as shown in figure 16.12.

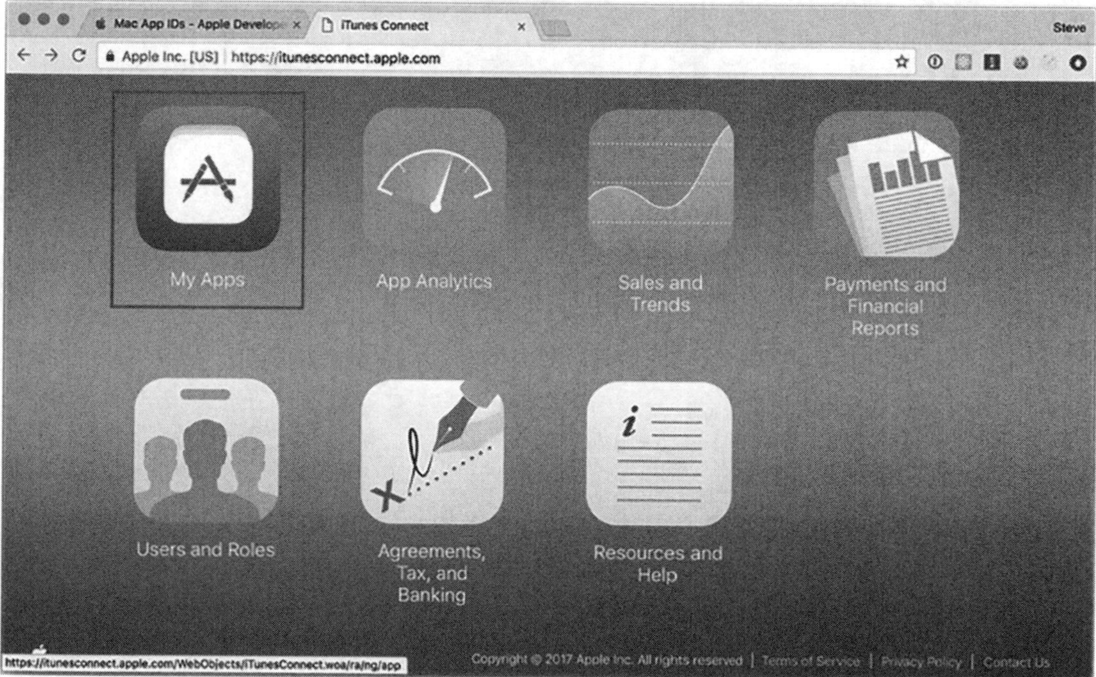

Figure 16.11 Select My Apps in iTunes Connect.

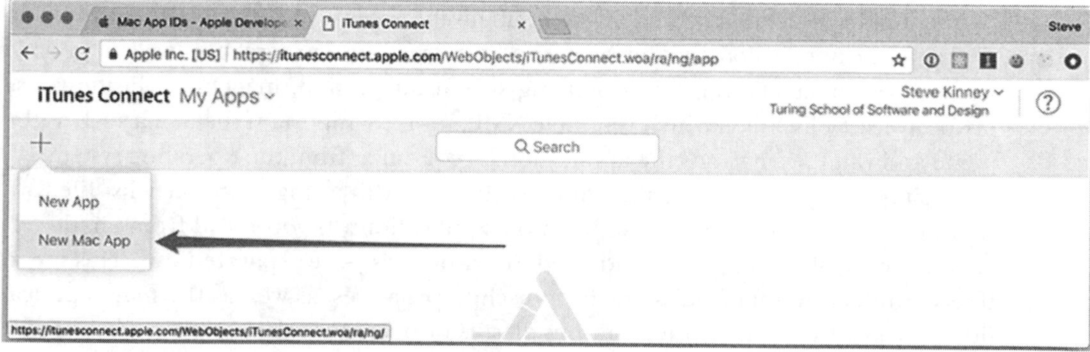

Figure 16.12 Add a new Mac application in iTunes Connect.

At this stage, as shown in figure 16.13, you are asked for some cursory information about your application: its name, primary language, the App ID description and suffix you created in the previous section, and more. The SKU is optional and is just used to identify application sales for the sake of accounting.

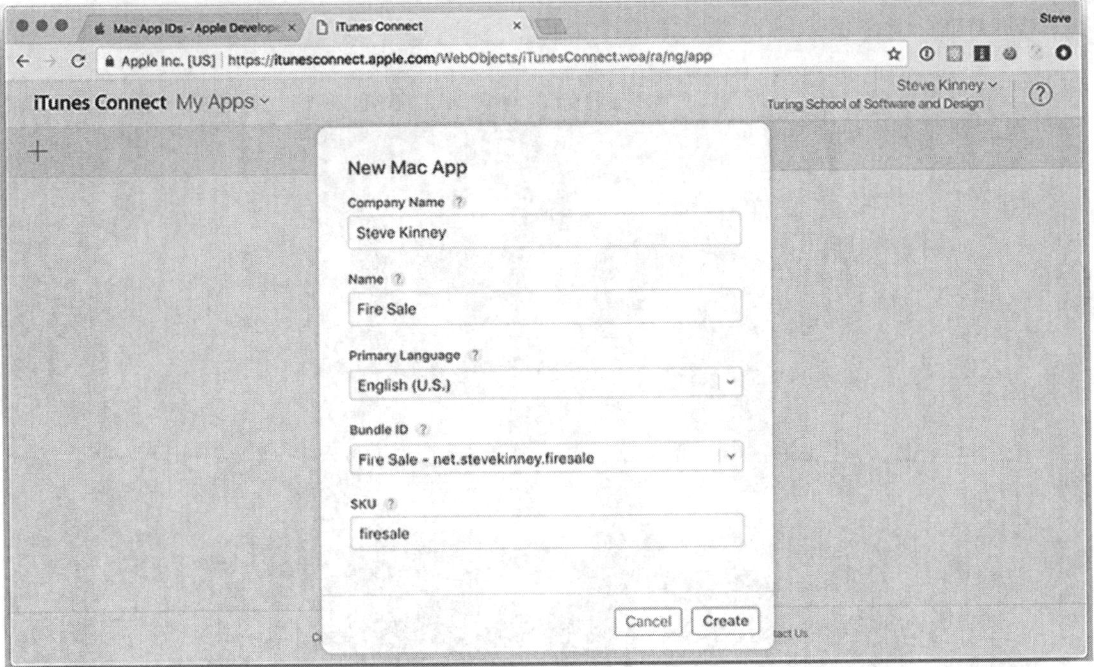

Figure 16.13 Provide details about the application in iTunes Connect.

16.1.4 Packaging your application for the Mac App Store

In chapter 14, we performed all of our configuration inline in the package.json file. To package our application for the Mac App Store, we need to sign it as well as provide some other metadata to aid in operating system integration. macOS applications use property list (.plist) files, which resemble XML, to store important metadata such as the name and what permissions the application is requesting from the operating system.

A simple application might be able to get away with a single property list file. But Electron applications aren't exactly simple applications. If you recall from chapter 1, each process—both the main and renderer processes—are separated out. This mean that we'll need to set permissions for our child processes, as well as the main application process. In addition, Electron bundles its own frameworks as well as libraries for media playback. These must be signed as well.

To accomplish this, we set up three property list files: info.plist stores the generic metadata for our application, parent.plist stores the sandbox permissions for the parent process, and child.plist stores the sandbox permissions for the child process. In this example, child processes extend the parent's permissions. These eventually are installed using a `build` script. As a result, I've decided to place each of these in a folder called ./scripts/mas. My naming conventions are not important. If you'd like to store these files somewhere else, that's fine. The Electron API Demos application stores the property lists in its assets folder. For the purposes of simplicity and clarity, I've chosen to keep all of the files in listings 16.1–16.3 in the same folder as the `build` script that we'll create together shortly.

Listing 16.1 Setting up the application: ./scripts/mas/info.plist

```
<?xml version="1.0" encoding="UTF-8"?>
<!DOCTYPE plist PUBLIC "-//Apple//DTD PLIST 1.0//EN"
     "http://www.apple.com/DTDs/PropertyList-1.0.dtd">
<plist version="1.0">
  <dict>
    <key>CFBundleURLTypes</key>
    <array>
      <dict>
        <key>CFBundleURLSchemes</key>
        <array>
          <string>firesale</string>
        </array>
        <key>CFBundleURLName</key>
        <string>Fire Sale</string>     <- This is the same as the productName field in your package.json.
      </dict>
    </array>
    <key>ElectronTeamID</key>
    <string>XD3V298ZRK</string>     <- Your Apple Team ID.
  </dict>
</plist>
```

Listing 16.2 Setting parent permissions: ./scripts/mas/parent.plist

```
<?xml version="1.0" encoding="UTF-8"?>
<!DOCTYPE plist PUBLIC "-//Apple//DTD PLIST 1.0//EN"
     "http://www.apple.com/DTDs/PropertyList-1.0.dtd">
<plist version="1.0">
  <dict>
    <key>com.apple.security.app-sandbox</key>
    <true/>     <- Mac App Store applications must use sandboxing.
    <key>com.apple.security.application-groups</key>     <- Allows access to the sandboxed containers of other applications by your team
    <string>XD3V298ZRK.net.stevekinney.firesale</string>     <- Identifies your team using the Team ID and bundle identifier
    <key>com.apple.security.files.user-selected.read-write</key>     <- Asks for permission to read and write files using the Open and Save dialog boxes
    <true/>
  </dict>
</plist>
```

All applications on the Mac App Store must enable *sandboxing*, which wraps each application into an isolated container and limits its ability to access the rest of the operating system. Apple does this in the name of security. That said, many applications can't do their jobs if isolated to a sandbox. Apple understands this and allows applications to clearly state what entitlements they need. We know that Fire Sale uses Open and Save dialog boxes to read and write from the filesystem, so we clearly state that we need that access.

One exception to sandboxing is that applications are allowed to reach into the containers of other applications created by the same developer. We never created tight integrations between Fire Sale and Clipmaster 900 or Jetsetter, but we may down the line. Stating the application group lets macOS know that this application is part of a family—even if it's a one-person family for now.

Listing 16.3 Extending permissions: ./scripts/mas/child.plist

```
<?xml version="1.0" encoding="UTF-8"?>
<!DOCTYPE plist PUBLIC "-//Apple//DTD PLIST 1.0//EN"
     "http://www.apple.com/DTDs/PropertyList-1.0.dtd">
<plist version="1.0">
  <dict>
    <key>com.apple.security.app-sandbox</key>
    <true/>
    <key>com.apple.security.inherit</key>
    <true/>
  </dict>
</plist>
```

Tells Apple that child processes will inherit the same permissions as the main process

With the three property lists in place, we use `electron-packager` to build the application. This approach is similar to the technique we used in chapter 14, with some important changes. First, we tell `electron-packager` that we're targeting the `mas` (Mac App Store) platform as opposed to `darwin` for regular macOS applications. We also script the rather tedious process of code signing all of the processes, frameworks, and libraries used by our application. This script uses the Xcode `codesign` command-line interface tool. This script is inspired by the approach used by the Electron Core Team to build the Electron API Demos application (https://github.com/electron/electron-api-demos). Make sure you have Xcode installed before running the script in the following listing. You also need to make sure you use the names of the certificates you generated earlier in this chapter.

Listing 16.4 The build script

```
#!/bin/bash

set -ex

APP="Fire Sale"

electron-packager . \
  "$APP" \
  --asar \
  --overwrite \
  --platform=mas \
```

This script runs similar to the build scripts used in package.json in chapter 14.

One minor change is that we're setting the platform to mas for the Mac App Store.

```
    --app-bundle-id=net.stevekinney.firesale \
    --app-version="$npm_package_version" \
    --build-version="1.0.0" \
    --arch=x64 \
    --icon=./icons/Icon.icns \
    --out=build \
    --extend-info=scripts/mas/info.plist
APP_PATH="./build/$APP-mas-x64/$APP.app"
RESULT_PATH="./build/$APP.pkg"
APP_KEY="3rd Party Mac Developer Application:
➥ Turing School of Software and Design (XD3V298ZRK)"
INSTALLER_KEY="3rd Party Mac Developer Installer:
➥ Turing School of Software and Design (XD3V298ZRK)"
FRAMEWORKS_PATH="$APP_PATH/Contents/Frameworks"
CHILD_PLIST="./scripts/mas/child.plist"
PARENT_PLIST="./scripts/mas/parent.plist"
```

Option takes a property list and merges it with the one included with Electron.

Location of the application after it has been built by electron-packager.

Destination for the installer after it has been prepared for the Mac App Store by Xcode.

Signed certificate for the application itself that we made earlier.

Signed certificate for the installer.

Path to Electron's frameworks and dependencies, which also need to be signed.

Property list to use for main and parent processes.

Property list to use for child processes and dependencies.

```
codesign -s "$APP_KEY" -f --entitlements "$CHILD_PLIST"
➥ "$FRAMEWORKS_PATH/Electron Framework.framework/Versions/A/Electron
➥ Framework"
codesign -s "$APP_KEY" -f --entitlements "$CHILD_PLIST"
➥ "$FRAMEWORKS_PATH/Electron
➥ Framework.framework/Versions/A/Libraries/libffmpeg.dylib"
codesign -s "$APP_KEY" -f --entitlements "$CHILD_PLIST"
➥ "$FRAMEWORKS_PATH/Electron
➥ Framework.framework/Versions/A/Libraries/libnode.dylib"
codesign -s "$APP_KEY" -f --entitlements "$CHILD_PLIST"
➥ "$FRAMEWORKS_PATH/Electron Framework.framework"
codesign -s "$APP_KEY" -f --entitlements "$CHILD_PLIST"
➥ "$FRAMEWORKS_PATH/$APP Helper.app/Contents/MacOS/$APP Helper"
codesign -s "$APP_KEY" -f --entitlements "$CHILD_PLIST"
➥ "$FRAMEWORKS_PATH/$APP Helper.app/"
codesign -s "$APP_KEY" -f --entitlements "$CHILD_PLIST"
➥ "$FRAMEWORKS_PATH/$APP Helper EH.app/Contents/MacOS/$APP Helper EH"
codesign -s "$APP_KEY" -f --entitlements "$CHILD_PLIST"
➥ "$FRAMEWORKS_PATH/$APP Helper EH.app/"
codesign -s "$APP_KEY" -f --entitlements "$CHILD_PLIST"
➥ "$FRAMEWORKS_PATH/$APP Helper NP.app/Contents/MacOS/$APP Helper NP"
codesign -s "$APP_KEY" -f --entitlements "$CHILD_PLIST"
➥ "$FRAMEWORKS_PATH/$APP Helper NP.app/"
codesign -s "$APP_KEY" -f --entitlements "$CHILD_PLIST"
➥ "$APP_PATH/Contents/MacOS/$APP"

codesign -s "$APP_KEY" -f --entitlements "$PARENT_PLIST" "$APP_PATH"

productbuild --component "$APP_PATH" /Applications --sign "$INSTALLER_KEY"
    "$RESULT_PATH"
```

Code-sign the parent application with the sandboxing entitlements included in parent.plist.

Uses Xcode to build the installer package.

16.1.5 Configuring application categories

We can include additional metadata in our property list that falls squarely under the category of "nice to have." Apple includes an exhaustive list of all of the options in their official documentation (http://mng.bz/2TDO), so I won't cover all of them here.

Listing 16.5 Adding applications to particular categories: ./scripts/info.plist

```
<key>NSHumanReadableCopyright</key>
<string>2017 Steve Kinney</string>
<key>LSApplicationCategoryType</key>
<string> public.app-category.developer-tools</string>
<key>LSApplicationSecondaryCategoryType</key>
<string public.app-category.productivity</string>
```

In the previous listing, we include metadata for the Mac App Store categories in which the application should be listed as well as some generic copyright information. You can find a full list of the available categories in Apple's official documentation (http://mng.bz/65Eg).

16.1.6 Register the application to open a file type

Fire Sale is an application that works with Markdown applications. In development, it was not listed as an application that could handle opening Markdown files. In addition, we could not drag a Markdown file onto the application icon in the dock. This limitation is because although we know that Fire Sale was built to work with Markdown files, macOS was not. To add support for a given file type—in this case, Markdown files—we add this code to ./scripts/mas/info.plist. The result is shown in figure 16.14.

Figure 16.14 Fire Sale is now registered with macOS as an application that can open Markdown files.

Listing 16.6 Setting Fire Sale to be available to open Markdown files: /script/info.plist

```
<key>CFBundleDocumentTypes</key>
<array>
<dict>
<key>CFBundleTypeExtensions</key>
```

Contains an array of strings of file extensions that the application should recognize

```
<array>
<string>markdown</string>
<string>mdown</string>
<string>md</string>
</array>
<key>CFBundleTypeRole</key>      <-- Tells macOS about the relationship between this application and the file type
<string>Editor</string>
<key>LSHandlerRank</key>         <-- Defines the priority in which this application should be listed for the respective file type
<string>Alternate</string>
</dict>
</array>
```

The `CFBundleDocumentTypes` contains an array of items that define the types of files that this application should be able to open. Fire Sale works only with Markdown files (and text files, technically), but an application like Atom, which works with a wide variety of file types, has a much longer list, which can be seen in its open source repository (http://mng.bz/zQ4B).

Each item in the `CFBundleDocumentTypes` dictionary contains a `CFBundleTypeExtensions` array, which lists the file types that the application should support. In addition, the `CFBundleTypeRole` key defines the application's relationship to the file type. Fire Sale edits Markdown files, so it makes sense that we've listed it as an editor. The available options are Editor, Viewer, Shell, and none.

Many applications can open a file type like Markdown. The `LSHandlerRank` attribute lets you decide what level of priority the operating system should provide for your application when the user double-clicks a file. `Owner` should be selected if the application creates a given file type. This is a good choice for a proprietary file type that can be opened only by a particular application. `Default` should be selected if the application is a good candidate for being the default application. Fire Sale is a great application, but it's likely that the user would prefer that—in general—the user would like Atom or Visual Studio Code to open upon double-clicking. This is why I chose `Alternate`.

You can define a number of other keys as well. For example, you could define the `CFBundleTypeIconFile` if you want all Markdown files to have a special icon that associates them with Fire Sale. A full list of the available options can be found in Apple's official documentation (http://mng.bz/4DTL).

16.2 Validating and uploading your application

Your application has been packaged and signed. Its entitlements have been defined. It is all ready to be uploaded to the Mac App Store. The next step, of course, is to upload the package to the store itself. You can do this using Xcode.

To get started, open Xcode and navigate to the Xcode application menu. Under Open Developer Tool, you find Application Loader, shown in figure 16.15. This is the helper application that uploads your Electron application.

After Application Loader opens, click Deliver Your App. As shown in figure 16.16, you are prompted to select the package that you want to upload—in this case, Fire Sale.pkg, located in ./build.

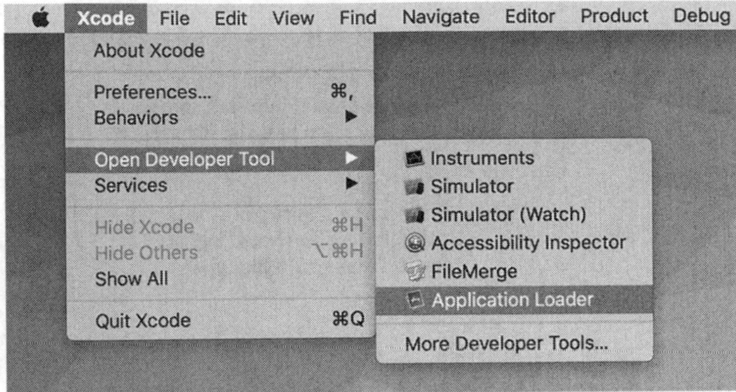

Figure 16.15 Use the Application Loader to upload your Electron application to the Mac App Store.

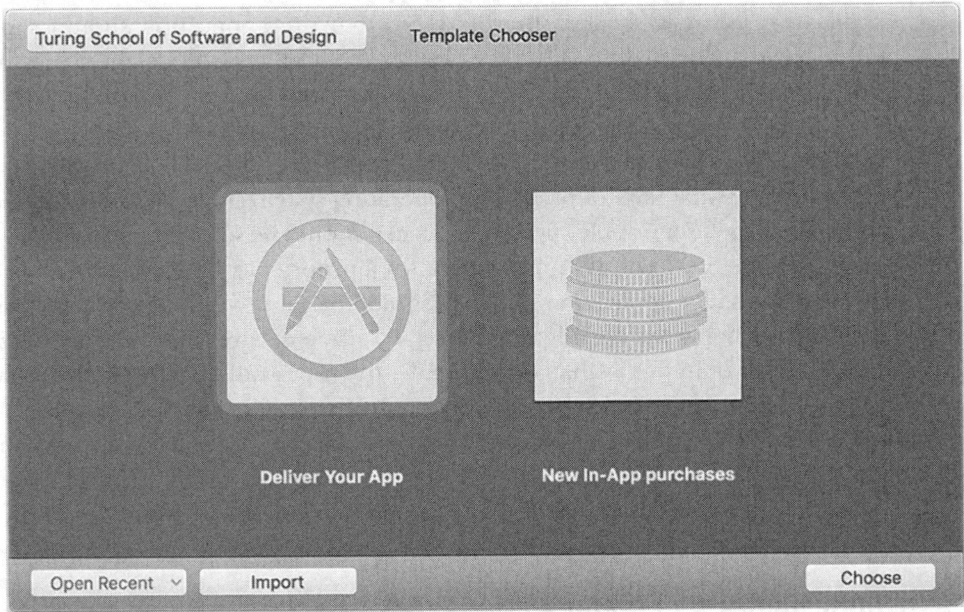

Figure 16.16 In this case, we're uploading a full application to the Mac App Store.

After you've chosen the package to upload, you can review its metadata, as shown in figure 16.17. If everything looks good, click Next to begin the upload process. It shouldn't take very long, but this is based—of course—on your connection speed and the size of the application package.

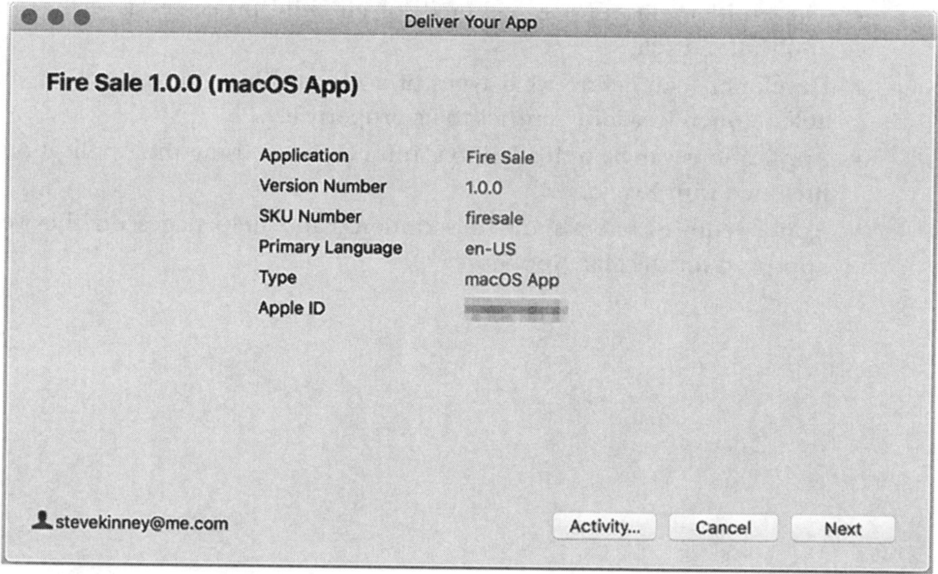

Figure 16.17 Verify that the application's metadata is correct.

16.3 Finishing touches

Apple wants to ensure the best possible experience for users. As a result, you must provide screenshots, descriptions, a link to a page where users can get help, and more. If you fail to do any of these, Apple will more than likely reject the application and ask you again to provide this information. I'm not going to go in depth in this book about adding screenshots, a home page, and documentation because it is both relatively straightforward as well as likely to change by the time the—possibly digital—ink dries on this page.

Summary

- All Mac App Store applications and their installers must be code signed to verify their authenticity.
- You can create certificate requests using Keychain Access, which is included in macOS.
- After you have a certificate request, you can upload it to Apple's developer platform to receive signed certificates.
- Applications must be registered with Apple through their developer platform.
- An application's Bundle ID is its unique identifier and is similar to a web domain but in reverse (e.g., `net.stevekinney.firesale`).
- Mac App Store applications must be sandboxed. Any entitlements needed must be defined in the property list.

- The entitlements must be defined for all child processes as well as the main application itself.
- Developers can define what types of a file an Electron application should be able to open by adding entries to its property list.
- Applications can be uploaded to iTunes Connect using the Application Loader included with Xcode.
- Apple requires screenshots, descriptions, and help pages on the web to be approved for the Mac App Store.

appendix
Code samples from Fire Sale and Clipmaster 9000

Fire Sale is an only slightly clever play on price markdowns—because it's a Markdown editor after all. Clipmaster 9000 is a simple UI for the Clipmaster application.

Code from the end of chapter 6

Listing 1 Fire Sale's main process: ./app/main.js

```
const { app, BrowserWindow, dialog } = require('electron');
const fs = require('fs');

const windows = new Set();
const openFiles = new Map();

app.on('ready', () => {
  createWindow();
});

app.on('window-all-closed', () => {
  if (process.platform === 'darwin') {
    return false;
  }
});

app.on('activate', (event, hasVisibleWindows) => {
  if (!hasVisibleWindows) { createWindow(); }
});

const createWindow = exports.createWindow = () => {
  let x, y;

  const currentWindow = BrowserWindow.getFocusedWindow();
```

```
  if (currentWindow) {
    const [ currentWindowX, currentWindowY ] = currentWindow.getPosition();
    x = currentWindowX + 10;
    y = currentWindowY + 10;
  }

  let newWindow = new BrowserWindow({ x, y, show: false });

  newWindow.loadURL(`file://${__dirname}/index.html`);

  newWindow.once('ready-to-show', () => {
    newWindow.show();
  });

  newWindow.on('close', (event) => {
    if (newWindow.isDocumentEdited()) {
      event.preventDefault();

      const result = dialog.showMessageBox(newWindow, {
        type: 'warning',
        title: 'Quit with Unsaved Changes?',
        message: 'Your changes will be lost permanently if you do not save.',
        buttons: [
          'Quit Anyway',
          'Cancel',
        ],
        cancelId: 1,
        defaultId: 0
      });

      if (result === 0) newWindow.destroy();
    }
  });

  newWindow.on('closed', () => {
    windows.delete(newWindow);
    stopWatchingFile(newWindow);
    newWindow = null;
  });

  windows.add(newWindow);
  return newWindow;
};

const getFileFromUser  = exports.getFileFromUser = (targetWindow) => {
  const files = dialog.showOpenDialog(targetWindow, {
    properties: ['openFile'],
    filters: [
      { name: 'Text Files', extensions: ['txt'] },
      { name: 'Markdown Files', extensions: ['md', 'markdown'] }
    ]
  });

  if (files) { openFile(targetWindow, files[0]); }
};
```

```
const openFile = exports.openFile = (targetWindow, file) => {
  const content = fs.readFileSync(file).toString();
  app.addRecentDocument(file);
  targetWindow.setRepresentedFilename(file);
  targetWindow.webContents.send('file-opened', file, content);
  startWatchingFile(targetWindow, file);
};


const saveMarkdown = exports.saveMarkdown = (targetWindow, file, content) =>
     {
  if (!file) {
    file = dialog.showSaveDialog(targetWindow, {
      title: 'Save Markdown',
      defaultPath: app.getPath('documents'),
      filters: [
        { name: 'Markdown Files', extensions: ['md', 'markdown'] }
      ]
    });
  }

  if (!file) return;

  fs.writeFileSync(file, content);
  openFile(targetWindow, file);
};

const saveHtml = exports.saveHtml = (targetWindow, content) => {
  const file = dialog.showSaveDialog(targetWindow, {
    title: 'Save HTML',
    defaultPath: app.getPath('documents'),
    filters: [
      { name: 'HTML Files', extensions: ['html', 'htm'] }
    ]
  });

  if (!file) return;

  fs.writeFileSync(file, content);
};

const startWatchingFile = (targetWindow, file) => {
  stopWatchingFile(targetWindow);

  const watcher = fs.watchFile(file, () => {
    const content = fs.readFileSync(file);
    targetWindow.webContents.send('file-changed', file, content);
  });

  openFiles.set(targetWindow, watcher);
};

const stopWatchingFile = (targetWindow) => {
  if (openFiles.has(targetWindow)) {
    openFiles.get(targetWindow).stop();
```

```
    openFiles.delete(targetWindow);
  }
};
```

Listing 2 Fire Sale's renderer process: ./app/renderer.js

```
const { remote, ipcRenderer } = require('electron');
const path = require('path');
const mainProcess = remote.require('./main.js');
const currentWindow = remote.getCurrentWindow();

const marked = require('marked');

const markdownView = document.querySelector('#markdown');
const htmlView = document.querySelector('#html');
const newFileButton = document.querySelector('#new-file');
const openFileButton = document.querySelector('#open-file');
const saveMarkdownButton = document.querySelector('#save-markdown');
const revertButton = document.querySelector('#revert');
const saveHtmlButton = document.querySelector('#save-html');
const showFileButton = document.querySelector('#show-file');
const openInDefaultButton = document.querySelector('#open-in-default');

let filePath = null;
let originalContent = '';

const isDifferentContent = (content) => content !== markdownView.value;

const renderMarkdownToHtml = (markdown) => {
  htmlView.innerHTML = marked(markdown, { sanitize: true });
};

const renderFile = (file, content) => {
  filePath = file;
  originalContent = content;

  markdownView.value = content;
  renderMarkdownToHtml(content);

  updateUserInterface(false);
};

const updateUserInterface = (isEdited) => {
  let title = 'Fire Sale';

  if (filePath) { title = `${path.basename(filePath)} - ${title}`; }
  if (isEdited) { title = `${title} (Edited)`; }

  currentWindow.setTitle(title);
  currentWindow.setDocumentEdited(isEdited);

  saveMarkdownButton.disabled = !isEdited;
  revertButton.disabled = !isEdited;
};
```

```
markdownView.addEventListener('keyup', (event) => {
  const currentContent = event.target.value;
  renderMarkdownToHtml(currentContent);
  updateUserInterface(currentContent !== originalContent);
});

newFileButton.addEventListener('click', () => {
  mainProcess.createWindow();
});

openFileButton.addEventListener('click', () => {
  mainProcess.getFileFromUser(currentWindow);
});

saveMarkdownButton.addEventListener('click', () => {
  mainProcess.saveMarkdown(currentWindow, filePath, markdownView.value);
});

revertButton.addEventListener('click', () => {
  markdownView.value = originalContent;
  renderMarkdownToHtml(originalContent);
});

saveHtmlButton.addEventListener('click', () => {
  mainProcess.saveHtml(currentWindow, htmlView.innerHTML);
});

ipcRenderer.on('file-opened', (event, file, content) => {
  if (currentWindow.isDocumentEdited() && isDifferentContent(content)) {
    const result = remote.dialog.showMessageBox(currentWindow, {
      type: 'warning',
      title: 'Overwrite Current Unsaved Changes?',
      message: 'Opening a new file in this window will overwrite your unsaved
     changes. Open this file anyway?',
      buttons: [
        'Yes',
        'Cancel',
      ],
      defaultId: 0,
      cancelId: 1,
    });

    if (result === 1) { return; }
  }

  renderFile(file, content);
});

ipcRenderer.on('file-changed', (event, file, content) => {
  if (isDifferentContent(content)) return;
  const result = remote.dialog.showMessageBox(currentWindow, {
    type: 'warning',
    title: 'Overwrite Current Unsaved Changes?',
    message: 'Another application has changed this file. Load changes?',
    buttons: [
```

```
      'Yes',
      'Cancel',
    ],
    defaultId: 0,
    cancelId: 1
  });

  renderFile(file, content);
});

/* Implement Drag and Drop */
document.addEventListener('dragstart', event => event.preventDefault());
document.addEventListener('dragover', event => event.preventDefault());
document.addEventListener('dragleave', event => event.preventDefault());
document.addEventListener('drop', event => event.preventDefault());

const getDraggedFile = (event) => event.dataTransfer.items[0];
const getDroppedFile = (event) => event.dataTransfer.files[0];

const fileTypeIsSupported = (file) => {
  return ['text/plain', 'text/markdown'].includes(file.type);
};

markdownView.addEventListener('dragover', (event) => {
  const file = getDraggedFile(event);

  if (fileTypeIsSupported(file)) {
    markdownView.classList.add('drag-over');
  } else {
    markdownView.classList.add('drag-error');
  }
});

markdownView.addEventListener('dragleave', () => {
  markdownView.classList.remove('drag-over');
  markdownView.classList.remove('drag-error');
});

markdownView.addEventListener('drop', (event) => {
  const file = getDroppedFile(event);

  if (fileTypeIsSupported(file)) {
    mainProcess.openFile(currentWindow, file.path);
  } else {
    alert('That file type is not supported');
  }

  markdownView.classList.remove('drag-over');
  markdownView.classList.remove('drag-error');
});
```

Code from the end of chapter 7

Listing 3 Fire Sale's application menu: ./app/application-menu.js

```
const { app, dialog, Menu } = require('electron');
const mainProcess = require('./main');

const template = [
  {
    label: 'File',
    submenu: [
      {
        label: 'New File',
        accelerator: 'CommandOrControl+N',
        click() {
          mainProcess.createWindow();
        }
      },
      {
        label: 'Open File',
        accelerator: 'CommandOrControl+O',
        click(item, focusedWindow) {
          if (focusedWindow) {
            return mainProcess.getFileFromUser(focusedWindow);
          }

          const newWindow = mainProcess.createWindow();

          newWindow.on('show', () => {
            mainProcess.getFileFromUser(newWindow);
          });
        },
      },
      {
        label: 'Save File',
        accelerator: 'CommandOrControl+S',
        click(item, focusedWindow) {
          if (!focusedWindow) {
            return dialog.showErrorBox(
              'Cannot Save or Export',
              'There is currently no active document to save or export.'
            );
          }
          mainProcess.saveMarkdown(focusedWindow);
        },
      },
      {
        label: 'Export HTML',
        accelerator: 'Shift+CommandOrControl+S',
        click(item, focusedWindow) {
          if (!focusedWindow) {
            return dialog.showErrorBox(
              'Cannot Save or Export',
              'There is currently no active document to save or export.'
            );
```

```
          }
          mainProcess.saveHtml(focusedWindow);
        },
      },
    ],
  },
  {
    label: 'Edit',
    submenu: [
      {
        label: 'Undo',
        accelerator: 'CommandOrControl+Z',
        role: 'undo',
      },
      {
        label: 'Redo',
        accelerator: 'Shift+CommandOrControl+Z',
        role: 'redo',
      },
      { type: 'separator' },
      {
        label: 'Cut',
        accelerator: 'CommandOrControl+X',
        role: 'cut',
      },
      {
        label: 'Copy',
        accelerator: 'CommandOrControl+C',
        role: 'copy',
      },
      {
        label: 'Paste',
        accelerator: 'CommandOrControl+V',
        role: 'paste',
      },
      {
        label: 'Select All',
        accelerator: 'CommandOrControl+A',
        role: 'selectall',
      },
    ],
  },
  {
    label: 'Window',
    submenu: [
      {
        label: 'Minimize',
        accelerator: 'CommandOrControl+M',
        role: 'minimize',
      },
      {
        label: 'Close',
        accelerator: 'CommandOrControl+W',
        role: 'close',
      },
```

```
      ],
    },
    {
      label: 'Help',
      role: 'help',
      submenu: [
        {
          label: 'Visit Website',
          click() { /* To be implemented */ }
        },
        {
          label: 'Toggle Developer Tools',
          click(item, focusedWindow) {
            if (focusedWindow) focusedWindow.webContents.toggleDevTools();
          }
        }
      ],
    }
  ];

  if (process.platform === 'darwin') {
    const name = 'Fire Sale';
    template.unshift({
      label: name,
      submenu: [
        {
          label: `About ${name}`,
          role: 'about',
        },
        { type: 'separator' },
        {
          label: 'Services',
          role: 'services',
          submenu: [],
        },
        { type: 'separator' },
        {
          label: `Hide ${name}`,
          accelerator: 'Command+H',
          role: 'hide',
        },
        {
          label: 'Hide Others',
          accelerator: 'Command+Alt+H',
          role: 'hideothers',
        },
        {
          label: 'Show All',
          role: 'unhide',
        },
        { type: 'separator' },
        {
          label: `Quit ${name}`,
          accelerator: 'Command+Q',
          click() { app.quit(); },
```

```
      },
    ],
  });

  const windowMenu = template.find(item => item.label === 'Window');
  windowMenu.submenu.push(
    { type: 'separator' },
    {
      label: 'Bring All to Front',
      role: 'front',
    }
  );
}

module.exports = Menu.buildFromTemplate(template);
```

Listing 4 Fire Sale's renderer process: ./app/renderer.js

```
const { remote, ipcRenderer } = require('electron');
const { Menu } = remote;
const path = require('path');
const mainProcess = remote.require('./main.js');
const currentWindow = remote.getCurrentWindow();

const marked = require('marked');

const markdownView = document.querySelector('#markdown');
const htmlView = document.querySelector('#html');
const newFileButton = document.querySelector('#new-file');
const openFileButton = document.querySelector('#open-file');
const saveMarkdownButton = document.querySelector('#save-markdown');
const revertButton = document.querySelector('#revert');
const saveHtmlButton = document.querySelector('#save-html');
const showFileButton = document.querySelector('#show-file');
const openInDefaultButton = document.querySelector('#open-in-default');

let filePath = null;
let originalContent = '';

const isDifferentContent = (content) => content !== markdownView.value;

const renderMarkdownToHtml = (markdown) => {
  htmlView.innerHTML = marked(markdown, { sanitize: true });
};

const renderFile = (file, content) => {
  filePath = file;
  originalContent = content;

  markdownView.value = content;
  renderMarkdownToHtml(content);

  updateUserInterface(false);
};
```

```
const updateUserInterface = (isEdited) => {
  let title = 'Fire Sale';

  if (filePath) { title = `${path.basename(filePath)} - ${title}`; }
  if (isEdited) { title = `${title} (Edited)`; }

  currentWindow.setTitle(title);
  currentWindow.setDocumentEdited(isEdited);

  saveMarkdownButton.disabled = !isEdited;
  revertButton.disabled = !isEdited;
};

markdownView.addEventListener('keyup', (event) => {
  const currentContent = event.target.value;
  renderMarkdownToHtml(currentContent);
  updateUserInterface(currentContent !== originalContent);
});

newFileButton.addEventListener('click', () => {
  mainProcess.createWindow();
});

openFileButton.addEventListener('click', () => {
  mainProcess.getFileFromUser(currentWindow);
});

saveMarkdownButton.addEventListener('click', () => {
  mainProcess.saveMarkdown(currentWindow, filePath, markdownView.value);
});

revertButton.addEventListener('click', () => {
  markdownView.value = originalContent;
  renderMarkdownToHtml(originalContent);
});

saveHtmlButton.addEventListener('click', () => {
  mainProcess.saveHtml(currentWindow, htmlView.innerHTML);
});

ipcRenderer.on('file-opened', (event, file, content) => {
  if (currentWindow.isDocumentEdited() && isDifferentContent(content)) {
    const result = remote.dialog.showMessageBox(currentWindow, {
      type: 'warning',
      title: 'Overwrite Current Unsaved Changes?',
      message: 'Opening a new file in this window will overwrite your unsaved
     changes. Open this file anyway?',
      buttons: [
        'Yes',
        'Cancel',
      ],
      defaultId: 0,
      cancelId: 1,
    });
```

```
    if (result === 1) { return; }
  }

  renderFile(file, content);
});

ipcRenderer.on('file-changed', (event, file, content) => {
  if (isDifferentContent(content)) return;
  const result = remote.dialog.showMessageBox(currentWindow, {
    type: 'warning',
    title: 'Overwrite Current Unsaved Changes?',
    message: 'Another application has changed this file. Load changes?',
    buttons: [
      'Yes',
      'Cancel',
    ],
    defaultId: 0,
    cancelId: 1
  });

  renderFile(file, content);
});

/* Implement Drag and Drop */
document.addEventListener('dragstart', event => event.preventDefault());
document.addEventListener('dragover', event => event.preventDefault());
document.addEventListener('dragleave', event => event.preventDefault());
document.addEventListener('drop', event => event.preventDefault());

const getDraggedFile = (event) => event.dataTransfer.items[0];
const getDroppedFile = (event) => event.dataTransfer.files[0];

const fileTypeIsSupported = (file) => {
  return ['text/plain', 'text/markdown'].includes(file.type);
};

markdownView.addEventListener('dragover', (event) => {
  const file = getDraggedFile(event);

  if (fileTypeIsSupported(file)) {
    markdownView.classList.add('drag-over');
  } else {
    markdownView.classList.add('drag-error');
  }
});

markdownView.addEventListener('dragleave', () => {
  markdownView.classList.remove('drag-over');
  markdownView.classList.remove('drag-error');
});

markdownView.addEventListener('drop', (event) => {
  const file = getDroppedFile(event);
```

```
  if (fileTypeIsSupported(file)) {
    mainProcess.openFile(currentWindow, file.path);
  } else {
    alert('That file type is not supported');
  }

  markdownView.classList.remove('drag-over');
  markdownView.classList.remove('drag-error');
});

ipcRenderer.on('save-markdown', () => {
  mainProcess.saveMarkdown(currentWindow, filePath, markdownView.value);
});

ipcRenderer.on('save-html', () => {
  mainProcess.saveHtml(currentWindow, htmlView.innerHTML);
});

const markdownContextMenu = Menu.buildFromTemplate([
  { label: 'Open File', click() { mainProcess.getFileFromUser(); } },
  { type: 'separator' },
  { label: 'Cut', role: 'cut' },
  { label: 'Copy', role: 'copy' },
  { label: 'Paste', role: 'paste' },
  { label: 'Select All', role: 'selectall' },
]);

markdownView.addEventListener('contextmenu', (event) => {
  event.preventDefault();
  markdownContextMenu.popup();
});
```

Code from the end of chapter 8

Listing 5 Fire Sale's renderer process: ./app/renderer.js

```
const { remote, ipcRenderer, shell } = require('electron');
const { Menu } = remote;
const path = require('path');
const mainProcess = remote.require('./main.js');
const currentWindow = remote.getCurrentWindow();

const marked = require('marked');

const markdownView = document.querySelector('#markdown');
const htmlView = document.querySelector('#html');
const newFileButton = document.querySelector('#new-file');
const openFileButton = document.querySelector('#open-file');
const saveMarkdownButton = document.querySelector('#save-markdown');
const revertButton = document.querySelector('#revert');
const saveHtmlButton = document.querySelector('#save-html');
const showFileButton = document.querySelector('#show-file');
const openInDefaultButton = document.querySelector('#open-in-default');
```

```
let filePath = null;
let originalContent = '';

const isDifferentContent = (content) => content !== markdownView.value;

const renderMarkdownToHtml = (markdown) => {
  htmlView.innerHTML = marked(markdown, { sanitize: true });
};

const renderFile = (file, content) => {
  filePath = file;
  originalContent = content;

  markdownView.value = content;
  renderMarkdownToHtml(content);

  showFileButton.disabled = false;
  openInDefaultButton.disabled = false;

  updateUserInterface(false);
};

const updateUserInterface = (isEdited) => {
  let title = 'Fire Sale';

  if (filePath) { title = `${path.basename(filePath)} - ${title}`; }
  if (isEdited) { title = `${title} (Edited)`; }

  currentWindow.setTitle(title);
  currentWindow.setDocumentEdited(isEdited);

  saveMarkdownButton.disabled = !isEdited;
  revertButton.disabled = !isEdited;
};

markdownView.addEventListener('keyup', (event) => {
  const currentContent = event.target.value;
  renderMarkdownToHtml(currentContent);
  updateUserInterface(currentContent !== originalContent);
});

newFileButton.addEventListener('click', () => {
  mainProcess.createWindow();
});

openFileButton.addEventListener('click', () => {
  mainProcess.getFileFromUser(currentWindow);
});

saveMarkdownButton.addEventListener('click', () => {
  mainProcess.saveMarkdown(currentWindow, filePath, markdownView.value);
});

revertButton.addEventListener('click', () => {
  markdownView.value = originalContent;
```

```
    renderMarkdownToHtml(originalContent);
  });

  saveHtmlButton.addEventListener('click', () => {
    mainProcess.saveHtml(currentWindow, htmlView.innerHTML);
  });

  const showFile = () => {
    if (!filePath) { return alert('This file has not been saved to the file
       system.'); }
    shell.showItemInFolder(filePath);
  };

  const openInDefaultApplication = () => {
    if (!filePath) { return alert('This file has not been saved to the file
       system.'); }
    shell.openItem(filePath);
  };

  showFileButton.addEventListener('click', showFile);
  openInDefaultButton.addEventListener('click', openInDefaultApplication);
  ipcRenderer.on('show-file', showFile);
  ipcRenderer.on('open-in-default', openInDefaultApplication);

  ipcRenderer.on('file-opened', (event, file, content) => {
    if (currentWindow.isDocumentEdited() && isDifferentContent(content)) {
      const result = remote.dialog.showMessageBox(currentWindow, {
        type: 'warning',
        title: 'Overwrite Current Unsaved Changes?',
        message: 'Opening a new file in this window will overwrite your unsaved
       changes. Open this file anyway?',
        buttons: [
          'Yes',
          'Cancel',
        ],
        defaultId: 0,
        cancelId: 1,
      });

      if (result === 1) { return; }
    }

    renderFile(file, content);
  });

  ipcRenderer.on('file-changed', (event, file, content) => {
    if (isDifferentContent(content)) return;
    const result = remote.dialog.showMessageBox(currentWindow, {
      type: 'warning',
      title: 'Overwrite Current Unsaved Changes?',
      message: 'Another application has changed this file. Load changes?',
      buttons: [
        'Yes',
        'Cancel',
      ],
```

```
    defaultId: 0,
    cancelId: 1
  });

  renderFile(file, content);
});

/* Implement Drag and Drop */
document.addEventListener('dragstart', event => event.preventDefault());
document.addEventListener('dragover', event => event.preventDefault());
document.addEventListener('dragleave', event => event.preventDefault());
document.addEventListener('drop', event => event.preventDefault());

const getDraggedFile = (event) => event.dataTransfer.items[0];
const getDroppedFile = (event) => event.dataTransfer.files[0];

const fileTypeIsSupported = (file) => {
  return ['text/plain', 'text/markdown'].includes(file.type);
};

markdownView.addEventListener('dragover', (event) => {
  const file = getDraggedFile(event);

  if (fileTypeIsSupported(file)) {
    markdownView.classList.add('drag-over');
  } else {
    markdownView.classList.add('drag-error');
  }
});

markdownView.addEventListener('dragleave', () => {
  markdownView.classList.remove('drag-over');
  markdownView.classList.remove('drag-error');
});

markdownView.addEventListener('drop', (event) => {
  const file = getDroppedFile(event);

  if (fileTypeIsSupported(file)) {
    mainProcess.openFile(currentWindow, file.path);
  } else {
    alert('That file type is not supported');
  }

  markdownView.classList.remove('drag-over');
  markdownView.classList.remove('drag-error');
});

const createContextMenu = () => {
  return Menu.buildFromTemplate([
    { label: 'Open File', click() { mainProcess.getFileFromUser(); } },
    {
      label: 'Show File in Folder',
      click: showFile,
```

```
        enabled: !!filePath
      },
      {
        label: 'Open in Default',
        click: openInDefaultApplication,
        enabled: !!filePath
      },
      { type: 'separator' },
      { label: 'Cut', role: 'cut' },
      { label: 'Copy', role: 'copy' },
      { label: 'Paste', role: 'paste' },
      { label: 'Select All', role: 'selectall' },
    ]);
};

markdownView.addEventListener('contextmenu', (event) => {
  event.preventDefault();
  createContextMenu().popup();
});

ipcRenderer.on('save-markdown', () => {
  mainProcess.saveMarkdown(currentWindow, filePath, markdownView.value);
});

ipcRenderer.on('save-html', () => {
  mainProcess.saveHtml(currentWindow, filePath, markdownView.value);
});
```

Listing 6 Fire Sale's application menu: ./app/application-menu.js

```
const { app, BrowserWindow, dialog, Menu, shell } = require('electron');
const mainProcess = require('./main');

const createApplicationMenu = () => {
  const hasOneOrMoreWindows = !!BrowserWindow.getAllWindows().length;
  const focusedWindow = BrowserWindow.getFocusedWindow();
  const hasFilePath = !!(focusedWindow &&
      focusedWindow.getRepresentedFilename());

  const template = [
    {
      label: 'File',
      submenu: [
        {
          label: 'New File',
          accelerator: 'CommandOrControl+N',
          click() {
            mainProcess.createWindow();
          }
        },
        {
          label: 'Open File',
          accelerator: 'CommandOrControl+O',
```

```
      click(item, focusedWindow) {
        if (focusedWindow) {
          return mainProcess.getFileFromUser(focusedWindow);
        }

        const newWindow = mainProcess.createWindow();

        newWindow.on('show', () => {
          mainProcess.getFileFromUser(newWindow);
        });
      },
    },
    {
      label: 'Save File',
      accelerator: 'CommandOrControl+S',
      enabled: hasOneOrMoreWindows,
      click(item, focusedWindow) {
        if (!focusedWindow) {
          return dialog.showErrorBox(
            'Cannot Save or Export',
            'There is currently no active document to save or export.'
          );
        }
        mainProcess.saveMarkdown(focusedWindow);
      },
    },
    {
      label: 'Export HTML',
      accelerator: 'Shift+CommandOrControl+S',
      enabled: hasOneOrMoreWindows,
      click(item, focusedWindow) {
        if (!focusedWindow) {
          return dialog.showErrorBox(
            'Cannot Save or Export',
            'There is currently no active document to save or export.'
          );
        }
        mainProcess.saveHtml(focusedWindow);
      },
    },
    { type: 'separator' },
    {
      label: 'Show File',
      enabled: hasFilePath,
      click(item, focusedWindow) {
        if (!focusedWindow) {
          return dialog.showErrorBox(
            'Cannot Show File\'s Location',
            'There is currently no active document show.'
          );
        }
        focusedWindow.webContents.send('show-file');
      },
    },
```

```
        {
          label: 'Open in Default Application',
          enabled: hasFilePath,
          click(item, focusedWindow) {
            if (!focusedWindow) {
              return dialog.showErrorBox(
                'Cannot Open File in Default Application',
                'There is currently no active document to open.'
              );
            }
            focusedWindow.webContents.send('open-in-default');
          },
        },
      ],
    },
    {
      label: 'Edit',
      submenu: [
        {
          label: 'Undo',
          accelerator: 'CommandOrControl+Z',
          role: 'undo',
        },
        {
          label: 'Redo',
          accelerator: 'Shift+CommandOrControl+Z',
          role: 'redo',
        },
        { type: 'separator' },
        {
          label: 'Cut',
          accelerator: 'CommandOrControl+X',
          role: 'cut',
        },
        {
          label: 'Copy',
          accelerator: 'CommandOrControl+C',
          role: 'copy',
        },
        {
          label: 'Paste',
          accelerator: 'CommandOrControl+V',
          role: 'paste',
        },
        {
          label: 'Select All',
          accelerator: 'CommandOrControl+A',
          role: 'selectall',
        },
      ],
    },
    {
      label: 'Window',
      submenu: [
        {
```

```
        label: 'Minimize',
        accelerator: 'CommandOrControl+M',
        role: 'minimize',
      },
      {
        label: 'Close',
        accelerator: 'CommandOrControl+W',
        role: 'close',
      },
    ],
  },
    {
    label: 'Help',
    role: 'help',
    submenu: [
      {
        label: 'Visit Website',
        click() { /* To be implemented */ }
      },
      {
        label: 'Toggle Developer Tools',
        click(item, focusedWindow) {
          if (focusedWindow) focusedWindow.webContents.toggleDevTools();
        }
      }
    ],
  }
];

if (process.platform === 'darwin') {
  const name = 'Fire Sale';
  template.unshift({
    label: name,
    submenu: [
      {
        label: `About ${name}`,
        role: 'about',
      },
      { type: 'separator' },
      {
        label: 'Services',
        role: 'services',
        submenu: [],
      },
      { type: 'separator' },
      {
        label: `Hide ${name}`,
        accelerator: 'Command+H',
        role: 'hide',
      },
      {
        label: 'Hide Others',
        accelerator: 'Command+Alt+H',
        role: 'hideothers',
      },
```

```
        {
          label: 'Show All',
          role: 'unhide',
        },
        { type: 'separator' },
        {
          label: `Quit ${name}`,
          accelerator: 'Command+Q',
          click() { app.quit(); },
        },
      ],
    });

    const windowMenu = template.find(item => item.label === 'Window');
    windowMenu.submenu.push(
      { type: 'separator' },
      {
        label: 'Bring All to Front',
        role: 'front',
      }
    );
  }

  return Menu.setApplicationMenu(Menu.buildFromTemplate(template));
};

module.exports = createApplicationMenu;
```

Listing 7 Fire Sale's main process: ./app/main.js

```
const { app, BrowserWindow, dialog, Menu } = require('electron');
const createApplicationMenu = require('./application-menu');
const fs = require('fs');

const windows = new Set();
const openFiles = new Map();

app.on('ready', () => {
  createApplicationMenu();
  createWindow();
});

app.on('window-all-closed', () => {
  if (process.platform === 'darwin') {
    return false;
  }
});

app.on('activate', (event, hasVisibleWindows) => {
  if (!hasVisibleWindows) { createWindow(); }
});

const createWindow = exports.createWindow = () => {
  let x, y;

  const currentWindow = BrowserWindow.getFocusedWindow();
```

```
  if (currentWindow) {
    const [ currentWindowX, currentWindowY ] = currentWindow.getPosition();
    x = currentWindowX + 10;
    y = currentWindowY + 10;
  }

  let newWindow = new BrowserWindow({ x, y, show: false });

  newWindow.loadURL(`file://${__dirname}/index.html`);

  newWindow.once('ready-to-show', () => {
    newWindow.show();
  });

  newWindow.on('focus', createApplicationMenu);

  newWindow.on('close', (event) => {
    if (newWindow.isDocumentEdited()) {
      event.preventDefault();

      const result = dialog.showMessageBox(newWindow, {
        type: 'warning',
        title: 'Quit with Unsaved Changes?',
        message: 'Your changes will be lost permanently if you do not save.',
        buttons: [
          'Quit Anyway',
          'Cancel',
        ],
        cancelId: 1,
        defaultId: 0
      });

      if (result === 0) newWindow.destroy();
    }
  });

  newWindow.on('closed', () => {
    windows.delete(newWindow);
    createApplicationMenu();
    newWindow = null;
  });

  windows.add(newWindow);
  return newWindow;
};

const getFileFromUser  = exports.getFileFromUser = (targetWindow) => {
  const files = dialog.showOpenDialog(targetWindow, {
    properties: ['openFile'],
    filters: [
      { name: 'Text Files', extensions: ['txt'] },
      { name: 'Markdown Files', extensions: ['md', 'markdown'] }
    ]
  });
```

```
  if (files) { openFile(targetWindow, files[0]); }
};

const openFile = exports.openFile = (targetWindow, file) => {
  const content = fs.readFileSync(file).toString();
  startWatchingFile(targetWindow, file);
  app.addRecentDocument(file);
  targetWindow.setRepresentedFilename(file);
  targetWindow.webContents.send('file-opened', file, content);
  createApplicationMenu();
};


const saveMarkdown = exports.saveMarkdown = (targetWindow, file, content) =>
    {
  if (!file) {
    file = dialog.showSaveDialog(targetWindow, {
      title: 'Save Markdown',
      defaultPath: app.getPath('documents'),
      filters: [
        { name: 'Markdown Files', extensions: ['md', 'markdown'] }
      ]
    });
  }

  if (!file) return;

  fs.writeFileSync(file, content);
  openFile(targetWindow, file);
};

const saveHtml = exports.saveHtml = (targetWindow, content) => {
  const file = dialog.showSaveDialog(targetWindow, {
    title: 'Save HTML',
    defaultPath: app.getPath('documents'),
    filters: [
      { name: 'HTML Files', extensions: ['html', 'htm'] }
    ]
  });

  if (!file) return;

  fs.writeFileSync(file, content);
};

const startWatchingFile = (targetWindow, file) => {
  stopWatchingFile(targetWindow);

  const watcher = fs.watchFile(file, () => {
    const content = fs.readFileSync(file);
    targetWindow.webContents.send('file-changed', file, content);
  });

  openFiles.set(targetWindow, watcher);
};
```

```
const stopWatchingFile = (targetWindow) => {
  if (openFiles.has(targetWindow)) {
    openFiles.get(targetWindow).stop();
    openFiles.delete(targetWindow);
  }
};
```

Completed code from the end of chapter 10

Listing 8 Clipmaster 9000's main process: ./app/main.js

```
const Menubar = require('menubar');
const { globalShortcut, Menu } = require('electron');

const menubar = Menubar({
  preloadWindow: true,
  index: `file://${__dirname}/index.html`,
});

menubar.on('ready', () => {
  const secondaryMenu = Menu.buildFromTemplate([
    {
      label: 'Quit',
      click() { menubar.app.quit(); },
      accelerator: 'CommandOrControl+Q'
    },
  ]);

  menubar.tray.on('right-click', () => {
    menubar.tray.popUpContextMenu(secondaryMenu);
  });

  const createClipping = globalShortcut.register('CommandOrControl+!', () =>
     {
    menubar.window.webContents.send('create-new-clipping');
  });

  const writeClipping = globalShortcut.register('CmdOrCtrl+Alt+@', () => {
    menubar.window.webContents.send('write-to-clipboard');
  });

  const publishClipping = globalShortcut.register('CmdOrCtrl+Alt+#', () => {
    menubar.window.webContents.send('publish-clipping');
  });

  if (!createClipping) { console.error('Registration failed',
     'createClipping'); }
  if (!writeClipping) { console.error('Registration failed',
     'writeClipping'); }
  if (!publishClipping) { console.error('Registration failed',
     'publishClipping'); }
});
```

Listing 9 Clipmaster 9000's renderer process: ./app/renderer.js

```
const { clipboard, ipcRenderer, shell } = require('electron');

const request = require('request').defaults({
  url: 'https://cliphub.glitch.me/clippings',
  headers: { 'User-Agent': 'Clipmaster 9000' },
  json: true,
});

const clippingsList = document.getElementById('clippings-list');
const copyFromClipboardButton = document.getElementById('copy-from-
     clipboard');

ipcRenderer.on('create-new-clipping', () => {
  addClippingToList();
  new Notification('Clipping Added', {
    body: `${clipboard.readText()}`
  });
});

ipcRenderer.on('write-to-clipboard', () => {
  const clipping = clippingsList.firstChild;
  writeToClipboard(getClippingText(clipping));
  new Notification('Clipping Copied', {
    body: `${clipboard.readText()}`
  });
});

ipcRenderer.on('publish-clipping', () => {
  const clipping = clippingsList.firstChild;
  publishClipping(getClippingText(clipping));
});

const createClippingElement = (clippingText) => {
  const clippingElement = document.createElement('article');

  clippingElement.classList.add('clippings-list-item');

  clippingElement.innerHTML = `
    <div class="clipping-text" disabled="true"></div>
    <div class="clipping-controls">
      <button class="copy-clipping">&rarr; Clipboard</button>
      <button class="publish-clipping">Publish</button>
      <button class="remove-clipping">Remove</button>
    </div>
  `;

  clippingElement.querySelector('.clipping-text').innerText = clippingText;

  return clippingElement;
};

const addClippingToList = () => {
  const clippingText = clipboard.readText();
```

```
  const clippingElement = createClippingElement(clippingText);
  clippingsList.prepend(clippingElement);
};

copyFromClipboardButton.addEventListener('click', addClippingToList);

clippingsList.addEventListener('click', (event) => {
  const hasClass = className => event.target.classList.contains(className);

  const clippingListItem = getButtonParent(event);

  if (hasClass('remove-clipping')) removeClipping(clippingListItem);
  if (hasClass('copy-clipping'))
     writeToClipboard(getClippingText(clippingListItem));
  if (hasClass('publish-clipping'))
     publishClipping(getClippingText(clippingListItem));
});

const removeClipping = (target) => {
  target.remove();
};

const writeToClipboard = (clippingText) => {
  clipboard.writeText(clippingText);
};

const publishClipping = (clippingText) => {
  request.post({ json: { clipping: clippingText } }, (err, response, body) =>
     {
    if (err) {
      return new Notification('Error Publishing Your Clipping', {
        body: JSON.parse(err).message
      });
    }

    const gistUrl = body.url;
    const notification = new Notification('Your Clipping Has Been Published',
     {
      body: `Click to open ${gistUrl} in your browser.`
    });

    notification.onclick = () => { shell.openExternal(gistUrl); };

    clipboard.writeText(gistUrl);
  });
};

const getButtonParent = ({ target }) => {
  return target.parentNode.parentNode;
};

const getClippingText = (clippingListItem) => {
  return clippingListItem.querySelector('.clipping-text').innerText;
};
```

index

Symbols

A

B

C

N

O

P

Q

R

S

T

U

V

W

X

Y